HUMAN RIGHTS IN AFRICA: FROM THE OAU TO THE AFRICAN UNION

This book examines the role of the Organization of African Unity, now the African Union, and how it has dealt with human rights since its inception in 1963. It is the only publication to consider this key African political institution from a human rights perspective. The author examines various themes including the rights of women, the rights of the child, the concept of democracy, and the right to development. Written by a leading human rights scholar, this book is essential reading for lawyers acting for African states, and for foreign governments and NGOs active in Africa, as well as being of interest to international and comparative human rights scholars.

DR RACHEL MURRAY is Reader in Law at the University of Bristol. She has worked previously at Birkbeck College, University of London, and at Queens University Belfast, where she was also the Assistant Director of the Human Rights Centre. She has published widely on the African human rights system, including a book written with Malcolm D. Evans, *The African Charter on Human and Peoples' Rights* (Cambridge University Press, 2002). She also works on national human rights commissions, having undertaken an evaluation of the Northern Ireland Human Rights Commission with Professor Stephen Livingstone.

HUMAN RIGHTS IN AFRICA

From the OAU to the African Union

RACHEL MURRAY

CAMBRIDGE
UNIVERSITY PRESS

CAMBRIDGE UNIVERSITY PRESS
Cambridge, New York, Melbourne, Madrid, Cape Town, Singapore, São Paulo

Cambridge University Press
The Edinburgh Building, Cambridge CB2 2RU, UK

Published in the United States of America by Cambridge University Press, New York

www.cambridge.org
Information on this title: www.cambridge.org/9780521839174

First published 2004

A catalogue record for this publication is available from the British Library

Library of Congress Cataloguing in Publication data
Murray, Rachel, Dr.
Human rights in Africa : from the OAU to the African Union / Rachel Murray.
p.   cm.
Includes bibliographical references and index.
ISBN 0-521-83917-3 (hb)
1. Human rights – Africa.   I. Title.
KQC572.M87   2004
342.608′5 – dc22   2004045822

ISBN-13 978-0-521-83917-4 hardback
ISBN-10 0-521-83917-3 hardback

Transferred to digital printing 2007

CONTENTS

ACKNOWLEDGEMENTS

This book would not have been possible without the kind and invaluable assistance of the OAU/AU staff. I would like to thank, in particular, Ben Kioko for all his advice, documentation and time spent assisting in this research. In addition, thanks must also go to Yetunde Teriba, Dr Kalimugogo and Mr Kouroma at the AU.

Also in Addis Ababa, Patrice Vahard of the UNHCHR and Beverley Byfield of UNHCR were both invaluable. Those at the African Commission on Human and Peoples' Rights have continued to be extremely helpful in providing me with documents and allowing me access to their meetings. Thanks must go in particular to Jan Jalloh, the Documentalist, in this respect. The trips to Addis Ababa and the headquarters of the OAU/AU would not have been possible without funding from SPTL and the SLSA, to whom I am very grateful.

I must also acknowledge the support and advice I received on drafts of the chapters from Dr Fareda Banda, Amanda Lloyd and Steven Wheatley. I am particularly grateful to Ibrahima Kane and Dr Kolawole Olaniyan for taking the time to read drafts of the entire manuscript and for their invaluable comments. Finola O'Sullivan at Cambridge University Press has provided constant encouragement, and Mary Starkey has been very accommodating.

Finally, thanks to Simon for his patience when I have had to put in the long hours.

ABBREVIATIONS

ACHPR	African Charter on Human and Peoples' Rights
ACJ	African Court of Justice
ACP	African, Caribbean and Pacific
ACRWC	African Charter on the Rights and Welfare of the Child
AEC	African Economic Community
AEL	Academy of European Law
AHSG	Assembly of Heads of State and Government of the OAU
AJICL	*African Journal of International and Comparative Law*
AJIL	*American Journal of International Law*
ANPPCAN	African Network for the Prevention and Protection against Child Abuse and Neglect
APC	African Population Commission
APRM	African Peer Review Mechanism
ASICL	African Society of International and Comparative Law
ASIL	American Society of International Law
AU	African Union
AWCPD	African Women's Committee on Peace and Development
BYIL	*British Yearbook of International Law*
CAR	Central African Republic
CCAR	Coordinating Committee on Assistance to Refugees
CEDAW	Convention on the Elimination of Discrimination Against Women
CSSDCA	Conference on Security, Stability, Development and Cooperation in Africa
DRC	Democratic Republic of Congo
ECA	Economic Commission for Africa
ECHR	European Convention on Human Rights
ECJ	European Court of Justice
ECOSOC	Economic and Social Council of the UN
ECOSOCC	Economic, Social and Cultural Council of the AU
EJIL	*European Journal of International Law*

EU	European Union
GA	General Assembly of the UN
HRLJ	*Human Rights Law Journal*
HRQ	*Human Rights Quarterly*
HSGIC	Heads of State and Government Implementation Committee
ICARA	International Conference on Assistance to Refugees in Africa
ICCPR	International Covenant on Civil and Political Rights
ICESCR	International Covenant on Economic, Social and Cultural Rights
ICLQ	*International and Comparative Law Quarterly*
ILM	International Legal Materials
ILO	International Labour Organisation
IOM	International Organisation for Migration
IUCN	International Union for the Conservation of Nature and Natural Resources
NIEO	New International Economic Order
IPEP	International Panel of Eminent Personalities
JAL	*Journal of African Law*
NEPAD	New Partnership for Africa's Development
NQHR	*Netherlands Quarterly of Human Rights*
NGOs	non-governmental organisations
OAU	Organization of African Unity
PSC	Peace and Security Council of the AU
RADIC	*African Journal of International and Comparative Law*
SADC	Southern African Development Community
UDHR	Universal Declaration of Human Rights
UNCRC	United Nations Convention on the Rights of the Child
UNEP	United Nations Environment Programme
UNHCR	United Nations High Commission for Refugees
UNICEF	United Nations International Childern's Emergency Fund
UNIFEM	United Nations Development Fund for Women
WILDAF	Women in Law and Development in Africa

Historical overview of human rights in the OAU/AU

Introduction

Human rights instruments and the organs that they created were for many years on the periphery of the political institutions under which they fell. This is despite the fact that the manner in which they are formulated and structured requires them to rely on these political institutions for their funding, nominations and appointments to their own organs and in some cases enforcement of their decisions.

Further, human rights as a discipline has evolved somewhat separately from international law, and international politics has been separated from international law. Thus, human rights have tended to have been dealt with by separate bodies created under the distinct human rights instruments and it is only recently that there has been an increased convergence of human rights into the mainstream of international organisations' thinking. Just as there has been a closer relationship between the European Convention on Human Rights (ECHR) and the European Union (EU),[1] so the African political organisation, the Organization of African Unity (OAU), which is now being transformed into the African Union (AU), illustrates this closer attention to human rights as falling within its remit. Whilst a separate instrument was adopted under the auspices of the OAU in 1981 specifically to deal with human rights (the African Charter on Human and Peoples' Rights (ACHPR)), it remained largely on the periphery of the OAU's attention until recently. Yet in later years the OAU organs developed an approach to human rights. This chapter will seek to chart the development of human rights within the OAU/AU from its inception in 1963 to the present day. It will examine the influences on the OAU/AU to deal with human rights and the trends which it has evidenced in selecting on what to focus.

---

[1] See, for example, P. Alston (ed.), *The EU and Human Rights* (Oxford: Oxford University Press, 1999).

The creation of the OAU and its structure

Whilst it is not the intention of this book to provide a detailed description of what led to the adoption of the OAU Charter in 1963,[2] a sketch of its development is useful. The background to the creation of the OAU can be traced back to a series of developments in various regions across the continent, with the various groupings among French-speaking countries,[3] East and Central Africa[4] and others pulling in slightly different directions.[5] A number of All-African Peoples' Conferences were held in the late 1950s and early 1960s with the aim of encouraging those who were not yet liberated to liberate themselves and to organise non-violent revolution in Africa. Even at this stage the seeds of some human rights issues that would find their way into the OAU can be discerned with condemnation of racism in South Africa, the call for the need for universal vote and concerns about religious separatism, among others.[6] States did not, however, agree on the nature of the regional organisation, with some falling into

[2] OAU Charter, adopted 25 May 1963, 3 ILM (1964) 1116. For this history to the background of the OAU see T. O. Elias, 'The Charter of the Organization of African Unity', *AJIL* 59 (1965) 243–67. For discussion of the OAU more generally see A. Chanda, 'The Organization of African Unity: An Appraisal', *Zambia Law Journal* 21–4 (1989–92) 1–29; H. Ait-Ahmed, *L'Afro-fascisme: les droits de l'homme dans la Charte et la pratique de l'OUA* (Paris: Harmattan, 1980); Boutros Boutros-Ghali, *L'Organization de l'Unité Africaine* (Paris: A. Colin Collection U, Series Institutions Internationales, 1969); C. O. C. Amate, *Inside the OAU: Pan-Africanism in Practice* (New York: St Martin's Press, 1986); Z. Cervenka, *The Organization of African Unity and its Charter* (New York: Praeger, 1968); M. A. Abdul-Razag, 'The OAU and the Protection of Human Rights in Africa' (Ph.D. thesis, University of Hull, 1988); D. Mazzeo (ed.), *African Regional Organizations* (Cambridge: Cambridge University Press, 1984); C. Nwankwo, 'The OAU and Human Rights', *Journal of Democracy* 4 (1993) 50–4.

[3] Groupings included the Brazzaville powers of the twelve French-speaking African states (Cameroon, Central African Republic (CAR), Chad, Congo, Dahomey, Gabon, Ivory Coast, Malagasy, Mauritania, Niger, Senegal, Upper Volta) meeting first in 1960.

[4] The Pan-African Movement of East and Central Africa (PAFMECA).

[5] In July 1959 the Sanniquellie Conference was held bringing together the governments of Liberia, Guinea and Ghana who pledged to work to set up a Community of Independent African States and decided to hold a conference in 1960. In August 1959 a conference was held in Monrovia of nine independent states (Ethiopia, Ghana, Guinea, Liberia, Libya, Morocco, Sudan, Tunisia and United Arab Republic) to look specifically at the Algerian question – to stop the war there and assist the nationalists, many of these states having recognised the Algerian provisional government. The first Conference of Independent African States took place in Accra, Ghana, in April 1958 (Ethiopia, Ghana, Liberia, Libya, Morocco, Sudan, Tunisia and United Arab Republic). See *International Organization* 16(2) (1962).

[6] Resolutions of the first All African Peoples' Conference held in Accra, 8–13 December 1958, see *International Organization* 16(2) (1962) 429–34, at 430.

the 'Monrovia' bloc,[7] favouring a 'more classical, "confederal" approach where, far from aiming at the integration of African states, sovereignty would be preserved in the framework of a much looser arrangement'.[8] In contrast, other states under the leadership of Ghana's President Nkrumah, in what became known as the 'Casablanca' bloc (United Arab Republic, Ghana, Guinea, Mali and Morocco), had signed the more federalist Casablanca Charter for economic cooperation, stressing elements of self-defence and the need to eliminate colonialism.[9] In Monrovia in May 1961 a pan-African conference was held in which twenty-two of the twenty-seven states in Africa that were independent at that time participated, although none from the Casablanca bloc. Some liberation movements were also admitted as observers. These states decided what sort of organisation they wanted, as Elias noted:

> The view was unanimous that a loose form of association of independent African states, based upon the principles of economic, cultural, scientific and technical cooperation among its members, was the ideal at which to aim. They one and all disavowed any intention to join any organisation of independent African states that would place the premium on political union supported by a military junta. It was generally felt that economic and technical development . . . should take precedence over political union, at least at this stage of the evolution of the newly independent states.[10]

One of the recommendations of the conference was that a Charter should be drawn up for an Organisation of African and Malagasy States.[11] Therefore, in January 1962 a second conference of the newly formed Assembly of Heads of States and Government was held in Lagos, Nigeria to look at drafting a Charter. Among other things it proposed the establishment of a Council of Ministers,[12] and this organ was mandated to meet in June in Lagos in 1962 to develop the Charter. The text of the Charter was

---

[7] Cameroon, CAR, Chad, Congo, Dahomey, Ethiopia, Gabon, Ivory Coast, Liberia, Libya, Malagasy, Mauritania, Niger, Nigeria, Senegal, Sierra Leone, Somalia, Togo, Tunisia and Upper Volta.

[8] P. Sands and P. Klein, *Bowett's Law of International Institutions*, 5th edn. (London: Sweet & Maxwell, 2001), chapter 10, at 244.

[9] Ibid. See also *International Organization* 16(2) (1962) 437–9.

[10] Elias, 'The Charter', at 243–4.   [11] *International Organization* 16(2) (1962) 439–43.

[12] It approved in principle a detailed Charter for an Organisation of Inter-African and Malagasy States with three organs, an assembly of heads of state, a council of ministers and a secretariat, with a Secretary General. It proposed setting up committees on certain issues, see *International Organization* 16(2) (1962) 439–43.

adopted at that meeting and at a further meeting in December of that year seventeen of the twenty-two states signed the Charter of the Organisation of African and Malagasy States, or Lagos Charter.[13] A third conference was held in Addis Ababa in Ethiopia. The Council of Ministers prior to that meeting had the task of joining the Casablanca Charter, the Lagos Charter and an Ethiopian draft (similar to the Lagos Charter) together in one document. The result was the Charter of the Organization of African Unity.[14] Elias notes that 'the plea of Ghana and of one or two other members for the establishment of a political union of Africa was firmly rejected by the conference'.[15] It would thus appear that although the wishes of the Monrovia group dominated, the OAU Charter was 'a product of compromise'.[16]

The OAU Charter provided for four principal institutions:[17] the Assembly of Heads of State and Government (AHSG), the Council of Ministers, the General Secretariat and the Commission of Mediation, Conciliation and Arbitration. The AHSG was the primary organ with final decision-making powers and the power to review the structure and functioning of the other organs.[18] It was composed of heads of state, or their representatives,[19] and required to meet at least once a year.[20]

The Council of Ministers was composed of the foreign ministers or their representatives and met at least twice a year,[21] usually in February and just prior to the Summit of the AHSG in June/July. It was responsible to the AHSG and its task was to prepare these Summits, implement the decisions of the AHSG and coordinate with it.[22] Again, as with the AHSG, there was one vote per state, but unlike the AHSG, voting on resolutions only required a simple majority.[23] In contrast to the AHSG, despite being

---

[13] The Casablanca bloc were still not present at any of these meetings.

[14] A Defence Commission was included among the specialised commissions to deal with the desire by the Casablanca bloc to have an African High Command.

[15] T. O. Elias, *Africa and the Development of International Law*, 2nd edn., ed. R. Akinjide (The Hague: Martinus Nijhoff, 1988), at 124. Elias notes that nowhere in the purposes of the OAU Charter 'is any reference made to political union of any kind; nor is the reference to co-operation "for defence and security" intended as relating to any idea of establishing an African High Command', Elias, 'The Charter', 243–67, at 251.

[16] G. Naldi, *The Organization of African Unity. An Analysis of its Role*, 2nd edn. (London: Mansell, 1999), at 2.

[17] Article 7.   [18] Article 8.   [19] Article 9.

[20] Article 9. It in fact rarely met more than this, although there was a provision in Article 9 for extraordinary sessions to be held. See Sands and Klein, *Bowett's Law*, at 246.

[21] Article 12. Again, it can hold extraordinary sessions.

[22] Article 13.   [23] Article 14. This also gives detail on quorum.

'the most dynamic organ of the OAU', it had limited powers,[24] although its role in economic and social matters was often seen as important.[25]

The Committee of Ambassadors offered advice to the Council of Ministers and AHSG and decided on issues to go on the agenda of the former. Given that ambassadors were in regular contact with the OAU Secretariat their role in placing human rights on the agenda of the Council of Ministers was crucial. This was particularly the case in respect of the work of the Central Organ on conflict, as Amnesty noted:

> The Ambassadors who are part of the Central Organ form an integral part of the early warning system. During the monthly meetings of the Central Organ of the Conflict Resolution Mechanism, their role should be to assess information on specific human rights situations indicating a possible conflict developing and they should be able to make recommendations to the appropriate organs of the OAU ... As they are central to the work of the Council, they can influence it to include a consideration of the human rights situation in Africa on the agenda of its meetings. They should include on the agenda of the Council situations where systematic human rights violations provides early warning of a possible conflict.[26]

The fourth organ mentioned expressly by the OAU Charter was the Commission of Mediation, Conciliation and Arbitration. The Charter did not define its composition or terms of reference, leaving this to a separate Protocol to be adopted by the AHSG. Although a Protocol was adopted,[27] this Commission was never actually established.

Also provided by the OAU Charter were a number of specialised commissions:[28] the Economic and Social Commission;[29] the Educational, Scientific, Cultural and Health Commission; and the Defence

---

[24] Sands and Klein, *Bowett's Law*, at 246; Elias, *Africa and the Development*, at 141–2.

[25] Amate, *Inside the OAU*, at 550–1.

[26] Amnesty International, *Organization of African Unity: Making Human Rights a Reality for Africans* (London: Amnesty International, August 1998) AI Index IOR 63/01/98, at 31.

[27] The Protocol stated that it would be composed of twenty-one members nominated by states and elected by the AHSG for five years and who have 'recognised professional qualifications', and that jurisdiction of the Commission was limited to only inter-state disputes. The Protocol set out the procedure for referring a dispute to the Commission. The President and Vice Presidents would be full time and other members are part time. It would consult with parties as to the best method of settling the dispute.

[28] Article 20.

[29] The Economic and Social Commission held its first meeting in Niamey in December 1963 and set out activities with the aim of setting up an African common market and free trade area. It also called for an all-African trade union organisation to be set up, and for a pan-African youth organisation, Amate, *Inside the OAU*, at 477.

Commission,[30] all of which were composed of the relevant ministers from each state.[31] In July 1964 the AHSG also set up a Transport and Communications Commission[32] and a Commission of African Jurists.[33]

The General Secretariat of the OAU was based in Addis Ababa and was the administrative headquarters of the OAU. It operated under the authority of the Secretary General of the OAU, who was appointed by the AHSG.[34] He was supported by Assistant Secretaries.[35] The Secretary General and his staff were supposed to be independent of states[36] and states themselves were under a duty not to interfere with their mandates.[37] The role of the Secretary General in developing a human rights policy of the OAU has gained increasing importance. One of the former Secretary Generals, Dr Salim Ahmed Salim, took a particular interest in human rights concerns.[38] His powers have been 'dependent on the Organization's "sovereign" political organs. This limited political role has been partly compensated by a factual development which, over the years, has seen the OAU's Acting President ("Président en exercice") increasingly representing the Organization in relations with third parties.'[39]

The General Secretariat was divided into various departments: political; administration and conferences; finance; economic development and cooperation; and education, scientific, cultural and social affairs.[40] The Legal Division of the Secretariat provided an overall role and in this respect was crucial in an examination of the approach of the OAU to human rights.

---

[30] The Defence Commission in the OAU Charter was not quite the African High Command envisaged by some African states at the time. Umozurike notes that it 'started off with no clear mandate and no direction' and only when Guinea was invaded by Portugal in 1970 did it have to respond. 'The Commission has not been directly connected with the liberation of colonial territories, a task assigned to the Liberation Committee', U. O. Umozurike, *International Law and Colonialism in Africa* (Enugu, Nigeria: Nwamife Publishers, 1979), at 99.

[31] Article 21.   [32] Resolution AHG/Res.20(I).   [33] Elias, 'The Charter', at 264–5.

[34] Article 16.   [35] Again appointed by the AHSG, OAU Charter, Article 17.

[36] 'In the performance of their duties the Secretary General and the staff shall not seek or receive instructions from any government or from any other authority external to the Organization. They shall refrain from any action which might reflect on their position as international officials responsible only to the Organization', Article 18(1).

[37] Article 18(2). See Functions and Regulations of the General Secretariat, on file with author.

[38] See, for example, Message by Dr Salim Ahmed Salim, OAU Secretary General on the Occasion of the 36th Anniversary of the Organization of African Unity, Addis Ababa, May 1999, p. 5; Address by HE Dr Salim Ahmed Salim, Secretary General of the Organization of African Unity to the International Conference on Africa, Africa at 40, London, 29 October 1997, at 2–3.

[39] Sands and Klein, *Bowett's Law*, at 247.

[40] *Functions and Regulations of the General Secretariat*, Article 15.

However, it is clear that its potential was not fully realised. As Amnesty indicates:

> The role of the Legal Division in regard to human rights issues beyond monitoring of ratifications and drafting of treaties is not very clear but it is understood that it also provides advice to the Secretariat on a range of issues pertaining to human rights including the rights of children and women and contributes to reports of the Secretary General on these issues.[41]

With the transformation of the OAU into the AU many of these organs and structures have been replaced or renamed. These will be described further below.

Human rights within the OAU

The provisions of the OAU Charter make little express mention of human rights. Instead they reflect the dominating concerns of Africa at that time, namely to ensure the independence of those African peoples who were still colonised, condemnation of apartheid regimes in southern Africa, and protecting the newly acquired statehood.[42] Thus, its provisions centre on issues such as the non-interference in internal affairs,[43] sovereign equality of states,[44] the fight against neo-colonialism,[45] self-determination in the state context,[46] and peaceful settlement of disputes.[47] Thus, at this stage, the OAU's focus was on protection of the state, not the individual,[48] and any concept of human rights within the OAU went little beyond the notion

---

[41] Amnesty International, *Organization of African Unity*, at 28.

[42] Furthermore, it has been suggested that the OAU was not initially willing to consider human rights, labelling them 'one of the main elements in the ideological armoury of imperialism', I. G. Shivji, *The Concept of Human Rights in Africa* (London: CODESRIA Book Series, 1989).

[43] Articles 3(1) and (2). Elias, as one of the drafters of the Charter, notes that 'the desire to be left alone, to be allowed to choose its particular political, economic and social systems and to order the life of its community in its own way, is a legitimate one for large and small states alike', Elias, 'The Charter', at 248. See also A. B. Akinyemi, 'The Organization of African Unity and the Concept of Non-Interference in Internal Affairs of Member States', *BYIL* 46 (1972–3) 393–400, at 393–5.

[44] Article 3(1).   [45] Preamble, Article 2(1)(d), Article 3(6).

[46] Preamble, Article 3(3).   [47] Article 3(4).

[48] For example, assassination is condemned in respect of subverting the state, 'unreserved condemnation . . . of political assassination as well as of subversive activities', Article 3(5). See also M.-C. D. Wembou, 'The OAU and International Law', in Y. El-Ayouty (ed.), *The Organization of African Unity after Thirty Years* (Westport, CT: Praeger, 1994) 15–26, at 17; K. Mathews, 'The Organization of African Unity', in Mazzeo (ed.), *African Regional Organizations*, 49–84, at 80.

of self-determination in the context of decolonisation and apartheid in
South Africa. As Mathews notes,

> the OAU Charter, for instance, does not contain any provision for the
> protection of the rights of the African masses . . . evidently the emphasis
> in 1963 was on the state rather than the people. As President Nyerere of
> Tanzania, one of the founding fathers of the OAU, has pointed out, the
> OAU Charter spoke for the African peoples still under colonialism or racial
> domination, but once the countries emerged to nationhood, the Charter
> stood for the protection of their heads of state and served as a trade union
> which protected them. In other words, the OAU appears to be an institution
> of the African heads of state, by the heads of state and for the heads of
> state.[49]

Thus, where other aspects of human rights are mentioned in the Charter
they are broad and general and related to the relationship among states.[50]
Although there is some note of ethnic divides: 'inspired by a common
determination to promote understanding among our peoples . . . in a
larger unity transcending ethnic and national differences', this is stressed
in respect of African unity as a whole, rather than from the perspective
of the impact upon the individual. Further, any threats to human rights
appeared to be reflected in the OAU Charter as coming from outside the
continent, something which African unity may help to prevent.[51] It was
clear, therefore, that state sovereignty was sacrosanct.[52]

These influences during the 1960s were to define the OAU's approach to
human rights issues for many years. Thus, from the point of view of human
rights, it was the two issues of self-determination and apartheid/racial
discrimination in southern Africa that were central to the OAU at its

---

[49] Mathews, 'The Organization of African Unity', at 79.
[50] For example, in the preamble it notes that states are 'conscious of the fact that freedom,
      equality, justice and dignity are essential objectives for the achievement of the legitimate
      aspirations of the African peoples'. Also, 'persuaded that the Charter of the UN and the
      UDHR, to the Principles of which we reaffirm our adherence, provide a solid foundation for
      peaceful and positive co-operation among states'; 'to promote international co-operation,
      having due regard to the Charter of the UN and the UDHR', Article 2(1)(e).
[51] 'Desirous that all African states should henceforth unite so that the welfare and well-being
      of their peoples can be assured . . . [and] to co-ordinate and intensify their co-operation
      and efforts to achieve a better life for the peoples of Africa', Article 2(1)(b). With this in
      mind states should thus coordinate their efforts, according to Article 2(2), specifically in
      the political, diplomatic, economic, educational and cultural, health, scientific and defence
      and security fields.
[52] C. Clapham, *Africa and the International System. The Politics of State Survival* (Cambridge:
      Cambridge University Press, 1996), at 115.

formation and which appear to have guided its approach to human rights throughout its later years. It is worth paying some attention to them in this respect.

The concept of self-determination

The history of colonisation to which nearly all of Africa had been subject, the resulting groupings among newly independent African states and the idea of a sense of African unity[53] were behind the creation of the OAU.[54] Indeed, it has been said that 'the Charter of the OAU is more than the constitution of an African regional organisation: it is a charter of liberation'.[55] This was reflected in the preamble of the OAU Charter which sought, as Naldi notes,

> to preclude external intervention in African affairs. This aim is linked to the goal of eradicating all forms of colonialism and neo-colonialism from Africa . . . This was a reference not only to the racist regimes of Southern Africa . . . but also to the policies by which external powers indirectly maintained or extended their influence over African countries. The eradication of colonialism in all its forms was therefore regarded as a necessary prerequisite to the attainment of the OAU's goals.[56]

The OAU spent many of its early years assisting in the liberation of colonised entities and giving assistance to liberation movements,[57] including funding their arms purchases and providing them with training.[58]

---

[53] Emerson attributes reasons for African unity to 'all Africans [having] a spiritual affinity with each other', but questions whether there is a presumption that Africans are all part of the same race, R. Emerson, 'Pan-Africanism', *International Organization* 16(2) (1962) 275–90, at 282.

[54] Naldi, *An Analysis*, at 1.

[55] J. Dugard, 'The Organisation of African Unity and Colonialism: An Inquiry into the Plea of Self-Defence as a Justification for the Use of Force in the Eradication of Colonialism', *ICLQ* 16 (1967) 157–90, at 158–9; G. L. Wilkins, *African Influence in the United Nations 1967–1975. The Politics and Techniques of Gaining Compliance to UN Principles and Resolutions* (Washington, DC: University Press of America, 1981), at 78–9.

[56] Naldi, *An Analysis*, at 3–4.

[57] For example, see Resolution on South Africa, CM/Res.1427(LVII).

[58] Z. Cervenka, 'Major Policy Shifts in the Organization of African Unity 1963–1973', in K. Ingham (ed.), *Foreign Relations of African States* (London: Butterworths, 1974) 323–44, at 330. I. Sagay, *International Law and the Struggle for the Freedom of Man in Africa* (Ife: Ife University Press, 1983). See GA Resolution 2625(XXV), 24 October 1970. Use of force to liberate is permitted in international law, and this has been confirmed for example in Conakry at the Conference of Afro-Asian Jurists, October 1964, Cairo Conference of Non-Aligned Movement, 1964 and in 1969 in the Lusaka Manifesto of OAU.

Thus, the OAU would appear to have supported the notion that there was a legal duty on states to end colonialism[59] and 'armed struggle has proven to be . . . a legitimate method of asserting the right of self-determination of a colonial or oppressed people'.[60] This anti-colonialism stance is reflected in the main human rights treaty for Africa, Article 20(2) ACHPR, which suggests that those under foreign domination can use any means to be free from it. This was supporting the notion that 'once people are recognised as having a right of self-determination, it follows logically and inevitably that they must also be legally entitled to resist any action aimed at denying them that right'.[61]

Resolutions were adopted on decolonisation[62] and the OAU created a Liberation Committee.[63] Despite some difficulties,[64] 'the OAU as a whole remained loyal to its self-assigned task of helping the people of the colonised territories of Africa to fight for their independence',[65] the Liberation Committee meeting regularly and ensuring that the issue was maintained on the agenda of the UN and OAU organs. Its recognition of liberation movements assisted in their obtaining assistance from other countries and access to the OAU and UN meetings and contributed

? Devil

[59] Legal Consequences Case, ICJ Rep (1971), p. 14 through military or other means.

[60] I Enemo, 'Self-Determination as the Fundamental Basis of the Concept of Legitimate Governance under the African Charter on Human and Peoples' Rights', in E. K. Quashigah and O. C. Okafor (eds.), *Legitimate Governance in Africa: International and Domestic Legal Perspectives* (The Hague: Kluwer Law International, 1999) 403–18, at 417.

[61] Ibid.

[62] For example, Resolution CIAS/Plen.2/Rev.2, adopted by the Founding Fathers of the OAU and thus the first resolution of the OAU. This 'reaffirmed that is the duty of all independent African states to support dependant peoples in Africa in their struggle for freedom and independence' and agreed unanimously to 'concert and coordinate their efforts' for independence; condemned 'flagrant violation of the inalienable rights of the legitimate inhabitants of the territories concerned' and called for colonial powers to 'take immediate measures' to end colonial domination.

[63] For information on its work see Amate, *Inside the OAU*, at chapter 8.

[64]   The persistent refusal by several member states to give the Liberation Committee the funds it needed to carry out the onerous task that had been entrusted to it coupled with the harsh criticisms by these very states of the performance of the Liberation Committee, would have killed the Committee within the first two or three years of its birth if it had not been sustained by the unquenchable desire and determination of the OAU as a whole to remove the stain of colonialism and white minority rule from the face of Africa,

Ibid., at 240

[65] Ibid., at 282–3.

towards defining what amounted to a liberation struggle[66] and setting out other standards for liberation movements. The southern Africa issue was at the forefront of such discussions.

However, self-determination even in the context of decolonisation had its limits. Prior to the attainment of independence of many African states, 'a general campaign of frontier rearrangement was under consideration',[67] and African leaders appeared to stress that colonial boundaries should be removed given that they were imposed without regard for the rights of the peoples living in the territories. However, on the creation of the OAU Charter, 'within a few years the atmosphere changed and more and more African states, upon obtaining independence, sanctioned the boundaries imposed by colonial powers'.[68] The OAU reflected this shift[69] and

> shied away from the earlier negative and radical approach and reversed their demand for the 'abolition' of the colonial boundaries, as the imme- diate 'union' of the African states was found to be premature and not fully accepted at the time. Above all, by this time almost half of the new African states had already been established within the pre-independence colonial boundaries. Therefore, the new African states instead chose the mainten- ance of these boundaries, but they did not specifically reject the necessity or the possibility of readjustments . . . It appears that the Charter merely stated the desires, intentions and consent of the member states to accept the existing territorial status quo. It did not refer to the colonial boundaries or boundary treaties specifically as such, though it was clear that that the ter- ritories of these states were defined by them. Similarly, the Organization of African Unity did not formally adopt the so-called uti possidetis doctrine, though in practice the political arrangements of the African states could have the same effect and interpretations of that doctrine. The Organiza- tion has been basically interested in preventing conflicts among the African states.[70]

---

[66] The Liberation Committee defined 'struggle' as 'any action, be it constitutional, psycholo- gical, political or military, carried out inside or outside a country with the aim of liberating it from foreign domination', as cited, ibid., at 284.

[67] M. Shaw, *Title to Territory in Africa. International Legal Issues* (Oxford: Clarendon Press, 1986), at 182. See All-Africa Peoples' Conference, Accra, 1958, which suggested changes to frontiers.

[68] Shaw, *Title to Territory*, at 183.

[69] Thus, the preamble to the OAU, 'determined to safeguard and consolidate hard-won independence as well as the sovereignty and territorial integrity of our states and to fight against neo-colonialism in all its forms', similarly Articles 2(1)(c), 3(3).

[70] Y. Makonnen, *International Law and the New States of Africa* (Addis Ababa: UNESCO, 1983), at 459–60.

Thus, as illustrated by the AHSG in its 1964 Resolution on the Intangibility of Frontiers,[71] it was clear that once independence had been gained the OAU upheld existing boundaries[72] on the basis of African unity and the need for peaceful settlement of disputes:

> Border problems constitute a grave and permanent factor of dissension; conscious of the existence of extra-African manoeuvres aiming at dividing the African states; considering further the borders of African states, on the day of their independence, constitute a tangible reality; recalling the establishment in the course of the Second Ordinary Session of the Council of the Committee of Eleven in charge of studying the means of strengthening African Unity; recognising the imperious necessity of settling, by peaceful means and within a strictly African framework, all disputes between African states; recalling further that all Member States have pledged, under Article VI, to scrupulously respect all principles laid down in Article III of the Charter of the Organization of African Unity; 1. solemnly reaffirms the strict respect by all Member States of the Organization for the principles laid down in Article III, para. 3 of the Charter of the Organization of African Unity; 2. solemnly declares that all Member States pledge themselves to respect the frontiers existing on their achievement of national independence.[73]

Others have argued that as the status of the principle of *uti possidetis* is questionable, African leaders were not necessarily simply applying the principle but 'being faced with serious problems if they were to reject the boundaries, they wisely resorted to political problems which might be said to have culminated in the emergence of what could be called African common law upon colonial boundaries'.[74] Thus, it appears to be more closely related to a desire to protect African unity: 'The artificial divisions and territorial boundaries created by the imperialist powers are

---

[71] AHG/Res.16(I), July 1964.
[72] One could say that the argument that state boundaries have been imposed on Africa does not hold up in reality: 'If it is remarkable that not a single federative scheme has been able to dent those "invalid" colonial boundaries, it is even more significant that there has not been a successful attempt to break out of those boundaries, to create a new state from within an old mold or to make a major boundary readjustment between states', T. Franck, 'Afference, Efference and Legitimacy in Africa', in Y. El-Ayouty and H. C. Brooks (eds.), *Africa and International Organization* (The Hague: Martinus Nijhoff, 1974) 3–10, at 4.
[73] AHG/Res.16(I), July 1964. Note also the Frontier Dispute case, *Burkina Faso v. Mali*, ICJ Reports, 1986, p. 554.
[74] Makonnen, *International Law*, at 458.

deliberate steps to abstract the political unity of the West African people.'[75] As Nkrumah stated:

> This fatal relic of colonialism will drive us to war against one another as our unplanned and uncoordinated industrial development expands, just as happened in Europe. Unless we proceed in arresting the danger through mutual understanding on fundamental issues, and through African Unity, which will render existing boundaries obsolete and superfluous, we shall have fought in vain for independence. Only African Unity can heal this festering sore of boundary disputes between our various states.[76]

It would also appear that this desire to maintain colonial boundaries was not really out of an obligation to the rules of state succession.[77] Thus, the OAU now stresses that one of the reasons for maintaining existing boundaries is because to allow otherwise may give encouragement to others to do the same.[78]

---

[75] Pan-African Congress, Manchester, 1945, cited in C. Legum, *Pan-Africanism* (New York: Praeger, 1965), at 153. See further,

> It is hereby resolved by the All African Peoples' Conference that the Conference (a) denounces artificial frontiers drawn by imperialist powers to divide the peoples of Africa, particularly those which cut across ethnic groups and divide people of the same stock; (b) calls for the abolition or adjustment of such frontiers at an early date to this problem founded upon the true wishes of the people; (c) calls upon the Independent States of Africa to support a permanent solution

> First All African Peoples' Conference, Accra, 5–13 December 1958, cited in Makonnen, *International Law*, at 458–9.

In addition, the Resolution on Somaliland had the same principle, Second All African Peoples' Conference, Tunis, 25–30 January 1960.

[76] K. Nkrumah, 'United we Stand', address, Proceedings of the Summit Conference of Independent African States, Addis Ababa, vol.1, section 2, Summit CIAS/GEN/INF/36, May 1963, at 7.

[77] Makonnen, *International Law*, at 460–2.

[78] As has been said in relation to the Comoros,

> The separatist Agenda is a serious threat to peace, security and stability of the Comoros and countries of the Indian Ocean in general. It would also be a very serious precedent likely to be emulated elsewhere in Africa and undermine one of the most fundamental principles of the OAU whose respect had greatly contributed to the maintenance of peace, security and stability on the Continent.

> Draft Decisions of the Sixty-Seventh Ordinary Session of the Council of Ministers, CM/DRAFT/DECISIONS(LXVII) REV.1, p. 9.

It goes on, 'reaffirms its total commitment to the unity and territorial integrity of the Comoros and to ensure that the unity and territorial integrity of the Comoros are preserved', at 10.

The OAU has consistently upheld this principle, despite criticisms that can be raised about the arbitrary nature in which these inherited colonial boundaries were imposed.[79] Thus, the OAU has subsequently rejected claims for independence for entities that exist within an OAU state, condemning such claims, for example, in Somalia,[80] Comoros[81] and Nigeria (Biafra). Some have argued that the acceptance by the majority of OAU members of the claims by the SADR against Morocco, which was then admitted as a member of the OAU, indicates 'an eloquent endorsement of a case of self-determination in post-independent Africa and an indication of a possible change in existing African perspectives on the principle'.[82] Given that this has not been applied elsewhere, however, the more credible explanation is, as Enemo argues, that

> it would be a mockery of the international legal order if a liberation movement like the Polisario of the SADR successfully secures the recognition of its movement with the rights and duties of a quasi-state but on successful conclusion of its struggle is denied the capacity to realise the fruits of its

[79] Shaw, *Title to Territory*, at 50. See also *Burkina Faso v. Mali*, ICJ Reports, 1986 554, at 566–7.

[80] Draft Decisions of the Sixty-Seventh Ordinary Session of the Council of Ministers, CM/DRAFT/DECISIONS(LXVII) REV.1, p. 14 'reaffirms the sovereignty, unity and territorial integrity of Somalia as one and indivisible state'. Decisions Adopted by the Sixty-Sixth Ordinary Session of the Council of Ministers, CM/Dec.330–363(LXVI), Dec.357 on Somalia.

[81]   The separatists' agenda equally constituted a serious precedent likely to compromise one of the most fundamental principles of the OAU – that of unity and territorial integrity – the respect of which had largely contributed to the maintenance of peace, security and stability in Africa. To conclude, they affirmed the need to do everything to ensure the respect for the unity and territorial integrity of the Comoros.
       Draft Rapporteur's Report of the Sixty-Seventh Ordinary Session of the Council of Ministers, CM/Plen/Draft/Rapt/Rpt(LXVII), at para. 116. See also Report of the Secretary General on the Situation in the Comoros, CM/2062 (LXVIII), paras. 2 and 3. Draft Rapporteur's Report of the Sixty-Seventh Ordinary Session of the Council of Ministers, CM/Plen/Draft/Rapt/Rpt(LXVII), at paras. 117 and 118(b) and (c); Decision on the Report of the Secretary General on the Conflict Situation in the Federal Islamic Republic of the Comoros (Doc.CM/2099(LXX)-c); OAU and Peace-Making (www.oau-oua.org/document/mechanism/english/mech16.htm); Communiqué of the Eighty-Third Ordinary Session of the Central Organ of the OAU Mechanism for Conflict Prevention, Management and Resolution at Ambassadorial Level, 3 June 2002, Central Organ/MEC/Amb/Comm.(LXXXIII).

[82] S. Blay, 'Changing African Perspectives on the Right of Self-Determination in the Wake of the Banjul Charter on Human and Peoples' Rights', *JAL* (1985) 147–59, at 157.

struggle. Therefore, such successful secessionist activities should be recognised and should be seen as legitimate under international law and also under the African Charter on Human and Peoples' Rights.[83]

Although the OAU has adopted a considerable number of resolutions supporting the right of the people of Palestine to self-determination and the 'legitimacy of the struggle',[84] on the whole in Africa, the OAU 'unequivocally rejects post-independent territorial claims' where these amount to changes in the territory.[85]

The notion of self-determination as a human right has gained increasing attention in international legal debate.[86] Although the right to self-determination in the context of decolonisation is now well established, and indeed the work of the OAU in this regard has been extremely important, the extent to which it can be applied beyond these situations is still not clear, either at the level of the OAU or internationally.[87] There is evidence, however, even early on in the work of the OAU, that the notion of self-determination is broader than claims for independence. In its Lusaka Manifesto adopted in 1969, for example, the OAU noted: 'All men are equal, and have equal rights to human dignity and respect, regardless of colour, race, religion or sex. We believe that all men have the right and the duty to participate as equal members of the society, in their own government.'[88]

---

[83] Enemo, 'Self-Determination', at 414.

[84] For example, see Draft Rapporteur's Report of the Sixty-Seventh Ordinary Session of the Council of Ministers, CM/Plen/Draft/Rapt/Rpt(LXVII), para. 200. See also Draft Decisions of the Sixty-Seventh Ordinary Session of the Council of Ministers, CM/DRAFT/DECISIONS(LXVII) REV.1, p. 4; Draft Resolution on the Question of Palestine, CM/Draft/Res.23(LXIII) Rev.1; Decision on the Report of the Secretary General on the Question of Palestine (Doc.CM/2104(LXX); Draft Resolution on the Situation in the Middle East, CM/Draft/Res.24(LXIII) Rev.1; Decision on the Report of the Secretary General on the Situation in the Middle East (Doc.CM/2103(LXX)), CM/Dec.457(LXX). Resolution on the Situation in the Middle East, CM/Res.1428(LVII).

[85] Enemo, 'Self-Determination', at 412–13.

[86] See, for example, K. Knop, *Diversity and Self-Determination in International Law* (Cambridge: Cambridge University Press, 2002); P. Alston, *Peoples' Rights* (Oxford: Oxford University Press, 2001); R. McCorquodale, *Self-Determination in International Law* (Dartmouth: Ashgate, 2000); T. D. Musgrave, *Self-Determination and National Minorities* (Oxford: Oxford University Press, 1997); C. Tomuschat, *Modern Law of Self-Determination* (Leiden: Brill, 1993); M. Pomerance, *Self-Determination in Law and Practice. The New Doctrine of the United Nations* (Leiden: Brill, 1982).

[87] Dugard, 'The Organisation of African Unity', at 159; Blay, 'Changing African Perspectives', at 147.

[88] The Lusaka Manifesto: A Policy Statement for Decolonisation in Respect of Southern Africa, adopted by a conference of fourteen African states in April 1969, adopted by the

Further, the OAU's attention to self-determination in the decolon-isation context arguably prompted its later expansion of the concept.[89] Firstly, it focused on independence and self-determination as a funda-mental right (but one owned by the state rather than the individual). Thus, in a resolution on the anniversary of the adoption of the UN General Assembly Resolution on Granting of Independence to Colonial Countries the Council of Ministers of the OAU noted that the General Assembly (GA) 'affirmed that the subjection of peoples to alien subju-gation, domination and exploitation constituted a denial of fundamental human rights and was contrary to the Charter of the United Nations'.[90] Furthermore,

> in the euphoria of the upsurge of nationalism and the struggle for freedom in this period, not much attention was given to the concepts of human rights or democracy. The cause of freedom and independence was itself a basic human right, of course, and the concentration was placed on this struggle . . . In the midst of the fast-moving events of the later 1950s and 1960s, it seemed almost irrelevant to ask what kinds of government would be established and how human rights would be protected after independence . . . There was an assumption that there was something inherent in traditional African organisations that would lead in the right direction.[91]

OAU and the UN, Resolution GA 2505, UN Doc.A/PV.1815, 20 November 1969. For text see Umozurike, *International Law*, appendix C.

[89] For example, 'reaffirms the right of each African people to choose its own political sys-tem', Draft Resolution on Measures to be Taken Against Neo-Colonialist Manoeuvres and Foreign Military Interventions in Africa, CM/Res.638(XXXI), para. 5.

[90] The continuation of colonialism in all its forms and manifestations, including racism, apartheid and the activities of foreign economic and other interests which exploit colonial peoples, as well as waging of colonial wars to suppress the national liberation movements of the colonial territories in Africa, is incompatible with the Charter of the United Nations, the Universal Declaration of Human Rights and the Declaration on the Granting of Independence of Colonial Countries and Peoples and poses a serious threat to international peace and security; reaffirms the inalienable rights of colonial peoples to struggle by all necessary means at their disposal against colonial powers which suppress their aspiration for freedom and independence.
Resolution on the Twentieth Anniversary of Adoption of Resolution 1514(XV) by United Nations General Assembly, CM/Res.793(XXXV), preamble and paras. 2, 3 and 5.

[91] G. M. Houser, 'Human Rights and the Liberation Struggle: The Importance of Creative Tension', in E. McCarthy-Arnolds, D. R. Penna and D. J. Cruz Sobrepeña (eds.), *Africa, Human Rights and the Global System. The Political Economy of Human Rights in a Changing World* (Westport, CT: Greenwood Press, 1994) 11–22, at 13.

Although clearly there was a 'contradiction often found between the struggle for independence and freedom on the one hand and gross violations of human rights in the midst of this struggle on the other',[92] at least the OAU was framing the issue in terms of human rights.

Secondly, the OAU does appear to consider that 'self-determination is a continuing matter, not a once-for-all constitution of the state'.[93] This had been reflected in its attention in more recent years to unconstitutional governments and issues of elections. Thus, self-determination could be said to be 'the historic root from which the democratic entitlement grew',[94] and that the anti-colonial movement was seen as a struggle for democracy and human rights,[95] prompting the OAU later to consider the concept of democracy and in turn human rights.

Lastly, in the course of the OAU considering self-determination as an independence issue it was also prompted to touch upon human rights issues. Thus, resolutions relating to African peoples who were still under colonial domination condemned the acts of the colonial powers which resulted in deaths, serious injuries and arbitrary detention, calling for individual prisoners to be set free and, for example, for the colonial rulers to pay 'ample compensation for the physical, material and mental sufferings endured by the victims'.[96] In the context, therefore, of the fight for independence it drew upon human rights standards to support its claims.[97]

Racism and apartheid in southern Africa

The second human rights-related issue that dominated the OAU at its inception, and for many years following, was how to deal with the South

---

[92] Ibid., at 15–16 and 17.

[93] J. Crawford, 'Democracy and the Body of International Law', in G. H. Fox and B. R. Roth (eds.), *Democratic Governance and International Law* (Cambridge: Cambridge University Press, 2000) 91–122, at 94.

[94] T. Franck, 'The Emerging Right to Democratic Governance', *AJIL* 86 (1992) 44–91, at 52.

[95] A. Aidoo, 'Africa: Democracy without Human Rights?', *HRQ* 15 (1993) 703–15, at 706.

[96] Resolution on Portugal's Act of Aggression against the Republic of Guinea, CM/Res.201(XIII).

[97] 'Reiterating its conviction that the total eradication of racial discrimination, apartheid and violations of the basic human rights of the peoples in colonial territories will be achieved by the greatest speed by the faithful and complete implementation of the Declaration', Resolution on the 20th Anniversary of Adoption of Resolution 1514(XV) by United Nations General Assembly, CM/Res.793(XXXV), preamble and para. 3.

African apartheid regime.[98] Resolutions adopted at its very first sessions concentrated on the situation noting that this was a 'serious threat to peace and international security', 'incompatible with its political and moral obligations as a member state of the United Nations' and a 'grave danger to stability and peace in Africa and in the world'.[99] It called on states of the OAU to respect sanctions against South Africa.[100] Similar resolutions were also adopted in respect of Rhodesia.[101]

What is apparent is that the OAU used human rights standards in the context of what was seen as a liberation struggle in South Africa. As a result it looked at a variety of human rights-related issues and in its condemnation of apartheid drew upon these as tools to support its position. It thus took the opportunity to condemn the events in South Africa and in the process linked human rights issues with what was happening.[102] It called for non-recognition of South African Bantustans,[103] expressed concern 'about the imposition of so-called self-government on the people of Namibia against their wishes', arguably introducing a wider notion of self-determination,[104] condemned the treatment of detainees (albeit political detainees) in prisons,[105] called for the 'unconditional

[98] Most of the resolutions adopted by the Council of Ministers and AHSG in the 1970s and 1980s relate to apartheid and decolonisation.
[99] Apartheid in South Africa, CM/Res.13(II).
[100] Sanctions were imposed by the OAU on Southern Rhodesia, and it threatened to sever diplomatic relations with the UK as well, ECM/Res.13(VI). The OAU also urged states not to recognise the white minority regime and to give aid to Zimbabwe in its struggle for independence, Resolution on Southern Rhodesia, CM/75(VI).
[101] 'A minority white settler government has been imposed upon the African peoples against their wishes.' This is said to threaten solidarity and the peace of Africa and the world, and the British government is called upon to prevent unilateral independence by a white minority, convene a conference and ensure one man one vote for independence. OAU states are required to reconsider diplomatic relations with Britain if these requests were ignored, Southern Rhodesia, CM/Res.14(II).
[102] Resolution on the Soweto Massacres in South Africa, CM/Res.476(XXVII); Resolution on Sanctions, CM/Res.553(XXIX), preamble.
[103] Resolution on Non-Recognition of South African Bantustans, CM/Res.492(XXVII). Also, 'considering that the Pretoria regime continues to pursue its hideous policy of Bantustanization which constitutes the complete denial of human rights and the right of self-determination', Resolution on South Africa, CM/Res.455(XXVI).
[104] Resolution on Namibia, CM/Res.537(XXVIII); Resolution on South Africa, CM/Res.538 (XXVIII), para. 2.
[105] Resolution on South Africa, CM/Res.538(XXVIII), para. 3; 'strongly condemns the continued imprisonment of hundreds of students and workers, the number of political prisoners and persecution of leaders such as Winnie Nomzano [sic] Mandela and Zeph Mothupeng [sic]; demands the immediate and unconditional release of all nationalist leaders serving terms of life imprisonment or long sentences who have been jailed

release of all political prisoners',[106] and expressed 'its deep concern over the trials conducted according to the arbitrary and inhuman laws of the government'.[107] Further, it condemned the 'loss of life and damage to property',[108] the killing of demonstrators[109] and unfair trials.[110] In the context of Rhodesia, for example, the OAU called on the UK government to suspend the 'present undemocratic constitution of 1961 and to convene a new constitutional conference for the purpose of preparing a Constitution founded on universal suffrage of all inhabitants of the territory'.[111] The Council of Ministers on several occasions was prepared to say that the 'atrocities perpetrated by the illegal racist minority regime in Rhodesia against the African people fighting for their freedom' were

---

since 1963 and pays tribute to their heroic struggles', Resolution on South Africa, CM/Res.554(XXIX), paras. 11–12. In respect of South Africa in 1989, the Council of Ministers noted that it was 'gravely concerned over the extension of the state of emergency, passing of death sentences on opponents of apartheid, continued detention without trial and intensified repression of all opponents of the minority racist regime; further concerned about the deteriorating health of political prisoners and detainees in apartheid prisons', Resolution on South Africa, CM/Res.1207(L), preamble. Further, 'demands that all prisoners and detainees in racist jails have access to proper medical care', Resolution on South Africa, CM/Res.1207(L), para. 6; 'Condemns the racist regime of South Africa for incarcerating South African patriots for over a quarter of a century under inhuman and harsh conditions which resulted in a sad deterioration of their health and, whilst welcoming the unconditional release of these stalwarts, some of whom have been rendered sick by adverse prison conditions, demands the immediate and unconditional release of all other political prisoners and detainees', Resolution on South Africa, CM/Res.1244(LI), para. 9.

[106] Resolution on Namibia, CM/Res.551(XXIX), para. 4(b); Resolution on Namibia, CM/Res.720(XXXIII), para. 4; Resolution on the Abduction and Detention of Victor Matlou of ANC by South African Police, CM/Res.767(XXXIV); Apartheid in South Africa, CM/Res.13(II); Southern Rhodesia, CM/Res.62(V).

[107] Apartheid and Racial Discrimination, CM/Res.31(II). The Council of Ministers condemned South Africa's arrests and trial of South West Africans arguing that this was 'unjust and illegal' in violation of UN resolutions demanding their release, Resolution on South West Africans Tried and Sentenced in South Africa, CM/Res.138(X).

[108] 'Strongly condemns the aggressive policies of the illegal South African occupation regime in Namibia reflected in its repeated acts of aggression against neighbouring states in particular Angola and Zambia, causing considerable loss of human life and damage to property', Resolution on Namibia, CM/Res.629(XXXI), para. 10; Resolution on the Current Situation in South Africa, CM/Res.956(XLI).

[109] Resolution on South Africa, CM/Res.636(XXXI), preamble.

[110] In 1967 the AHSG adopted a resolution on the trial of South West Africans in South Africa noting it was 'violating normal legal procedures and denying the said nationals any access to witnesses or family connections both of which are necessary for preparing effectively for their legal defence', asking the UN to stop the trial, Resolution on South West Africans on Trial in South Africa, AHG/Res.50(IV).

[111] General Resolution on Southern Rhodesia, ECM/Res.11(V).

'crimes against humanity'.[112] It also called on other African states to try to secure the release of detainees fighting for national liberation.[113] Later resolutions reiterated these issues, adding also that African governments should combat 'any policy based on racial discrimination'.[114] It thus had broadened its consideration not only to racial discrimination in general[115] but also to touch upon issues such as refugees[116] and human rights.

Although for many years such issues were always stressed within the context of apartheid and the struggle for independence,[117] in the course of thirty years the South African issue prompted the OAU to consider human rights issues in general as it sought to use all the means at its disposal to condemn the apartheid regime. When apartheid ended it was then difficult for African states to say human rights were just a domestic concern. As Clapham notes:

[112] Resolution on Rhodesia, CM/Res.135(X). It also said the same in respect of Portugal, Resolution on Territories under Portuguese Domination, CM/Res.137(X). A massacre in Mozambique by South Africa was said in 1987 to be a crime against humanity, Declaration on the Massacre at Homoine in the People's Republic of Mozambique, CM/ST.24 (XLVI).

[113] Resolution on Territories under Portuguese Domination, CM/Res.137(X); Resolution on Apartheid and Racial Discrimination, CM/Res.242/Rev.1(XVII); Resolution on Zimbabwe, CM/Res.267(XIX). Solemn Declaration on General Policy, CM/ST.9(XXI); 'Reaffirms the policy of apartheid is a crime against the conscience and dignity of the whole mankind and is incompatible with the Charters of the United Nations and the OAU and the Universal Declaration of Human Rights', Resolution on the Situation in Southern Africa, CM/Res.936(XL), para. 9.

[114] Apartheid and Racial Discrimination in the Republic of South Africa, CM/Res.48(IV); Apartheid and Racial Discrimination in the Republic of South Africa, CM/Res.66(V); Resolution on South Africa, CM/Res.554(XXIX), paras. 1–3.

[115] Resolution on Sanctions, CM/Res.553(XXIX), preamble. The AHSG also adopted a resolution relating to racial discrimination against black Americans in the USA in 1964, Racial Discrimination in the United States of America, AHG/Res.15(I); see also Resolution on Apartheid and Racial Discrimination, CM/Res.102(IX).

[116] In respect of a resolution on Zimbabwe in 1980 the Council of Ministers noted issues like 'right of return of all Zimbabwean exiles and refugees', 'deeply indignant at the reports of torture and harassment of refugees returning to Southern Rhodesia', Resolution on Zimbabwe, CM/Res.766(XXXIV), and further, 'reaffirming the fact that the oppressive system of apartheid colonialism and racism constitute major causes for the exodus of refugees in Southern Africa'. See also Resolution on the Root Causes of Refugees in Africa, CM/Res.987(XLII).

[117] 'Calls on OAU member states to intensify the international campaigning for the immediate and unconditional release of all political prisoners, detainees, people under house arrest and other forms of restriction in South Africa and appeals to African and friendly states to campaign for the granting of prisoner of war status to all freedom fighters captured by the enemy', Resolution on South Africa, CM/Res.636(XXXI), para. 12.

In bringing their outrage to the attention of an external and especially Western audience, however, African governments and other anti-apartheid campaigners both explicitly breached the frontiers of juridical sovereignty and raised issues relating to the treatment of individuals which could equally be raised with reference to their own states. Once the human rights records of African-ruled states started to attract external attention, it was correspondingly harder to claim the protection of sovereign statehood.[118]

Other issues prompting the OAU to deal with human rights

It is also worth mentioning a number of other smaller issues which had some impact on the OAU choosing to consider human rights as part of its remit. Firstly, the work of the International Labour Organisation (ILO) and other international organisations prompted the OAU organs to consider issues like workers' rights from an early stage in its history.[119] Events and conferences held at the international level (some of which were held in Africa) in which African states were involved also prompted the OAU to consider some aspects of human rights. This can be seen, for example, in the chapters on the rights of women and of the child.[120] Secondly, the decision of the OAU organs during the 1980s to grant observer status to NGOs may also have had some (much lesser) role to play when those, albeit a very limited number, were admitted on the basis of their role in human rights.[121]

---

[118] Clapham, *Africa*, at 189.

[119] For example, in a Resolution on the relationship with the OAU and ILO the Council of Ministers, 'appreciating the work done by the ILO in the field of employment promotion and the improvement of working and living conditions of workers' and 'recalling the urgent need for Africa to implement the Declaration and Programme of Action on the establishment of the New International Economic Order', recommended that there be a working relationship between the two bodies set up, the ILO to provide more technical cooperation to African states, Resolution on the Relations between the OAU and ILO, CM/Res.446(XXV).

[120] See chapters 5 and 6.

[121] In 1986 the OAU gave observer status to the African Jurists Association, noting that it was 'conscious of the beneficial role that the Association can play with regard to the promotion and protection of human rights and other legal issues in Africa', Resolution on the Application of African Jurists Association for Observer Status, CM/Res.1036(XLIII). In 1992 the Council of Ministers granted observer status to the Social and Democratic Inter-African organisation, 'taking note of the importance of the objectives of the Socialist and Democratic Inter-African in particular the promotion of African unity, promotion of the respect of human rights and fundamental liberties as well as the strengthening of inter-African

Beyond these issues, however, little attention was paid to human rights until the end of the Cold War in the early 1990s.[122]

Landmark developments in the OAU's approach to human rights

The African Charter on Human and Peoples' Rights (ACHPR)

From the late 1970s onwards a number of important events define the OAU/AU move to increased attention to human rights. Encouragement at the UN level for regional human rights mechanisms, NGO lobbying and a recognition by some African leaders themselves that human rights in another state were also their concern fed into the adoption by the OAU of the African Charter on Human and Peoples' Rights (ACHPR) in 1981.[123] With its coming into force in 1986, human rights were thus officially recognised in the OAU, albeit still in a rather limited fashion given the independent focus of the Charter and its weak enforcement mechanisms. Its Commission, an independent body of eleven experts, was, however, headquartered in The Gambia, a factor which would not help to integrate its work in the rest of the OAU's organs in Addis Ababa, and which has exacerbated its isolation over the years both theoretically

and international cooperation', Resolution on the Request for an OAU Observer Status Submitted by the Socialist and Democratic Inter-African, CM/Res.1383(LV), preamble. In 1994 the Council of Ministers gave observer status to the African Society of International and Comparative Law (ASICL), noting the importance of its objectives such as 'international law, the protection of public liberties and the improvement of the administration of justice', Resolution on the Granting of OAU Observer Status to the African Society of International and Comparative Law, CM/Res.1540(LX), preamble. In a resolution relating to the cooperation with the International Commission of Jurists, the Council of Ministers noted that 'Considering the mandate of the ICJ and its important role in the promotion and protection of Human Rights in Africa and especially in the support rendered towards the establishment and functioning of the African Commission on Human and Peoples' Rights' and 'Considering also that the principles and objectives governing the activities of the ICJ are in conformity with the principles and purposes of the OAU', 'Taking into account the need to enhance the cooperation between the OAU and International Commission of Jurists in the field of human rights in Africa'. It then approved a draft cooperation agreement between them, Resolution on the Proposed Cooperation Agreement between the Organization of African Unity and the International Commission of Jurists, CM/Res.1675(LXIV), preamble.

[122] See J. Oloka-Onyango, 'Human Rights and Sustainable Development in Contemporary Africa: A New Dawn or Retreating Horizons', Human Development Report 2000 Background Paper (UNDP, 2000), http://www.undp.org/docs/publications/background_papers/Oloka-Onyango2000.html.

[123] Adopted 27 June 1981, 21 ILM (1982) 58.

and practically from the work of the rest of the OAU, despite the latter's formal role in the examination of the Commission's documents and financing of its activities.[124] Some of the bodies within the OAU Secretariat Headquarters in Addis Ababa which one might expect to liase with the African Commission appear to have little knowledge of its work.[125] Whilst the African Charter could therefore be said to be some recognition that human rights in one state were matters of concern to other states, it was argued that this was not accompanied by an effective enforcement mechanism within the Charter.[126] Certainly the OAU had turned a blind eye to atrocities committed by Bokassa in the Central African Republic and Idi Amin in Uganda,[127] yet the decision to adopt this Charter, its subsequent coming into force in 1986 and the work of its Commission have had a considerable impact on the OAU/AU and at the very least have ensured that human rights were then a constant, albeit perhaps sidelined, feature on the agenda of the OAU bodies.[128] Unfortunately, as the chapter on the African Charter indicates,[129] there does appear to have been a presumption that human rights issues will be dealt with by the African Commission in Banjul. Resolutions adopted by the OAU organs relating to the work of the African Commission and in the adoption of its reports have generally, therefore, been limited to formalities, supporting the idea of the Commission and that it should be strengthened in general, urging states to ratify the Charter and subsequent instruments and submit their reports to the Commission.[130] Over the years, however, the fact that its reports were on the agenda of the OAU organs and the adoption of

---

[124] ACHPR, Articles 33–44 and 59.

[125] Indeed, when the Commission presented its Draft Protocol on the Rights of Women to the OAU General Secretariat it was asked to revise it further in light of parallel discussions which had taken place at the OAU, Draft Protocol to the African Charter on Human and Peoples' Rights on the Rights of Women in Africa [Final Version], CAB/LEG/66.6; Drafting Process of the Draft Protocol on the Rights of Women in Africa, DOC/OS(XXVII)/159b. See chapter 2 below.

[126] Clapham, *Africa*, at 191.

[127] Akinyemi, 'The Organization of African Unity', at 393.

[128] Even when the ACHPR was in the process of being debated, it received relatively little attention at the level of the Council of Ministers and AHSG, resolutions merely referring to its development: for example, in its first specific resolution on human rights in 1980, Decision 115(XVI) of the AHSG; Resolution on Human and Peoples' Rights, CM/Res.792(XXXV).

[129] Chapter 2.

[130] Resolution on the African Commission on Human and Peoples' Rights, CM/Res.1379 (LV); Decision on the Fifteenth Annual Activity Report of the African Commission on Human and Peoples' Rights, AHG/Dec.171(XXXVIII). See further, chapter 2.

additional protocols to the African Charter, requiring the involvement of the OAU, have had some influence on the way in which the latter has approached human rights.

In July 1998 a Protocol establishing an African Court on Human and Peoples' Rights was adopted by the Assembly of the OAU.[131] This provides for an independent eleven-member court with both advisory and contentious jurisdiction over the rights in the ACHPR. States,[132] the African Commission on Human and Peoples' Rights, African intergovernmental organisations, NGOs and individuals are permitted to submit cases direct to the Court alleging violations of the ACHPR.[133] It can receive requests for advisory opinions from an OAU state, the OAU and its organs, or 'any African organisation recognised by the OAU'.[134] The Protocol has now received the required number of ratifications to come into force.[135]

Five years later the Assembly of the AU also adopted another Protocol that had been initiated by the African Commission on Human and Peoples' Rights. The Protocol on the Rights of Women in Africa[136] provides for a wide range of rights for women, including elimination of harmful practices,[137] equal rights in marriage,[138] participation in decision making,[139] protection in armed conflicts,[140] as well as rights to education and training, economic and social welfare rights, and the right to health.[141] There are also provisions on food security, adequate housing, healthy and sustainable environment, and sustainable development.[142] The Protocol is to be enforced by the African Commission on Human and Peoples' Rights, using the existing mechanisms of state reporting under

---

[131] Protocol to the African Charter on Human and Peoples' Rights on the Establishment of an African Court on Human and Peoples' Rights, OAU/LEG/AFCHPR/PROT(III), adopted by the Assembly of Heads of State and Government, 34th session, Burkina Faso, 8–10 June 1998.

[132] Only those that have lodged a case with the Commission, those against which a case has been lodged at the Commission, and those whose citizens are victims of human rights violations, Article 5(1)(b)–(d).

[133] Only 'relevant NGOs with observer status before the Commission' can submit cases 'directly before the Court', and only individuals where the states have made declarations accepting the jurisdiction of the Court in these instances, Article 5(3) and Article 34(6).

[134] Article 4.

[135] Article 34(3). The states who have so far ratified are: Algeria, Burkina Faso, Burundi, Comonos, Côte d'Ivoire, DRC, The Gambia, Lesotho, Libya, Mali, Mauritius, Rwanda, Senegal, South Africa, Togo and Uganda.

[136] Protocol to the African Charter on Human and Peoples' Rights on the Rights of Women in Africa, adopted by the Assembly of the African Union, Mozambique, July 2003.

[137] Article 5.　　　[138] Article 6.　　　[139] Article 9.　　　[140] Article 11.

[141] Articles 12, 13 and 14.　　　[142] Articles 15–19.

the Charter.[143] The Commission will interpret provisions of the Protocol until the African Court on Human and Peoples' Rights comes into force.[144]

The 1990 Declaration and other events in the 1990s

The end of the Cold War and the imposition of economic conditions for the granting of aid by the World Bank and other donors has been important in shaping the approach of the OAU to human rights.[145] In its seminal Declaration in 1990 on the Political and Socio-Economic Situation in Africa and the Fundamental Changes taking Place in the World[146] the AHSG noted the changes in the relationship with the West to one of cooperation and the end of the Cold War. Several themes are apparent from this Declaration and feature in the later work of the OAU organs. It reflects a more holistic approach to human rights concerns and combines a number of issues that were relevant at the time. These included globalisation and the impact of the 'increasing global tendency towards regional integration and the establishment of trading and economic blocs'[147] on Africa. Secondly, it noted development and socio-economic issues; economic performance had decreased with the resulting impact on health, housing and education of the people. The OAU thus reaffirmed that Africa's development 'is the responsibility of our governments and our peoples. We are now more than before determined to lay solid foundation for self-reliant, human-centred and sustainable development on the basis of social justice and collective self-reliance.'[148] This increased attention by the OAU to issues of development[149] would appear as a theme in the OAU's later work. Thirdly, the impact of refugees and conflicts was also apparent.[150] Lastly,

---

[143] ACHPR, Article 62, see Protocol, Article 26(1).
[144] Protocol, Articles 27 and 32.   [145] See Clapham, *Africa*, at 192.
[146] Declaration on the Political and Socio-Economic Situation in Africa and the Fundamental Changes Taking Place in the World, 11 July 1990, 26th session of AHSG.
[147] Ibid.   [148] Ibid.
[149] Resolution on the Permanent Sovereignty of African Countries over their Natural Resources, CM/Res.245(XVII); Resolution on the African Charter for Popular Participation in Development and Transformation, CM/Res.1286(LII), preamble.
[150]   We therefore renew our determination to work together towards the peaceful and speedy resolution of all the conflicts on our continent. The resolution of conflicts will be conducive to the creation of peace and stability . . . and will also have the effect of reducing expenditure on defence and security thus releasing additional resources for socio-economic development. We are equally determined to make renewed efforts to eradicate the root causes of the refugee problem. It is only

the Declaration also noted the importance of democracy and popular participation, this again being tied with the aim of achieving economic progress:

> It is necessary to promote popular participation of our peoples in the processes of government and development. A political environment which guarantees human rights and the observance of the rule of law, would assure high standards of probity and accountability particularly on the part of those who hold public office. In addition, popular based processes would ensure the involvement of all including in particular women and youth in development efforts. We accordingly recommit ourselves to the further democratisation of our societies and to the consolidation of democratic institutions in our countries. We reaffirm the right of our countries to determine, in all sovereignty, their system of democracy on the basis of socio-cultural values, taking into account the realities of each of our countries and the necessity to ensure development and satisfy the basic needs of our peoples. We therefore assert that democracy and development should go together and should be mutually reinforcing.[151]

In 1990 the African Charter on the Rights and Welfare of the Child (ACRWC) was adopted[152] as a way of promoting the UN Convention on the Rights of the Child in Africa.[153] This Charter provided for a separate eleven-member independent Committee to promote, protect and interpret the rights in the instrument. The Charter eventually came into force nine years later and its Committee met first in spring 2002.

Further moves in the late 1990s again indicated a shift to the OAU seeing human rights as part of its remit. At this time the OAU organised a series of conferences for ambassadors and ministers specifically on human rights.[154] In the resulting recommendations states committed

---

> through the creation of stable conditions that Africa can fully harness its human and material resources and direct them towards development.
>
> Declaration on the Political and Socio-Economic Situation in Africa and the Fundamental Changes Taking Place in the World, 11 July 1990, 26th session of AHSG.

[151] Ibid.   [152] 26th Session AHSG, OAU Doc. CAB/LEG/24.9/49 (1990).

[153] See chapter 6.

[154] Resolution on the Ministerial Conference on Human Rights in Africa, CM/Res.1673 (LXIV), preamble. The OAU Ministerial Conference on Human Rights was held in April 1999 in Grand Bay, Mauritius. See also Introductory Note to the Report of the Secretary General, Sixty-Ninth Ordinary Session of the Council of Ministers, Addis Ababa, Ethiopia, 19–23 March 1999, paras. 296–8.

themselves to 'ensure that the recommendations contained in the Grand Bay (Mauritius) Declaration and Plan of Action are reflected in all the relevant programmes of the OAU and, to put in place the necessary mechanisms for appropriate follow-up action on the implementation of the Declaration and Plan of Action'.[155] The resulting Grand Bay Declaration and Plan of Action indicated a shift from human rights being seen as the domain of the African Commission in Banjul to a more integrated perspective within the OAU itself, and marked an important turning point in the OAU's recognition of its role in this regard.[156] Thus in 1998 at its Summit the AHSG noted expressly the role of women, the need to 'work towards the establishment and consolidation of effective democratic systems, taking into account the socio-cultural realities of our states, with all actors of the civil society', the importance of working 'towards the establishment and consolidation of a credible and independent justice accessible to all; ensure respect for human rights and fight impunity', among other issues.[157]

Thus, whilst by the late 1990s other themes were getting the attention of the OAU, the adoption of the Algiers Declaration[158] in 1999 reflected the idea that the OAU had moved beyond simply considering the self-determination issue:

> We believe that human rights have undergone major positive changes since the independence of African countries ... The liberation movements of our peoples, the efforts of our countries of the OAU to codify and implement these rights, as well as the current dynamic process of establishing new democratic spaces in Africa have contributed to a very large extent to these changes.

The Declaration also recognised the contribution of the ACHPR, the Protocol on the African Court and the Grand Bay Declaration and the Plan of Action which 'eloquently testify to Africa's contribution to the promotion and protection of the noble cause of human rights'. It did not stop there, however, but went further to consolidate the responsibility of the OAU:

---

[155] Decision on the Report of the Secretary General on the Ministerial Conference on Human Rights (Doc.CM/2123(LXX)), CM/Dec.475(LXX).

[156] Ibid.: 'calls upon all member states, the OAU and all relevant UN agencies and other international partners to implement it'.

[157] Ouagadougou Declaration, AHG/Decl.1(XXXIV), para. 1.

[158] Algiers Declaration, AHG/Decl.1(XXXV).

We, however, recognise that much remains to be done to bring these developments to the level of our own expectations and the legitimate aspirations of our peoples. We are aware of these limitations and determined
not to relent in our efforts to transcend them. In this spirit we reiterate
our commitment to the protection and promotion of human rights and
fundamental freedoms. We emphasise the indivisibility, universality and
inter-dependence of all human rights, be they political and civil or economic, social and cultural or even individual or collective. We call upon
the international community to ensure that they are not used for political
purposes.[159]

Conference on Security, Stability, Development and Cooperation in Africa (CSSDCA)

In 1991 President Museveni, then Chairman of the OAU, proposed a meeting on Security, Stability, Development and Cooperation in Kampala. This
Conference looked at how to deal with development, security and stability and adopted the Kampala Document which included the 1990 OAU
Declaration on Socio-Economic Changes as well as the African Charter
on Popular Participation in Development. This Kampala Document was
presented to the OAU AHSG in Nigeria in 1991, although it was not
adopted, but referred to the Council of Ministers. It was only in July 1999
at the 1999 Summit that the Nigerian president called for it to be looked
at again and relaunched the impetus.

At the Extraordinary Summit in September 1999 in Sirte, Libya, it was
decided to hold a ministerial Conference on Security, Stability, Development and Cooperation in Africa (CSSDCA) and this was formally
endorsed by the AHSG of the OAU. The first ministerial meeting of the
CSSDCA was held in Nigeria from 8–9 May 2000 and at the following July
Summit of the OAU in Togo in 2000 a Solemn Declaration was adopted
by the OAU organs. It was agreed that there would be a standing conference at the level of heads of state every two years, and the first one took
place in South Africa in July 2002. Experts' meetings were held in South
Africa and Ethiopia prior to this in December 2001 and May 2002 to discuss the security and stability issues. The aims of these were to develop
a Memorandum of Understanding on the issues, to submit to the OAU
76th Council of Ministers session for approval. It was intended that the
CCSDCA would form a more binding element in the AU, perhaps as an
Annex to the Constitutive Act.

[159] Ibid.

What is important in this context is that central to the CSSDCA are a number of human rights components. Thus the Draft Memorandum of Understanding on Security, Stability, Development and Cooperation in Africa's[160] 'core values' includes reference to the 'impact of refugees and displaced persons on security, natural resources, spread of arms and weapons, good governance and human rights, rejection of unconstitutional changes of government, respect and promotion of human rights, rule of law and equitable social order, eradication of corruption, no political organisation on basis of race, religion', as well as reference to 'transparent electoral processes, development, cooperation and integration'. Commitment to these core values is pledged by states that they should, among other things, 'promulgate constitutions with Bills of Rights, free and fair elections, separation of powers, multiparty systems, free expression, independent judiciary, popular participation, civilian authority, protection of human rights, establishment of African Court on Human and Peoples' Rights, improve good governance, promote and protect rights and welfare of the African child'.

Further, a number of indicators were developed under the CSSDCA which are important for human rights. Concrete obligations of states include ratification and implementation of human rights instruments by particular dates,[161] that they take national measures,[162] including setting

---

[160] See www.au2002gov.za/docs/background/cssdca.htm.

[161] For example, that all states ratify the OAU Convention on Refugees by 2003 and take national measures to give effect to its provisions. Further, states should implement the provisions of the Charter for Popular Participation in Development 'by creating more enabling conditions for increased participation of women, the youth and civil society organisations', para. 22. States were to ratify the African Charter on the Child by 2003, the Optional Protocol to the UN Convention on the Rights of the Child and ensure its implementation by 2005 and take effective plans for demobilisation of soldiers; and all provisions of the ACHPR by 2003, as well as other international instruments and implement such along with the Grand Bay Declaration and Plan of Action. All states were to ratify the Optional Protocol to Convention on the Elimination of Discrimination Against Women (CEDAW) by 2005.

[162] By 2004 states should have adopted 'the fundamental tenets of democratic society . . . namely, a Constitution and a Bill of Rights provision, where applicable, free and fair elections, an independent judiciary, freedom of expression and subordination of the military to legitimate civilian authority, rejection of unconditional changes of government, and implement these principles by 2005, where they are not already applicable', para. 14. By 2004, states should have elaborated principles of good governance, para. 15; incorporate into national laws habeas corpus or detention without trial and prohibited of torture, etc. by 2004, para. 25; take measures by 2005 to promote equality of women and 'ensure the representation of women in all national institutions, as well as abrogate discriminatory

up domestic institutions,[163] that the OAU/AU review human rights standards and make the necessary changes[164] and support bodies that protect human rights.[165]

Implementation of the CSSDCA process is to be achieved by legislation and other measures, the designation of focal points in states to coordinate and monitor implementation of CSSDCA and the creation of national coordinating committees. Current knowledge and best practice on democratic practices, human rights and good governance should be disseminated and the CSSDCA Unit should be enlarged; it is now a part of the Commission of the AU. Performance will be monitored by a standing conference on CSSDCA at Summit level every two years, with review meetings of plenipotentiaries in between these meetings. The national units would work with the CSSDCA unit, and with the process of peer scrutiny and national mechanisms would produce country reports, with input from civil sector and others. The CSSDCA Unit would coordinate with international bodies and the visitation panels composed of eminent Africans would carry out assessments on the spot every two years. This process of peer review is likely to be of increased importance, particularly with the NEPAD developments and increased integration between the two.[166] The role of the organs like the African Commission on Human and Peoples' Rights is of huge potential importance.

---

laws in African countries against women', and also adopt and ratify the Protocol on the rights of women and the instruments for their protection, para. 26.

[163] States should by 2003 have set up independent electoral commissions or other mechanisms 'to ensure free and fair elections in all African countries', para. 18; and each state should set up an independent commission to determine prison conditions and Parole Board by 2005, para. 28.

[164] For example, that the OAU review the Convention on Refugees by 2005 to adapt it to current circumstances and to strengthen oversight mechanisms in respect of giving the Secretariat statistics on human rights protection, separating armed elements from the refugee population, and measures to compel rebel groups to respect the rights of refugees, returnees and displaced persons. Further, The AU should

> adopt and standardise by 2003, guidelines for independent and effective observations of elections in AU member states with the provision of an effective electoral unit within the AU commission. The guidelines must include provisions for strengthening civil society and local monitoring groups in individual African countries and the continent as a whole to support the process of ensuring free and fair elections.

para. 19

[165] All states are to submit periodic reports to the African Commission by 2004 and the Commission is to be given adequate resources by 2006, para. 26.

[166] See below.

Transformation from OAU to AU

The OAU has recently gone through a process of transformation to become the African Union (AU). In Libya on 9 September 1999 the OAU's Assembly of Heads of State and Government at their Fourth Extraordinary Summit adopted the Sirte Declaration proposing an Inter-African Union. Legal experts and parliamentarians met in Ethiopia in April and in Tripoli at the end of May 2000 and their report was considered by the First OAU Ministerial Meeting on the Implementation of the Sirte Declaration.[167] In July 2000 in Lomé, Togo, the Constitutive Act of the Union was adopted.[168] The Act provides for transitional arrangements whereby the OAU Charter remains operative for one year 'for the purpose of enabling the OAU/AEC to undertake the necessary measures regarding the devolution of its assets and liabilities to the Union and all matters relating thereto'.[169]

The AU also accelerates the process of economic unity begun by the Treaty on the African Economic Community (AEC). In this sense it is taking the wider political and economic view that the EU now encompasses, indeed it was the EU that was said to have served as the AU's model.[170] Some have noted 'the subtle and sometimes overt references which are frequently made in the AEC treaty of Abuja to the structure and policies of the EU. A perusal of the treaty leaves no doubt that the architects of the Abuja treaty hoped to replicate the EU's structure, policies and success, but on an African landscape.'[171]

Whilst the EU may be seen as a beacon for economic success, it may be less likely to suggest to those seeking to replicate it that human rights should be at the forefront of their considerations. The EU, despite its

---

[167] Report of the Ministerial Conference on the Establishment of the African Union and Pan-African Parliament, CM/2162(LXXII).

[168] See appendix II.   [169] Constitutive Act, Article 33(1).

[170] Although others have argued that in fact the EU was not the only regional influence and models from ASEAN were also of use, see Inter-Africa Group/Justice Africa, 'The Architecture and Capacity of the African Union. African Development Forum (ADF III) Economic Commission for Africa', Issues Paper for the African Union Symposium, at 3.

[171] O. A. Babarinde, 'Analyzing the Proposed African Economic Community: Lessons from the Experience of the European Union', paper for the Third ECSA-World Conference on The European Union in a Changing World, sponsored by the European Commission, D-G X, Brussels, 19–20 September 1996, http://www.ecsanet.org/conferences/babarinde.htm, at 5. He goes on to argue that there are 'limits to the parallels that can be drawn between the EU and the proposed AEC ... the stated goals may be too ambitious, albeit not impossible, to achieve, given the recent socio-political and economic trends which predominate in Africa'.

considerable reputation, has been criticised for failing to adopt a coherent approach to human rights. As Alston and Weiler state:

> The human rights policies of the European Union are beset by a paradox. On the one hand, the Union is a staunch defender of human rights in both its internal and external affairs. On the other hand, it lacks a comprehensive or coherent policy at either level and fundamental doubts persist whether the institutions of the Union possess adequate legal competence in relation to a wide range of human rights issues arising within the framework of Community policies.[172]

The role of Libya in the establishment of an African Union also has implications for its future. Initially Arabic nations were, unsuccessfully, encouraged to adopt something similar.[173] Concerns have been raised about the extent to which Libya, whose recent treatment of black Africans has come under considerable criticism,[174] is able to promote an African organisation, one of whose central planks should be human rights for all Africans.[175] However, it is important to stress that although Libya may have been at the forefront of the OAU/AU transition, it has not been the only state to have played a key role and it would be wrong to say that the AU is simply a Libyan creation. It is the result of a long process of OAU/AEC initiatives.

The provisions of the resulting Constitutive Act suggest that human rights will indeed play a greater role in the work of the Union than they did in the OAU. Thus, the preamble of the Act recalls 'the heroic struggles waged by our peoples and our countries for economic independence, human dignity and economic emancipation'. Human rights are mentioned specifically with states being 'determined to promote and protect human and peoples' rights, consolidate democratic institutions and culture and to ensure good governance and the rule of law'. The central Objectives, in Article 3, and Principles, in Article 4, of the Union

---

[172] P. Alston and J. H. H. Weiler, 'An "Ever Closer Union" in Need of a Human Rights Policy: The European Union and Human Rights', in Alston (ed.), *The EU and Human Rights* 3–68, at 6. For other discussions of the EU and human rights see A. Clapham, 'A Human Rights Policy for the European Community', *Yearbook of European Law* 10 (1990) 309–49; D. Marantis, 'Human Rights, Democracy and Development: The European Community Model', *Harvard Human Rights Journal* 7 (1994) 1–32, at 7; N. Neuwahl and A. Rosas (eds.), *The European Union and Human Rights* (The Hague: Martinus Nijhoff, 1995).

[173] See http//www.africanews.org. Indeed, Qadhafi wanted them to join the AU and many have questioned his objectives in doing so.

[174] See, for example, allegations of racist attacks against sub-Saharan Africans, 'Libya', *Amnesty International, Annual Report 2001*, AI Index: POL 10/001/2001.

[175] See also *The Times*, 22 January 2003.

noted that the Union's aims include not only achieving 'greater unity and solidarity between the African countries and the peoples of Africa' and accelerating development but also the need to 'promote peace, security and stability on the continent'.[176] It is recognised that there is a need to 'encourage international co-operation, taking due account of the Charter of the United Nations and the Universal Declaration of Human Rights' and 'promote and protect human and peoples' rights in accordance with the African Charter on Human and Peoples' Rights and other relevant human rights instruments'.[177] Thus states should respect the need for 'peaceful coexistence of member states and their right to live in peace and security',[178] promote gender equality, have 'respect for democratic prin-ciples, human rights, the rule of law and good governance', respect the sanctity of life and condemn unconstitutional changes of government.[179]

Also relevant are the requirements to 'promote co-operation in all fields of human activity to raise the living standards of African peoples' and to 'work with relevant international partners in the eradication of pre-ventable diseases and the promotion of good health on the continent'.[180]

On the face of it, therefore, the Constitutive Act of the AU appears to give an important place to human rights and an indication that they will play a significant role in the AU. However, there has been considerable concern that institutions such as the African Commission on Human and Peoples' Rights and the proposed African Court on Human and Peoples' Rights do not appear to feature in the Act. Whilst some fear that this meant these bodies were being sidelined or forgotten under these new structures,[181] it perhaps indicates lack of coherence in the Act as a whole to the previous structures of the OAU, when other organs, such as the Central Organ, were also omitted.[182] Indeed, the OAU/AU organs have continually stressed that it is for the African Commission on Human and

---

[176] Article 3(f).   [177] Article 3(e) and (h).   [178] Article 4(i).

[179] Article 4(l), (m), (o) and (p).   [180] Articles 3(k) and (n).

[181] The Sirte Declaration went a little further, with the AHSG noting the violations of human and peoples' rights that continued on the continent and specifically stated: 'We also recommit ourselves to ensure the early establishment of the African Court on Human and Peoples' Rights', Draft Sirte Declaration, Fourth Extraordinary Summit of the Assembly of Heads of State and Government, 8–9 September 1999, Sirte, Libya, EAHG/Draft/DECl.(IV) Rev.1, para. 14.

[182] For example, the Council of Ministers has asked that the Secretary General take mea-sures to assure the place of the African Population Commission and the OAU Labour and Social Affairs Commission in the AU, Decision on the Place of the African Pop-ulation Commission (APC) in the African Union, AHG/Dec.176(XXXVIII); Decision on the Place of the OAU Labour and Social Affairs Commission in the African Union, AHG/Dec.177(XXXVIII).

Peoples' Rights first to consider its place within the Union and to inform the AU organs accordingly.

What is perhaps more concerning is that, despite being mentioned in the substantive provisions of the Act, in relation to the mandates of the various institutions within the Union, human rights are not listed under any of them expressly. The most one can presume is to infer that they might be covered by the mandate of these bodies. The Assembly, as the supreme body of the Union, seems to reflect the AHSG under the OAU. The functions of the Executive Council in Article 13 provide that it should coordinate and take decisions on 'policies in areas of common interest' and lists 'environmental protection, humanitarian action and disaster response and relief', 'education, culture, health', 'nationality, residency and immigration', 'social security ... child care policies as well as policies relating to the disabled and handicapped'.[183] Similarly the Act establishes a number of Specialised Technical Committees[184] and it is possible that those on Health, Labour and Social Affairs, and on Education, Culture and Human Resources, may cover human rights.

Other institutions of the Union include a Pan-African Parliament and a Court of Justice. The latter is charged under Article 26 with interpreting any aspect of the Act.[185] It is possible that this body and the proposed African Court on Human and Peoples' Rights will exist side by side, which has worked well in the European system, with the European Court of Human Rights and the European Court of Justice (ECJ).[186] The latter in fact has developed a closer relationship with the jurisprudence of the former and shown itself willing to take a more human rights approach to its cases. As the ECJ has held:

> It is well settled that fundamental rights form an integral part of the general principles of law whose observance the Court ensures. For that purpose, the Court draws inspiration from the constitutional traditions common to the Member States and from the guidelines supplied by international treaties for the protection of human rights on which the Member States

---

[183] Article 13(e), (h), (j), (k) of the Constitutive Act respectively.

[184] This are committees on: Rural Economy and Agricultural Matters; Monetary and Financial Affairs; Trade, Customs and Immigration; Industry, Science and Technology, Energy, Natural Resources and Environment; Transport, Communications and Tourism; Health, Labour and Social Affairs; Education, Culture and Human Resources', Article 14.

[185] Protocol of the African Court of Justice, adopted July 2003, Decision on the Draft Protocol of the Court of Justice of the African Union, Dec.EX/CL/59(III), Assembly/AU/Dec.24(II).

[186] See R. Murray, 'A Comparison between the African and European Courts of Human Rights', *African Human Rights Law Journal* 2(2) (2002) 195–222.

have collaborated or of which they are signatories. In this regard, the Court has stated that the Convention has special significance.[187]

The relationship between the African Court of Justice (ACJ) and the African Court on Human and Peoples' Rights will be examined in greater detail in chapter 2.

There will also be a Permanent Representatives Committee, an Economic, Social and Cultural Council (an advisory body of social and professional groups) and financial institutions.

The Act provides for a Pan-African Parliament, in Article 17, 'to ensure the full participation of African peoples in the development and economic integration of the continent'.[188] Its powers are determined by a Protocol to the Act. This Parliament has its basis in the Treaty of the AEC and it is a Protocol to this Treaty which has created the Pan-African Parliament mentioned in the Constitutive Act. This Protocol was drafted at the same time as the Constitutive Act[189] and has now been adopted by the OAU AHSG.[190] Among Parliament's Objectives are to 'promote the principles of human rights and democracy in Africa' and to 'encourage good governance, transparency and accountability in Member States'.[191] It is composed of five representatives from each state who should include at least one woman in their delegation and 'must reflect the diversity of political opinions in each National Parliament or other deliberative organ'.[192] However, the members vote in their own capacity and cannot hold executive or judicial offices in their home states at the same time.[193] It is intended that the Parliament will eventually have legislative powers, according to Article 11 of the Protocol, although in its first five years it will have consultative and advisory powers only.[194]

This Parliament is perceived to mirror that of the EU,[195] which, it has been said, plays an essential role in ensuring the democratic nature

---

[187] Opinion 2/94, Accession by the Communities to the Convention for the Protection of Human Rights and Fundamental Freedoms, [1996] ECR I-1759, para. 33.

[188] Constitutive Act, Article 17(1).   [189] Tripoli, 29 May–2 June 2000, CM/2162(LXXII).

[190] At its Fifth Extraordinary Summit, Sirte, Libya, February–March 2001: Decision on the Draft Protocol to the Treaty Establishing the African Economic Community Relating to the Pan-African Parliament, Doc.EAHG/3(V), EAHG/Dec.2(V).

[191] Protocol to the Treaty Establishing the African Economic Community Relating to the Pan-African Parliament, CM/2198(LXXIII), Annex I, Articles 3(2) and (3).

[192] Protocol on the Pan-African Parliament, Article 4.   [193] Ibid., Articles 6 and 7.

[194] The Protocol requires a simple majority to come into force and this was achieved in November 2003, see Press Release 093/2003.

[195] 'The Dream of an African Parliament', 27 February 2001, http://allafrica.com/stories/200102270364.html.

of the EU in that 'democratic institutions have a special duty to take care of fundamental rights'[196] and the Parliament is 'the international institution which is able to distinguish between the individual interests of the states and the common interests of mankind'.[197] There is concern that the African equivalent will not be able to represent the many millions of individuals in Africa.[198]

A Peace and Security Council of the AU has also been established.[199] Its task is to take decisions on conflict prevention, management and resolution, and Article 1 of the Protocol provides that it is 'a collective security and early-warning arrangement to facilitate timely and efficient response to conflict and crisis situations in Africa'. Other bodies would assist the work of the Council including, as provided in Article 2, the Commission, a Panel of the Wise, a Continental Early Warning System, an African Standby Force and a Special Fund. Among its aims would be to develop a common defence policy and 'promote and encourage democratic practices, good governance and the rule of law, protect human rights and fundamental freedoms, respect for the sanctity of human life and international humanitarian law, as part of efforts for preventing conflicts'.[200] The principles guiding it in Article 4 of the Protocol expressly include the Universal Declaration of Human Rights (UDHR) and 'respect for the rule of law, fundamental human rights and freedoms, the sanctity of human life and international humanitarian law'. The Council is composed of fifteen states reflecting the geographical regions of the continent[201] and who are committed, among others, to principles of democratic governance, the rule of law and human rights.[202] The Council under Article 7 of the Protocol can authorise peace missions, recommend to the Assembly that the AU

---

[196] E. Boumans and M. Norbart, 'The European Parliament and Human Rights', *NQHR* 7 (1989) 35–56, at 37.

[197] P. van Dijk, 'The Law of Human Rights in Europe – Instruments and Procedures for a Uniform Implementation', *AEL* 6(2) (1997) 22–50. See further discussions on the EU Parliament, K. St C. Bradley, 'Reflections on the Human Rights Role of the European Parliament', in Alston (ed.), *The EU and Human Rights* 839–58.

[198] Larger states would prefer representation on the Parliament to reflect population, although many smaller states want equality. However, decisions on such important issues have been postponed until the Union is functioning.

[199] May 2004. See also Protocol Relating to the Establishment of the Peace and Security Council of the African Union, 9 July 2002.

[200] Ibid., Article 3(f).

[201] As noted below, it is likely that the Heads of State Implementation Committee (HSIC) of NEPAD may transform itself into this Council.

[202] Protocol Relating to the Establishment of the Peace and Security Council of the African Union, 9 July 2002, Article 5(2)(g).

intervene in certain situations in respect of grave crimes, including crimes against humanity, impose sanctions on unconstitutional changes in government and 'follow-up, within the framework of its conflict prevention responsibilities, the progress towards the promotion of democratic practices, good governance, the rule of law, protection of human rights and fundamental freedoms, respect for the sanctity of human life and international humanitarian law by Member States'. Article 19 specifically provides that it will 'seek close cooperation' with the African Commission on Human and Peoples' Rights 'in all matters relevant to its objectives and mandate' and that Commission should also inform the Council of relevant issues. The Protocol replaced the Cairo Declaration of 1993 and previous OAU resolutions and decisions on conflict prevention, management and resolution.[203] The Protocol required a simple majority of AU states to ratify it in order to come into force.

The Economic Social and Cultural Council (ECOSOCC) is an advisory organ[204] composed of 150 civil society organisations including those representing women, children, elderly, disabled, professional groups, NGOs, workers, employers, traditional leaders, academics, religious and cultural organisations.[205] Among its functions are the promotion of human rights, the rule of law, good governance and gender equality.[206] This offers considerable hope not only for increased civil society participation in the AU but also the possibility of another avenue by which human rights matters can be raised.

The Secretariat of the AU, based in Addis Ababa, is the Commission of the AU[207] and it is composed of a Chair, Deputy Chair and eight other Commissioners.[208] The members of the Commission in the performance of their tasks are not permitted to receive instructions from government or other external authorities.[209] The Commissioners should as a group reflect the regions of the continent and there is a requirement that there is at least one woman from each region.[210] Commissioners are nominated by the regions from among nationals of member states and elected by

---

[203] Ibid., Article 22.   [204] Constitutive Act, Article 22.

[205] Draft Statutes of the Economic Social and Cultural Council, Exp/Draft/ECOSOCC Statutes/Rev.2, Article 2.

[206] Ibid., Article 5(5).

[207] Statutes of the Commission, ASS/AU/2(I)-d. Note that this book will refer to 'the Commission of the African Union' in respect of this body; and the 'African Commission on Human and Peoples' Rights' in respect of the organ established under the ACHPR.

[208] Statutes of the Commission, ASS/AU/2(I)-d, Article 2.   [209] Ibid., Article 4(1).

[210] Ibid., Article 6.

the states, and are responsible for implementation of decisions over the specific remits for which they are appointed.[211] Article 12 provides for a number of 'portfolios' for the Commission and these include one on Political Affairs which covers 'Human Rights, Democracy, Good Governance, Electoral Institutions, Civil Society Organizations, Humanitarian Affairs, Refugees, Returnees and Internally Displaced Persons'.[212] Although gender is considered to be 'cross-cutting through all the portfolios of the Commission, a special unit has been established in the Office of the Chairperson to coordinate all activities and programmes of the Commission related to gender issues'.[213]

New Partnership for Africa's Development (NEPAD)

In parallel to the OAU/AU transformation has been the recent contribution of what is known as the New Partnership for Africa's Development (NEPAD). NEPAD merges the previous Millennium Partnership for Africa's Recovery Programme (MAP)[214] and the Omega Plan, finalised in July 2001. It was created by African leaders and addresses economic and social development for the continent and how Africa can build partnerships elsewhere. Its goals are sustainable development, eradication of poverty and stopping Africa's marginalisation in globalisation. One of the important aspects of NEPAD is that it recognises that development is impossible unless there is democracy and respect for human rights. Its Democracy and Political Governance Initiative notes the ACHPR, ACRWC, UN instruments including human rights instruments, and other OAU initiatives taken by OAU organs. The Initiative confirms the commitment of heads of state to various aspects of human rights including

---

[211] Ibid., Article 11.
[212] The others are: Peace and Security (Conflict Prevention, Management and Resolution, and Combating Terrorism . . .); Infrastructure and Energy (Energy, Transport, Communications, Infrastructure and Tourism . . .); Social Affairs (Health, Children, Drug Control, Population, Migration, Labour and Employment, Sports and Culture . . .); Human Resources, Science and Technology (Education, Information Technology Communication, Youth, Human Resources, Science and Technology . . .); Trade and Industry (Trade, Industry, Customs and Immigration Matters . . .); Rural Economy and Agriculture (Rural Economy, Agriculture and Food Security, Livestock, Environment, Water and Natural Resources and Desertification . . .); and Economic Affairs (Economic Integration, Monetary Affairs, Private Sector Development, Investment and Resource Mobilization . . .).
[213] The Directorate on Gender and Development, Article 12(3), Statutes of the Commission.
[214] MAP, March 2001, was a pledge by African leaders in respect of their participation in the international economic and political order.

the rule of law; the equality of all citizens before the law and the liberty of the individual; individual and collective freedoms, including the right to form and join political parties and trade unions, in conformity with the constitution; equality of opportunity for all; the inalienable right of the individual to participate by means of free, credible and democratic political processes in periodically electing their leaders for a fixed term of office; and adherence to the separation of powers, including the protection of the independence of the judiciary and of effective parliaments.[215]

There is also a commitment to combat corruption. It makes it clear that restoring stability is necessary for sustainable development, good governance, human rights and democracy. It places particular importance on human rights:

> In the light of Africa's recent history, respect for human rights has to be accorded an importance and urgency all of its own. One of the tests by which the quality of a democracy is judged is the protection it provides for each individual citizen and for the vulnerable and disadvantaged groups. Ethnic minorities, women and children have borne the brunt of the conflicts raging on the continent today. We undertake to do more to advance the cause of human rights in Africa generally and, specifically, to end the moral shame exemplified by the plight of women, children, the disabled and ethnic minorities in conflict situations in Africa.[216]

It stresses further the important role of women in this regard. The Action Plan adopted requires states to ensure that 'respective national constitutions reflect the democratic ethos and provide for demonstrably accountable governance', that political representation is promoted, 'thus providing for all citizens to participate in the political process in a free and fair political environment' and that there is 'strict adherence to the position of the African Union (AU) on unconstitutional changes of government and other decisions of our continental organization aimed at promoting democracy, good governance, peace and security'. Further, states are required to 'strengthen and, where necessary, establish an appropriate electoral administration and oversight bodies, in our respective countries and provide the necessary resources and capacity to conduct elections which are free, fair and credible' and to 'heighten public awareness of the African Charter on Human and Peoples' Rights, especially in our educational institutions'. Provisions on good governance require states to ensure, among other things, an 'accountable, efficient and effective civil service', 'ensure the effective functioning of parliaments and other

[215] AHG/235(XXXVIII), Annex I.   [216] Ibid., para. 1.

accountability institutions in our respective countries, including parliamentary committees and anti-corruption bodies; and ensure the independence of the judicial system that will be able to prevent abuse of power and corruption'.

It also makes specific commitments with regard to human rights including support for civil society organisations,[217] 'support the Charter, African Commission and Court on Human and People's Rights as important instruments for ensuring the promotion, protection and observance of Human Rights', the strengthening of cooperation with international organisations such as the UN High Commission for Human Rights; and to 'ensure responsible free expression, inclusive of the freedom of the press'.

Implementation is to be achieved through a Heads of State and Government Implementation Committee (HSGIC) chaired by Nigeria and with Senegal and Algeria as Vice Chairs, with seventeen other states representing different geographical areas of Africa. It reports to the AU Summit and its aim is to look at strategy and set up mechanisms for reviewing progress. There is also a Steering Committee, composed of the personal representatives of the five initiating presidents (Algeria, Egypt, Nigeria, Senegal, South Africa). It has been dominated by South Africa where its secretariat is presently based.

NEPAD is voluntary, unlike the CSSDCA under the AU proper. States have to sign up to a review process[218] known as the African Peer Review Mechanism (APRM), which requires that states, after eight months, submit to a base review and then reviews at three years and five years. There is also the possibility of ad hoc reviews. The country reviews are to be done by the Panel of Eminent Experts and teams from other institutions such as the African Commission on Human and Peoples' Rights, the Pan-African Parliament and ECOSOCC.[219] The benchmarks recently adopted indicate a number of 'key objectives for democracy and political governance' which include reduction of conflicts, constitutional democracy, promotion of economic, social, cultural, civil and political rights, separation of powers, fighting corruption, and protection of the rights of

---

[217] To 'facilitate the development of vibrant civil society organizations, including strengthening human rights institutions at the national, sub-regional and regional levels'.

[218] Sixteen so far have done so.

[219] The Panel has now been appointed and is composed of Ms Marie-Angelique Savané (Chairperson), Prof. Adebayo Adedeji, Ambassador Bethuel Kiplagat, Mr Mourad Medelci, Dr Dorothy Njeuma, Dr Chris Stals and Dr Graca Machel. There is no member of the African Commission on Human and Peoples' Rights on the Panel.

women, children, the vulnerable and refugees.[220] The standards adopted include OAU/AU instruments as well as those of the UN, and the criteria require ratification of these instruments, the reflection of the standards in the constitution and the extent to which the rights are realised in the particular country. Originally, the UN Economic Commission for Africa was going to be used for the peer review but due to concerns by Nigeria that this would render the process too Western dominated, there has been a requirement that peer review will take place under the AU CSSDCA Unit.[221] Thus, whilst the NEPAD process, with its secretariat presently in Pretoria, is perceived to have been dominated by South Africa, this change moves it back under the auspices of the AU.[222] This should avoid confusion over the exact position of NEPAD under the AU and any concerns over duplication and competition.[223] The AU has the further benefit of being obligatory whereas NEPAD is only voluntary.[224]

---

[220] Objectives, Standards, Criteria and Indicators for the African Peer Review Mechanism (APRM), NEPAD/HSGIC-03–2003/APRM/ Guideline/OSCI, 9 March 2003.

[221] J. Cilliers, 'NEPAD's Peer Review Mechanism' (Pretoria: Institute for Security Studies Paper 64, November 2002) at 4, www.iss.co.za.

[222] Cilliers notes that

> although nominally part of the AU Commission, the NEPAD HSIC originally proposed that the APRM secretariat be independent of the Commission in its management, operations and funding, which will come directly from participating member governments. The head of the APRM Secretariat will report directly to the NEPAD HSIC, including by way of annual reports. This strange arrangement reflected the compromise that had emerged in respect to the initial idea of locating the APRM secretariat outside of the AU Commission. The 5th HSIC meeting during November 2002 now provides for the full integration of the APRM secretariat into the AU structures and process and future decisions may also see the end of the HSIC as a semi-separate governing body.

Ibid., at 4

[223] Thus,

> the existence of a separate NEPAD governing and implementation structure that operated in parallel to the Commission of the AU had been a source of considerable tension between NEPAD, the continental organisation and those African countries who have little interest in subscribing to the process of peer review. To compound these tensions the Rome meeting of the NEPAD HSIC also agreed that the separate NEPAD secretariat established in South Africa would continue to exist after the AU Summit in Durban and only be reviewed in Maputo during the Summit of 2003. Ultimately the NEPAD secretariat would, of course, relocate to Addis Ababa or could constitute a satellite office of the Commission, but as an integral part of the AU Commission. This understanding has subsequently been reaffirmed by the communiqué following the Abuja HSIC meeting in November.

Ibid., at 3

[224] Ibid., at 5–6.

Despite these problems, NEPAD has been significant in the international attention that it has managed to maintain on Africa:

> Had it not been for NEPAD under the leadership of President Mbeki, Africa would have suffered severe marginalisation after the events of 11th September 2001. Instead it was the focus of discussions at the G8 in Canada and will be again in France in 2003 . . . In the process considerable focus has been placed on those features of globalisation that perpetuate African poverty . . . While not sufficient, NEPAD has done much to attract continued development assistance at a time when the attention of key donor countries has been diverted by military priorities. Perhaps most important of all, is that NPEAD has spurred action within the African Union, reflected in the speed with which the Protocol on the establishment of the AU Peace and Security Council was finalised. Eventually NEPAD will be seen to have made a key contribution in the transition from the OAU to the African Union, and even more specifically to the process of value building and coherence in preparation of the establishment of the Peace and Security Council.[225]

Given that peer review appears now to be consolidated in the AU and the focus throughout both the AU and the NEPAD processes on human rights, this signifies once more an attempt to have a more integrated response to human rights across the continental institutions as a whole. Once again, there is potential for a more coordinated approach to human rights and their implementation and, once more, the role of institutions like the African Commission on Human and Peoples' Rights is likely to become central.

Internal issues

Whilst these developments took place at the regional level, it is also important to note several influences from the domestic setting. As will be further considered in chapter 4, the conflicts that have taken place across Africa have had an impact on the OAU/AU's decision to look at human rights. Although the OAU has been criticised for its failure to prevent or manage these crises effectively, they have prompted it to reflect later on these events from a human rights angle. For example, the genocide in Rwanda in 1994 led to the OAU appointing an independent committee whose report stressed the importance of human rights violations in this context.[226] The

---

[225] Ibid.
[226] The International Panel of Eminent Personalities to Investigate the Genocide in Rwanda and the Surrounding Events, Report on the Genocide in Rwanda, July 2000:

wars in Liberia,[227] the DRC[228] and Sierra Leone,[229] in particular, have also been ongoing influences.

Relationship of the OAU/AU with other international organisations

It would not be appropriate to leave an introduction on human rights within the context of the OAU/AU without making some mention of the role of the latter in the international arena.

Despite Africa often being seen as 'a recipient of, rather than a contributor to, the development of international law',[230] the importance of the OAU/AU and its organs in advancing international human rights law should not be forgotten.[231] As has been noted, 'the common positions taken by OAU members within the UN have even made it possible for the African organisation to exercise a significant influence on the evolution of international law in that field'.[232] In the context of the struggle for decolonisation, for example, the African voice in the international arena was very powerful in prompting the UN to take action. Similarly, lobbying by African states helped to ensure enlargement of membership of UN bodies.[233] One of the reasons for these achievements, however, may have been more to do with Africa's lack of, rather than real, political power. As

---

http://www.internetdiscovery.org/forthetruth/Rwanda-e/EN-III-T.htm. See chapter 4 for more discussion.

[227] See, for example, Resolution on Liberia, CM/Res.1585(LXII).

[228] See, for example, The Situation in the Great Lakes Region, the Democratic Republic of Congo, CM/Dec.353(LXVI); Report of the Secretary General on the Situation in the Democratic Republic of Congo, CM/2099(LXX)-d.

[229] See, for example, Decision on the Report of the Secretary General on the Situation in Sierra Leone, CM/Dec.454(LXX); Report of the Secretary General on the Conflict Situation in Sierra Leone, CM/2099(LXX)-f; Decision on Sierra Leone, CM/2164(LXXII)-e.

[230] A. P. Mutharika, 'The Role of International Law in the Twenty-First Century: An African Perspective', Fordham International Law Journal 18 (1995) 1706; T. Maluwa, 'International Law Making in the Organisation of African Unity: An Overview', RADIC 12 (2000) 201–25, at 201.

[231] Elias, Africa and the Development, at chapter 1. See also K. C. Dunn, 'Introduction: Africa and International Relations Theory', in K. C. Dunn and T. M. Shaw, Africa's Challenge to International Relations Theory (Basingstoke: Palgrave, 2001) 1–10.

[232] Sands and Klein, Bowett's Law, at 248.

[233] T. Hovet, 'Effect of the African Group of States on the Behaviour of the United Nations', in El-Ayouty and Brooks (eds.), Africa, 11–17, at 13. See also Mathews, 'The Organization of African Unity', at 72; R. A. Akindele and B. A. Akinterinwa, 'Reform of the United Nations: Towards Greater Effectiveness, Enhanced Legitimacy Profile and Equitable Regionally-Balanced Membership in an Enlarged UN Security Council', in G. A. Obiozor and

Clapham notes, Africa's entry into the world scene dominated by Cold War alliances also benefited the continent as it had more freedom than perhaps others:

> Whereas in many parts of the world, moreover, the formal recognition of state sovereignty was in practice deeply compromised by superpower competition, and the resulting need for weak states to seek external protection, African states were relatively free. They did not form part of that 'backyard' or reserved domain ... Put simply, African states were accorded an international freedom of action which largely reflected the fact that they did not matter very much.[234]

More recently, African initiatives have been important in ensuring increased attention, among economic institutions such as the World Bank and WTO, to the interests of developing states.[235] This appears to have been done in collaboration with other regional groupings, such as Arab nations and Asia,[236] where the 'deep rooted historical, political, cultural, economic and other links' have been stressed.[237] In this sense, it has been argued that

> it is not difficult to establish a verifiable, direct link between cultural/racial factors and the direction of African foreign policy. This linkage cannot be dismissed easily for it was, in part, similar factors that shaped European attitudes and policies towards Africa. Thus, if one conceives African nationalism as opposition to and refusal to submit to alien political control involving racial injustice and cultural debasement, then Pan-Africanism is the most concrete expression of it ... in essence, Pan-Africanism is a struggle for racial justice, dignity and a new role for Africa in the world community. Viewed in this way, Pan-Africanism was to enable Africans to 'rejoin and recreate history'. It was to provide the ideological framework

A. Ajala (eds.), *Africa and the United Nations System: The First Fifty Years* (Lagos: Nigerian Institute of International Affairs, 1998) 200–31, at 206.

[234] Clapham, *Africa*, at 42.

[235]   The concern of the African states with these kind of activities has meant that the UN role in encouraging economic and social cooperation has been one of more direct involvement than the role of coordination that was originally conceived ... [the influence of African states] has meant that the major proportion of the UN activity is concerned with direct involvement in development rather than the coordination of activities of the international organisations.

Hovet, 'Effect of the African Group', at 15

[236] Draft Resolution on Afro-Arab Co-operation, CM/Draft/Res.16(LXIII) Rev.1; Draft Resolution on Strengthening Relations between African and Asian Countries and Organizations, CM/Draft/Res.20(LXIII) Rev.1.

[237] Resolution on Afro-Arab Co-operation, CM/Res.1440(LVII).

for the elimination of oppression and rapidly transform the oppressed. But more than anything, it is a positive defence against the humiliation Africans and Africans in the Diaspora have suffered for centuries.[238]

The work of the Africa Group[239] at the UN has helped to ensure an African perspective is fed into various bodies.[240] As a result,

> by coming together under the umbrella of the OAU, the states of Africa have obviously got much more out of the UN, both collectively and individually, than would otherwise have been the case. With their collective voice, they have persuaded the UN to listen to them and to do for them much more than they would have been able to do by and for themselves.[241]

The approach of the OAU to the UN has always been one of support and it has become increasingly concerned about its marginalisation.[242] Clearly, as will be seen in chapter 4, when it comes to conflict situations, the OAU has seen itself as playing a secondary role to the UN. The OAU's relationship with the UN's Economic Commission for Africa (ECA) has been an interesting one, with some states wishing to see a close relationship between the ECA and the OAU,[243] and others not wanting the latter to

---

[238] E. K. Dumor, *Ghana, OAU and Southern Africa. An African Response to Apartheid* (Accra: Ghana Universities Press, 1991) at 26–7.

[239] Made up of permanent representatives to the UN.

[240] This 'remains the main instrument for pursuing the aims and objectives of the OAU in the forum of the UN'. 'The African group at the UN has the advantage of having the bulk of issues that it brings before the UN and its component organs clearly defined for it in advance of the decisions and resolutions adopted by the highest political authority of its member states, the OAU Assembly of Heads of State', Amate, *Inside the OAU*, at 197. See also W. W. Nyangoni, *Africa in the United Nations System* (Cranbury, NJ: Associated University Presses, 1985); see Report of the Committee on South West Africa Concerning Implementation of General Assembly Resolutions 1569(XV) and 1596(XV), GAOR, Sixteenth Session, Suppl.No.12A(A/4926), at 18–19.

[241] Amate, *Inside the OAU*, at 568.

[242] Algiers Declaration, AHG/Decl.1(XXXV):
We note with grave concern the growing marginalisation of the United Nations and its role under the Charter for the maintenance of international peace and security and the promotion of international co-operation for development. We declare that the unilateral use of force in international relations, outside the duly conferred mandate of the United Nations Security Council, opens the way to practices inimical to world peace and security. We reaffirm our commitment to respect for the major role and responsibilities of the United Nations and its Security Council in the maintenance of international peace and security.

[243] J. O. C. Jonah, 'The UN and the OAU: Roles in the Maintenance of International Peace and Security in Africa', in El-Ayouty and Brooks (eds.), *Africa* 127–51, at 131.

dominate. As a result, there has been some concern in the past by the ECA that it was being seen as subordinate to the OAU.[244]

However, the attention paid to Libya by the international community has affected relationships between African states and the UN as a whole. When the UN adopted sanctions against Libya following the Lockerbie issue, the OAU stood firmly behind Libya: reaffirming 'its solidarity with the Great Libyan Arab Jamahiriya [the OAU] commends its efforts and numerous initiatives taken in the search of solution to the crisis; deplores the maintenance of sanctions against Libya despite that country's flexibility and efforts in meeting the conditions set by the United Nations Security Council for lifting the sanctions'.[245] The action against Libya was seen as being against African as a whole: 'Consider that any act aimed at destabilising and undermining the Libyan Arab Jamahiriya constitutes an affront to the collective aspiration of Africa and African peoples towards the attainment of self esteem, dignity and independence.'[246] The OAU Assembly thus decided in June 1998 that it would not comply with the UN sanctions.[247] As Sands and Klein note:

> It may prove to be difficult to assess the precise influence of this decision on the lifting of sanctions by the Council later that year. Nevertheless, it cannot be excluded that such a course of conduct might influence the practice of other regional organisations which may be concerned about the legality of some of the decisions taken by the UN Security Council, particularly in the absence of any system of checks and balances or of judicial review of its acts.[248]

---

[244] 'Spokesmen for the ECA made it known that the ECA could not be limited to play only the role of a consultant and work for the OAU only when it was called upon to do so . . . they would not have the ECA relegated to taking instructions from the OAU and certainly not from the OAU General Secretariat', Amate, *Inside the OAU*, at 546.

[245] Draft Resolution on the Dispute between the Great Libyan Arab Jamahiriya and the United States of America, the United Kingdom and France, CM/Draft/Res.28(LXIII) Rev.1. See also Draft Declaration of the Thirty-Third Ordinary Session of the OAU Assembly of Heads of State and Government on the Dispute between the Libyan Arab Jamahiriya and the United States of America and Great Britain, AHG/Draft/Decl.2(XXXIII) Rev.2: calls for a 'just and fair trial' by the Scottish judges, para. 4. Because of lack of solution at that stage it notes: 'This has led to an impasse and, as a result, the entire people of Libya have not only been held hostage for five years, but have also been subjected to collective suffering because of accusations none of the two countries concerned have been able to substantiate.'

[246] Special Motion of Thanks to the Leader of the Great Socialist Libyan Jamahiriya Brother Muammar Al Ghaddafi Adopted by the Fifth Extraordinary Session of the Assembly of Heads of State and Government, EAHG/Dec.4(V).

[247] Sands and Klein, *Bowett's Law*, at 245.   [248] Ibid.

Libya has capitalised on its African support by spearheading the moves to the AU. In this context, in August 2002 African states nominated Libya to chair of the UN Human Rights Commission, despite criticisms from the international community.[249]

The OAU/AU and African states clearly still see their position within the international arena as a disadvantaged one, criticising the UN for failing to pay the same degree of attention to African problems as to those of others. The OAU has focused on trying to get African candidates into positions at the UN and other international organisations.[250] In addition, there is a clear indication of the perception among African states that the international community should be assisting them in respect of conflicts and development and that this comes, in part, from the colonisation context and the debt owed to Africa as a result: 'In the wake of the upsurge in the activities of pro-democracy movements and the increasing struggle for democratisation in Africa, there has emerged a new expectation amongst many Africans of a role for the international community to assist in the democratisation process of these countries.'[251] Yet the UN has been eager to stress that 'Africa must look at itself' and 'look beyond its colonial past for the causes of current conflicts'.[252] In this regard, therefore, the adoption of NEPAD has been hailed by the UN and Western leaders as a positive programme for cooperation on development with Africa, particularly with its focus on finding African solutions to the problems faced.

Conclusion

This book argues that, despite this inauspicious start, the OAU/AU has paid considerable attention to human rights. The Addis Ababa organs have looked at a variety of human rights issues which will be explored in chapters 3 to 8. These include the concept of democracy, human rights in times of conflict, the position of women, children and refugees, and the relationship between human rights and development. What the book also hopes to illustrate, however, is that this work has often been ad hoc.

---

[249] See Human Rights Watch, 'Libya Should not Chair UN Human Rights Commission', 9 August 2002.

[250] See, for example, Decision on African Candidatures for Posts within the United Nations System and Other International Organisations, CM/Dec.484(LXX).

[251] E. K. Quashigah, 'Legitimate Governance in Africa: The Responsibility of the International Community', in Quashigah and Okafor (eds.), Legitimate Governance 461–85, at 461–2.

[252] The Causes of Conflict and Promotion of Durable Peace and Sustainable Development in Africa, Secretary General's Report to the UN Security Council, 16 April 1998, para. 12.

New standards have been elaborated and new institutions created without any real attempt to build upon or consolidate what has gone before. The most obvious institution under the remit of the OAU/AU to have taken a leading role and operated at the centre of such developments was the African Commission on Human and Peoples' Rights. Yet, as is examined in chapter 2, it has functioned on the periphery of the OAU/AU structure and its ability, at present, to act as an effective coordinating body must be questioned. The recent addition of yet more institutions, including the African Court on Human and Peoples' Rights, has happened without any degree of consideration as to their coordination. Serious attention must now be given to mapping out the responsibilities of each AU institution and clarifying the human rights standards which have been developed to ensure a bright future for human rights in Africa.

The relationship between the OAU/AU and the African Commission on Human and Peoples' Rights

In 1981 the OAU adopted the African Charter on Human and Peoples' Rights (ACHPR). It is seen as the primary instrument for the promotion and protection of human rights in Africa. It came into force in 1986[1] and all OAU/AU states are now party to it. The ACHPR provides for an eleven-member independent Commission, based in Banjul, The Gambia, to monitor implementation of its provisions.[2] In addition, in 1998 the OAU AHSG adopted the Protocol to the African Charter establishing an African Court on Human and Peoples' Rights.[3] As at the time of writing this Protocol had just received the necessary number of ratifications to come into force.[4]

In order to put this book, examining the role of the OAU/AU in human rights, into context, the ACHPR must be mentioned. This chapter will not, however, focus on the work of the Commission or the provisions of the Charter which has been covered in detail elsewhere.[5] Instead it will attempt to place the work of the Commission within the context of its parent organisation, the OAU/AU, to consider the OAU/AU's role in facilitating the functioning of the Commission and the integration of the Commission's work throughout the rest of the organs of the OAU/AU.

It is also essential to mention in this context the two ministerial conferences on human rights held at the levels of the OAU and AU, in Grand

---

[1] OAU Doc. CAB/LEG/67/3 rev. 5, 21 ILM (1982) 58.   [2] ACHPR, Article 30.

[3] Protocol to the African Charter on Human and Peoples' Rights on the Establishment of an African Court on Human and Peoples' Rights, OAU/LEG/AFCHPR/PROT(III), adopted by the Assembly of Heads of State and Government, Thirty-Fourth Session, Burkina Faso, 8–10 June 1998.

[4] See below.

[5] See for example, R. Murray, *The African Commission on Human and Peoples' Rights and International Law* (Oxford: Hart Publishing, 2000); M. Evans and R. Murray (eds.), *The African Charter on Human and Peoples' Rights. The System in Practice 1986–2000* (Cambridge: Cambridge University Press, 2002); E. Ankumah, *The African Commission on Human and Peoples' Rights. Practices and Procedure* (The Hague: Martinus Nijhoff, 1996).

Bay, Mauritius, and Kigali, Rwanda, which have had a positive impact in consolidating the relationship between the Commission and the OAU/AU organs.[6] There were a number of reasons for holding these conferences at this time. Firstly, high-level political conferences had been held elsewhere – for example, in 1993 in Vienna – and a new breed of African leaders were influential in pushing forward the democratic agenda and attention to human rights, and therefore breaking with the idea that human rights should always be dealt with defensively. Further, the African Commission on Human and Peoples' Rights itself saw these conferences at the level of the OAU/AU as a way of promoting and strengthening its own work. It is also crucial to mention the influence of NGOs that encouraged the holding of these conferences. The resulting Declarations and Plan of Action from each of the conferences form an important part of the OAU/AU's work on human rights and consolidate the link between the Addis Ababa and Banjul organs.

As the book illustrates, however, whether these declarations have been realised in practice is questionable. Although some of the instruments mentioned in both the Grand Bay and Kigali Declarations have now come into force, most of the recommendations still require implementation. The conferences evidence at least ministerial recognition of human rights in the context of the OAU/AU and of the relationship between themselves and the African Commission on Human and Peoples' Rights. It is also hopeful that there is a commitment to the holding of such conferences on a regular basis.

The African Commission as an organ of the OAU: the OAU and its obligations under the African Charter on Human and Peoples' Rights

As with other human rights treaties, the ACHPR is thus under the ultimate authority of the political OAU, and now AU, and the OAU/AU is given certain responsibilities in relation to its functioning. It is the aim of this section to examine the official obligations and whether there is any other influence on their relationship.

The ACHPR provides for a wide spectrum of human and peoples' rights. These include not only civil and political rights, but also economic, social and cultural rights and rights of a people. The promotion

---

[6] See Grand Bay (Mauritius) Declaration and Plan of Action, CONF/HRA/DECL(I); Kigali Declaration, MIN/CONF/HRA/Decl.1(I).

and protection of these rights is overseen by the African Commission on Human and Peoples' Rights, established under the Charter. It has a mandate in Article 45 to collect documents, undertake research, organise seminars, disseminate information, collaborate with relevant organisations, lay down principles and give recommendations to government.

States are expressly required under the Charter to submit to the Commission every two years reports on the legislative and other measures they have taken to implement the Charter.[7] The Commission is also able to receive complaints from states, and has developed a mechanism by which individuals, NGOs and others can submit communications to it, alleging violations by states parties of the Charter provisions.[8] In the course of its work it has adopted a number of resolutions on particular human rights themes[9] and in relation to particular states.[10] The appointment of Special Rapporteurs from among its members on Summary Arbitrary and Extrajudicial Executions, Prisons and other Conditions of Detention and on the Rights of Women have also enabled these areas to be developed. The creation of Working Groups composed of NGOs and Commissioners to examine issues such as freedom of expression, indigenous populations/communities and fair trial have also made important contributions.[11] There has been important jurisprudence on human and peoples' rights standards emanating from the Commission as a result. The Commission sits twice a year in meetings across the African continent and has a permanent headquarters based in The Gambia.

The official role of the OAU under the ACHPR

As with the European, Inter-American and UN human rights mechanisms, the ACHPR and its Commission are established under the auspices of a political body, in the case of Africa the OAU. The Commission's effectiveness in promoting and protecting human rights therefore depends, to

---

[7] Article 62.   [8] Articles 47–59.
[9] See, for example, Resolution on Guidelines and Measures for the Prohibition and Prevention of Torture, Cruel, Inhuman or Degrading Treatment or Punishment in Africa, 32nd Session of the Commission, October 2002; Resolution on HIV/AIDS Pandemic – Threat against Human Rights and Humanity, 29th Session of the Commission, May 2001.
[10] For example, Resolution on Compliance and Immediate Implementation of the Arusha Peace Agreement for Burundi, 28th Session of the Commission, November 2000; Resolution on Côte d'Ivoire, 28th Session of the Commission, November 2000.
[11] See, for example, Resolution on Freedom of Expression, May 2001; Resolution on the Rights of Indigenous People/Communities in Africa, November 2000.

a certain extent, on whether the necessary support is provided by the OAU.[12]

Whilst there is a recognition that there must be some political involvement in order for these independent mechanisms to function properly, it is also recognised that this must not go too far. The independence of the organ must be maintained in order for it to achieve its aims of promotion and protection. The concern is, however, that this balance is often not achieved. In this regard the African Commission has been criticised for its lack of independence.[13] The relationship between the Commission and the OAU is clearly important here.

The OAU has certain obligations under the African Charter. The transition to the AU has not been accompanied by a review of the Commission's Rules of Procedure or Charter which are now out of date with regard to the institutions that exist under the AU structures. This examination will therefore look at the previous OAU mechanisms and, where possible, consider the present position. The Commission needs urgently to consider reviewing the Rules of Procedure and the AU needs to consider amendments to the Charter to confirm the position under the new arrangements.

Appointment of Commissioners and staff

Article 33 of the African Charter requires that Commissioners will be elected by secret ballot by the OAU Assembly from a list of those nominated by states. The Secretary General then has a role in supervising the nomination process and elections under Articles 34–40 of the African Charter. Until recently the election process took place at the level of Heads of State but at the July 2001 Summit it was decided that this took up too much of their time and that the elections for AU Commissioners, African Commissioners on Human and Peoples' Rights and the Committee on the Child be done through the Executive Council and then approved by the Assembly. This process was followed in the elections in Maputo in July 2003. All states who have the right to sit on AU organs (i.e. who have not been suspended) are present during the election process as it is an item

---

[12] L. Henkin, 'International Law: Politics, Values and Functions', *Collected Courses of the Hague Academy of International Law* 216 (1989) 3–416, at 252.

[13] Although this has also been apparent with other regional bodies as well; see, for example, D. W. Cassel, 'Somoza's Revenge: A New Judge for the Inter-American Court of Human Rights', *HRLJ* 13(4) (1992) 137–40.

on the agenda. The ballot process is carefully scrutinised to ensure it is not interfered with. It would appear to be taken seriously.

However, it is clear that states have in the past perceived the position of Commissioner to be less than prestigious and therefore not taken a great deal of effort either to nominate persons or to nominate appropriate ones. The AU informs states of vacancies six months before the Summit and gives them three months to submit nominations, with CVs. At the most recent round of elections in July 2003, more information was available from the OAU/AU on the candidates nominated by states.[14] As well as existing members, whose terms had expired and who were requesting re-election,[15] the other candidates were a mixture of those with human rights backgrounds[16] and government appointments.[17] There was no suggestion that the latter were not eligible for candidature despite their obvious status as government appointees. The explicit nature of the Rules of Procedure for the African Committee on the Rights and Welfare of the Child clearly have assisted in preventing such nominations on that Committee and give provision for the AU to intervene.[18] Unfortunately there is no equivalent in the African Commission's Rules of Procedure and the Commission itself can do very little about its membership, particularly when ambassadors, as existing members of the Commission, are unlikely to support any changes. The OAU/AU, however, does appear to

[14] Report of the Interim Chairperson on the Election of the Members of the African Commission on Human and Peoples' Rights, EX/CL/57(III) Rev.1.

[15] Commissioners Ben Salem, Tunisia; Badawi El-Sheikh, Egypt, neither of whom were elected.

[16] Mrs Reine Alapini Gansou, Benin: a lawyer, she has worked with WILDAF on women's rights and other human rights matters. Ms Sanji Monageng, Botswana: Executive Secretary of the Law Society, has also been up for nomination to UN CEDAW Committee. She was elected to the African Commission. Dr Alain Didier Olinga, Cameroon: has written academic articles on human rights and is a law professor in human rights. Mr Ibrahim Idris, Ethiopia: Director of the Human Rights and Peace Centre, Dean of the Law Faculty, Addis Ababa University. Dr Willy Munyoki Mutunga, Kenya: board member of the Kenya Human Rights Commission, lawyer, chairs other human rights organisations as well. Mr Mohamed Abdullahi Ould Babana, Mauritania: magistrate, who was elected to the African Commission. He has attended previous sessions of the Commission as a representative of the government of Mauritania. Mr Bahame Tom Mukirya Nyanduga, Tanzania: Tanganyika Law Society, who was also elected to the African Commission.

[17] Mr Eugene Nindorera, Burundi: Human Rights Minister. Mr Abdi Ismail Hersi, Djibouti: Director General of the Ministry of Justice. Mrs Sylvie Kayitesi Zainabo, Rwanda: in Ministry of Environment, Secretary of State and Chairperson of the National Human Rights Commission of Rwanda. Dr Abdelaziz Mahmoud Buhedma from Libya was also appointed to the Commission.

[18] See chapter 6.

see it as the task of the Commission to highlight this difficulty formally to it and to request its assistance. The Commission, however, despite some informal statements, does not appear to have been willing to do this publicly.[19]

Article 31 makes it clear that the Commissioners should be of particular standing and independent and impartial. Article 31 requires that the members be from 'amongst African personalities of the highest reputation, known for their high morality, integrity, impartiality and competence in matters of human and peoples' rights; particular consideration being given to persons having legal experience'. It is clear that the appointments have not always been from those with the highest reputation in human rights.[20] In order to reduce the chance of this happening, it is essential that NGOs and others lobby at the domestic level for the appointment of appropriate members.

Article 31 also requires that Commissioners serve in their personal capacity.[21] There has been an ongoing debate about the extent of present and previous Commissioners' independence, with many holding positions, sometimes senior, in governments at the same time as sitting on the Commission.[22] This has led to difficulties and some indications that Commissioners fail to take an impartial view in relation to state compliance with obligations under the Charter. It is essential that states nominate individuals with a sufficient degree of independence and that the OAU/AU organs ensure that this is the case. Amnesty also says that there can be difficulties if Commissioners simultaneously hold positions in the UN, as this may detract from their work.[23]

Under Article 41 of the ACHPR, the Secretary General of the OAU appoints the Secretary to the Commission. This is an important job, as it is full time, unlike that of the Commissioners, and this individual is responsible for the daily management and functioning of the Commission. It would seem to be important that those who occupy this post be free from government control, although this is not an explicit requirement

---

[19] Interview with Ben Kioko, September 2003.

[20] See in respect of the recent round of appointments, above.

[21] Article 31(2).

[22] For example, Andrew Chigovera was, when he was initially appointed to the Commission, also the Attorney General of Zimbabwe at the time.

[23] Amnesty International, *Organization of African Unity*, at 6–7. An example here is the late Blondin Beye who sat on the Commission for many years, but for a large part of that time was also Special Representative of the UN Secretary General for Angola. He attended very few of the sessions of the African Commission on Human and Peoples' Rights while holding his UN appointment.

in the Charter. The individual should also be sufficiently experienced and accountable to the OAU/AU. They should reside in Banjul and be there the majority of the time. Yet in reality, there have been considerable concerns about the capacity of some of the individuals who have been appointed as Secretary to the Commission to be independent of their governments, and many occupied senior positions in government before working at the Commission.

The OAU/AU is also required to appoint staff to the Commission. The staffing levels of the Commission have fluctuated over the years and have generally been seen as inadequate, forcing the Commission to rely on funding by outside donors to provide additional staff. This problem of limited funding is, however, faced by the OAU/AU as a whole.

Funding

Article 41 of the ACHPR provides that the Commission will be funded by the OAU. It has been a constant criticism that the OAU has consistently failed to provide adequate resources, and the Commission has constantly drawn the attention of the OAU to this.[24] As the Commission noted to the Council of Ministers in 1998, it 'could not carry out quite a number of activities, despite their importance, owing to the paucity of the human, financial and material resources needed to ensure its smooth-running'.[25] Further, it had only two jurists despite the amount of work and it noted further:

> In the budgetary appropriations for the Commission there is no provision for human rights protection and promotion activities which constitute the corner stone of its mandate. Consequently it was also not possible to organise planned seminars aimed at human rights promotion; it was not possible for members of the Commission to make scheduled visits to states parties; there was much delay in the publication of the Commission's magazine; communication between Commission members on the one hand, and between these members and the Secretariat, on the other, as well as contacts between the Commission, states parties and other partners, were seriously hampered by lack of financial resources. These constraints have been faced by the Commission throughout its ten years of existence.[26]

---

[24] See Annual Activity Reports, http://www.achpr.org/html/annualactivityreports.html.
[25] Interim Report on the Activities of the African Commission on Human and Peoples' Rights, CM/2056(LXVII), para. 22.
[26] Ibid.

The Commission has thus consistently called on the OAU organs to provide it with 'adequate human, financial and material resources to enable it to function effectively':[27] 'The African Commission hereby makes an urgent appeal to this august Council to find in its present session an appropriate and definitive solution to this problem which has tended to become endemic.'[28]

However, while requests have been made on paper, the Commission has done little more. It is essential that the Commission takes a more proactive approach and takes more responsibility for its budget. The Commission has relied on funding and provision of staff and equipment from other sources.[29] In turn, this has led to some feeling that the Commission is not African owned. In addition, despite outside funding, the Commission still suffers significantly from a lack of permanent staff and adequate resources at its Secretariat. This does nothing to ensure the long-term stability of resources which funding from the OAU/AU would provide.

The Council of Ministers and AHSG in response to the financial concerns of the Commission have made rather general statements urging that, for example, the Commission be strengthened,[30] and that 'adequate resources should be provided urgently to the African Commission to enable it to effectively carry out its mandate in accordance with the relevant resolutions of the ASHG and charges the Advisory Committee and the General Secretariat to take appropriate measures in this regard for the biennium 1998–2000'.[31] Although it was suggested in 1994 that an

---

[27] AHG/Res.188(XXV) and AHG/Res.227(XXIX), AHG/Res.230(XXX), AHG/Res.250(XXXI), Dec. AHG/Dec.123(XXXIII).

[28] Dec. AHG/Dec.123(XXXIII).

[29] For example, the EU, Danida, see Fifteenth Annual Activity Report of the African Commission on Human and Peoples' Rights, 2001–2, http://www.achpr. org/15th_Annual_ Activity_Report-_AHG.pdf, paras. 48–58.

[30] Decision on the Tenth Annual Activity Report of the African Commission on Human and Peoples' Rights, AHG/Dec.123(XXXIII).

[31] Draft Decisions of the Sixty-Seventh Ordinary Session of the Council of Ministers, CM/DRAFT/DECISIONS(LXVII) REV.1, CM/Draft/Dec.26(LXVII). Interim Report on the Activities of the African Commission on Human and Peoples' Rights (Doc.CM/ 2056(LXVII)); Resolution on Measures Taken to Implement Resolution AHG/Res.230 (XXX) Relating to the Strengthening of the African Commission on Human and Peoples' Rights and the Establishment of an African Court of Human and Peoples' Rights, CM/Res.1674(LXIV), preamble; Resolution on the African Commission on Human and Peoples' Rights. Twenty-Ninth Ordinary Session of the Assembly of Heads of State and Government of the Organization of African Unity, 28–30 June 1993, Cairo, http://www1.umn.edu/humanrts/africa/resafchar29th.html. 'Resolved to provide the

experts meeting be held to consider how to enhance the efficiency of the African Commission, this does not appear to have been done.[32] On a more positive note, the OAU/AU recently agreed to increase the budget to the Commission enabling it, among other things, to extend the time for its sessions from ten to fifteen days.

Although the budget for the OAU/AU has increased from $30m. under the OAU to $43m. for 2003–4, the lack of funding is a problem for the OAU/AU in general, with many states being in arrears. The issue of finding alternative sources of funding has been under consideration.[33] This is clearly now a high priority for the AU.

Examination and adoption of the Commission's reports

There are several provisions of the ACHPR which make it clear that the African Commission is ultimately accountable to the OAU, particularly the AHSG. The corollary to this is that the OAU/AU should therefore be the final port for the enforcement of the Commission's decisions and some of the responsibility for doing so should rest with it.

Article 54 requires that the Commission submit to each session of the AHSG a report of its activities. This is reaffirmed by Rule 79 of the Commission's Rules of Procedure. The Rules of Procedure seem to imply that it is the Chairman of the OAU, rather than the Chairman of the Commission, who publishes the report after its consideration, and, secondly, that it would only require the consideration of the OAU, not its actual approval.[34] However, the way in which Article 59 of the ACHPR has been interpreted[35] has meant that the report is not made public until approved

Commission with the resources necessary for its effective functioning with a view to attaining its assigned objectives', Resolution Relating to the African Commission on Human and Peoples' Rights, AHG/Res.188(XXV). Resolution on the African Commission on Human and Peoples' Rights, Twenty-Eighth Ordinary Session of the Assembly of Heads of State and Government of the Organization of African Unity, 29 June–1 July 1992, Dakar, http://www1.umn.edu/humanrts/africa/resafchar28th.html.

[32] Resolution on the African Commission on Human and Peoples' Rights, AHG/Res.230 (XXX).

[33] Some ideas included imposing a tax on flights into Africa, but this raised problems of states who had fewer visitors and whether they should therefore pay the same.

[34] Rule 79 reads: '(1) As stipulated in Article 54 of the Charter, the Commission shall each year submit to the Assembly, a report on its deliberations, in which it shall include a summary of the activities. (2) The report shall be published by the Chairman after the Assembly has considered it.'

[35] Article 59 reads: '(1) All measures taken within the provisions of the present Chapter shall remain confidential until the Assembly of Heads of State and Government shall otherwise decide. (2) However the report shall be published by the Chairman of the Commission

by the AHSG. This was of considerable concern in the early years of the Commission when it was feared that states would refuse to adopt a report which contained allegations against them of violations of human rights. However, in practice this has not really been an issue. For many years the report was just adopted without debate, usually late in the evening, after other, more high-profile, business was done.[36] This, in turn, however, led to concerns that while one would not wish to argue that it should be prevented from publication on the basis of concerns of states at this level, the report's effectiveness was being diminished by not being subjected to any scrutiny.

In 1996 the Secretary General of the OAU suggested that the full debate on the report of the African Commission on Human and Peoples' Rights should take place before the Council of Ministers, rather than the Assembly, as the Council had more time to discuss such matters. There had been initial concerns that placing reports before the Council of Ministers could mean that the Council could prevent anything its members did not like going before the Assembly of Heads of State. However, in practice this process has been even more of a disadvantage. All issues that appear before the Assembly come through the Council of Ministers, and the recommendations and resolutions that the Assembly adopts rely heavily on what the Council of Ministers have suggested. Heads of state do not draft, they simply approve what has gone before. The Council of Ministers, and the ambassadors, are often more approachable and decisions made at ambassadorial level are fed into the Council of Ministers and then on to the heads of state.

The suggestion that the Council of Ministers examine the Commission's report, despite being approved, was not actually carried out. When questioned about this staff at the AU said that it was presumed that if the Commission wanted the procedure to be adopted it should initiate it through a resolution requesting that the Council of Ministers take over the main debate. It would appear that the Commission never did write this resolution. However, in July 2003 the Executive Council of the AU was mandated by the Assembly to consider the ACHPR annual reports and report to the Assembly on them.[37] Although the discussion of

upon the decision of the Assembly of Heads of State and Government. (3) The report on the activities of the Commission shall be published by its Chairman after it has been considered by the Assembly of Heads of State and Government. '

[36] Interview with Ben Kioko, September 2003.

[37] Assembly/AU/Dec.6(II), Draft Decision on the Sixteenth Annual Activity Report of the African Commission on Human and Peoples' Rights – Doc. Assembly/AU/7(II).

the Commission's report at this Summit was limited, at least this statement is a step in the right direction.

A further problem is that the reports and other documents of the Commission do not provide sufficient detail on the situation in particular countries to enable the AU organs to take any effective decision.[38] It has been suggested that it would be useful to have an executive summary of the Commission's report and a clear indication of what action is required by the AU organs as a consequence.

The Rules of Procedure make it clear that it is the Commission that must disseminate the report. This has clearly not been done as effectively as it could have been. Given that the report is considered at the OAU/AU, it would be appropriate for it to disseminate it among states at this time and among other organs of the OAU/AU. In Lusaka in July 2001 at the Summit of the Assembly of the OAU it was decided that states should bear the responsibility of popularising the AU in their own states, especially as the budget of the AU restricts its ability to print for outside sources.

Neither the AU organs nor the African Commission on Human and Peoples' Rights appear to be willing to take responsibility or the initiative to make the necessary changes to make more effective use of the documentation and findings of the Commission.

Enforcing state obligations

Throughout the Charter there is reference to the role of the OAU organs in terms of enforcing the decisions of the Commission. In this regard the OAU/AU organs have made general calls for states to cooperate with the Commission.[39] This has included calling on states to ratify the Charter and instruments adopted by the Commission which, in some instances, has been relatively successful.[40]

Under Article 58 of the ACHPR, the Commission 'shall draw the attention of the Assembly of Heads of State and Government to these special cases' of 'the existence of a series of serious or massive violations' of the Charter. The Assembly can then request the Commission to undertake an in-depth study of the cases and to report to it with recommendations. Article 58(3) also provides for cases of emergency to be submitted by the Commission to the Assembly which can request a study. The African

---

[38] Amnesty International, *Organization of African Unity*, at 11.

[39] Resolution on the African Commission on Human and Peoples' Rights, AHG/Res.240 (XXXI).

[40] For example, all AU states are party to the ACHPR.

Commission has, on several occasions, referred a number of cases to the Assembly under Article 58.[41] The Assembly, however, made no response in relation to any of these submissions. The reasons for this seem to be more procedural. It would appear that requests to the Assembly were only made as part of the Annual Activity Report of the Commission, not highlighted expressly and not referred to in other documentation. Because of the lack of attention to the detail of the Report during Assembly debates, the length of the Commission's reports and the failure to highlight these requests specifically, such statements were never discussed. Further, the resolutions whereby the Assembly adopts the Report of the Commission are usually drafted by the Commission itself, and the Commission, while it has used this opportunity to call the attention of the Assembly to other matters, does not appear to have used it in respect of Article 58 issues. The Commission could therefore have done more itself to encourage action by the Assembly in this regard.

As noted above, states are obliged to submit reports every two years under Article 62 of the Charter on the measures they have taken to implement its provisions. Unfortunately, while the record has improved in recent years, most states are behind in their obligations in this regard.[42] While the Commission itself has taken certain actions to try to remedy this situation, some of which have been successful,[43] it is also argued that the OAU/AU organs have a role to play: 'Fulfilling obligations under the African Charter is central to implementation of the principles of the OAU Charter.'[44] The OAU/AU organs should therefore be mentioning such obligations when meeting with states and ensuring implementation of the Commission resolutions on overdue reports.[45] In addition, Rule 81(3) of the Commission's Rules of Procedure provide for the Commission to go through the Secretary General to inform states of its wishes on what should be in the reports, and Rule 86 enables general observations of the Article 62 reports from the Commission to be transmitted

---

[41] For example, Communication 102/93, *Constitutional Rights Project and Civil Liberties Organisation* v. *Nigeria*, Twelfth Annual Activity Report of the African Commission on Human and Peoples' Rights, Annex V, AHG/215(XXXV); Communications 64/92, 68/92 and 78/92, *Krishna Achuthan, and Amnesty International* v. *Malawi*, Seventh Annual Activity Report of the African Commission on Human and Peoples' Rights, ACHPR/RPT/7th.

[42] See Sixteenth Annual Activity Report of the African Commission on Human and Peoples' Rights, 2002–3, Annex II.

[43] See M. Evans, T. Ige and R. Murray, 'The Reporting Mechanism of the African Charter on Human and Peoples' Rights', in Evans and Murray (eds.), *The African Charter* 36–60.

[44] Amnesty International, *Organization of African Unity*, at 12.   [45] Ibid.

to the Assembly, which it has started to do. In this regard, one would expect the Assembly at least to have a more active role. However, all the OAU/AU organs appear to have done is to comment briefly and make general statements for states to submit their reports 'as [soon as] possible if they have not yet done so' and to seek help from the Commission if they were having trouble doing so.[46] Again, given that it is apparent that the African Commission on Human and Peoples' Rights drafts the resolution for the OAU/AU Assembly to later adopt,[47] the Commission could be more robust here.[48]

The Commission publishes its decisions on its communications in its Annual Activity Report. The Commission's Rules of Procedure require that its observations on the cases be communicated through the Secretary General to the Assembly, as well as the state or states involved.[49] In response to this, the Chairman of the OAU or the Assembly can request

[46] Resolution on the African Commission on Human and Peoples' Rights, Twenty-Eighth Ordinary Session of the Assembly of Heads of State and Government of the Organization of African Unity, 29 June–1 July 1992, Dakar, http://www1.umn.edu/humanrts/africa/resafchar28th.html. See also Draft Decisions of the Sixty-Seventh Ordinary Session of the Council of Ministers, CM/DRAFT/DECISIONS(LXVII) REV.1, CM/Draft/Dec.26(LXVII), Interim Report on the Activities of the African Commission on Human and Peoples' Rights (Doc.CM/2056(LXVII)).

[47] For example, Resolution on Overdue Reports, Twenty-Eighth Ordinary Session of the Assembly of Heads of State and Government of the Organization of African Unity, 29 June–1 July 1992, Dakar, http://www1.umn.edu/humanrts/africa/resoverdue.html. See also Resolution on the African Commission on Human and Peoples' Rights, Twenty-Ninth Ordinary Session of the Assembly of Heads of State and Government of the Organization of African Unity, 28–30 June 1993, Cairo, http://www1.umn.edu/humanrts/africa/resafchar29th.html. Resolution on Human and Peoples' Rights, AHG/Res.202(XXVII), para. 2. Resolution on the African Commission on Human and Peoples' Rights, AHG/Res.207(XXVIII).

[48] For example, in one of the resolutions the Commission drafted for adoption by the OAU organs it called on states to implement Article 26 of the ACHPR by setting up national institutions, ensuring human rights was included in the curriculum of education and training of law-enforcement officials under Article 25 of the ACHPR and that the right of receipt of information was guaranteed under Article 9 of the ACHPR. It has also requested 'states to include in their education programs specific measures to encourage a thorough understanding of issues relating to human rights and encourages them to pursue their efforts in order to take into account, within the framework of the training of officers-in-charge of Armed Forces, Law Enforcement and of all other relevant branched, appropriate elements concerning human rights', Resolution on the African Commission on Human and Peoples' Rights, Twenty-Eighth Ordinary Session of the Assembly of Heads of State and Government of the Organization of African Unity, 29 June–1 July 1992, Dakar, http://www1.umn.edu/humanrts/africa/resafchar28th.html; Resolution on the Promotion of Human Rights in Africa, CM/Res.1420(LVI), para. 4. Resolution on the African Commission on Human and Peoples' Rights, AHG/Res.207(XXVIII), paras. 2–4.

[49] Commission's Rules of Procedure, Rule 120(2).

an in-depth study from the Commission on the cases.[50] Whether this is something different from the Article 58 report is not clear, but the wording in Rule 120(3) 'in accordance with the provisions of the Charter' suggests it is not. In addition, the whole Annual Report of the Commission must be presented to the OAU organs under Article 59 of the Charter. The Commission at present does not have a follow-up procedure to monitor compliance with its decisions, although it has begun considering this and states have made mention of it in their statements during the Commission's meetings.[51] Given that the reports now contain the only public official reproduction of the Commission's decisions, one would expect that this would be considered carefully by the OAU/AU organs on their approval of its adoption. Specific cases, however, are not discussed at OAU/AU meetings as they are included in the Annual Activity Report which is not discussed in detail, as noted above.

As the role of the Committee of Ministers has shown in the European Convention on Human Rights,[52] the impact that political organs can have on ensuring compliance with decisions of an independent human rights body can be considerable. The most the OAU/AU appears to have done is to request states to 'designate high ranking officials to act as focal points in the relation between the Commission and the States as such focal points would facilitate the follow up on the Commission's recommendations and contact between states and the Commission'.[53] The OAU/AU organs have an important role to play in this regard but have failed to act proactively. The African Commission on Human and Peoples' Rights could assist by making its documentation and findings more accessible, providing a summary and expressly listing recommendations to the Assembly in its resolutions.

Assisting in its investigations

Article 46 permits the Commission in the consideration of communications to approach the Secretary General, among others, for information. The extent to which this occurs is not clear, although it would appear to be limited given that the OAU/AU organs have not gone beyond general

---

[50] Ibid., Rule 120(3).
[51] See R. Murray, 'Report of the 31st Ordinary Session of the African Commission on Human and Peoples' Rights, South Africa, May 2002', on file with author.
[52] ECHR, Article 54.
[53] Resolution on the African Commission on Human and Peoples' Rights, AHG/Res.227 (XXIX).

statements calling on states to collaborate with the Commission and its Special Rapporteurs, for example.[54]

Assisting in arriving at an amicable solution

The inter-state communication procedure in Articles 47–54 envisages a clear role for the Secretary General of the OAU.[55] Although there have been very few of these cases before the Commission[56] one might expect more involvement of the OAU/AU organs. There appears to have been little connection, however, between the Banjul and Addis Ababa organs in this regard.

Attendance at the Commission's sessions

Article 42(5) of the ACHPR permits the Secretary General of the OAU to attend the Commission's sessions and present statements to the sessions of the Commission if invited to do so by the Chairman,[57] but not, however, to participate in its deliberations or to vote. It has been recommended that the Secretary General take advantage of this provision and attend in person or at least send a representative on a regular basis.[58] Although

---

[54] Resolution on the African Commission on Human and Peoples' Rights, Thirtieth Ordinary Session of the Assembly of Heads of State and Government of the Organization of African Unity, 13–15 June 1994, Tunis, http://www1.umn.edu/humanrts/africa/resafchar30th.html.

[55] Article 47 reads:

> If a State Party to the present Charter has good reasons to believe that another State Party to this Charter has violated the provisions of the Charter, it may draw, by written communication, the attention of that State to the matter. This Communication shall also be addressed to the Secretary General of the OAU and to the Chairman of the Commission. Within three months of the receipt of the Communication, the State to which the Communication is addressed shall give the enquiring State, written explanation or statement elucidating the matter. This should include as much as possible, relevant information relating to the laws and rules of procedure applied and applicable and the redress already given or course of action available.

Article 49 reads: 'Notwithstanding the provisions of Article 47, if a State Party to the present Charter considers that another State Party has violated the provisions of the Charter, it may refer the matter directly to the Commission by addressing a communication to the Chairman, to the Secretary General of the Organisation of African unity and the State concerned.'

[56] No inter-state communication has been carried through to completion, although several states have started the process before the Commission. For example, Ethiopia and Eritrea have suggested using the Commission's procedures in this regard, and the DRC submitted a case before Rwanda, Uganda and Burundi in 1999, Communication 227/99, which has yet to be dealt with fully by the Commission.

[57] Commission's Rules of Procedure, Rule 22.

[58] Amnesty International, *Organization of African Unity*, at 11.

there have been occasions on which the Secretary General himself and his representatives have attended the Commission's meetings,[59] this has not been a particularly regular occurrence.

Apart from the very first meeting of the Commission, which Article 64(2) of the ACHPR deems shall be convened by the Secretary General and at the Headquarters of the OAU, when the Rules of Procedure of the Commission were amended they removed the primary role of the Secretary General in the organisation of meetings. This is now the task of the Secretary and Chair of the Commission, although there must be consultation with the Secretary General of the OAU who can change 'under exceptional circumstances' the starting date after discussion with the Chair.[60] Similar involvement is required for extraordinary sessions.[61] The Chairman of the OAU is also one of the individuals who can request an extraordinary session to be held[62] but whether he has ever done this is not clear.[63]

Meetings have been held all over Africa. The Commission has therefore not followed its Rules of Procedure strictly; they require that sessions are held at the Commission's headquarters, and there is no indication whether it has consulted with the Secretary General in making these decisions.[64] The AHSG, Council of Ministers and Secretary General can propose items to be included on the agenda of the Commission.[65] Whether they have done so is not clear. The Rules of Procedure of the Commission also require the provisional agenda to be sent to the OAU Chairman.[66]

There are requirements which involve the Secretary General in terms of the minutes of the sessions under Rule 39 of the Commission's Rules, although in practice no minutes are produced by the Commission.[67] There is a requirement that the Commission submit a report to the Chairman of the OAU on the deliberations of each session.[68] One presumes that this is the final communiqué, but there is also a report produced by the Commission which is not made public. Although documentation in

---

[59] For example, at the 25th Session of the Commission in Burundi in April/May 1999.
[60] Commission's Rules of Procedure, Rules 2(2) and (3).
[61] Ibid., Rule 3(2).   [62] Ibid., Rule 3(1)b.
[63] Two extraordinary sessions have been held so far, one in June 1989 to examine the Rules of Procedure of the Commission, and the second in December 1995 to look at the situation in Nigeria, among others.
[64] Commission's Rules of Procedure, Rule 4.   [65] Ibid., Rule 6.   [66] Ibid., Rule 7.
[67] It is notable that minutes of the private sessions and official decisions and reports do not require expressly to be distributed to the OAU, ibid., Rules 40 and 42.
[68] Ibid., Rule 41. Rules of Procedure.

general appears to be sent from the Commission to the AU and primarily to its Office of the Legal Counsel, it is not disseminated across other AU bodies.

Encouraging ratification of other instruments

The OAU is the depository for treaties adopted under the regional mechanism[69] and has taken a clear role in encouraging ratification of these instruments. This has included encouraging states to ratify the instruments in which the Commission played a part in drafting, such as the Protocol on the Rights of Women in Africa.

The ACHPR provides that amendment of the Charter shall be done through the OAU Assembly.[70] States should send written requests, not to the Commission, but to the Secretary General of the OAU. There is some role for the Commission in this process, in that the AHSG cannot consider the draft until all states and the Commission have seen it and had a chance to comment upon it. Both the Protocols on the Court and the Rights of Women saw the involvement of the African Commission in the process before their consideration at ministerial level and their eventual adoption by the Assembly.[71]

Enhancing interpretation of the ACHPR

There is the possibility of the OAU taking a more proactive role in the interpretation of human rights and in directing human rights issues to the Commission. In Article 45(3) and (4) of the ACHPR the Commission is mandated to interpret the provisions of the ACHPR at the request of, among others, an institution of the OAU and to 'perform any other tasks which may be entrusted to it by the Assembly of Heads of State and Government'. This gives the OAU/AU the opportunity to use the Commission to examine particular human rights issues, but there is no indication that it appears to have been used.

---

[69] ACHPR, Article 63.   [70] Ibid., Article 68.

[71] See, for example, Draft Protocol to the African Charter on Human and Peoples' Rights on the Rights of Women in Africa, [Final Version], 13 September 2000, CAB/LEG/66.6; Government Legal Experts Meeting on the Question of the Establishment of an African Court on Human and Peoples' Rights, 6–12 September 1995, Cape Town, Report, OAU/LEG/EXP/AFC/HPR(I), reproduced in *African Journal of International and Comparative Law* 8(2) (1996) 493–500. See in respect of the drafting of the Protocol on the Court, J. Harrington, 'The African Court on Human and Peoples' Rights', in Evans and Murray (eds.), *The African Charter* 305–34.

There has been very little evidence of OAU/AU organs using the jurisprudence of the Commission and the provisions of the Charter in their work, beyond mere reference to the Charter itself. There is no indication that the OAU/AU organs have knowledge of a comprehensive database of Commission decisions upon which they could build their own interpretations and no real attempt to draw upon the documentation or work of the Commission. Whether the Commission's documentation is used appears to depend more on chance than any systematic attempt to strengthen institutional knowledge.

In the same vein, it would appear that while the African Commission on Human and Peoples' Rights is known in the OAU/AU Addis Ababa organs, it is not seen as a point of authority for interpretation of human rights issues in general. As a result, it does not seem to be called upon by OAU/AU organs to provide an authoritative interpretation of various human rights issues, for example. This would, arguably, help strengthen its authority and independence. Yet it does not appear that the Commission has a high enough profile and its documentation is simply not that well known.

Facilitating the functioning of the Commission

There is a possibility of the Commission setting up working groups which can meet, if the Secretary General has been consulted, outside sessions.[72] This requirement to consult is presumably due to the financial burden which these might impose on the OAU. The Commission has made use of this process by appointing several working groups, although whether it requested the permission of the Secretary General is not clear, especially given that funding for the meetings appears to have come from other sources, not the OAU/AU.[73]

In an interesting development and an indication of how much the OAU organs could become involved if they so wished, the Assembly in 1996 adopted a resolution calling on the Commission to suspend review of granting observer status for NGOs until criteria had been clarified.[74] This seemed to be the outcome of concerns by governments of the influence of NGOs in the work of the Commission. The Commission as a result did suspend consideration of applications for a number of sessions, until

---

[72] Commission's Rules of Procedure, Rule 28(2).

[73] For example, support for the Working Group on Free Expression has come from the NGO Article 19.

[74] Annual Activities of the African Commission on Human and Peoples' Rights, AHG/Dec.126(XXXIV), paras. 3, 4, 6 and 7.

it adopted criteria in 1998.[75] While this actually resulted in a positive measure, as until that point the criteria had not been clear, it is clearly unacceptable for there to be this level of interference with the Commission's work.

Role of OAU Secretariat and its Secretary General

The initial Rules of Procedure of the African Commission on Human and Peoples' Rights perceived a more central role for the Secretary General of the OAU, although when amended at the eighteenth session of the Commission, many of these tasks were given to the Secretary of the African Commission instead. As seen above, the Secretary General still, however, has a role in many aspects of the Commission's work. Under the AU it is presumed that this position will be taken over by the Chairperson of the AU Commission.

The Mauritius Plan of Action recognised the need to strengthen cooperation with the Commission: 'the OAU Secretariat's involvement in its activities related to human and peoples' rights with regard to, among other things, conflict prevention and management, refugees and displaced people, observation of elections and the establishment of the African Economic Community'.[76] In the Kigali Declaration this was further consolidated by calling on 'the AU policy organs to provide the African Commission with suitable Headquarters, an appropriate structure and adequate human and financial resources for its proper functioning, including the establishment of a Fund to be financed through voluntary contributions from Member States, international and regional institutions' and 'the AU Policy Organs to review the operation and composition of the African Commission on Peoples' Rights with a view to strengthening its independence and operational integrity and ensuring appropriate gender representivity and to report on the progress made to the appropriate AU Organs as soon as possible'.[77]

Rule 73 of the Rules of Procedure of the African Commission on Human and Peoples' Rights permits 'Specialised Institutions' of the OAU to have a relationship with the Commission.[78] It also envisages a role for the

---

[75] Resolution on the Cooperation between the African Commission on Human and Peoples' Rights and NGOs having Observer Status with the Commission, October 1998.

[76] Mauritius Plan of Action, section IV(b), para. 54.

[77] Kigali Declaration, paras. 23 and 24.

[78] The 'specialised agencies' of the OAU include, for example, the African Accounting Council, the Pan-African News Agency and the African Bureau for Educational Sciences.

Secretary General to consult with such bodies before an item is placed on the Commission's agenda as submitted by them and also for it to be involved if the proposals relate to additional activities of the OAU. There is also a role for these specialised institutions to receive Article 62 reports from the states and comment upon them.[79] This has never been used. There is also the possibility of inter-governmental organisations which have been given permanent observer status by the OAU to participate in the Commission's sessions 'on issues falling within the framework of activities of these organisations'.[80]

The African Court on Human and Peoples' Rights

In 1998 the OAU Assembly adopted the Protocol to the ACHPR establishing an African Court on Human and Peoples' Rights. As noted above, the drafting of this Protocol, although initiated at the level of the African Commission, was finalised through the OAU. Since 1998 the African Commission has been discussing the need to ensure the requisite number of ratifications to ensure that the Protocol comes into force. However, debate at the sessions has often concluded in statements that the Commission does not have the resources to undertake such a campaign, and that the responsibility must fall to the OAU/AU. With the assistance of NGOs and Western governments, the OAU/AU has encouraged states to ratify the Protocol and this has been met with recent success, with the level of ratification required for it to come into force having been satisfied.[81]

One concern of the OAU/AU has been, however, ensuring adequate funding for the Court.[82] This has been particularly pressing given the adoption of new organs under the transformation to the AU, and in particular in defining the role of the new African Court of Justice (ACJ). The relationship between the two has yet to be clarified and at one stage it was suggested that the Court on Human and Peoples' Rights should become a sub-chamber of the ACJ.[83] While it was finally decided that a

---

[79] Commission's Rules of Procedure Rule 82.

[80] Ibid., Rule 74(1).

[81] Algeria, Burkina Faso, Burundi, Comoros, Côte d'Ivoire, DRC, The Gambia, Lesotho, Libya, Mali, Mauritius, Rwanda, Senegal, South Africa, Togo and Uganda.

[82] The OAU is required to fund the Court under Article 32 of the Protocol.

[83] Although states were still urged to ratify the Protocol on the African Court on Human and Peoples' Rights, Report of the Meeting of Experts of the 1st AU Ministerial Conference on Human Rights in Africa, Kigali, 5–6 May 2003, EXP/CONF/HRA/RPT.(II), para. 53.

separate human and peoples' rights court was necessary,[84] the financial implications of such have still to be settled.[85] The funding issue, however, is something that must be tackled by the AU as a whole, rather than using it as an argument for not having two organs if so required. It is important that the AU consider what can be done to increase states' contributions and how should this be worked on first. So, if states reduced their military spending and paid up all their arrears to the AU, there would be sufficient money to pay off the AU debts and finance other projects. The debate should therefore be where to put the money now and how to ensure that states reduce military spending.

Under the Protocol establishing the African Court on Human and Peoples' Rights, the OAU/AU has various functions. It can request an advisory opinion 'on any legal matter relating to the Charter or any other relevant human rights instruments';[86] and can submit a case to the Court.[87] The Secretary General of the OAU requests nominations for judges to the Court and prepares a list of candidates for the Assembly, which then elects them.[88] The Assembly also has the power to set aside a decision of the judges for suspension or removal of judges from the Court.[89] It is the Assembly that will determine the seat of the Court[90] and the Court is to report annually to it.[91] Decisions of the Court will be transmitted to the Council of Ministers of the OAU which will monitor its execution.[92]

Is the African Commission and Court/Charter known to other OAU bodies?

It would appear that despite being an organ of the OAU/AU, the African Commission on Human and Peoples' Rights is not well known among the Addis Ababa bodies. In order for human rights to be integrated across the

---

[84] The reasons given were that it could tackle issues of impunity and corruption; it could interpret treaties under the AU relating to human rights; and it could set precedents, especially within conflict situations.

[85] Information on the Financial Implications of the Adoption of the Protocol on the Establishment of the African Court on Human and Peoples' Rights, CM/2083(LXVIII). It noted at para. 4 that financial implications depended upon where the court would sit and staffing levels. It provides an estimate of the costs and of what staff might be required. It is interesting that in the short term no allocation is made for a legal officer, only later, at 7–8.

[86] Protocol, Article 4.   [87] Ibid., Article 5(1).

[88] Ibid., Articles 13 and 14. The Secretary General also has a role when a seat becomes vacant, Article 20.

[89] Article 19.   [90] Article 25.   [91] Article 31.   [92] Article 30.

whole spectrum of the OAU/AU's work, however, it is essential that this is changed. As Amnesty notes, such cooperation 'would go a considerable way towards bridging the information and conceptual gulf that exists between the two institutions'.[93]

There appears to be limited provision of information between the Addis Ababa organs and the Commission, with the Commission liaising mostly with the Legal Division of the OAU/AU but its documents and work not being disseminated further than this. Documents of the African Commission on Human and Peoples' Rights tend to be distributed at the Summit meetings and are therefore picked up by the various OAU/AU bodies, but often not referred to beyond this. Attendance of OAU/AU representatives at Commission meetings has been limited and the Commissioners, similarly, have not been regularly involved in the meetings of Addis Ababa organs.

As a result, there has been little attempt to integrate the Commission's jurisprudence into the rest of the OAU/AU work. Although there are references by the OAU/AU organs to the African Charter and its provisions or the mere existence of the Commission on Human and Peoples' Rights, there are hardly any to the work of the Commission in interpreting them. There is thus practically no reference to Commission resolutions or decisions on particular issues which may be relevant.[94]

Conclusion: the place of the ACHPR under the AU

Now that the Constitutive Act has been adopted, the time is ripe for the African Commission on Human and Peoples' Rights and the prospective Court to consider in detail their future place within the AU. Apart from the pressing need to amend its Rules of Procedure and Charter to reflect the new institutional arrangements, the African Commission on Human and Peoples' Rights and AU need to go further and consider how the position of the Commission can be consolidated and strengthened. Despite attention to the changes taking place in Addis Ababa for several years, and the Kigali Ministerial Conference on Human Rights calling for action from the Commission,[95] the African Commission has so far failed to see the

---

[93] Amnesty International, *Organization of African Unity*, at 10.

[94] One of the very few examples is the Report of the Secretary General on the Issue of Landmines and International Efforts to Reach a Total Ban, CM/2009(LXVI), para. 7, which notes the adoption of a resolution by the African Commission in 1995 and cites from it.

[95] To review the Charter in the light of the changes under the AU. The AU Should also review the structure of the African Commission on HPR in the light of the setting up of the AU

urgency of discussing this matter further. Given the numerous bodies that exist now in the AU with some remit for human rights, including the development of the African Peer Review Mechanism (APRM) under NEPAD,[96] and the rhetoric given to human rights standards across the Union as a whole, the African Commission on Human and Peoples' Rights is in an ideal position to assert itself as the authoritative voice on human rights for the continent. In doing so it could place the African Court on Human and Peoples' Rights in an equally, if not more, prominent position. The Commission must also carefully examine its role and relationship with the new African Court.

At present, however, the African Commission is not in an ideal position to take on this role. The further dilution of its resources through the establishment of other bodies and the failure to refer to its work by existing OAU/AU bodies suggest that it is not reasonable to expect it to function as an effective coordinating institution at the moment. Various measures need to be taken to ensure that it can fulfil this role, including ensuring the independence and integrity of its members. The same issues are also likely to arise with the African Court on Human and Peoples' Rights, and it is naïve to think that its establishment alone will be the panacea for the failures of the Commission.

It is essential that the AU sees the African Commission and Court on Human and Peoples' Rights occupy a central role in the AU's overall strategy on human rights. As the Assembly noted in July 2003, the African Commission on Human and Peoples' Rights should spearhead these developments and 'enhance interaction and coordination with the different organs of the African Union in order to strengthen the African Mechanism for the Promotion and Protection of Human and Peoples' Rights'.[97]

The failure of the OAU/AU so far to take account of the Commission's work seem to be historical and procedural, rather than deliberate. In the climate of the AU process and the good will that is there to strengthen

---

Commission, Report of the Meeting of Experts of the First AU Ministerial Conference on Human Rights in Africa, Kigali, 5–6 May 2003, EXP/CONF/HRA/RPT.(II), para. 28.

[96] Recommendations from the meeting of the AU first ministerial conference on human rights concluded that further consideration needed to be given to implementing the Grand Bay Decision and Plan of Action and that they should also consider how this would work with the APRM, guidelines should be developed to assist states to report on such matters, and setting up mechanisms so states could review their own performance and that of other states, Report of the Meeting of Experts of the First AU Ministerial Conference on Human Rights in Africa, Kigali, 5–6 May 2003, EXP/CONF/HRA/RPT.(II).

[97] Assembly/AU/Dec.6(II), Draft Decision on Sixteenth Annual Activity Report of the African Commission on Human and Peoples' Rights – Doc. Assembly/AU/7(II).

human rights protection in the AU, the African Commission has a role to play in driving its own position in this. The AU has made it clear that it is now up to the Commission to decide on how it wishes to be seen within the Union. The Commission must take this opportunity seriously if it is not to be sidelined and become irrelevant under the new structures. So far it has not taken any initiative in this regard. Unfortunately, the Addis Ababa organs, while one might have expected some action on their part as well, appear to have been unwilling to do so. At present, therefore, while there may be a recognition of the need to change, this is not being accompanied by the necessary practical measures to implement such.

The link between human rights and democracy

Introduction

> Democracy and human rights have historically been regarded as distinct
> phenomena occupying different areas of the political sphere: the one a
> matter of the organisation of government, the other a question of individual
> rights and their definition . . . Today this separation is no longer tenable,
> if indeed it ever was . . . the type of political system within a country is far
> from irrelevant to the standard of human rights its citizens enjoy.[1]

The increasing importance since the end of the Cold War of linking the
concept of democracy[2] with human rights can be seen at the level of the
UN,[3] regionally[4] and can be seen at the OAU.[5] The fact that the OAU spent

---

[1] D. Beetham, 'Democracy and Human Rights: Civil and Political, Economic, Social and Cultural', in J. Symonides (ed.), *Human Rights: New Dimensions and Challenges* (Dartmouth: Ashgate, 1998) 71–98, at 71–2.

[2] See S. Marks, *Riddle of All Constitutions. International Law, Democracy and the Critique of Ideology* (Oxford: Oxford University Press, 2000); D. Held, *Models of Democracy* (London: Polity Press, 1996).

[3] See Vienna Declaration and Plan of Action from the 1993 World Conference on Human Rights, General Assembly Resolution 49/30, December 1994; General Assembly Resolution on Enhancing the Effectiveness of the Principle of Periodic and Genuine Elections, 1988; UN Commission on Human Rights Resolution 2000/47; UN Commission on Human Rights Resolution 2001/41; UN Commission on Human Rights Resolution 2001/36.

[4] See D. Shelton, 'Representative Democracy and Human Rights in the Western Hemisphere', *HRLJ* 12 (1991) 353–9; OAS Declaration The Santiago Commitment to Democracy and Renewal of the Inter-American System, 3rd Plenary Session, 4 June 1991; OAS General Assembly Resolution, Representative Democracy, Res.AG/RES.1080(XXI-0/91), 5th Plenary Session, 5 June 1991; OAS Declaration of Managua for Promotion of Democracy and Development, 4th Plenary Session, 8 June 1993.

[5] S. M. Makinda, 'Democracy and Multi-Party Politics in Africa', *Journal of Modern African Studies* 34(4) (1996) 555–73, at 555. See also K. Tomasevski, *Between Sanctions and Elections: Aid Donors and their Human Rights Performance* (New York: Continuum International Publishing Group, 1997); K. Sikkink, 'The Power of Principled Ideas: Human Rights Policies in the United States and Europe', in J. Goldstein and R. Keohane (eds.), *Ideas and Foreign Policy: Beliefs, Institutions and Political Change* (Ithaca: Cornell University Press, 1995); A. Clapham, 'Where is the EU's Human Rights Common Foreign Policy and How

many years focusing on decolonisation as an aspect of self-determination, an issue which then became more or less obsolete, is also a factor that prompted it to expand such a concept to consideration of more internal issues.[6] At the same time economic development was also becoming an issue for the OAU with the era of globalisation. As the former Secretary General of the OAU illustrated:

> The issue of democratisation and good governance has been on the OAU's agenda for the last several years. In the process, we have endeavoured to promote these objectives within the limits of our resources and capacity. In this regard we have been encouraged by the growing recognition by our member states that the roots of economic development and political stability must be planted in good and responsive governance. Indeed, contrary to the impressions that many have created, that the process of democratisation has been imposed on African countries, it is a fact that the efforts to create more humane societies on our Continent, have been the logical outcome of the long yearning of our people, demonstrated during the era of the anti-colonial struggle, to have more say in determining how they should be governed and by whom. Democracy in Africa, in spite of a few setbacks here and there, is surely taking root.[7]

It is in this context that the OAU has over the years stressed the importance of democracy as applicable to African states and has developed some standards as to what constitutes a democratic state. Although there is

---

is it Manifested in Multilateral Fora?', in Alston (ed.), *The EU and Human Rights* 621–49, at 627.

[6] Indeed, this trend has been apparent from the international arena where the right to self-determination has been interpreted to encompass standards on democratic governments and the manner in which they come to power.

> The ICCPR itself requires the introduction of democratic principles, including the right to vote and to be elected at genuine periodic elections. For those states not party to the International Covenant it is not clear that an obligation to introduce democratic government exists; indeed it is possible to conceive, certainly in states with small populations, systems of government, other than democracy, in which the people may freely determine their political status and freely pursue their economic, social and cultural development in compliance with the right to self-determination.

> S. Wheatley, 'Democracy and International Law: A European Perspective',
> *ICLQ* 51 (2002) 225–47, at 232–3

See Human Rights Committee, statement on the Congolese report, UN Doc.CCPR/C/79/Add.118, para. 20.

[7] Address by HE Dr Salim Ahmed Salim, Secretary General of the Organization of African Unity to the International Conference on Africa, Africa at 40, London, 29 October 1997.

some degree of discretion accorded to states in this context,[8] and the OAU has recognised that the notion of democracy is difficult to define, it has stressed that it is something to which African states should be committed:[9]

> We seem not to have a precise understanding or even an appropriate working definition of what Africa perceives as democracy. The Westminster model of democracy seems to have caused more confusion about democracy in Africa than to support the legitimate aspirations and demands of the African people in their nation building endeavours. The confusion is not so much about the principles of democracy but rather on what democracy is all about . . . The confusion notwithstanding, most African countries have over the years embarked on the democratisation process.[10]

In this regard, the OAU has considered not only the 'more process oriented terms' such as elections and how they are conducted,[11] but also

---

[8]   We at the OAU have been working on the assumption that while the fundamental principles of democracy and good governance are universal, their application vary from country to country. On this understanding, countries are entitled to pursue goals and objectives of a democratic disposition on the basis of their socio-cultural values, taking into account specific realities. Indeed, the dimension of cultural values and historical experiences are relevant in the application and consideration of democracy in our societies . . . But while there are universal values which are the common heritage of humanity, there are no ready made recipes for democracy and governance. Each society should generate its home grown modalities for forging ahead in democracy and good governance on the basis of universally recognised principles.

Ibid.
As with the UN, there is no one single model of a democratic system, it is 'not a model to be copied by a goal to be attained', UN Secretary General, 'Support by the United Nations of the Efforts of Governments to Promote and Consolidate New or Restored Democracies', UN Doc.A/52/513, 21 October 1997, para. 27. Also, Universal Declaration on Democracy, adopted by the Inter-Parliamentary Council, 161st session, Cairo, 16 September 1997, *NQHR* 18(1) (2000) 127–30, para. 2.

[9] A. Aidoo, 'Africa', at 704–5. S. Kaballo, 'Human Rights and Democratization in Africa', in D. Beetham (ed.), Politics and Human Rights, Special Issue, *Political Studies* 43 (1995) 189–203.

[10] 'Addressing the Challenges of Peace and Security in Africa', Conflict Management Center, Occasional Paper Series No. 1/1999 has a separate section on 'Good governance, human rights and conflict management', at 14 ff.

[11] For example, Fox argues that 'international law's modest approach to democratisation, therefore, has focused on electoral processes', G. H. Fox, 'The Right to Political Participation in International Law', in G. H. Fox and B. R. Roth (eds.), *Democratic Governance and International Law* (Cambridge: Cambridge University Press, 2000) 48–90, at 49. See Wheatley, 'Democracy'.

has been willing to consider wider issues[12] such as the social structure of the particular country, freedom of expression[13] and, wider still, the democratic nature of institutions such as the UN at the international level. It has thus addressed, in part, the concerns of those who argue that democracy is more than just elections[14] but also what amounts internally to the right to 'freely determine their political status and freely pursue their economic, social and cultural development'.[15] Its important recent Declaration on the Framework for an OAU Response to Unconstitutional Changes in Government[16] reflects this wider perception, noting the need to set down some clear guidelines for states:

> Beyond invoking relevant Declarations issued by various sessions of our Assembly and the Council of Ministers, consideration could be given to the elaboration of a set of principles on democratic governance to be adhered to by all Member States of the OAU. These principles are not new; they are, as a matter of fact, contained in various documents adopted by our Organization. What is required here is to enumerate them in a coherent manner which will bear witness to our adherence to a common concept of democracy and will lay down the guiding principles for the qualification of a given situation as constituting an unconstitutional change. In this regard, and without being exhaustive, we have also agreed on the following principles as a basis for the articulation of common values and principles for democratic governance in our countries.

This chapter will discuss the way in which the OAU initially focused on changes in government and elections, before turning to wider

---

[12] P. Ocheje, 'Exploring the Legal Dimensions of Political Legitimacy: A "Rights" Approach to Governance in Africa', in Quashigah and Okafor (eds.), *Legitimate Governance in Africa* 165–205, at 189; C. R. Ezetah, 'Legitimate Governance and Statehood in Africa: Beyond the Failed State and Colonial Self-Determination', in Quashigah and Okafor (eds.), *Legitimate Governance in Africa*, 419–59.

[13] Franck, 'Emerging Right', at 52.

[14] Democracy is to do with 'the structures of participation (electoral and procedural), provisions for separation of powers, and mechanisms of accountability. Human rights, on the other hand, have to do with basic freedoms (individual or collective), principles of equity and equality, and the preservation of human life and dignity', Aidoo, 'Africa', at 705–6. See also *Socialist Party and Others* v. *Turkey*, European Court of Human Rights, Reports 1998-III; Franck, ' Emerging Right', at 79–80.

[15] Articles 1 ICCPR and ICESCR are linked closely to democratic government, Wheatley, 'Democracy', at 230; E. Daes, 'Explanatory Note Concerning the Draft Declaration on the Rights of Indigenous Peoples', UN Doc.E/CN.4/Sub.2/1993/26/Add.1, 19 July 1993, para. 17. See also Human Rights Committee, General Comment No. 12, on Article 1, UN Doc.HRI/GEN/1/Rev.1 at 12 (1994), para. 4.

[16] AHG/Decl.5(XXXVI).

considerations. Although, as will be seen below, the OAU/AU have shown some degree of commitment in articulating standards, when it comes to implementation of these, the measures taken are very weak.

Military coups and changes to government

Much of the OAU's attention has been focused on unconstitutional changes of government. Since African states began to attain their independence there has been a proliferation of dictatorships across the continent as well as ongoing conflicts.[17] This issue has received an increasing amount of the OAU's attention, as reflected in the adoption by the AHSG in June 1997 of a Decision on the Unconstitutional Changes of Government in Africa.[18] Changes to 'constitutional' government have been deemed to be unlawful by the OAU and are listed in its Declaration on the Framework for an OAU Response to Unconstitutional Changes in Government[19] as:

i. a military coup d'état against a democratically elected Government;
ii. intervention by mercenaries to replace a democratically elected Government;
iii. replacement of democratically elected Governments by armed dissident groups and rebel movements;
iv. the refusal by an incumbent government to relinquish power to the winning party after free, fair and regular elections.

This list does not seem to include, however, unconstitutional changes to non-democratic governments and similarly does not really detail what amounts to a democratic government. Thus, there have been various attempts by states to prevent the attendance at OAU summits of heads of state who have acquired power as a result of a coup.[20] Yet, as

---

[17] Y. El-Ayouty, 'An OAU for the Future: An Assessment', in El-Ayouty, *OAU after Thirty Years* 179–93, at 188.

[18] Decision on the Unconstitutional Changes of Government in Africa, AHG/Dec.150 (XXXVI), 33rd Ordinary Session in Harare, June 1997. See also Statement by Dr Salim Ahmed Salim, Secretary General of the OAU on the Assassination of President Ibrahim Mainassara Bare of the Republic of Niger, 10 April 1998; Press Release No. 22/99, 22 March 1999, www.oau-oua.org/document/press/press8.htm.

[19] Declaration on the Framework for an OAU Response to Unconstitutional Changes in Government, AHG/Decl.5(XXXVI).

[20] At the first meeting of the OAU various countries opposed Togo attending as there had been a coup there. This happened again in respect of the overthrow of Nkrumah in Ghana in 1966 and the overthrow by Idi Amin of Obote in Uganda in 1971.

Akinyemi notes, 'no hard and definite conclusions can be drawn from these episodes . . . for OAU discussion to take place, three conditions must be present: the coup, two rival delegations turn up at an OAU conference, and sponsors for both delegations. In other cases of coup d'état, a combination of the latter two conditions has been missing.'[21] Certainly, this has not always applied and the focus in this context seems to be on the nature of coming to power, not other factors.

Other documents indicate, however, that the OAU has condemned on numerous occasions the taking of power through 'violent' or 'unconstitutional' means.[22] Thus, where 'legitimate' governments have been overthrown,[23] and where there has been assassination of political leaders, this has been deemed to be unconstitutional by the OAU.[24]

The OAU has condemned coups and military takeovers[25] which have taken place in many states such as Sierra Leone, DRC, Niger, Guinea

---

[21] Akinyemi, 'The Organization of African Unity', at 399.

[22] See, for example, Statement by Salim Ahmed Salim, Secretary General of the OAU on the Assassination of President Ibrahim Mainassara Bare of the Republic of Niger, 10 April 1998, Press release.

[23] Draft Rapporteur's Report of the Sixty-Seventh Ordinary Session of the Council of Ministers, CM/Plen/Draft/Rapt/Rpt(LXVII), para. 121 notes that the start of the crisis in Sierra Leone began with the 'violent overthrow of the legitimate government of President . . . Kabbah'.

[24] See for example, Statement by Dr Salim Ahmed Salim, Secretary General of the OAU on the Assassination of President Ibrahim Mainassara Bare of the Republic of Niger, 10 April 1998:

> I wish in particular to urge the political leaders of Niger to engage in immediate consultations and dialogue in order to ensure that the laid down constitutional procedures are followed, in resolving the political crisis that has resulted from the President's assassination . . . It is my fervent hope that they will endeavour to overcome their current crisis and ensure that their country is returned to the path of constitutional rule and that they will be able to chart the future through a democratic process.

At its 73rd Session the Central Organ of the OAU considered the situation in DRC and 'strongly condemns the assassination of President Laurent Désiré Kabila, which is a flagrant violation of the principles of the OAU, and Decision 142 on unconstitutional changes', Communiqué of the Seventy-Third Ordinary Session of the Central Organ of the OAU Mechanism for Conflict Prevention, Management and Resolution at Ambassadorial Level, Addis Ababa, 29 January 2001.

[25] Report of the Plenary, CM/PLEN/RPT(LXIII), where the minister noted that 'given the large number of conflicts in Africa [he] called for the enhancing of the capacity of the AOU Mechanism for Conflict . . . The new trend of military takeovers had serious implications for the democratic process and conflicts', at para. 20. Other organs have held that military coups violate the right to self-determination, such as the Human Rights Committee under the ICCPR, Chile, fourth periodic report, UN Doc.CCPR/C/95/Add.1, para. 11.

Bissau,[26] the Comoros and CAR.[27] Coups have been seen as resulting in 'flagrant violations of the basic principles of our continental Organization and of the United Nations . . . [and are] unacceptable and anachronistic, which is in contradiction of our commitment to promote democratic principles and conditions'.[28] Various reasons have been given for this attention to coups and unlawful seizure of power. Thus, it is considered that coups 'irrespective of the perpetrators . . . undermined confidence in Africa's capacity to establish and sustain democracy'.[29] In addition, they are seen as contrary to the rule of law and to the expression of the will of the people: 'We reaffirm that coups are sad and unacceptable developments in our Continent, coming at a time when our people have committed themselves to respect of the rule of law based on [the] people's will expressed through the ballot and not the bullet.'[30]

In this sense it is not just violent coups that should be prohibited,[31] but any takeover of power from an elected government. A similar approach can be gleaned from other regional systems.[32]

---

[26] Report of the Secretary General on the Situation in Guinea Bissau, CM/2099(LXX)-e, para. 6.

[27] See, for example, Introductory Note of the Secretary General to the Seventy-Fourth Ordinary Session of the Council of Ministers, at 41.

[28] Declaration on the Framework for an OAU Response to Unconstitutional Changes. See also UN GA Resolution A/RES/45/151, 18 December 1990, Respect for the Principle of National Sovereignty and Non-Interference in the Internal Affairs of States in their Electoral Processes.

[29] Draft Rapporteur's Report of the Sixty-Seventh Ordinary Session of the Council of Ministers, CM/Plen/Draft/Rapt/Rpt(LXVII), para. 138.

[30] Declaration on the Framework for an OAU Response to Unconstitutional Changes. Such reasoning was reaffirmed in relation to Sierra Leone, Communiqué Issued by the Thirty-Third Ordinary Session of the Central Organ of the OAU Mechanism for Conflict Prevention, Management and Resolution at Ambassadorial Level, Harare, Monday 26 May 1997, Central Organ/MEC/AMB/Comm.(XXXIII), paras. 3–5.

[31] Statement by Salim Ahmed Salim, Secretary General of the OAU on the Assassination of President Ibrahim Mainassara Bare of the Republic of Niger, 10 April 1998, Press Release.

[32] For example, Schnably notes the fact that the requirement in Article 23 of the OAS Charter cannot be derogated from suggests that 'the American Convention implicitly condemns all coups'. He talks further of the Protocol of Washington, GA Sixteenth Special Session in Connection with the Amendments to the Charter of the Organization, OEA/Ser.P, OAS Doc.AG/doc.11(XVI-E/92) (1992), but argues that this has not yet been invoked. Note also OAS GA Resolution 1080 Representative Democracy, AG Res.1080(XXI-0/91), OEA/Ser.P, OAS Doc.AG/RES.1080(XXI-0/91) (1991); Santiago Commitment to Democracy and Renewal of the Inter-American System, June 1991, OAS GAOR, Twenty-First Session, OEA/Ser.P/AG doc.2734/91 (June 4 1991). As Schnably states in respect of the OAS: 'both Resolution 1080 and the Protocol cover classic military coups . . . Both . . . may encompass more than coups', noting the term 'interruption' of the political process in

There is some suggestion that as a 'coup against elected governments could no longer be tolerated by our countries',[33] it is therefore lawful to overthrow a military regime. Thus, the Council of Ministers, for example in respect of Sierra Leone, 'welcomed the overthrow of the military junta which has opened the way for the reinstatement of the democratically elected government of President Ahmad Tejan Kabbah . . . [and] congratulates and highly commends ECOWAS and ECOMOG and reiterates its full support [to them] to bring an end to the crisis . . . through the early restoration of constitutional order and the reinstatement of the legitimate government'.[34]

Action taken by the OAU in response to an unconstitutional change in government has included the suggestion that the Central Organ of the OAU Mechanism for Conflict 'reactivate, as a matter of urgency, the Committee on Anti-Constitutional Changes, in order to finalise its work in the light of the Harare Declaration, in particular the measures to apply in coup d'état situations occurring in member states'.[35]

However, while there would appear to be no role, in theory, according to the OAU, for the military in government in Africa (and on this basis few governments would be perceived as legitimate),[36] the reality demonstrates total disregard for this approach.[37]

Although in international law the recognition of a new government by states is automatic upon it obtaining power through constitutional means, where the government is not there constitutionally,[38] 'the international

Resolution 1080. Further, 'logically it would be possible to regard the military-backed illegal dissolution of the legislature as an "overthrow" – a subversion – of democracy by force', S. Schnably, 'Constitutionalism and Democratic Government in the Inter-American System', in Fox and Roth (eds.), *Democratic Governance* 155–98, at 163–7.

[33] Report and Decisions of the Eighth Ordinary Session of the Conference of African Ministers of Information, 17–19 June 1997, Cairo, CIM/8 RPT.(VIII), para. 19.

[34] Draft Decisions of the Sixty Seventh Ordinary Session of the Council of Ministers, CM/DRAFT/DECISIONS(LXVII) REV.1, at 11.

[35] Decision on Un-Constitutional Changes in Member States, CM/Dec.483(LXX).

[36] Enemo, 'Self-Determination', at 407.

[37] However, one must distinguish between the international norm and enforcement of that norm and the extent to which the norm itself is invalidated by its non-application. See E. K. Quashigah and O. C. Okafor, 'Legitimate Governance in Africa – International and Domestic Legal Perspectives: An Introduction', in Quashigah and Okafor (eds.), *Legitimate Governance in Africa* 3–19, at 17.

[38] Montevideo Convention, Article 1. In international law whether states recognise another government depends on whether the latter has 'effective control' over the territory of the state, H. Lauterpacht, *Recognition in International Law* (Cambridge: Cambridge University Press, 1947), at 98. As Murphy notes, in line with the Estrada Doctrine, how a government comes to power is a matter for national law and thus any questioning of it is an interference

community does not refuse to recognise governments simply by virtue of their being non-democratic'.[39] However, 'if it can be shown that one of the criteria in "recognition" practice by states is whether the entity is democratic, this would be powerful evidence that democracy is on its way to becoming a global entitlement'.[40] In this context, unfortunately, it would appear that the OAU only considers what is democratic in its narrow sense, namely 'primarily in situations where a democratic government is internally overthrown by non-democratic (often military) authorities',[41] rather than in its wider context.[42]

The OAU has called on other states not to recognise unconstitutional regimes and has argued there is a duty on other states not to cooperate with such a regime and also to support the people towards restoring democracy.[43] In addition, the OAU has also suggested there may be a duty to intervene. In its Declaration on the Framework for an OAU Response to Unconstitutional Changes in Government,[44] the AHSG details a procedure in the event of an unconstitutional change of government. This includes initial condemnation by the current Chairman and Secretary General of the OAU who should also 'convey a clear and unequivocal warning to the perpetrators of the unconstitutional change that, under no circumstances, will their illegal action be tolerated or recognized by the OAU . . . [and] should urge for consistency of action at the bilateral, inter-state, sub-regional and international levels'.[45] The Central Organ would then meet to discuss the issue and after condemning the change it has a number of options including giving the regime six months to

with its sovereignty, S. D. Murphy, 'Democratic Legitimacy and the Recognition of States and Governments', in Fox and Roth (eds.), *Democratic Governance* 123–54, at 142. See also P. C. Jessup, 'The Estrada Doctrine', *AJIL* 25 (1931) 719.

[39] Murphy, 'Democratic Legitimacy', at 143–5.

[40] Ibid. See also Wheatley, 'Democracy', at 232.

[41] Murphy gives examples of where states have rallied against a non-democratic government but says that 'it is difficult to see that the international community has taken the second step of crystallising this notion as a legal norm, or is even over time moving toward such a norm', Murphy, 'Democratic Legitimacy', at 146–7.

[42] Ibid., at 128–30.

[43] For example, see Decisions Adopted by the Sixty-Sixth Ordinary Session of the Council of Ministers, CM/Dec.330–363(LXVI), Dec.356 on Sierra Leone; Communiqué Issued by the Thirty-Third Ordinary Session of the Central Organ of the OAU Mechanism for Conflict Prevention, Management and Resolution at Ambassadorial Level, Harare, Monday 26 May 1997, Central Organ/MEC/AMB/Comm.(XXXIII), para. 6.

[44] AHG/Decl.5(XXXVI).

[45] Declaration on the Framework for an OAU Response to Unconstitutional Changes in Government.

'restore constitutional order', during which time the regime would be prohibited from participating in the OAU Policy Organs including in meetings of the Central Organ, Council of Ministers and AHSG, although its membership and obligations towards the OAU will remain.[46] During this time the Secretary General should

> gather facts relevant to the unconstitutional change of Government and establish appropriate contacts with the perpetrators with a view to ascertaining their intentions regarding the restoration of constitutional order in the country; the Secretary-General should seek the contribution of African leaders and personalities in the form of discreet moral pressure on the perpetrators of the unconstitutional change in order to get them to cooperate with the OAU and facilitate the restoration of constitutional order in the Member State concerned; the Secretary-General should speedily enlist the collaboration of the Regional Grouping to which the 'country in crisis' belongs.[47]

After the six months, sanctions could be imposed on the regime if it has not complied with the requirement to restore constitutional order, and its continued suspension from OAU Policy Organs will apply. The Declaration states that such sanctions 'could include visa denials for the perpetrators of an unconstitutional change, restrictions of government-to-government contacts, trade restrictions, etc.'[48] In this respect, however, it reiterates that 'careful attention should be exercised to ensure that the ordinary citizens of the concerned country do not suffer disproportionately on account of the enforcement of sanctions'. The measures will be implemented by the Central Organ and a sanctions sub-committee would be established under it, composed of five members to monitor compliance with any decision taken and make recommendations.[49] The CSSDCA and NEPAD processes and recent amendments in relation to the AU may help to ensure greater enforcement. The AU mechanisms and provisions of the Constitutive Act appear to place considerable, weight on excluding governments who have come to power by unconstitutional means, although it is unfortunate, however, that the opportunity was not taken to ensure, for example as happens with the EU, that a requirement of accession to the AU should be that a state must be democratic.[50] In practice, however,

---

[46] Ibid.   [47] Ibid.   [48] Ibid.   [49] Ibid.
[50] See Inter-Africa Group/Justice Africa, 'The Architecture and Capacity of the African Union. African Development Forum (ADF III) Economic Commission for Africa', Issue Paper for the African Union Symposium.

the AU has already excluded some governments from participating in its organs due to their unconstitutional nature.[51]

The election process

There is a general agreement that democratic elections should be 'free and fair' and give expression to the 'will of the people'.[52] This has been affirmed by the OAU organs,[53] and reiterated in its recent Declaration on the Principles Governing Democratic Elections in Africa[54] and in the CSSDCA process.[55] The OAU has said that there should be free choice as to who governs a state[56] in full recognition of voting rights.[57] On

[51] Once the AU condemns a coup, the state in question is suspended from participating in the AU organs. Comoros was suspended, until the agreement was implemented, as was Côte d'Ivoire and Madagascar until they remedied the situations. Two other states, CAR and Guinea Bissau, remain suspended, see, e.g., Decision on the Comoros (CM/2164(LXXII) -c), CM/Dec.523(LXXII), which applied the Unconstitutional Changes in Government principles here: 'Expresses concern that no significant progress has been made towards the return of the Comoros to constitutional order as called for in the Algiers Decisions on Unconstitutional Changes of Government, and requests the Secretary-General to continue to engage the Comorian parties with a view to ensuring a speedy return to constitutional rule.'

[52] See Wheatley, 'Democracy', at 236–9. See UDHR, Article 21(3). See also ICCPR, Article 25 and ECHR, Protocol 1, Article 3; ACHPR, Article 23(1); UN General Assembly Resolution 46/137; UN Resolution 45/150, Enhancing the Effectiveness of the Principle of Periodic and Genuine Elections, GA Resolutions A/RES/45/150, 18 December 1990.

[53] Introductory Note to the Report of the Secretary General, Thirty-Second Ordinary Session of AHSG, Sixty-Fourth Ordinary Session of Council of Ministers, July 1996; Report of the Secretary General on the Situation in Guinea Bissau, CM/2099(LXX)-e, para. 37. Draft Resolution on Sierra Leone, CM/Draft/Res.25(LXIII) Rev.1. See in particular, Declaration on the Principles Governing Democratic Elections in Africa, AHG/Decl.1(XXXVIII).

[54] Declaration on the Principles Governing Democratic Elections in Africa, AHG/Decl. 1(XXXVIII).

[55] The national constitution should stipulate inter alia that the citizens of participating members have the right to participate in free and fair elections in their countries through an election based on a secret ballot and universal adult suffrage. By the same token, every citizen of a participating member state has the right to stand for election of public office and participate in the affairs of the state. The presence of international observers in national elections is desirable, as it will enhance the credibility of election process and results.

Africa Moves to Launch a Conference on Security, Stability, Development and Cooperation in Africa (CSSDCA), http://www.au2002.gov.za/docs/key_oau/cssdca.htm, at 2.B.

[56] See, for example, Report of the Secretary General on the Situation in Somalia, CM/2099(LXX)-g, para. 3.

[57] Draft Resolution on the Question of Palestine, CM/Draft/Res.23(LXIII) Rev.1; UN GA Resolution A/RES/45/151, 18 December 1990, Respect for the Principle of National

several occasions the OAU has stated that elections should reflect the wishes of the people of the state.[58] Therefore, as stated by the Inter-American organs, where there is 'some consistency between the will of the voters and the result of the election', elections could be said to be 'authentic',[59] where 'the exercise of political rights is an essential element of representative democracy, which also presupposes the observance of other human rights'.[60]

The OAU has paid considerable attention to the way in which elections are held and certainly seems to see them as 'aimed at achieving a representative government and representative governance has become an index for democratic governance'.[61] In the numerous resolutions adopted in the issue, culminating in the Declaration on the Principles Governing Democratic Elections in Africa, the OAU has held that elections should comply with certain standards, an approach in line with international standards.[62] This is despite it having recognised, as has the UN,[63] there

     Sovereignty and Non-Interference in the Internal Affairs of States in their Electoral Processes; UN Resolution 45/150, Enhancing the Effectiveness of the Principle of Periodic and Genuine Elections, GA Resolution A/RES/45/150, 18 December 1990; ICCPR, Article 25.

[58] Press Release 15/99, 2 March 1999: on Obasanjo's election victory in Nigeria it noted the 'orderly conduct of the elections and the conclusion . . . that the elections and its outcome despite some evident shortcomings, reflected the wishes of the Nigerian people and their desire to bring about a peaceful and successful transfer of power to a democratically elected government'.

[59] Mexico Elections Decision, Cases 9768, 9780, 9828, Inter-American Commission on Human Rights, 97, 108, OEA/Ser.L/V/11.77, doc.7, rev.1 (1990).

[60] Ibid., para. 44.   [61] Quashigah, 'Legitimate Governance in Africa', at 469.

[62] For example, summarising the various treaties, Fox concludes that they generally require several things for a free and fair election: '(1) universal and equal suffrage; (2) a secret ballot; (3) elections at reasonable periodic intervals; and (4) an absence of discrimination against voters, candidates or parties', Fox, 'The Right to Political Participation', at 69. See also Inter-American Commission Mexico Elections Cases, paras. 44–78.

[63] The UN has also held that 'all states enjoy sovereign equality and that each state has the right freely to choose and develop its political, social, economic and cultural systems; recognising that there is no single political system or electoral method that is equally suited to all nations and their people', Resolution 45/150, Enhancing the Effectiveness of the Principle of Periodic and Genuine Elections, GA Resolution A/RES/45/150, 18 December 1990. Thus, the UN has held that 'principles of national sovereignty and non-interference in the internal affairs of any state should be respected in the holding of elections', UN GA Resolution A/RES/45/151, 18 December 1990, Respect for the Principle of National Sovereignty and Non-Interference in the Internal Affairs of States in their Electoral Processes. Electoral systems, according to the European Court of Human Rights, can change 'from place to place and from time to time', *Mathieu-Mohin and Clerfayt*, Series A, No. 113, European Court of Human Rights (1987), para. 54. In this respect, the UN has affirmed that 'it is the concern solely of peoples to determine methods and

should be some degree of flexibility in how elections are run.[64] These standards will be examined in turn.

There would appear to have to be multi-party elections[65]

Although Article 25 of the ICCPR does not clarify whether multi-party elections are required,[66] the Human Rights Committee 'has consistently expressed skepticism that "genuine" one-party elections are possible'[67] and has also held that a one-party state will not be democratic.[68] A similar line has been followed by the Inter-American Commission.[69] Despite Africa often being seen as synonymous with one-party rule,[70] and although 'the swing to multipartyism in Africa today cannot be any

to establish institutions regarding the electoral process, as well as to determine the ways for its implementation according to their constitutional and national legislation', UN GA Resolution A/RES/45/151.

[64] 'The OAU has welcomed the transition to democracy it being understood that transition is in accordance with the socio-cultural values of each of the member states', Dr Salim Ahmed Salim, Secretary General of the OAU, Address to the 7th Pan-African Congress, Kampala, 3–8 April 1994, at 8.

[65] Report of the Plenary, CM/PLEN/RPT(LXIII); Introductory Note to the Report of the Secretary General, Thirty-Second Ordinary Session of AHSG, Sixty-Fourth Ordinary Session of Council of Ministers, July 1996.

[66] Article 23(1) ACHR; Article 25(1) ICCPR; Fox, 'The Right to Political Participation', at 55.

[67] Fox, 'The Right to Political Participation', at 57. He cites Communication No. 314/1988, UN Doc.CCPR/C/48/D/314/1988 (1993) about Zambian elections, holding 'the Committee observes that restrictions on political activity outside the only recognised political party amount to an unreasonable restriction on the right to participate in the conduct of public affairs', Communication No. 314/1988, para. 6.6. See also Human Rights Committee, General Comment 25.

[68] *Bwalya v. Zambia*, UN Human Rights Committee, Communication No.314/1988, Decision of 14 July 1993, 14 *HRLJ* (1993) 408.

[69] Mexico Elections Cases.

[70] See International Commission of Jurists, *Human Rights in One Party State* (London: ICJ, 1978); J. K. Nyerere 'Democracy and the Party System', in J. K. Nyerere, *Freedom and Unity: A Selection from Writings and Speeches, 1952–1966* (New York: Oxford University Press, 1966); Y. Khushalani, 'Human Rights in Africa and Asia', *HRLJ* 4 (1983) 403–42; S. V. Mubako, 'Zambia's Single Party Constitution: A Search for Unity and Development', *Zambia Law Journal* 5 (1973) 67–85; P. Msekwa, 'The Doctrine of the One-Party State in Relation to Human Rights and the Rule of Law' in ICJ, *Human Rights* 33–35; B. P. Wanda, 'The One-Party State and the Protection of Human Rights in Africa with Particular Reference to Political Rights', *AJICL* 3(4) (1991) 756–70, at 767. Makinda, 'Democracy', at 557–8. See also I. Wallerstein, 'The Decline of the Party in Single-Party African States', in J. Palambara and M. Weiner (eds.), *Political Parties and Political Development* (Princeton: Princeton University Press, 1966) 201–14.

guarantee for human rights',[71] there are numerous references throughout the OAU's documents to the need for multi-party elections.[72] In addition, the OAU has required that there be involvement of political parties in the process.[73] Thus, in relation to the Great Lakes region and the DRC, the Council of Ministers urged the government 'to associate all political forces in the process leading to the organisation of these elections; appeals to member states and the international community provide the new government with all the necessary assistance during the transitional period in order to enable it to prepare the organisation and holding of democratic, free and fair elections'.[74]

Fairness of elections to be measured by international community and population of the state

There has been some suggestion that fairness is measured not only by the international community,[75] but also by the population of the state, an

---

[71] Aidoo, 'Africa', at 708. See also Wanda, 'The One-Party State', at 756–7. Makinda, 'Democracy', at 568.

[72] For example, Dr Salim Ahmed Salim, noting democratisation as one of the priorities for Africa, considered Africa's 'second wind of change, involving a transformation to multi-party system of government'. See also Introductory Note to the Report of the Secretary General, Thirty-Second Ordinary Session of AHSG, Sixty-Fourth Ordinary Session of Council of Ministers, July 1996, where the Secretary General noted: 'African states continued on the path of promoting democracy and respect for human rights. This is partly demonstrated by the fact that many of our countries have held multi-party elections.'

[73] The UN has noted that 'periodic and genuine elections' include 'an electoral process that provides an equal opportunity for all citizens to become candidates and put forward their political views, individually and in co-operation with others as provided in national constitutions and laws'. See also, the UN 'solemnly declares that only the total eradication of apartheid and the establishment of a non-racial, democratic society based on majority rule, through the full and free exercise of adult suffrage by all the people in a united and non-fragmented South Africa, can lead to a just and lasting solution', UN GA Resolution A/RES/45/151, 18 December 1990, Respect for the Principle of National Sovereignty and Non-Interference in the Internal Affairs of States in their Electoral Processes.

[74] Decisions Adopted by the Sixty-Sixth Ordinary Session of the Council of Ministers, CM/Dec.330–363(LXVI), Dec.353.

[75] Resolution on the Situation in Angola, CM/Res.1432(LVII): 'mindful that the multi-party elections held . . . were internationally recognised as free and fair'. Resolution on Frontline and Other Neighbouring States, CM/Res.1434(LVII): 'commends the people of Angola for the great spirit of civility and political maturity demonstrated throughout the electoral process, particularly during the elections held on 29 and 30 September 1992; strongly urges UNITA to accept the outcome of the elections of 29 and 30 September, which were consider [sic] free and fair by the United Nations and the international community'.

indication of its importance both internationally and domestically. For example, the Central Organ noted in respect of Sierra Leone

> that it was only fourteen months ago that the people of Sierra Leone held general elections which were declared by Africa and the international community as a whole to be free and fair. That democratic process resulted in the election of President Tejan Kabbah and the national Parliament. The Central Organ further recalled that those elections represented the determination of the people of Sierra Leone to take charge of their own destiny even in the midst of very difficult circumstances. They are hailed as a triumph not only for the people of Sierra Leone but also for the process of democratisation in the continent.[76]

Fairness depends on percentage who voted and their education

In addition, the OAU organs have also suggested that whether elections are free and fair could be said to depend on the 'percentage of the population that registered and voted', as well as their 'level of education':

> Election per se does not necessarily constitute democracy. It is merely a process towards democracy . . . In most African states one has to look not into the percentage of the population that registered and voted . . . Moreover one has also to consider the level of education of the . . . voters and their understanding of democracy as a major tool in national development process. Significantly even the 10% of voters may not be a representative sample of the general population. Often they belong to the elite and they have capacity to manipulate electoral process and to buy votes.[77]

The OAU has thus suggested that an 'all-inclusive process' is a requirement of democracy.[78] The UN has also held that 'the right of everyone to take part in the government of his or her country is a crucial factor in the

---

[76] Communiqué Issued by the Thirty-Third Ordinary Session of the Central Organ of the OAU Mechanism for Conflict Prevention, Management and Resolution at Ambassadorial Level, Harare, Monday 26 May 1997, Central Organ/MEC/AMB/Comm.(XXXIII), para. 2.

[77] Addressing the Challenges of Peace and Security in Africa, at 15.

[78] It welcomed the 'commitment of all the Comorian Parties to work towards a lasting resolution of the crisis in their country on the basis of respect for the unity and territorial integrity of the Archipelago, the return of constitutional legality and an all-inclusive process', Decision on the Islamic Federal Republic of the Comoros, CM/Dec. 571(LXXIII). The right of political participation is found in various other international instruments: UDHR, Article 21(3); ICCPR, Articles 25(a) and (b) and aspects of other human rights such as equality before the law, etc.

effective enjoyment by all of a wide range of other human rights and fundamental freedoms, embracing political, economic, social and cultural rights'.[79] This will require 'an electoral process that provides an equal opportunity for all citizens to become candidates and put forward their political views, individually and in co-operation with others, as provided in national constitutions and laws'.[80] Thus the OAU has reiterated the right of an individual 'to participate freely in the government or his or her country, either directly or through freely elected representatives in accordance with the provisions of the law' and the 'right to fully participate in the electoral processes of the country, including the right to vote or be voted for, according to the laws of the country and as guaranteed by the Constitution, without any kind of discrimination'.[81]

Elections should be peaceful

The OAU organs have also required that for elections to be free and fair there must be disarmament of warring factions,[82] violence should be prohibited[83] and there should be non-interference by the media or foreign investment interests.[84] For example, the Council of Ministers deplored in relation to elections in Zimbabwe in June 2000 'the attempts by some foreign interests, through the massive injection of resources and manipulation of the media to interfere in and influence the outcome

[79] GA Resolution, A/RES/45/150, 18 December 1990, Enhancing the Effectiveness of the Principle of Periodic and Genuine Elections, 45th Session.

[80] Ibid.

[81] Declaration on the Principles Governing Democratic Elections in Africa, para. III.

[82] Decisions Adopted by the Sixty-Sixth Ordinary Session of the Council of Ministers, CM/Dec.330–363(LXVI), Dec.355 on Liberia notes 'the encouraging process so far achieved in the Liberian peace process through the disarmament of all the warring factions, the establishment of an Independent Electoral Commission, the reconstitutions of the Supreme Court of Liberia, the enlargement of ECOMOG and its full deployment all over the territory, thus creating the necessary conditions for the conduct of free and fair elections'.

[83] 'No individual or political party shall engage in any act that may lead to violence or deprive others of their constitutional rights and freedoms. Hence all stakeholders should refrain from, among others, using abusive language and/or incitement to hate or defamatory allegations and provocative language. These acts should be sanctioned by designated electoral authorities', Declaration on the Principles Governing Democratic Elections in Africa, para. IV.

[84] 'In covering the electoral process, the media should maintain impartiality and refrain from broadcasting and publishing abusive language, incitement to hate, and other forms of provocative language that may lead to violence', ibid., para. IV.

of the elections as a threat to national independence'.[85] This was not, however, backed up in real terms by any effective enforcement action. The Secretary General has expressed concern where armed forces are involved.[86] In addition, 'every candidate and political party shall respect the impartiality of the public media by undertaking to refrain from any act which might constrain or limit their electoral adversaries from using the facilities and resources of the public media to air their campaign messages'.[87]

Impartial institutions

The UN has recognised the importance of having independent strong institutions.[88] The OAU has held that there must be an independent national electoral commission and reconstitution of the courts in each state.[89] Thus, states should 'establish where none exist, appropriate institutions where issues such as codes of conduct, citizenship, residency, age requirements for eligible voters, compilation of voters' registers, etc. would be addressed' and 'establish impartial, all-inclusive, competent and accountable national electoral bodies staffed by qualified personnel, as well as competent legal entities including effective constitutional courts to arbitrate in the event of disputes arising from the conduct of elections'.[90] Furthermore, this requires that 'every individual and political party participating in elections shall recognize the authority of the Electoral Commission or any statutory body empowered to oversee the electoral process and accordingly render full cooperation to such a

---

[85] Decision on Developments in Zimbabwe, CM/Dec.544(LXXII). A similar approach has been adopted by the UN which has affirmed that 'any extraneous activities that attempt, directly or indirectly, to interfere in the free development of national electoral processes, in particular in the developing countries, or that intend to sway the results of such processes, violate the spirit and letter of the principles established in the Charter' and 'strongly appeals to all states to abstain from financing or providing, directly or indirectly, any other form of overt or covert support for political parties or groups and from taking actions to undermine the electoral processes in any country', UN GA Resolution A/RES/45/151, 18 December 1990, Respect for the Principle of National Sovereignty and Non-Interference in the Internal Affairs of States in their Electoral Processes.

[86] Introductory Note to the Report of the Secretary General, Thirty-Second Ordinary Session of AHSG, Sixty-Fourth Ordinary Session of the Council of Ministers, July 1996.

[87] Declaration on the Principles Governing Democratic Elections in Africa, para. IV.

[88] See, for example, General Assembly Resolution A/50/332.

[89] Decisions Adopted by the Sixty-Sixth Ordinary Session of the Council of Ministers, CM/Dec.330–363(LXVI), Dec.355 on Liberia.

[90] Declaration on the Principles Governing Democratic Elections in Africa, para. III.

Commission/Body in order to facilitate their duties',[91] and that 'every citizen and political party shall accept the results of elections proclaimed to have been free and fair by the competent national bodies as provided for in the Constitution and the electoral laws and accordingly respect the final decision of the competent Electoral Authorities or, challenge the result appropriately according to the law'.[92]

Wider protection of human rights

The OAU has also recognised the need to protect human rights in general during times of elections, and the rights to freedom of expression, association and movement in particular. It has called on states to 'safeguard the human and civil liberties of all citizens including the freedom of movement, assembly, association, expression, and campaigning as well as access to the media on the part of all stakeholders, during electoral processes' and to 'promote civic and voters' education on the democratic principles and values in close cooperation with the civil society groups and other relevant stakeholders'.[93] Individuals should have a 'right to free association and assembly in accordance with the law', 'freedom to establish or to be a member of a political party or Organization in accordance with the law' and 'individuals or political parties have the right to freedom of movement, to campaign and to express political opinions with full access to the media and information within the limits of the laws of the land'.[94] In addition, 'individual or political parties shall have the right to appeal and to obtain timely hearing against all proven electoral malpractices to the competent judicial authorities in accordance with the electoral laws of the country'.[95]

Prevention of fraud

States should 'take all necessary measures and precautions to prevent the perpetration of fraud, rigging or any other illegal practices throughout the whole electoral process, in order to maintain peace and security'.[96] In addition, 'all stakeholders in electoral contests shall publicly renounce the practice of granting favours, to the voting public for the purpose of influencing the outcome of elections'.[97]

---

[91] Ibid., para. IV.   [92] Ibid.   [93] Ibid., para. III.
[94] Ibid.   [95] Ibid.   [96] Ibid.   [97] Ibid.

Adequate security and funding

The OAU has recognised the impact that the security situation and financial resources can have on the fairness of elections. It has thus required states to 'ensure the availability of adequate logistics and resources for carrying out democratic elections, as well as ensure adequate provision of funding for all registered political parties to enable them organise their work, including participation in electoral process' and 'ensure that adequate security is provided to all parties participating in elections'.[98]

Elections should be transparent

The OAU has also required that elections should be held in openness.[99] In this respect the OAU has stated that states should 'ensure the transparency and integrity of the entire electoral process by facilitating the deployment of representatives of political parties and individual candidates at polling and counting stations and by accrediting national and/other observers/monitors'.[100] Furthermore, 'candidates or political parties shall have the right to be represented at polling and counting stations by duly designated agents or representatives'.[101]

In this regard, the role of international institutions and the OAU is an important factor[102] and seeks to ensure the integrity of the process and assure the public of the importance of their involvement.[103] The OAU has

---

[98] Ibid.

[99] Decisions Adopted by the Sixty-Sixth Ordinary Session of the Council of Ministers, CM/Dec.330–363(LXVI), Dec.353 on the situation in the Great Lakes region and in the DRC 'calls upon the government of DRC and all the political forces of that country to show the spirit of openness, compromise and reconciliation in order to ensure a smooth transition to democratic and constitutional rule'. Other international bodies have said that election must be regular, Article 25(1) ICCPR; Article 23(1) ACHR.

[100] Declaration on the Principles Governing Democratic Elections in Africa, para. III.

[101] Ibid.

[102] Geisler notes that the elections in 1991 in Zambia when it transformed to a multiparty system were the first to be monitored in this way: 'It marked the beginning of an era of confidence in the possibilities of democratic change, and confirmed the positive influence that international observers can have on such processes. Their presence was henceforth considered an essential precondition for acceptable transitional multi-party elections.' She now notes that while such election observers were initially tolerated by the governments, now they are seen as foreign interference, G. Geisler, 'Fair? What has Fairness got to do with it? Vagaries of Election Observations and Democratic Standards', *Journal of Modern African Studies* 31(4) (1993) 613–37, at 613–14.

[103] See for example, NDI Handbook, *How Domestic Organizations Monitor Elections. An A-Z Guide*, chapter 1, www.un.org/Depts/dpa/ead.

monitored elections in many states,[104] and countries sometimes request observer missions from the OAU for election monitoring.[105] As the previous Secretary General, Dr Salim Ahmed Salim, has noted, 'the Secretariat has been encouraged to monitor and to assist, whenever possible, the democratic process. Monitoring of elections has now become a regular activity of the Secretariat.'[106] The OAU has stated that 'to be effective, the OAU seeks to ensure that its approval of electoral processes reflects the conduct of free and fair elections, rather than being a rubber stamp for elections that are flawed, and that due process is followed. Ideally, the OAU should not endorse any elections in which it has not had a monitoring presence from the beginning.'[107] Citing the UDHR, ICCPR and the right of citizens to participate freely in the government of their choice in the ACHPR, the OAU has stressed that elections were 'the basis of the authority of any representative government' and 'an important dimension in conflict prevention, management and resolution'.[108]

[104] See, for example, Introductory Note to the Report of the Secretary-General, Sixty-Ninth Ordinary Session of the Council of Ministers, Addis Ababa, 19–23 March 1999, para. 299; Report of the Sixty-Fourth Ordinary Session of the Council of Ministers, CM/Rpt(LXIV), at 22; Report of Secretary General on the Process of Election Monitoring by OAU; Introductory Note of the Secretary General to the Seventy-Fourth Ordinary Session of the Council of Ministers, at 66ff.; Report of the Secretary General on the Situation in the Comoros, Central Organ/MEC/MIN/3(V); Communiqué of the Eighty-Third Ordinary Session of the Central Organ of the OAU Mechanism for Conflict Prevention, Management and Resolution at Ambassadorial Level, 3 June 2002, Central Organ/MEC/Amb/Comm.(LXXXIII).

[105] For example, Introductory Note of the Secretary General to the Seventy-Fourth Ordinary Session of the Council of Ministers, at 65, noted that Benin, Uganda and Chad had requested missions.

[106] Secretary General of the OAU addresses the Seventh Pan-African Congress, Kampala, 3–8 April 1994, at 8. Lessons from a Decade of Conflicts: Prospects of Peace and Security by the Year 2000. A Presentation by His Excellency Salim Ahmed Salim, Secretary General, Conference of African Ministers of Planning and UNDP Resident Representatives, 31 January–2 February, Ouagadougou, at 23:

> In this regard, issues of governance and the building and/or strengthening of democratic institutions is also critical in conflict prevention, management and resolution. The OAU has in this regard continued to support the democratic transition in Africa. The Organization has been able to observe, upon invitation, 41 elections or referenda in 28 member states . . . It is, indeed encouraging to note that member states are increasingly entrusting the OAU with the responsibility of observing elections. The challenge facing the OAU is to assist in sustaining this momentum.

[107] Supporting Democratic Processes in Africa. Electoral Assistance, Observation and Supervision (www.oau-oua.org/document/mechanism/english/mech03.htm). See UN GA Resolution A/RES/46/137, 17 December 1991, Enhancing the Effectiveness of the Principle of Periodic and Genuine Elections.

[108] Declaration on the Principles Governing Democratic Elections in Africa.

Although the UN believes electoral monitoring 'should remain an exceptional activity of the Organization to be undertaken in well-defined circumstances, primarily in situations with a clear international dimension',[109] elections have been seen by the international community as an issue which may in certain circumstances go beyond the state itself, to justify monitoring by international and regional bodies.[110]

While the OAU has developed norms and guidelines on which it conducts its missions and evaluation,[111] some issues still remain vague. As Geisler notes: 'As democratic processes have been reduced to the holding of internationally observed multiparty elections with no agreement on the definition and principles of democracy, the discourse on "good governance" has remained "a divisionary, unrewarding and in the end frivolous pursuit".'[112]

It is encouraging to note, therefore, that more recently, in the context of the OAU seeming to see its remit as broader than just intervening in exceptional circumstances, it has developed further principles for monitoring elections on the continent, adopting in July 2002 a Declaration on the Principles Governing Democratic Elections in Africa. Besides setting out rights and duties of individuals and states during elections, including that states 'ensure the transparency and integrity of the entire electoral process by facilitating the deployment of representatives of political parties and individual candidates at polling and counting stations and by accrediting national and/other observers/monitors',[113] it reiterated the role of the OAU in election monitoring as being part of the democratic process as a whole: 'We request the OAU to be fully engaged in the strengthening of the democratisation process, particularly by observing and monitoring elections in our Member States.'[114]

---

[109] UN GA Resolution A/RES/46/137, 17 December 1991, Enhancing the Effectiveness of the Principle of Periodic and Genuine Elections. See also UN GA Resolution A/RES/45/150, 18 December 1990, Enhancing the Effectiveness of the Principle of Periodic and Genuine Elections, 'underscore the duty of each member of the international community to respect the decisions taken by other states in freely choosing and developing their electoral institutions'.

[110] The UN has stressed that 'the international community should continue to give serious consideration to ways in which the United Nations can respond to the requests of Member states as they seek to promote and strengthen their electoral institutions and procedures', UN GA Resolution A/RES/45/150.

[111] Geisler notes 'election observation has been called an "at best imperfect art", and the lack of any internationally accepted norms and guidelines as to what constitutes free and fair elections greatly contribute to its present imperfections', Geisler, 'Fair?', at 617.

[112] Ibid., at 633–4.

[113] Declaration on the Principles Governing Democratic Elections in Africa, para. III.

[114] Ibid., para. V.

The Declaration provided that there should be intervention by the OAU/AU at the early stages of elections: 'in order to ensure that elections are truly free and fair, electoral observation must begin at the earlier stages, that is when electoral lists are being compiled', then moves on to discuss the limitations of its own capacity for being involved in elections at the early stages. It then lists among its priorities strengthening of electoral commissions and national election-monitoring mechanisms and the 'strengthening of institutions that will promote democracy, rebuild and consolidate judiciaries and legislative institutions'.[115] The OAU/AU's aim in part, therefore, is self-sufficiency of the electoral process. This reflects a trend of the UN away from 'large-scale verification missions to smaller and more economical assistance projects' with more emphasis on capacity building.[116] As indicated by the UN this 'will also contribute to the credibility of the process, which should alleviate the earlier perceived need for international election observers. The creation of permanent electoral institutions and the enhanced credibility of the electoral process are essential elements in creating sustainable electoral systems.'[117]

Further, a Memorandum of Understanding between the OAU General Secretariat and Host Country on election monitoring provides that invitations are sent by states to the OAU at least two months in advance of the election; that states should not charge OAU observers and 'facilitate easy access of observers/monitors to locations of electoral events/activities and unhindered in the performance of their tasks'; and that the General Secretariat could decline an invitation to monitor elections 'which in its considered opinion do not measure up to the normative standards enunciated in this Declaration'.[118] This clearly goes beyond the OAU being involved in just 'exceptional circumstances' to something that is considered the norm.

The OAU Secretariat was requested to obtain extra funds to implement the Declaration on democratic elections and to research whether to set up a Democratisation and Electoral Assistance Fund and a Democratisation and Election Monitoring Unit. The Secretariat would also compile a register of African experts on election monitoring as observers and work

---

[115] Supporting Democratic Processes in Africa. Electoral Assistance, Observation and Supervision (www.oau-oua.org/document/mechanism/english/mech03.htm). UN GA Resolution A/RES/46/137, 17 December 1991, Enhancing the Effectiveness of the Principle of Periodic and Genuine Elections.

[116] Ibid., para. 27.   [117] Ibid., para. 32.

[118] Declaration on the Principles Governing Democratic Elections in Africa, para. V.

on standards and procedures for selecting those chosen as OAU observers. It was also required to promote cooperation with NGOs and international organisations and to publish reports on monitoring of elections.[119] In July 2002 the Council of Ministers decided to set up this election-monitoring unit within the Office of the Commission responsible for Political Affairs 'to be responsible for coordinating and streamlining participation in election monitoring in collaboration with the competent authorities of the countries concerned', noting 'the importance of the OAU involvement in election observation and monitoring as well as the promotion and advancement of the political process in Africa through the use of a more credible and effective approach'.[120] It stressed that the election observation team would be composed of representatives of the OAU Secretariat and others 'experienced and competent in the area of election monitoring', selected from the OAU states, which should include women. Those giving members should also pay their costs, and the team would report to the Secretary General who would report to the Council of Ministers.[121]

Clearly there are still problems[122] and the OAU in the past has been strong on rhetoric but weak on enforcement of its standards. It is hoped, however, given the reference to the various rights of the individual in the Declaration that more attention will be placed on such issues in the future. Indeed, the fact that some of the members of the African Commission on Human and Peoples' Rights have been asked to take part in these observer missions illustrates that the OAU may at least see elections as having a human rights dimension.[123] Certainly, this has not been the case

---

[119] Ibid., para. VI.

[120] Decision on the Establishment of Election Monitoring Unit in Africa, Doc. CM/2264 (LXXVI) Add.4, CM/Dec.686.

[121] Ibid.

[122] As the Assistant Secretary General noted at the Council of Ministers 76th session in July 2002,

> the absence of clear mandate spelt out in a decision or declaration indicating, in unambiguous terms, the aims and objectives of OAU election monitoring missions; the lack of institutional capacities to effectively undertake activities geared to strengthening democratic processes in Africa; lack of adequate financial resources to enable the Organization undertake its mission effectively and to cover all the critical aspects of the electoral process; namely voter registration, declaration of results, including electoral campaign and the actual casting of votes.

> Report of the Seventy-Sixth Ordinary Session of the Council of Ministers, July 2002, CM/Rpt(LXXVI), para. 92.

[123] There are a number of results. One is that such intervention has enabled interpretation of rights relating to elections. As Fox notes, '[as] election monitoring has entered the mainstreaming of UN assistance to developing countries, a link to treaty-based

in the past, as the reports of the missions from the Secretary General often noted what happened on such missions and problems that arose, but did not always pass detailed comment on whether the elections were satisfactorily carried out or not.[124] As Amnesty International noted several years ago, 'the OAU initiatives in election monitoring have amounted to little more than watching the process of voting. It has ignored the environment which is essential for any free and fair elections, including respect for human rights such as the exercise of the right to freedom of association and freedom of expression.'[125] Amnesty at that time urged the Conflict Division to consider the situation in the country at the time before making recommendations as to how human rights can be respected in preparing for elections: 'An assessment of the freedom and fairness of the elections will never be credible without an assessment of the human rights context in which the elections took place.'[126]

Thus, it is hoped that the moves by the OAU over the years and the setting out of a more standardised approach to election monitoring in the Declaration will move away from what it had done in the past, namely: 'depending on the situations and on the requests of Member States' the composition and number have varied, as the Secretary General has admitted: 'We have not reached the stage of standardizing our election monitoring operations.' While the financial resources of the OAU may have a part to play in this regard, the Secretary General has also acknowledged that these observer teams 'have not been able to be as effective as we would wish', although they have played a 'constructive role in supporting the efforts towards democratisation in our Member States and contributing to the promotion of a democratic culture in our Continent'.[127]

participatory rights has emerged. UN missions have implicitly affirmed the interpretations of participating rights first articulated by human rights treaty bodies. They have also cast themselves as enforcing a right to political participation.' He says that 'the Secretary-General has regarded electoral assistance as aiding in establishment of the democratic institutions contemplated by human rights instruments', noting that the UN has defined human rights standards in elections 'solely by reference to human rights instruments', Fox, 'The Right to Political Participation', at 70 and 80 and at footnote 181.

[124] Introductory Note of the Secretary General to the Seventy-Fourth Ordinary Session of the Council of Ministers, at 65 makes no comment in relation to elections observed in Benin, Uganda and Chad, despite describing some problems that occurred.

[125] Amnesty International, *Organization of African Unity*, at 23.   [126] Ibid.

[127] Introductory Note to the Report of the Secretary General, Council of Ministers Sixty-Ninth Ordinary Session, March 1999, paras. 299–302.

Elements of democracy in African states

As the rest of this book notes, the OAU/AU organs have considered human rights to be an important element of a state's obligation. One of the ways in which they have done this is through developing and expanding on this concept of what constitutes a democratic state.

As noted above, there have been concerns expressed that attention is often shown to the election process but not to other issues of human rights or democratic institutions in the day-to-day running of a country.[128] As the UN Human Rights Commission has clarified, elections are part of a 'broader process that strengthens democratic principles, values, institutions, mechanisms and practices which underpin formal democratic structures and the rule of law'.[129] Thus, sometimes, despite a commitment to democracy, states have

> all too often been characterised by a mere commitment to the enthronement of, and emphasis on, formal elective processes; procedures that do not necessarily ensure that *substantive* changes in the lives of the citizens of the relevant country are realised. In too *many* cases the establishment of formal democratic institutions has not led to the securement of respect for larger freedom, human rights and even development.[130]

It is therefore essential that elections and voting are seen as only one of the features necessary for democracy.[131] Elections should not been seen in isolation but should be 'part of a holistic process of democratic transition and governance'.[132] Thus states have been called on by the UN Human Rights Commission to 'consolidate democracy through the promotion of

---

[128] Aidoo argues that political parties are often not concerned with issues of human rights, only in so far as they impinge on elections. The issue is therefore left to human rights NGOs, Aidoo, 'Africa', at 708.

[129] 'Continuing Dialogue on Measures to Promote and Consolidate Democracy', Commission on Human Rights Resolution 2001/41, para. 4.

[130] Quashigah and Okafor, 'Legitimate Governance', at 8. See also M. wa Mutua, 'The Ideology of Human Rights: Toward Post Liberal Democracy?', in Quashigah and Okafor (eds.), *Legitimate Governance in Africa* 109–64, at 119.

[131] It has thus been asked 'whether the right to vote is, in itself, the *panacea* for Africa's socio-economic and political problems; whether it is not merely one of the many *resources* that most Africans might utilise in their struggle for legitimate governance and even development', Quashigah and Okafor, 'Legitimate Governance', at 8.

[132] 'Seminar on Interdependence between Democracy and Human Rights: The UN System and Promotion of Democracy: Achievements and Challenges', Paper prepared by the United Nations Department of Political Affairs, Geneva, 25–26 November 2002, at 5.

pluralism, the protection of human rights and fundamental freedoms, maximising the participation of individuals in decision-making and the development of competent and public institutions, including an independent judiciary, effective and accountable legislature and public service and an electoral system that ensures periodic, free and fair elections'.[133] More recently the OAU has paid attention to many of these issues in defining what amounts to a 'democratic state'. As the Secretary General noted in 1997:

> We at the OAU consider governance as the totality of the exercise of authority in the management of a country's affairs comprising of the complex mechanisms, processes and institutions through which citizens and groups articulate their interests, exercise their legal rights and mediate their differences . . . Democracy had often been understood as the participation of people in electing a government of their choice through the ballot box. Elections are, indeed a crucial stage in the democratic process . . . But, while elections are necessary, they, by themselves do not provide sufficient condition for the building of democracy and good governance . . . Perhaps more critical than the electoral process, which we consider to be vital, is the need to build viable institutions to sustain democracy and promote good governance . . . the need to strengthen the quality of leadership so as to ensure the promotion of [a] people centred decision-making process. This of course calls for greater transparency in decision-making as well as accountability . . . power must be vested in the people and not in their leaders.[134]

In this respect, the OAU's Declaration on the Framework for an OAU Response to Unconstitutional Changes in Government[135] notes a number of factors necessary to 'provide a solid underpinning to the OAU's agenda of promoting democracy and democratic institutions in Africa'. Further, as the CSSDCA process indicates, 'lack of democracy in which people freely participate in government, denial of personal liberties, abuse of religion, precedence given to military expenditure over other sectors of national life and the lack of proper administrative machinery for the control and management of public funds are some of the deep-rooted

---

[133] Promoting and Consolidating Democracy, Commission on Human Rights Resolution 2000/47, para. 1.
[134] Address by HE Dr Salim Ahmed Salim, Secretary General of the Organization of African Unity to the International Conference on Africa, Africa at 40, London, 29 October 1997, at 3–4.
[135] AHG/Decl.5(XXXVI).

causes of insecurity.[136] Its Stability Calabash also stresses the importance of 'popular participation in governance: active and genuine participation of the citizens of every country in the governance of public affairs has to be fostered' and where political parties are established they 'should not be created on religious, ethnic, regional or racial basis and considerations and these should not be exploited by leaders'.[137]

In thus interpreting what amounts to a democratic state, the OAU organs have thus noted various elements.[138]

A constitution

As Gutto has noted, 'ideally constitutions . . . are the appropriate legal repository for the principal institutions of governance and their role and functions'.[139] The OAU has appeared to suggest that a written constitution is important: the 'adoption of a democratic Constitution: its preparation, content and method of revision should be in conformity with generally acceptable principles of democracy',[140] although alone, this is clearly insufficient.[141] Thus, the constitution

> must in the very first instance imply that a society acknowledges its constitution as a living standard with which the conduct of public behaviour should conform and against which it must be evaluated. The minimum evidence of adherence to the principles of constitutionalism is therefore public respect for the constitution, in whatever form, of the society of which one is a member.[142]

As the CSSDCA process requires, there should be a 'freely promulgated constitution with Bill of Rights provisions', namely that 'every state should

---

[136] CSSDCA, Security Calabash, part B.   [137] Ibid., Stability Calabash.

[138] For information on the UN approach see, for example, Continuing Dialogue on Measures to Promote and Consolidate Democracy, Commission on Human Rights Resolution 2001/41; 'Seminar on the Interdependence between Democracy and Human Rights', 25–26 November 2002, and papers from this conference.

[139] S. Gutto, 'Current Concepts, Core Principles, Dimensions, Processes and Institutions of Democracy and the Inter-Relationship between Democracy and Modern Human Rights', Seminar on the Interdependence between Democracy and Human Rights, Geneva, 25–26 November 2002, www.unhchrh.ch, para. 16.

[140] Declaration on the Framework for an OAU Response to Unconstitutional Changes in Government.

[141] H. W. O. Okoth-Ogendo, 'The Quest for Constitutional Government', in G. Hyden, D. Olowu and H. W. O. Okoth-Ogendo (eds.), *African Perspectives on Governance* (Trenton, NJ: Africa World Press, 2000) 33–60, at 33–4, and 40–1. See also Enemo, 'Self-Determination', at 403.

[142] Okoth-Ogendo, 'The Quest', at 35–6.

have a constitution that is promulgated after thorough national debate
and adopted by an assembly of freely elected representatives of the people.
Such a Constitution should contain a Bill of Rights.'

Separation of powers, rule of law and independence of the judiciary

'Empowered and effective legislatures and judiciaries are core institutions
of good governance'.[143] Thus, reflecting the position adopted by the UN,[144]
according to the OAU, separation of powers and independence of the
judiciary are other factors for a democratic state.[145] In this respect there
should be 'security of tenure for officers in the judiciary':

> Not only should the legislative and executive branches of government unfet-
> ter the actions of the officers of the bench, but also their tenure should be
> guaranteed and provided for in the national constitutions. A Judicial Com-
> mission should exercise decisions relating to the removal of officers from
> the bench. Independence of the judiciary must be effected through an invi-
> olate tenure of offices, and through stable emoluments guaranteed by an
> act of parliament.[146]

Support for civil society, opposition parties and popular participation

Popular participation is clearly important in the democratic process.[147]
The OAU has called for the 'promotion of political pluralism or any other
form of participatory democracy and the role of the African civil society, including enhancing and ensuring gender balance in the political

---

[143] Gutto, 'Current Concepts', para. 20.
[144] See Basic Principles on the Independence of the Judiciary, General Assembly Resolution
40/32, 28 November 1985; Resolution 40/146, December 1985; UN Economic and Social
Rights Committee, E/C.12/1/Add.48, 1 September 2000, para. 19.
[145] Declaration on the Framework for an OAU Response to Unconstitutional Changes in
Government. This is reflected in the ACHPR itself, particularly Article 26, as Aginam
notes, 'Article 26 of the African Charter has made the role of the courts in the realization
of legitimate governance a critically important one', O. Aginam, 'Legitimate Governance
under the African Charter on Human and Peoples' Rights', in Quashigah and Okafor
(eds.), *Legitimate Governance in Africa* 345–74, at 357.
[146] Africa Moves to Launch CSSDCA, at 2.B.
[147] See, for example, Strengthening of Popular Participation, Equity, Social Justice and Non-
Discrimination as Essential Foundations of Democracy, Commission on Human Rights
Resolution 2001/36; UN Human Rights Committee, case against Colombia, 25 September
1992, CCPR/C/79 Add.3, para. 3; UN Human Rights Committee, Niger, 29 April 1993,
CCPR/C/79 Add.17, para. 3; UN Committee on Economic, Social and Cultural Rights,
E/C.12/1995/5, para. 23.

process'.[148] In addition, it also noted the 'the principle of democratic change and recognition of a role for the opposition'.[149] With the requirement that there be 'plural political structures', the CSSDCA has clarified that 'every country would ensure that there is no hindrance to alternative ideas, institutions and leaders competing for public support. In the case of multiparty pluralism, this principle requires that every participating member should ensure the separation of party from the state.' Furthermore, there should be limits to the tenures of elected politicians, with 'periodic renewal of the mandate of political leaders. At the same time, the tenure of elected leaders in various branches of government should be constitutionally limited to a given number of years.'[150]

The OAU has even gone so far as to suggest a particular type of electoral system, namely proportional representation:

> With respect to electoral mechanism that promotes maximum participation of all groups in their Government, the principle of proportional representation should be adopted, taking into consideration the peculiar situation of each country. The principle of proportional representation should be applied for legislative elections. To foster stability in governance of national affairs, governments should ensure that in making appointments, due regard is given to equitable representation at the central, regional and local levels.[151]

The importance of genuine NGOs in respect of popular participation cannot be overemphasised: 'a society and polity does not necessarily require explicit human rights nongovernmental organisations so long as "freedom of association" . . . or "political pluralism" . . . prevails. In the absence of such conditions . . . the role of non-governmental organisations becomes all the more central.'[152]

---

[148] Declaration on the Framework for an OAU Response to Unconstitutional Changes in Government.

[149] Ibid. 'There can be no democracy without pluralism', *Socialist Party and Others* v. *Turkey*, European Court of Human Rights, Reports 1998-III, para. 41. The European Court of Human Rights has also said that Article 11 ECHR includes political parties, *Refah Partisi (Welfare Party) and Others* v. *Turkey*, Application Nos. 41340/98 and 41342-4/98, decision of 31 July 2001, at para. 44. Aidoo also argues that multipartyism is not a guarantee of human rights protection, Aidoo, 'Africa', at 708.

[150] Africa Moves to Launch CSSDCA, at 2.B.   [151] Ibid.

[152] H. Scoble, 'Human Rights Non-Governmental Organizations in Black Africa; Their Problems and Prospects in the Wake of the Banjul Charter', in C. E. Welch and R. I. Meltzer (eds.), *Human Rights and Development in Africa* (Albany: State University of New York Press, 1984) 177–203.

There should also be 'civilian democratic authority'.[153] Therefore, the OAU has stressed 'the necessity of promoting popular participation in the process of government'[154] and in decision making and development.[155] This should include participation in political and socio-economic development and decentralisation of power.[156] As the Secretary General of the OAU has stated:

> Most African countries have over the years embarked on the democratisation process and have increasingly accepted the need for popular participation of their people in development . . . what is commonly agreed is that a democratic government exists to uphold and enforce a certain kind of society, a certain set of relations between individuals, a certain set of rights and claims that people have on each other both directly and indirectly through their rights to property. What this means is that a democratic government is a government that guarantees the fundamental freedoms and with that has the capacity to dispense a just, fair and transparent management and control of production relations between individuals and within societies. In other words, a government that operates on the basis of politics of exclusion or a government that does not allow popular participation in development or a government that does not represent the will of the people however defined is by all standards not a democratic government.[157]

This requires a 'bottom-up' approach, partnership with all sections of society and building and strengthening democratic institutions.[158] The

---

[153] Report of the Plenary, CM/PLEN/RPT(LXIII), para. 20. As Wheatley notes, 'a democratic government is one in which political power is based on the will of the people, and which provides all citizens the opportunity to participate equally in the political life of their societies. A regime may be termed "democratic", then, if it embodies, within its institutions and mechanisms, the twin principles of political equality and popular sovereignty,' Wheatley, 'Democracy', at 235.

[154] Resolution on the African Commission on Human and Peoples' Rights, Twenty-Eighth Ordinary Session of the Assembly of Heads of State and Government of the Organization of African Unity, 29 June–1 July 1992, Dakar, http://www1.umn.edu/humanrts/africa/resafchar28th.html.

[155] M. Byers and S. Chesterman, '"You the People": Pro-Democratic Intervention in International Law', in Fox and Roth (eds.), *Democratic Governance* 259–92, at 261.

[156] Addressing the Challenges of Peace and Security in Africa, at 11, talks about avoiding conflicts, popular participation, inclusion in the process of government and development: 'The decentralisation of power through political popular participation with and involvement in the political and socio-economic development, decision-making process, is the antidote, to potential internal conflict. The security of the state lies with its people, and this presupposes their ability, determination, commitment and desire to protect.'

[157] Ibid., separate section on 'Good governance, human rights and conflict management', at 14 ff.

[158] Lessons from a Decade of Conflicts, at 23. See African Charter for Popular Participation in Development which was adopted by the OAU AHSG in 1989.

role of women in this respect has been recognised by the OAU,[159] requiring states to pay particular attention to the position of women, and to 'encourage the participation of African women in all aspects of the electoral process in accordance with the national laws'.[160] The CSSDCA clarified that 'all the existing laws that discriminate against women should be abrogated and juridical instruments and mechanisms that will guarantee and preserve the rights of women should be adopted. The United Nations Convention on the elimination of discrimination against women should be ratified by and applied in all African countries'.[161] Furthermore, it is also important to consider the role of youth and education:

> The future of Africa will be in the hands of the youth of today. Educational systems should incorporate in their curricula, teachings in African values, cultures, history, philosophy, etc. Research in African humanities should be given no less attention than the pursuit of science and technology. In the face of escalating education costs, strategies should be devised to ensure the acquisition of basic education by all youth. Education is a prerequisite to the full and effective participation of people in the democratic process and all efforts should be made to eliminate illiteracy.[162]

Protection of human rights, in particular the right to free expression

More generally, and more recently, however, the OAU has consolidated this closer link between democracy and human rights, stressing that the protection of human rights, is essential for a democracy,[163] namely,

---

[159] African Charter for Popular Participation in Development and Transformation, Arusha, February 1990 (International Conference on Popular Participation in the Recovery and Development Process in Africa, UN and others), A/45/427, 22 August 1990, www.africaaction.org/african-initiatives/charter.htm.

[160] Declaration on the Principles Governing Democratic Elections in Africa, para. III. See similar approach by UN Committee under CEDAW, General Recommendation No. 23, A/52/38, 1997.

[161] Africa Moves to Launch CSSDCA, at 2.B.   [162] Ibid.

[163] As the African Charter for Popular Participation in Development and Transformation states:

> We believe that for people to participate meaningfully in their self-development, their freedom to express themselves and their freedom from fear must be guaranteed. This can only be assured through the extension and protection of people's basic human rights and we urge all Governments to vigorously implement the African Charter on Human and People's Rights and the Universal Declaration of Human Rights, the Convention on the Rights of the Child, the ILO Convention No. 87 concerning Freedom of Association and Protection of the Right to Organize and the Convention on the Elimination of All Forms of Discrimination Against Women.'

'constitutional recognition of fundamental rights and freedoms in conformity with the Universal Declaration of Human Rights of 1948 and the
African Charter on Human and Peoples' Rights of 1981' as well as the
'guarantee and promotion of human rights'.[164] The Secretary General of
the OAU has summarised the position thus:

> It is important to note that the issue of human rights has increasingly
> become an important agenda of the OAU . . . The OAU member states
> have recognised that the process of democratisation and building good
> governance go hand in hand with the observance of and respect for human
> rights. In many of the OAU member states we note the emergency and
> to some extent proliferation of institutions dealing with the promotion of
> human rights and respect of the rule of law . . . But it cannot be disputed
> that OAU member states have explicitly or implicitly come to accept the
> standards set out in the UDHR, the ICESCR and the ICCPR. Indeed, in
> articulating the purposes of the OAU, the founding fathers of our conti-
> nental organisation decided to include in the Charter the promotion of
> unity, the solidarity of African states, the co-ordinating and intensifica-
> tion of co-operation and efforts to achieve [a] better life for the people of
> Africa and the promotion of international co-operation, having due regard
> to the Charter of the UN and the UDHR. In doing so, the African leaders
> were encouraging the promotion and protection of human rights within
> member states. They were advocating the right to life, liberty and security
> of the person, equality before the law, the right to freedom of movement,
> assembly and association, and the right to take part in government. The
> founding fathers were also advocating the right to work, the right to form
> and join trade unions, the right to education, and the right to participate
> freely in the cultural life of the community. This means that the OAU and its
> member states recognised the imperative need of promoting the standards
> that together constitute what is commonly known as [the] International
> Bill of Rights.[165]

---

[164] Declaration on the Framework for an OAU Response to Unconstitutional Changes in
Government. See also UN Declaration on the Principles of International Law Concerning
Friendly Relations, GA Res. 2625 (XXV) 24 October. The right to self-determination in
the Convention on the Elimination of Racial Discrimination has also been interpreted
as requiring the government 'to represent the whole population without discrimination
as to race, colour, descent or national or ethnic origin', General Recommendation (21),
Right to Self-Determination, 15 March 1996, para. 4. As Wheatley notes, states' reports
considered by the Human Rights Committee indicate that 'the effective implementation
of the (internal) right of the people to self-determination requires the introduction of a
democratic government', Wheatley, 'Democracy', at 232.

[165] Addressing the Challenges of Peace and Security in Africa, at 14 ff. and 22.

As with the UN,[166] the OAU has looked specifically in this regard to the need for the state to 'guarantee of freedom of expression and freedom of the press, including guaranteeing access to the media for all political stake-holders'.[167] This is in line with European Court of Human Rights rulings which have held that democracy 'thrives on freedom of expression'[168] and freedom of the press 'affords the public one of the best means of discovering and forming an opinion of the ideas and attitudes of political leaders'.[169] Thus, the CSSDCA requires that there be 'annual publication of records of compliance with human rights instruments'; also

> The charter and mandate of The African Commission on Human and Peoples Rights (ACHPR) should be expanded for ACHPR to undertake an annual assessment of human rights record of each African country and publish its findings. The monitoring role prescribed for the ACHPR is not intended to be exercised only in situations of human rights violations but as an annual routine and applied to all African signatory states of the CSSDCA process. The establishment of [an] African court of justice on Human Rights within the framework of ACHPR is recommended. The court will adjudicate between governments and people's rights. ACHPR should be funded separately drawing upon the funds of international organizations and other independent sources.[170]

It further required the signature, ratification and implementation of legal instruments for promoting and protecting human rights,[171] 'freedom from arbitrary arrest and detention',[172] 'establishment and protection of

---

[166] UN Human Rights Committee, Communication 628/1995, *Tae Hoon Park* v. *Republic of Korea*, 20 October 1998.

[167] Declaration on the Framework for an OAU Response to Unconstitutional Changes in Government.

[168] *Socialist Party and Others* v. *Turkey*, para. 45.

[169] The press have a right to give political information and public have a right to receive such, *Lingens* v. *Austria*, European Court of Human Rights, Series A, No. 103, paras. 41 and 42.

[170] Africa Moves to Launch CSSDCA, at 2.B.

[171] An important element in fostering stability is to protect and promote human rights of individual citizens. This not only assures the individual of his rights and dignity but also enables him to actualise his full potential which itself is necessary for socio-economic development. Therefore, every participating state would be required to sign, ratify and implement African and other relevant international legal instruments in the field of human rights.

Ibid.

[172] No citizen should be subject to arbitrary arrest or detention without trial or subject to trial and other forms of human or cruel treatment. Provisions for habeas mandamus and habeas corpus should be made in national codes or laws. Legal aid

organs for monitoring accountability' and their independence,[173] independence of the civil service[174] and protection of trade union rights.[175]

Democratic institutions

Strong and democratic institutions have been seen as one of the key elements of democracy,[176] and the OAU has also stressed the need for such organs[177] that safeguard human rights and 'considerably reduce the risks of unconstitutional change on our Continent'.[178] This has, however, been centred around the need to avoid unconstitutional events.[179] Such institutions should be 'representative of our peoples and receiving their active participation would further contribute to the consolidation of modern

> services for those who cannot provide legal services for them should be funded from public revenue. All participating African countries should remove from their statute books all laws authorising detention without trial.
>
> Ibid.

[173]   Institutions that promote accountability in public service should be established. These include board of audits for public expenditure, code of conduct bureau should be given adequate protection through measures that enable independent financing and guarantee tenures for the officers of the institutions. The financing of organs of adjudication and accountability (courts, audit board, code of conduct bureaux or ombudsman) should be paid from consolidated revenue funds not subject to arbitrary interference by executive fiat.

Ibid.

[174] 'An independent civil service having a guaranteed security of tenure, salary and pension with members nominated on professional grounds by an independent Civil Service Commission. Removal of a Civil Servant must be exercised solely by an independent Civil Service Commission', ibid.

[175] 'In order to ensure industrial peace and harmony, which is a prerequisite for economic growth and development, all governments should respect trade union rights in accordance with ILO conventions and recommendations', ibid.

[176] UN GA Resolution 56/96.

[177] Decision AHG/Dec.142(XXXV); see also Report of the Secretary General on the Situation in Guinea Bissau, CM/2099(LXX)-e, para. 6 noted that the AHSG had responded earlier to the crisis: 'They also urgently called for the respect for the democratically elected institutions and appealed to the people of Guinea Bissau to rally behind the government of President Vieira.' It noted that the Ceasefire Agreement was based on principles including the following, para. 17: 'reaffirmation of the official recognition of the democratic institutions and legality', as well as conditions for the return of refugees and displaced persons.

[178] Declaration on the Framework for an OAU Response to Unconstitutional Changes in Government. See this similar requirement in the Universal Declaration on Democracy, paras. 9–10.

[179] Introductory Note to the Report of the Secretary General, Thirty-Second Ordinary Session of AHSG, Sixty-Fourth Ordinary Session of the Council of Ministers, July 1996, para. 8.

African states underpinned by the rule of law, respect for the fundamental rights and freedoms of the citizens and the democratic management of public affairs'.[180]

Good governance and combating corruption

In more recent years the OAU/AU has seen the link, on paper, between corruption, human rights and democracy.[181] In its Draft OAU/AU Convention on Combating Corruption,[182] for example, the preamble notes the OAU/AU is

> cognizant of the fact that the Constitutive Act of the African Union inter alia, calls for the need to promote and protect human and peoples' rights, consolidate democratic institutions and culture and ensure good governance and the rule of law; aware of the need to respect human dignity and to foster the promotion of economic, social and political rights in conformity with the provisions of the African Charter on Human and Peoples' Rights and other relevant human rights instruments; . . . underlined the need to observe principles of good governance, the primacy of law, human rights, democratisation and popular participation by the African peoples in the process of governance.

In drafting the Convention,[183] the Secretary General was requested to convene, in cooperation with the African Commission on Human and Peoples' Rights, 'a high level meeting of experts to consider ways and means of removing obstacles to the enjoyment of economic, social and cultural rights including the fight against corruption and impunity and propose appropriate legislative and other measures'.[184] There was a recognition of the impact of corruption on economic and social rights, as reflected

---

[180] Algiers Declaration, AHG/Decl.1(XXXV).

[181] The Secretary General of the OAU, Mr Amara Essy, 'noted that corruption undermined the confidence of the people in public institutions, contributed to abuse of human rights and the escalation of conflicts on the continent', Report of the Experts Meeting to Consider the OAU/AU Convention on Combating Corruption, 26–29 November 2001, Expt/OAU/Conv/Comb/Corruption/Rpt.1(I), para. 9.

[182] Draft OAU/AU Convention on Combating Corruption, DOC/OS(XXXI)/INF.52.

[183] The result of a Resolution of the AHSG, Resolution AHG/Dec.126(XXXIV).

[184] Members of the African Commission attended the Experts' Meeting at which the Convention was drafted. A statement was made by Commissioner El-Hassan in this regard. In his speech 'he characterised corruption as an obstacle to the enjoyment of human rights in general, and particularly, economic, social and cultural rights as well as an obstacle to the socio-economic development of the African continent', Report of the Experts' Meeting to Consider the OAU/AU Convention on Combating Corruption, 26–29 November 2001, Expt/OAU/Conv/Comb/Corruption/Rpt.1(I), para. 5.

in its Objectives[185] and Principles.[186] The Convention is to be enforced by an Advisory Board on Corruption within the OAU/AU, under Article 20, which will be composed of eleven independent experts. This Board has promotional and advisory capabilities and is specifically required by Article 20(5)(g) to 'build partnerships with the African Commission on Human and Peoples' Rights, African civil society, government, intergovernmental and non-governmental organisations to facilitate dialogue in the fight against corruption'.[187] Clearly human rights issues, on paper, appear to be given attention across the AU's work, but the extent to which this will be actually implemented in practice is still to be seen. The powers of the Board are, arguably, not strong, suggesting that the rhetoric will not be followed by enforcement.

Importance of sustainable development

The UN and others have stressed the integral part that democracy plays in ensuring sustainable development.[188] In this respect the OAU has recognised that human rights should not just include civil and political rights but also economic, social and cultural rights.[189] The increasing

---

[185] The need to 'promote socio-economic development by removing obstacles to the enjoyment of economic, social and cultural rights as well as civil and political rights', Article 2(4).

[186] Article 3 requires firstly that states should undertake to abide by 'respect for democratic principles and institutions, popular participation, the rule of law and good governance' and secondly 'respect for human and peoples' rights in accordance with the African Charter on Human and Peoples' Rights and other relevant human rights instruments'. Among the provisions defining corruption and dealing with the role of the media, there are minimum guarantees for a fair trial which require that any person alleged to have committed offences shall received a fair trial in accordance with the African Charter and other international human rights instruments that have been recognised by the relevant parties.

[187] States are required to tell the Board of progress made in compliance with the Convention, under Article 20(7) at least once a year.

[188] For issues of development and human rights see chapter 8. See also, for example, 'Strengthening of Popular Participation, Equity, Social Justice and Non-Discrimination as Essential Foundations of Democracy', Commission on Human Rights Resolution 2001/36; G. Bauer, 'Namibia in the First Decade of Independence: How Democratic?', *Journal of Southern African Studies* 27(1) (2001) 33–55, where she notes the impact of economic development on democracy in Namibia; P. Chabal, 'The Quest for Good Government and Development in Africa: Is NEPAD the Answer?', *International Affairs* 78(3) (2002) 447–62.

[189] See, for example, D. Beetham, 'Democracy and Human Rights: Contrast and Convergence', Office of the High Commissioner for Human Rights, Seminar on the Interdependence between Democracy and Human Rights, Geneva, 25–26 November 2002, para. 10.

link between democracy and development can be seen clearly in the CSS-DCA and NEPAD processes. The latter has been much lauded by Western leaders and the international institutions.[190] Thus, its Democracy and Political Governance Initiative requires that states 'will also undertake a series of commitments towards meeting basic standards of good governance and democratic behaviour while, at the same time, giving support to each other'[191] focusing in particular on institutional reforms in 'administrative and civil services; strengthening parliamentary oversight; promoting participatory decision-making; adopting effective measures to combat corruption and embezzlement; and undertaking judicial reforms'.[192] Further, the Declaration on Democracy, Political, Economic and Corporate Governance,[193] in support of democracy and the democratic process, besides reference to promotion and protection of human rights in general, instructs states to

> ensure that our respective national constitutions reflect the democratic ethos and provide for demonstrably accountable governance; promote political representation, thus providing for all citizens to participate in the political process in a free and fair political environment; enforce strict adherence to the position of the African Union (AU) on unconstitutional changes of government and other decisions of our continental organization aimed at promoting democracy, good governance, peace and security; strengthen and, where necessary, establish an appropriate electoral administration and oversight bodies, in our respective countries and provide the necessary resources and capacity to conduct elections which are free, fair and credible; reassess and where necessary strengthen the AU and sub-regional election monitoring mechanisms and procedures; and heighten public awareness of the African Charter on Human and Peoples Rights, especially in our educational institutions.[194]

Other elements

In addition to the above, the OAU has said that it was 'convinced that an increase in, and expansion of the spaces of freedom . . . would further contribute to the consolidation of modern African states underpinned by the rule of law, respect for the fundamental rights and freedoms of the

---

[190] See A. Sen, *Development as Freedom* (Oxford: Oxford University Press, 2000) UNDP, Millennium Declaration, September 2000; UNDP, 'Deepening Democracy in a Fragmented World', Human Development Report (New York: UNDP, 2002).
[191] NEPAD, para. 82.   [192] Ibid., para. 83.   [193] AHG/235(XXXVIII), Annex I.
[194] Ibid., para. 13.

citizens and the democratic management of public affairs'.[195] Further, the OAU envisages that some legislative reform may also be required for a state to be democratic.[196]

Democracy in the OAU/AU and international community

'It follows that the processes of democratisation at country level have to be complemented by a democratisation of the institutions involved in the regulation and enforcement at the international level . . . There is now a growing recognition of the interdependence of democratisation at the national and international levels.'[197] A criticism of the OAU has been its detachment from the people which is it supposed to govern. In addition, while some NGOs have observer status before the OAU/AU, these have not been human rights organisations.[198] Clearly, granting observer status to NGOs is not sufficient to ensure participation of Africans in general in the work of the OAU/AU. Although lack of transparency and involvement of the general population of states has been a criticism directed at a number of international organisations,[199] it is perhaps even more difficult, given the social and political realities, for the average African to understand and to get involved in the work of the organs of the OAU/AU. Its meetings are often conducted confidentially and its documents difficult to obtain. The OAU/AU has, however, given the impression more recently that civil society should play an increasingly important role;[200] in June 2001 and again in 2002 it held two OAU Civil Society Conferences. However, in general the AU has been government driven and much more needs to be done to ensure involvement from the ground.[201]

---

[195] Algiers Declaration.
[196] Declaration on the Framework for an OAU Response to Unconstitutional Changes in Government.
[197] Beetham, 'Democracy and Human Rights: Contrast and Convergence', para. 34.
[198] Although it is possible that those who were involved had some impact on the OAU's approach to human rights, see chapter 1. It is to be noted that there are considerable difficulties for an NGO to gain observer status, as the criteria, such as obtaining the support of a number of African governments, can be very restrictive.
[199] T. Pogge, 'Creating Supra-National Institutions Democratically: Reflections on the European Union's "Democratic Deficit"', Journal of Political Philosophy 5(2) (1997)3–25; P. C. Schmitter, How to Democratize the European Union . . . And Why Bother? (Lanham: Rowman & Littlefield, 2000).
[200] The 'OAU has made strong efforts to enlist the African population', Introductory Note of the Secretary General to the Seventy-Fourth Ordinary Session of the Council of Ministers.
[201] See Inter-Africa Group/Justice Africa, 'The Architecture and Capacity of the African Union', paras. 2 and 3.

The role of the Pan-African Parliament is also potentially important in this respect[202] but whether this will actually achieve increased involvement of Africans in the AU is debatable,[203] certainly in the short term. Beyond this institution, it is difficult to see evidence of involvement of African populations in practice. The OAU was little known across the continent and, while the AU has made some attempt to increase its profile, much more needs to be done to ensure its visibility.

Also of interest is the international dimension of democracy,[204] and the OAU has been looking at this issue since its inception and Africans started to gain their independence and participate on the international scene. Its lobbying clearly had some part to play in some successes in changing the composition of UN bodies, and it has focused its attention on organs such as the Security Council[205] and the 'need to democratise' these organs:

> The increase in the membership of and equitable representation on the Security Council has become imperative because of the need to democratise the Council and make it more effective and transparent. The democracy that is currently being preached at the national level should prevail in the international system. It is therefore necessary to review the composition and the decision-making process of the Security Council... Ultimately with the progress in the democratisation of the international system, permanent membership and the right of veto would be reviewed and all members of

---

[202] Decision on the Report of the Secretary General on the Draft Co-operation Agreement between the OAU and the Union of African Parliaments (Doc.CM/2124(LXX)-c), CM/Dec.476(LXX); Decision on the Establishment of the African Union and the Pan-African Parliament, AHG/Dec.143(XXXVI).

[203] See chapter 1.

[204] The Universal Declaration on Democracy also has 'the International Dimension of Democracy', in which it notes that

> democracy must also be recognised as an international principle, applicable to international organisations and to states in their international relations. The principle of international democracy does not only mean equal or fair representation of states; it also extends to the economic rights and duties of states. The principles of democracy must also be extended to the international management of issues of global interest and the common heritage of mankind, in particular the human environment.

> paras. 24 and 25

[205] 'The composition of the Security Council should be further democratised to reflect current reality that has emerged with the end of the Cold War, the increase in the number of states members of the UN and the need to improve the Council's functioning, methods of work and relationship with states which are not members of the Security Council', Report of the African Group at the United Nations Regarding Proposals on the Concept and Modalities of Rotation as well as its Application to the Two Permanent Seats for Africa at the Security Council, CM/2065(LXVIII) Rev.1, para. 1.

the Security Council would be elected according to the principle of equitable geographical representation in order to ensure their accountability to all members of the UN, on whose behalf they assume primary function of maintaining international peace and security in accordance with the provisions of the Charter.[206]

Conclusion

The concept of self-determination was initially expanded to prompt the OAU to focus on elections and the manner in which governments came to power as an element of what constituted a democratic state. Over more recent years it has been willing to examine wider issues including the way in which countries are run. In some respects the OAU/AU, as elsewhere,[207] has interpreted this to encompass a variety of human rights issues. But, as before, any attention to human rights has been secondary, developed as a consequence of the OAU organs' concentration on other matters. With recent changes in respect of the AU and its

---

[206] Draft Declaration on the Reform of the Security Council Submitted by the African Group in New York, AHG/Draft/Decl.3(XXXIII). The Common African Position on this matter is that the Security Council should be expanded to twenty-six members with Africans having at least two permanent seats and two non-permanent seats, with the same powers for all members. There was a Harare Declaration in 1997 which established this position, Draft Harare Declaration of the Assembly of Heads of State and Government of the OAU on the Reform of the UN Security Council, AHG/Draft/Decl.3(XXXIII) Rev.3: 'reiterating the need to democratise the [Security] Council and make it more efficient and transparent'. African states should also decide how seats should be rotated between them, Report of the African Group at the United Nations Regarding Proposals on the Concept and Modalities of Rotation as well as its Application to the Two Permanent Seats for Africa at the Security Council, CM/2065(LXVIII) Rev.1. The African Group at the United Nations has noted: 'The idea of a rotating permanent seat is a novel one conceived by African Heads of State to satisfy their desire to be represented on the Security Council in an equitable manner. The fundamental principle underlying the idea is that no African should claim a permanent seat for itself in perpetuity. The seat would therefore belong to Africa as a collectivity and not to an individual country', at 16.

[207] See 'Promotion and Consolidation of Democracy', Working Paper by Mr Manuel Rodríguez Cuadros on the measures provided in the various international human rights instruments for the promotion and consolidation of democracy, in accordance with the mandate contained in decision 2000/116 of the Sub-Commission on the Promotion and Protection of Human Rights, E/CN.4/Sub.2/2001/32, 5 July 2001; 'Promotion and Consolidation of Democracy', expanded working paper by Mr Manuel Rodríguez Cuadros on the measures provided in the various international human rights instruments for the promotion and consolidation of democracy, in accordance with the mandate contained in decision 2000/116 of the Sub-Commission on the Promotion and Protection of Human Rights, E/CN.4/Sub.2/2002/36, 10 June 2002.

Constitutive Act, in particular with the CSSDCA process and NEPAD, the potential to maintain the link between democracy and human rights is large. A Commissioner on Political Affairs has been created, whose portfolio will cover human rights, democracy, good governance and electoral institutions, among other things,[208] and there are explicit references in the Constitutive Act to democracy and human rights as well as 'Condemnation and rejection of unconstitutional changes of governments' in its Principles and the power to suspend states from the Union who come to power through unconstitutional means.[209] The reference not only to the importance of human rights and to the 'establishment and strengthening of democratic structures and good governance based on common tenets', as well as 'the rejection of unconstitutional changes of government in any African country as a threat to order and stability in the African continent as a whole' and 'the conduct of electoral processes in a transparent and credible manner and a concomitant obligation by the parties and candidates to abide by the outcome of such processes in order to enhance national and continental stability' among the core values in the Draft Memorandum of Understanding on Security, Stability, Development and Cooperation in Africa indicates that what is judged to be democratic by the CSSDCA may be viewed holistically.

Yet this rhetoric has so far not been accompanied by enforcement. True, the AU organs have continued to support the concept of democracy and free and fair elections, endorsing the findings of a recent Conference on Elections, Democracy and Good Governance,[210] and called for its communiqué conclusions to be implemented. The Executive Council also requested that the Commission of the AU convene an experts meeting to examine the documents from the conference and that the AU will formulate a document on Democracy and Governance as a result.[211] Yet at this stage, the AU needs to make sure that its standards are consolidated and actually implemented in reality. There needs to be greater attention to the mechanisms and machinery under the AU to do so.

The CSSDCA at least sets out some performance indicators in this regard which may help to translate such standards into reality. These include, for example, that states

---

[208] Statutes of the Commission, ASS/AU/2(I)-d, Article 12.
[209] Constitutive Act, Article 30.
[210] Decision on the Report of the Interim Chair on the Conference on Elections, Democracy and Good Governance, 7–10 April 2003, Assembly/AU/Dec.18(II).
[211] Decision on the Report of the Interim Chair of the Conference on Elections, Democracy and Good Governance, 7–10 April 2003, Doc.EC/CL/35(II), EX/CL/Dec.31(III).

by 2004 adopt, and in some cases recommit to, the fundamental tenets of a democratic society as stipulated in the CSSDCA Solemn Declaration as an African common position, namely, a Constitution and a Bill of Rights provision, where applicable, free and fair elections, an independent judiciary, freedom of expression and subordination of the military to legitimate civilian authority; rejection of unconstitutional changes of government; and implement these principles by 2005, where they are not already applicable.[212]

With regard to democratisation and good governance states should:

Elaborate by 2004 principles of good governance based on [a] commonly agreed set of indicators to be included in national legislations, including decentralization of administration and effective, transparent control of state expenditure. By 2003, all African countries should enact legislation to provide for the impartiality of the public service, the independence of the judiciary and the necessary autonomy of public institutions such as the Central bank and the office of the Auditor-general.[213]

There should also be a Code of Conduct for Political Office Holders by 2005 in each state, the establishment of an anti-corruption commission by 2004 and independent national electoral commissions by 2003 'and/or other appropriate mechanisms and institutions to ensure free and fair elections in all African countries'.[214] Further, states are required to

adopt and standardise by 2003, guidelines for independent and effective observations of elections in AU Member States, with the provision of an effective electoral unit within the AU Commission. The guidelines must include provisions for strengthening civil society and local monitoring groups in individual African countries and the continent as a whole to support the process of ensuring free and fair elections. The Commission should be gradually equipped and funded to conduct independent election observation by 2003. The reports of the various election observation teams of the AU should be made public.[215]

There should be arrangements for the disclosure of campaign funding sources and state funding for all political parties by 2004, as well as conclusion by 2004 of 'appropriate arrangements, including electoral reforms, for the institution of more inclusive systems of government'.[216] Legislation should have been adopted by 2004 on 'the formation and operation of

---

[212] CSSDCA Declaration, part III, para. 14.   [213] Ibid., para. 15.
[214] Ibid., paras. 16–18.   [215] Ibid., para. 19.   [216] Ibid., paras. 20 and 21.

political parties to ensure that such parties are not formed and operated on the basis of ethnic, religious, sectarian, regional or racial extremism and establish a threshold of voter support as criteria for public funding, without compromising freedom of association and the principle of multi-party democracy'.[217] With regard to popular participation states are required to have implemented the provisions of the Charter for Popular Participation for development and transformation in Africa 'by creating more enabling conditions for increased participation of women, the youth and civil society organizations'.[218] The CSSDCA monitoring process is also to be used itself 'to establish best current knowledge and practices that would strengthen democratic practices, the protection of human rights and the promotion of good governance in the continent'.[219]

The fact that the African Commission on Human and Peoples' Rights is the obvious body to which the CSSDCA peer review process will look means that its decisions on military coups as violations of human rights and wider jurisprudence on human rights in African states will hopefully become of increasing importance and increasingly integrated into the AU.

While this is laudable, the issue must now be, is the AU going to build upon the standards already set by the OAU organs, which would make sense, or just keep adding to the rhetoric? While the CSSDCA offers hope for some development of institutional memory, in terms of implementation many of its deadlines are already past or so close that their likelihood of being complied with is minimal. The AU needs to pay much greater attention now to defining more realistic goals and setting up an effective machinery for their oversight and enforcement.

---

[217] Ibid., para. 23.   [218] Ibid., para. 22.   [219] Ibid., para. 7.

The relationship between conflict and human rights

This chapter will not assess the OAU/AU's involvement in conflict situations per se,[1] but the extent to which a human rights perspective has been taken in dealing with conflict situations. As will be seen, the OAU/AU has taken an ad hoc approach in this regard, paying human rights some attention but with more focus on humanitarian standards and no coherent attempt to link the two overall. The recent attention to terrorism has, however, evidenced a human rights perspective.

Human rights and conflicts

Traditionally, state responsibilities during times of conflict fell within the domain of humanitarian law, with states being able to derogate from certain human rights norms under human rights treaties during times of war or other public emergency.[2] This dichotomy between humanitarian and human rights law is often apparent in the OAU's approach; and where it considers the former,[3] the latter is often forgotten. This may be explained

---

[1] See, for example, A. Adedeji, *Comprehending and Mastering African Conflicts. The Search for Sustainable Peace and Good Governance* (London: Zed Books, 1999); A. B. Bozeman, *Conflict in Africa. Concepts and Realities* (Princeton: Princeton University Press, 1976); A. Mazrui, 'Towards Containing Conflict in Africa: Methods, Mechanisms and Values', *East African Journal of Peace and Human Rights* 2 (1995) 81–90; M. Mekenkamp, P. van Tongeren and H. van de Veen, *Searching for Peace in Africa. An Overview of Conflict Prevention and Management Activities* (Utrecht: European Platform for Conflict Prevention and Transformation, 1999).

[2] See, for example, D. Fleck (ed.), *Handbook of Humanitarian Law of Armed Conflicts* (Oxford: Oxford University Press, 1995); T. Meron, 'On the Inadequate Reach of Humanitarian and Human Rights Law in the Need for a New Instrument', *AJIL* 77 (1983) 589; W. Solf, 'Human Rights in Armed Conflict: Some Observations on the Relationship between Human Rights Law and the Law of Armed Conflict', in H. Han (ed.), *World in Transition: Challenges to Human Rights, Development and World Order* (Washington, DC: University Press of America, 1979) 41–53.

[3] 'Makes an urgent appeal for the respect of the provisions of the Geneva Conventions on International Humanitarian Law', Decision on the Situation in the Mano River

by the fact that the OAU is often trying to manage or resolve conflicts, rather than having time to prevent them.[4]

Yet there has been an increasing trend by the OAU/AU to recognise the relationship between conflicts and human rights. Thus, at a keynote speech in March 1995 Dr Salim Ahmed Salim, then Secretary General of the OAU, noted the importance of human rights and standards such as 'accountability to the public, transparency of government activities, independent and honest judiciary, enforcement of rules and regulations, provision of social and economic services, democratisation, press free-dom, curbing militarism and improving accountability and control in areas such as public employment and private as well as public finance'[5] in preventing and resolving conflicts. This approach was reflected most clearly in the Declaration creating the Conflict Mechanism in 1993 which saw human rights as a central issue.[6] In addition, the African Commission on Human and Peoples' Rights envisaged a role for itself in determining human rights implications in times of conflict, stressing in particular that the lack of derogation provision in the ACHPR meant that states could not derogate from rights during times of war or peace.[7] While the African

Sub-Region, CM/Dec. 572 (LXXIII). See also Report of the Seventy-Third Ordinary Session of the Council of Ministers, February 2001, CM/Rpt(LXXIII), para. 59; Communiqué, Ninety-First Ordinary Session of the Central Organ of the Mechanism for Conflict Prevention, Management and Resolution at Ambassadorial Level, 2 April 2003, Central Organ/MEC/AMB/Comm.(XCI), para. iii.

[4] Thus, it has called for training, for example, for troops on the 'concept and conduct of peace support operations', and such training should include international human-itarian law, but has not made any specific reference to human rights, Report of the Second Meeting of the Chief of Defence Staff of the Central Organ of the OAU Mechanism for Conflict Management and Resolution, OAU/CHST/CO/RPT(II), para. 34.2.

[5] State, Sovereignty and Responsibility. A Keynote Address by Dr Salim Ahmed Salim, OAU Secretary General, to the African Conference on Peacemaking and Conflict Resolution, Durban, 20–23 March 1995, Press and Information Division, April 1995, at 5.

[6] The objective of early-warning information is to prevent perceived or actual threat to the values of the Organization as contained in its Charter. The values range from the protection of human and peoples' rights, promotion of democracy and security for all and the building of regional collective security to guarantee the promotion of peace, security, stability and development in the Continent.

In respect of who will collect such information, it lists the need to build links with specialists such as human rights monitoring groups, Cairo Declaration of the Assembly of Heads of State and Government on the Establishment of a Mechanism for Conflict Prevention, Management and Resolution, AHG/DECL.3(XXIX), at 7 and 8.

[7] 'The African Charter, unlike other human rights instruments, does not allow for states parties to derogate from their treaty obligations during emergency situations. Thus, even a civil war in Chad cannot be used as an excuse by the state violating or permitting violations

Commission talked about establishing an Early Intervention Mechanism in times of massive human rights violations, including reporting such situations to the Assembly under Article 58,[8] this and other attempts by some at the OAU Secretariat to ensure increased coordination between the African Commission on Human and Peoples' Rights and the Conflict Mechanism do not appear to have got off the ground.

OAU/AU general involvement in conflict

Although the OAU has consistently stressed the principle of peaceful settlement of disputes,[9] it has had a poor record in terms of involvement in Africa's conflicts.[10] This has been attributed to the non-intervention clause in the OAU Charter,[11] and the fact that it was never intended to be a peacekeeper but a body to promote African unity.[12] Thus, while the OAU

> provides a unique meeting place for African national leaders and is well suited for conflict management by summit diplomacy . . . The presence of other heads of state means that there are numerous potentially helpful third parties easily and readily available to assist in bringing these leaders together. The climate at OAU summit meetings may be propitious for such efforts to initiate settlements as a fraternal atmosphere usually prevails... As most of the meetings and gatherings are closed to the press, such private diplomacy is further eased... The OAU is then well suited to assist in conflict management when the major issue is one that can be negotiated between representatives, preferably heads of state, of member nations. The OAU is less useful in conflicts where national leaders cannot be brought together

of rights in the African Charter', Communication No.74/92, *Commission Nationale des Droits de l'Homme et des Libertés* v. *Chad*, Ninth Annual Activity Report of the African Commission on Human and Peoples' Rights, 1994–5.

[8] See Reflection on the Establishment of an Early Intervention Mechanism in Cases of Massive Human Rights Violations, Twenty-Fourth Ordinary Session, Banjul, 22–31 October 1998, DOC/OS/52(XXIV), reprinted in R. Murray and M. Evans, *Documents of the African Commission on Human and Peoples' Rights* (Oxford: Hart Publishing, 2001), at 757.

[9] Indeed, this is apparent prior to the OAU's creation, see Pact of the Arab League, Article 5; Bandung Declaration 1955, UN Doc.A/C.6/L.537/Rev.I, Part B(b)2; First Conference of Independent African States, Accra, April 1958: Resolution on the Exchange of Views on Foreign Policy. See Z. Cervenka, 'The Role of the OAU in the Peaceful Settlement of Disputes', in El-Ayouty and Brooks (eds.), *Africa* 48–68.

[10] J. O. C. Jonah, 'The OAU: Peacekeeping and Conflict Resolution', in El-Ayouty (ed.), *OAU after Thirty Years* 3–14, at 9.

[11] Ibid.   [12] Cervenka, 'The Role of the OAU', at 53.

and/or where there is need that the third party control material resources. The OAU pattern of conflict management can best be characterised as that of settlement *within* the organisation rather than *by* the organisation.[13]

Despite the OAU Charter providing for a role for the OAU in finding African solutions to conflict situations on the continent through the creation of the Commission of Mediation, Conciliation and Arbitration,[14] this body was never used and there was no real role formulated for the OAU in internal conflicts.[15] Although there was some evidence of the OAU becoming actively engaged in conflicts during its first ten years, its ability to deal with civil wars, which most of Africa's more recent conflicts have been, has been very limited.[16] It was particularly unfortunate, therefore, that during the Cold War the OAU was left to deal with conflicts in Africa.[17]

Failures of the OAU during the Cold War 'dictated caution in future post-Cold War peacekeeping activities'[18] and, as outside powers gauged their 'attitude toward African problems based on the posture of the OAU',[19] after the Cold War there was an emphasis on finding 'African solutions to African problems'.[20]

The OAU, in contrast, has preferred to stress the primary role of the UN in preventing, managing and resolving conflicts in Africa,[21] and lack of funding and logistical support has also prompted the OAU to request UN

---

[13] B. D. Meyers, 'Intraregional Conflict Management by the Organization of African Unity', *International Organization* 28(3) (1974) 345–73, at 369.

[14] OAU Charter, Article 19.

[15] Sands and Klein, *Bowett's Law* chapter 10, at 248.

[16] Meyers, 'Intraregional Conflict Management', at 368. See also A. Alao, 'The Role of African Regional and Sub-Regional Organisations in Conflict Prevention and Resolution', Working Paper No. 23, *New Issues in Refugee Research* (New York: UNHCR, July 2000), www.unhcr.ch, at 8.

[17] The OAU sent a peacekeeping force to Chad in respect of its civil war during the Cold War, Alao, 'The Role of African Regional and Sub-Regional Organisations', at 9. See also B. Andemicael, *Peaceful Settlement among African States: Roles of the United Nations and the Organization of African Unity* (New York: UN Institute for Training and Research, 1972), at 45.

[18] Alao, 'The Role of African Regional and Sub-Regional Organisations', at 9.

[19] Jonah, 'The OAU', at 11–12.

[20] B. Andemicael, 'OAU–UN Relations in a Changing World', in El-Ayouty (ed.), OAU *after Thirty Years* 119–38, at 120–1.

[21] M. Malan, 'The OAU and Subregional Organisations. A Closer Look at the Peace Pyramid', Occasional Paper No. 36 (Pretoria: Institute for Security Studies, January 1999), http://www.iss.co.za/Pubs/PAPERS/36/Paper36.html, at 4.

assistance in peacekeeping operations.[22] Failures of the UN – for example, in the Congo – have, however, encouraged African states to try to establish their own African arrangements.[23] Into the gap have stepped sub-regional bodies which have tended to be seen as 'a possible first line of reaction where the OAU is unable to act'.[24] As Malan notes,

> the OAU seems to have been relegated to a conflict management role as an intermediary – between the UN and its higher moral authority for ensuring international peace and security on the one hand, and the sub regional organisations with their perceived greater political will and executive power on the other hand. This notion has found various expressions – from talk of 'layered responses' to African conflicts, to ideas of pyramidal conflict management structures for the continent.[25]

Overall, therefore, the OAU/AU appears to view its ability to deal with conflict situations as dependent upon outside assistance,[26] whether that be from the UN or other organisations such as the EU.[27] As a result, however, 'regional military involvement in conflict resolution has been ad hoc and not in accordance with a specific operating programme'.[28] Further, sub-regional bodies have not always been best placed to deal with conflict situations. Besides issues of limited financial means and regional political powerful states, among others, 'regional organisations face a problem of legitimacy if they are perceived to be acting without the authorisation of the global organisation – the United Nations – particularly where the action entails the use of force'.[29] This is exacerbated further with the 'web of controversy and mutual distrust' in the relationship between the UN and those sub-regional bodies. Thus, African organisations have felt that the UN has not taken African problems seriously and that it has not encouraged local initiatives. On the other hand, the UN considers that undemocratic governments were a key issue in conflicts and therefore

---

[22] For example, in relation to Chad, Jonah, 'The OAU', at 8.
[23] Ibid., at 4.   [24] Malan, 'The OAU and Subregional Organisations', at 5.
[25] Ibid., at 2.
[26] Assembly/AU/Dec.16(II), Draft Decision on the Establishment by the European Union of a Peace Support Operation Facility for the African Union.
[27] 'Requests the EU to examine the possibility of setting up a Peace Support Operation Facility (PSOF), to fund peace support and peace keeping operations conducted under the authority of the AU, thereby enhancing the capacity of the Union to fully play its role in the promotion of peace, security and stability in Africa', ibid.
[28] Malan, 'The OAU and Subregional Organisations', at 2; Alao, 'The Role of African Regional and Sub-Regional Organisations', at 7.
[29] Alao, 'The Role of African Regional and Sub-Regional Organisations', at 19–21.

until this was rectified by states the UN could do little to assist, and that the African organisations themselves were corrupt and badly managed.[30]

Organs responsible for conflict and their remit on human rights

Besides the defunct Commission of Mediation, Conciliation and Arbitration, a number of other organs under the OAU/AU have taken a role in conflict.

Role of Secretary General and Chair

The tendency elsewhere in regional organisations is that states often prefer informal structures for resolving conflicts, perhaps explaining why the mechanism for mediation never got off the ground in the OAU.[31] Instead the OAU has focused on using its Chairperson as 'a focal point for the resolution of a number of African disputes'.[32] There has been some confusion over the respective roles of the Chairperson and Secretary General and, although initially the Secretary General's role was administrative, over the years this has become more political.[33] Where they have worked together it has been a good arrangement, but there are no formal guidelines on when and how they should do so.[34]

Some Secretary Generals have been outspoken on certain issues; for example, Salim Ahmed Salim is said to have taken a 'positive view of human rights and, through his statements to the meetings of the political organs, has urged member states of the OAU to respect human rights'.[35] It is particularly important in maintaining the credibility of the OAU/AU on such matters that it is seen to publicly condemn atrocities.[36] However, there was evidence that his attention was not focused evenly and that those states that were more influential have been less likely to attract public statements by the Secretary General.[37] There is a clear basis under the Constitutive Act now for the Chairman of the AU Commission to intervene and comment on violations. Certainly, given the roles of the Secretary General and Chairman of the AU Commission in the ACHPR, it is arguable that they have a clear legal, if not moral, obligation to comment on any violations.[38]

---

[30] Ibid., at 22.   [31] Jonah, 'The OAU', at 4.   [32] Ibid., at 5.
[33] Ibid. He or she is required to be impartial, see OAU Charter, Article 18(1).
[34] Jonah, 'The OAU', at 5–6.
[35] Amnesty International, *Organization of African Unity*, at 16.
[36] Ibid.   [37] Ibid., at 17.   [38] Ibid. See chapter 2.

Conflict mechanism

In 1993 the AHSG adopted a Declaration on the Establishment within the OAU of a Mechanism for Conflict Prevention, Management and Resolution.[39] The Conflict Mechanism operated under two bodies, the Central Organ and the Conflict Management Division/Centre. The Central Organ was composed of the sixteen states that were elected every year to the Bureau of the Assembly of the OAU. The Conflict Management Centre was the secretariat of the Mechanism.

There does appear to have been an attempt at the level of the Secretariat of the OAU to link the work of the African Commission on Human and Peoples' Rights with that of the Conflict Management Division, particularly in the area of early warning. However, this was not fully realised. The Commission was not taken seriously by the conflict organs, and the reports on conflict situations that were presented to the OAU Council of Ministers and AHSG did not detail human rights violations.[40] Thus, 'while attention may correctly have been focused in the report on issues such as the primary health care system and sanitation, the failure to address other human rights issues such as the rebuilding of national institutions, including the judicial system, to protect human rights and prevent further violations, is a serious oversight'.[41] In addition, the reports failed to give a wider picture of the situation, essential in preventing conflicts occurring.[42]

On transformation to the AU, the Central Organ was officially incorporated as one of the organs of the AU,[43] but only after reference had been omitted to it in the Constitutive Act. The Organ remained until the Protocol on the Peace and Security Council received the required number of ratifications to come into force.[44] This happened at the end of December 2003.

IPEP

In the wake of the 1994 genocide in Rwanda, in 1998 the OAU established an International Panel of Eminent Personalities to Investigate the

---

[39] June 1993, Cairo.   [40] Amnesty International, *Organization of African Unity*, at 19.
[41] Ibid., at 19–20.   [42] Ibid., at 20.
[43] Decision AHG/Dec.160(XXXVII), as an organ under Article 5(2) of the Constitutive Act.
[44] Decision on the Establishment of the Peace and Security Council of the African Union, ASS/AU/Dec.3 (I).

Genocide in Rwanda and the Surrounding Events.[45] Its task was to 'establish the facts about how such a grievous crime was conceived, planned and executed, investigate and determine culpability for the failure to enforce the Genocide Convention in Rwanda and in the Great Lakes Region and to recommend measures aimed at redressing the consequences of the genocide and at preventing any possible recurrence of such a crime'.[46] In doing so, it was asked to look at the following actors' roles: UN; OAU; internal and external forces; NGOs; African and non-African leaders; and governments, individually or collectively.[47]

It produced its report in July 2000, in which it condemned the actions not only of the UN but also the OAU and other actors, finding that the OAU had failed to examine the human rights situation in Rwanda, which could have helped prevent the crisis.[48]

CSSDCA process

The CSSDCA process is a clear indication of the increased willingness to see human rights and conflict, among others, as interrelated. Thus, the Solemn Declaration recognises the importance of the human rights instruments and documents adopted under the OAU including the ACHPR, the Protocol establishing the African Court on Human and Peoples' Rights and the Decision on Unconstitutional Changes of Government, 'for ensuring the promotion, protection and observance of human rights as an integral part of our Organization's wider objective of promoting collective security for durable peace and sustainable development'.[49] It reiterates the 'inter-linkage between peace, stability, development, integration and cooperation'.[50] The Declaration displays a number of

---

[45] Establishment of the Panel of Eminent Personalities to Investigate the Genocide in Rwanda and the Surrounding Events, Doc. CM/2063(LXVIII), CM/Dec.409(LXVIII).

[46] Report of the Secretary General on the Establishment of an International Panel of Eminent Personalities to Investigate the Genocide in Rwanda and the Surrounding Events, CM/2048(LXVII), para. 7.

[47] Ibid., para. 9.

[48] 'Africa cannot count on the world outside to solve its crises. It is largely on its own. This is at least as true in ending human rights abuses as in ending conflicts,' International Panel of Eminent Personalities, Report on the Genocide in Rwanda, July 2000, para. 21.12. The report is available at http://www.internetdiscovery.org/forthetruth/Rwanda-e/EN-III-T.htm.

[49] CSSDCA Solemn Declaration, AHG/Decl.4(XXXVI), para. 2.   [50] Ibid., para. 7.

themes, including a recognition of the impact of stability in one African country for its neighbours and the region; the need to seek 'African solutions to African problems'; that 'democracy, good governance, respect for human and peoples' rights and the rule of law are prerequisites for the security, stability and development of the Continent'; and that 'the responsibility for the security, stability and socio-economic development of the Continent lies primarily with African States'.

While human rights standards are expressly linked with 'specific principles' in respect of security[51] and stability,[52] the Plan of Action sets out specific requirements for states. These include provisions on strengthening democratic institutions;[53] involving civil society;[54] upholding the rule of law; combating racism and protecting human rights;[55] and ensuring the 'equitable distribution of national income and wealth as well as transparency in the exploitation of Africa's resources',[56] among others.

AU organs: the Peace and Security Council (PSC)

The Constitutive Act provides for a Peace and Security Council, and its Protocol was adopted in July 2002.[57] Among the Objectives of this PSC of the AU, in Article 3, is a reference in the final paragraph to 'promote

[51] This 'implies individual and collective responsibilities exercised within the basic framework of the African Charter on Human and Peoples Rights and other relevant international instruments', Ibid., para. 10.

[52] 'Noting that stability requires that all States be guided by strict adherence to the rule of law, good governance, peoples participation in public affairs, respect for human rights and fundamental freedoms, the establishment of political organizations devoid of sectarian, religious, ethnic, regional and racial extremism', Ibid., para. 11.

[53] 'Intensify efforts aimed at enhancing the process of democratization in Africa. In this regard, the strengthening of institutions that will sustain democracy on the continent including the holding of free and fair elections should be encouraged; Adopt and implement a set of guidelines for dealing with unconstitutional and undemocratic changes in Africa in line with the Decisions that we took during the 35th Ordinary Session of our Assembly held in Algiers in 1999,' Ibid., para. 15.

[54] 'Encourage the participation and contribution of Civil Society in our States, to the efforts to bring about further democratization in our Continent; Recommit ourselves to the promotion of Good Governance, a culture of peace and accountability by leaders and officials, as a shared community value; encourage civic education on good governance and the promotion of African values in African institutions and schools', ibid., para. 15.

[55] 'Such as the freedom of expression and association, political and trade union pluralism and other forms of participatory democracy', Ibid., para. 15.

[56] Ibid.

[57] Decision on the Establishment of the Peace and Security Council of the African Union, ASS/AU/Dec.3(I), para. 3. See also CM/Dec.31(LXXVI) Rev.1.

and encourage democratic practices, good governance and the rule of law, protect human rights and fundamental freedoms, respect for the sanctity of human life and international humanitarian law, as part of efforts for preventing conflicts'.[58] In its Principles, Article 4, it is to be guided by the UN Charter and UDHR (although not expressly the ACHPR) and 'respect for the rule of law, fundamental human rights and freedoms, the sanctity of human life and international humanitarian law'. The Union has the right to intervene 'in respect of grave circumstances, namely: war crimes, genocide and crimes against humanity as well as a serious threat to legitimate order to restore peace and stability to the member state of the Union upon the recommendation of the Peace and Security Council' as detailed in Article 4(h) of the Constitutive Act. In terms of electing members of the Council criteria include that the state should show 'respect for constitutional governance, in accordance with the Lomé Declaration, as well as the rule of law and human rights'.[59] In March 2004 the Executive Council elected the first states to the PSC and the PSC held its first meeting, where it adopted its Rules of Procedure. It has powers to anticipate events that may lead to genocide and crimes against humanity, recommend the intervention of the Union if there were war crimes, genocide and crimes against humanity, impose sanctions on unconstitutional changes in government and follow up in terms of conflict prevention issues of human rights, among other things.[60] The Commission of the AU is also to provide training in humanitarian law and human rights law to civilian and military personnel in these cases.[61] There is specific reference to the need for it to develop a relationship with the African Commission on Human and Peoples' Rights in which it should 'seek close cooperation' and the Commission should tell the Council of any relevant issues.[62]

The Chairman of the Assembly of the AU was asked to set up a group of experts to examine the possibility of having a common African defence and security policy.[63] This meeting noted that

> it was important to take cognisance of existing positions such as the African Charter on Human and Peoples' Rights, the New Partnership for Africa's Development (NEPAD) and the Convention on Terrorism . . . the need for

---

[58] Protocol Relating to the Establishment of the Peace and Security Council of the African Union, Article 3(f).
[59] Ibid., Article 5(2)(g).   [60] Ibid., Article 7.
[61] Ibid., Article 13(13).   [62] Ibid., Article 19.
[63] Decision on the Situation in Madagascar, ASS/AU/Dec.7(I), July 2002.

all deliberations to be guided by the necessity to respect human rights, as this would play a role in preventing violent conflicts. Clear emphasis also needed to be placed on the peaceful resolution of conflicts both within and between states.[64]

Further, 'bad governance, human rights abuses and unconstitutional changes of government, were also identified as some of the internal threats to Africa's security'.[65] It was also proposed that a Common African Defence and Security Policy should offer the individual African protection from tyrannical governments by allowing other African governments to intervene under the auspices of the AU. A contrary view was, however, expressed to the effect that 'a balance should be effected between protecting the sovereignty of the state in question and protecting the individual rights of its citizens which were allegedly infringed'.[66] In the Policy Framework for the Establishment of the African Standby Force and Military Staff Committee, the African Military Experts recommended that the Chairperson of the Commission should submit reports on various matters to the PSC, including on humanitarian developments and human rights.[67] There is also the requirement in peace support operations that there should be training in humanitarian law.[68]

At least here, and with the CSSDCA process, the AU seems increasingly to see a link between human rights and conflict and suggests that human rights will be integral to the remit of the PSC. While institutional support for this connection between human rights and conflict is perhaps starting to get off the ground, it is worth examining the extent to which, in substantive terms, human rights standards are seen as central to the OAU/AU when it has dealt with conflicts in the past.

Human rights approaches in conflict

The OAU/AU has said that human rights violations are one of the causes of conflicts in Africa. Thus, it has referred to, for example, treatment of

---

[64] Report of the Meeting of Experts on a Common African Defence and Security Policy, 27–29 March 2003, Randburg, South Africa, Exp/Mtg/CADSP/Rpt.(I), para. 13.

[65] Ibid., para. 29.   [66] Ibid., para. 38.

[67] Policy Framework for the Establishment of the African Standby Force and Military Staff Committee, Submitted by African Military Experts to African Chiefs of Defence Staff, 12–14 May 2003, Exp/ASF-MSC/2(I), para. 3.17.

[68] African Standby Force and Military Staff Committee, Part II-Annexes, 12–14 May 2003, Exp/ASF–MSC/2(I), para. 17.2.

minority groups as a contributing factor in the development of conflicts. As the Secretary General stated:

> While one of the major sources of internal conflicts has been on the distribution of power and control over resources, the tendency to affirm one's identity by rejecting outside cultural influence has also been a factor in internal conflicts. Moreover, failure to provide opportunity for minority groups to participate actively in the exercise of political power has contributed to the social division and has led to claims of self-determination.[69]

Democratisation is also seen as central to preventing conflict[70] and here the Secretary General has stated:

> Indeed, the prospects of peace and security in Africa are discernible in the process of democratisation which is now taking root in Africa. Clearly this is one area which the OAU intends to pursue vigorously as it is obvious that the democratisation of political life in African countries and the building of democratic institutions, a culture of tolerance and respect for human rights are a prerequisite for peace, security, and development in the continent. Both the Charter of the OAU and the African Charter on Human and Peoples' Rights recognise the imperative necessity of respect for human and peoples' rights as a prerequisite for building peace, security and stability within African societies.[71]

In this regard it would seem to be important that any early-warning system takes account of human rights violations, these having been recognised

---

[69] Lessons from a Decade of Conflicts: Prospects of Peace and Security by the Year 2000. A Presentation by His Excellency Salim Ahmed Salim, Secretary General, Conference of African Ministers of Planning and UNDP Resident Representatives, 31 January–2 February, Ouagadougou, at 6. See also Report of the Secretary General on the Situation in Angola, CM/2099(LXX)-a, at 2; Report of the Secretary General on the Situation in Somalia, CM/2099(LXX)-g, para. 14.

[70] For example, Addressing the Challenges of Peace and Security in Africa, Conflict Management Center, Occasional Paper Series No.1/1999, notes at 10: 'Good governance, democracy and respect for fundamental freedoms are major elements in defining security in Africa.' Further, at 17:
> The propensity for human disaster requiring humanitarian intervention of international dimension in Africa, is often the result of the absence of good governance and effective mechanisms to ensure the respect for human rights and fundamental freedoms. The perception of the Continent as a Continent in crisis and a theater of humanitarian disaster are more often than not linked to what is often referred to as a crisis of democracy in Africa.

[71] Lessons from a Decade of Conflicts, at 26.

as potential causes of conflict. The OAU has recognised in developing its Early Warning System that

> the objective of early-warning information is to prevent perceived or actual threat to the values of the Organization as contained in its Charter. The values range from the protection of human and peoples' rights, promotion of democracy and security for all and the building of regional collective security to guarantee the promotion of peace, security, stability and development in the Continent.[72]

It also suggested ways of strengthening expertise from the outside: 'A continent wide network of specialists in various state agencies, academic institutions, human rights monitoring groups, local NGOs and civil societies are important contacts in strengthening the gathering of information for an OAU early-warning system.'[73] Similarly, the African Commission on Human and Peoples' Rights developed an Article 58 early-warning system which made some reference to the role of the OAU organs.[74] Yet neither appears to have amounted to much in reality.

In brokering peace agreements the OAU/AU has sometimes required human rights commitments to be part of the deal. Thus, parties to a conflict have been required, for example, to ensure a 'commitment to put an end to measures directed against the civilian population and to address the negative socio-economic impact of the crisis on the civilian population, particularly the deportees; deployment of a team of Human Rights Monitors; . . . mobilisation of resources for the resettlement of the displaced persons'.[75] There has also been considerable attention to restoration of democratic institutions.[76] However, these attempts have tended to be rather ad hoc.

Conversely, it has also recognised that conflicts themselves result in human rights violations. However, this, again, has not been consistently applied by the OAU/AU. Often, for example, it has simply made references to general condemnation of 'all acts of violence and mass murder' during

---

[72] See www.oau-oua.org/document/mechanism/english/mech02.htm.
[73] Ibid.   [74] See above.
[75] Introductory Note to the Report of the Secretary General, Sixty-Ninth Ordinary Session of the Council of Ministers, Addis Ababa, 19–23 March 1999, para. 137. See also 'Stresses that a durable settlement in Burundi must be based on democracy and security for all', Resolution on Burundi, CM/Res.1649(LXIV), para. 3.
[76] See, for example, Resolution on Liberia, CM/Res.1585(LXII), para. 14; Report of the Secretary General on the Conflict Situations in Africa (Doc.CM/2004(LXVI), The Situation in the Great Lakes Region, the Democratic Republic of Congo (Doc.CM/2004(LXVI)), CM/Dec.353(LXVI), paras. (b), (c) and (d).

times of conflict[77] or 'untold human suffering including the deaths of hundreds of thousands of people, and massive human displacements'.[78] Thus, on many occasions the human rights situation in a conflict has only really been mentioned in passing,[79] or ignored completely.[80]

However, where it has paid human rights some attention, the OAU/AU has seen fit to condemn states and other parties to a conflict for, among other things, 'the gross violations of human rights and international humanitarian law',[81] calling on them, for example, to 'conduct an investigation into political prisoners and prison conditions and repeal of laws hindering political activity'.[82] There has been some attention to the impact

---

[77] Report of the Secretary General on the Situation in the Democratic Republic of Congo, CM/2099(LXX)-d, para. 17. See also Decision on the Report of the Secretary General on the Situation in Sierra Leone (Doc.CM/2099(LXX)-f), CM/Dec.454(LXX); Report of the Secretary General on the Conflict Situation in Sierra Leone, CM/2099(LXX)-f, para. 1. See also, 'There is also the humanitarian and human rights situation which is quite disturbing', Introductory Note of the Secretary General to the Seventy-Fourth Ordinary Session of the Council of Ministers. In Draft Decisions of the Sixty Seventh Ordinary Session of the Council of Ministers, CM/DRAFT/DECISIONS(LXVII) REV.1, at 8, the Council of Ministers 'calls on the belligerents to adopt a cease fire and respect the rights of the individual'. In relation to Angola the Secretary General has noted that 'the devastating impact [of the war] on the humanitarian situation in that country . . . raise[s] serious concerns over the security of the civilian population caught in the crossfire of hostilities. The safety of children is cause for even greater concern. Hundreds of children continue to be abducted by UNITA and more generally are subject to deliberate physical abuse and indiscriminate attacks', Introductory Note of the Secretary General to the Seventy-Fourth Ordinary Session of the Council of Ministers, at 28. See also Report of the Secretary General on Sierra Leone, Central Organ/MEC/MIN/2E(V), para. 5.

[78] Introductory Note of the Secretary General to the Seventy-Fourth Ordinary Session of the Council of Ministers, at 32. See also Report of the Secretary General on the Situation in the Comoros, CM/2062(LXVIII), which notes the state of chaos on the island:

> Such a situation which arose from the apathy demonstrated by the population, cannot be divorced from the consequent increase in acts of repression against all those expressing the least opposition to the separatist view and from the persistent refusal by the separatists to authorise the resumption of free movement of persons between Anjouan and the other islands of the Archipelago.

para. 14

See also Report of the Secretary General on the Situation in Burundi, Central Organ/MEC/MIN/2A(V): mentions, para. 5.

[79] Introductory Note of the Secretary General to the Seventy-Fourth Ordinary Session of the Council of Ministers, at 16.

[80] See, for example, ibid., at 17–26; Report of the Secretary General on the Situation in Liberia, Central Organ/MEC/MIN/2C(V).

[81] Introductory Note of the Secretary General to the Seventy-Fourth Ordinary Session of the Council of Ministers, at 18–19.

[82] Ibid.

of weapons on rights,[83] particularly with regard to the rights of the child.[84] While the OAU has referred to a 'right to peace'[85] and there is reference to such in the ACHPR,[86] it can hardly be said to have elaborated on its content any further. More frequent than reference to human rights violations, however, are references to violations of humanitarian law.[87]

Responsibilities for human rights protection during conflicts

Where the OAU/AU has recognised human rights as an issue in conflict situations, it has been prepared to say that the responsibility falls on a variety of actors. Thus, rebel groups have been called upon to protect human rights;[88] on other occasions it has been prepared to say that

---

[83] Report of the Secretary General on the Issue of Landmines and International Efforts to Reach a Total Ban, CM/2009(LXVI); Draft Decisions of the Sixty Seventh Ordinary Session of the Council of Ministers, CM/DRAFT/DECISIONS(LXVII) REV.1, at 18; Decision on the 'First Meeting of States parties to the Convention on the Prohibition of the Use, Stockpiling, Production and Transfer of their Anti-Personnel Mines and on the Destruction', AHG/Dec.135(LXX).

[84] 'Thus, the Assembly emphasised the impact of the proliferation, circulation and illicit traffic in light weapons on the conscription of an increasing number of child-soldiers, the psychological trauma resulting thereof and the need to observe the provisions of the African Charter on the Rights and Welfare of the Child and the Convention on the Rights of the Child', Report of the Secretary General on the Preparation for the Ministerial Conference on Small Arms and Light Weapons, CM/2165(LXXII).

[85] 'Pursue initiatives aimed at strengthening the efforts invested in member states, regional organizations and the international community to promote an environment of peace and stability for the development of Africa and sensitise public opinion to recognise the right to peace as a fundamental right of the human person', Decision on the Strengthening of OAU/UNESCO Cooperation (Doc.CM/2097(LXX) Add.3), CM/Dec.480(LXX).

[86] ACHPR, Article 23.

[87] Introductory Note of the Secretary General to the Seventy-Fourth Ordinary Session of the Council of Ministers, at 9, notes the Central Organ's 'grave concern about the humanitarian situation and repeated violations of international humanitarian law committed in the DRC', calling on all parties to comply with humanitarian law obligations.

[88] Decision on Somalia, M/2164(LXXII)-f), CM/Dec.526(LXXII), para. 3; Decision on the Report of the Secretary General on the Situation in the Democratic Republic of Congo (DRC), Doc. CM/2254(LXXVI)-b, CM/Dec.663, para. 18; Communiqué of the Eighty-Third Ordinary Session of the Central Organ of the OAU Mechanism for Conflict Prevention, Management and Resolution at Ambassadorial Level, 3 June 2002, Central Organ/MEC/Amb/Comm.(LXXXIII); Decision on the Situation in Madagascar, ASS/AU/Dec.7(I). It has also called for the 'trial of the leadership of the RUF and urges the United Nations to bring to trial the leadership of the RUF, for their crimes against humanity and human rights violations and urges the United Nations Security Council to take appropriate measures in this regard', Decision on Sierra Leone (CM/2164(LXXII)-e), CM/Dec.525(LXXII), para. 12.

individuals have responsibility for violations of international human rights and humanitarian law.[89] The OAU has supported the establishment of the International Criminal Court.[90]

Terrorism

More recently, in the light of international events, the OAU/AU has focused its attention on terrorism. In this context, human rights have played a role. In 1999 the OAU adopted its own Convention on the Prevention and Combating of Terrorism. This treaty provides a definition of terrorism,[91] and sets out areas of cooperation for states parties. Provisions include those on state jurisdiction, extradition and extraterritorial investigations. There is no mechanism for enforcement, despite attempts to establish such,[92] and thus the roles of the PSC and the AU Commissioner on Peace and Security will be particularly important.[93] The Convention entered into force in December 2002.[94]

It is to be welcomed that influences of human rights are evident in various provisions of the Convention. The preamble confirms that terrorism 'is a serious violation of human rights and, in particular, the rights

[89] Decision on the Report of the Secretary General on the Conflict Situation in Angola (Doc.CM/2099(LXX)-a), CM/Dec.450(LXX). The Secretary General also recommended that the Council of Ministers 'strongly condemn Mr Jonas Savimbi and his UNITA group for waging a campaign of indiscriminate attacks and terror against the civilian population in Angola; for the killing, maiming and the displacement of innocent women and children, the abduction of foreigners, the shooting down of UN planes and other crimes', Report of the Secretary General on the Situation in Angola, CM/2099(LXX)-a, at 2; Decision on the Report of the Secretary General on the Conflict Situation in Angola (Doc.CM/2099(LXX)-a), CM/Dec.450(LXX), preamble. See also The Situation in Angola, CM/Dec.442(LXIX).

[90] Draft Decisions of the Sixty-Seventh Ordinary Session of the Council of Ministers, CM/DRAFT/DECISIONS(LXVII) REV.1, at 37 takes note of the statement of Senegal to ensure that an African conference is held on the International Criminal Court and 'strongly supports the establishment of an International Criminal Court', urging states to adopt the Rome Statute.

[91] Article 1(3)(a).

[92] See Decision on the Report of the Interim Chairperson on the Draft Protocol to the AU Convention on the Prevention and Combating of Terrorism, EX/CL/Dec.2032.

[93] This is affirmed by Article 7 of the Protocol of the Peace and Security Council and the Plan of Action.

[94] As of December 2003 the following states had ratified the Convention: Algeria, Angola, Burkina Faso, Burundi, Cape Verde, Comoros, Egypt, Equatorial Guinea, Eritrea, Ethiopia, Ghana, Guinea, Kenya, Lesotho, Libya, Madagascar, Malawi, Mali, Mauritius, Mozambique, Nigeria, Rwanda, SADR, Senegal, Seychelles, South Africa, Sudan, Tanzania, Togo and Tunisia.

to physical integrity, life, freedom and security'. Article 7 requires that those suspected of terrorist offences be able to communicate with and be visited by representatives of their state 'to protect that person's rights', to be assisted by a lawyer of their choice and to be informed of these rights. The Convention makes it clear, however, that 'notwithstanding the provisions of Article 1, the struggle waged by peoples in accordance with the principles of international law for their liberation or self-determination, including armed struggle against colonialism, occupation, aggression and domination by foreign forces shall not be considered as terrorist acts'.[95]

Particularly important is the inclusion of Article 22 which states that 'nothing in this Convention shall be interpreted as derogating from the general principles of international law, in particular the principles of international humanitarian law, as well as the African Charter on Human and Peoples' Rights'. However, as Human Rights Watch notes, it is disappointing that human rights standards on due process, fair trial and protection from torture in particular were not more explicitly laid out in the Convention.[96]

Further initiatives on terrorism include the decision to establish an African Centre for the Study and Research on Terrorism.[97] The OAU also adopted a Plan of Action on the Prevention and Combating of Terrorism in September 2002,[98] although reference to human rights and democratic principles is not explicit.

These developments are important, not only in ensuring long-term stability for the continent, but also in the potential role of the AU organs in ensuring compliance with human rights standards in the context of terrorism.

Conclusion

While there does appear to be some recognition of the impact of conflict on human rights, there is little indication that the close monitoring of human rights violations may be a useful indicator of conflicts and a way of preventing them. As a result, the approach has been rather disappointing.

---

[95] Article 3.
[96] Human Rights Watch, 'Letter to Mozambique President Chissano, New Chair of the African Union', 20 August 2003, http://www.hrw.org/press/2003/08/au082003ltr.htm.
[97] Decision on Terrorism in Africa, Assembly/AU/Dec.15(II).
[98] Plan of Action of the African Union High Level Inter-Governmental Meeting on the Prevention and Combating of Terrorism in Africa, Mtg/HLIG/Conv.Terror/Plan(I).

Human rights are by no means integral to the decisions of the OAU, rather they seem to have arisen by chance.

There needs to be more work done at the AU on elaborating standards of human rights in respect of conflict situations. Although the history of the Central Organ's involvement in human rights matters is not promising, the provisions in place with respect to the PSC and the work of the CSSDCA process are more specific and offer some hope that human rights will have increased attention under the new organs. Clearly, therefore, the PSC would have good reason to see human rights as integral to its mandate, and it needs to be encouraged to see human rights as an important part of its work.

5

Women and the OAU/AU

Although there is no mention of gender in the OAU Charter itself,[1] the OAU has paid increasing attention to the position of women.[2] More recently, there has been an attempt to mainstream a gender perspective across all fields of the OAU/AU's work, but it has paid particular attention to their rights in times of conflict, and their right of participation and role in development. The recent adoption of a Protocol on the Rights of Women in Africa to the ACHPR, and gender being a specific principle of the Union as indicated by the Constitutive Act, are also to be noted. The rights of women seem to be something on which the OAU/AU has taken some concerted action.

However, as will be seen, while the attention is to be commended, its approach does seem to evidence a rather stereotypical presumption of the role of women in society. Similarly, while there is clear rhetoric of the need to support women and increase their participation and protection of their rights, particularly at the international level, less attention has been paid to the position of rural women.

The reasons for the OAU/AU paying attention to the position of women seem to come from various sources. Certainly, early on its work, the participation of the OAU in international conferences led it to adopt resolutions relating to the rights of women as a follow-up.[3] In addition, the role of

---

[1] Indeed, it has been said by one member of the African Commission on Human and Peoples' Rights that women were neglected in the drafting of the Charter and that this was one of the reasons for its downfall, Commissioner Ondziel-Gnelenga, at the 29th Session of the African Commission on Human and Peoples' Rights in Libya, see transcripts of the debate on the AU, on file with author. The Ghana–Guinea–Mali Union, also known as Union of African States, held a meeting in April 1961 and the presidents of these three countries signed a charter of Union of African States which came into effect in July that year. There was some mention of the position of women in the provisions but it was rather limited. This was not fed into the final OAU Charter.

[2] See, for example, Decision on Women and Gender, CM/Dec.579(LXXIII).

[3] For example, in a Resolution in 1979, it noted the UN World Conference of Women on Equality, Development and Peace in Denmark that was due to be held in 1980, Resolution on

women in the African liberation struggle did not go unrecognised by the OAU.[4] The activities and lobbying of a number of women's organisations, despite few having observer status with the OAU, has also had an impact.[5] More recently, the need for the OAU to react to conflicts and economic development of the continent has also prompted it to look at the rights of women from these perspectives.

Right of participation

As has been noted by those writing on the position of women in Africa, not only are women ignored in traditional democratic discourse, 'their oppression and subordination in male-dominated patriarchal societies has also kept them outside the parameters of formal politics'.[6] To remedy this situation international human rights law has recognised that it may be necessary to take positive action to give effect to the principle of equality in favour of a group that has been disadvantaged.[7] This, however, must be

---

World Conference of Women on Equality, Development and Peace, CM/Res.711(XXXII), preamble. See also Resolution for the International Women's Year, CM/Res.395(XXIV); Resolution on the World Conference of the United Nations Decade for Women: Equality, Development and Peace, Copenhagen, CM/Res.876(XXXVII); Resolution for the International Women's Year, CM/Res.390(XXIV).

[4] It noted 'the active participation of women in the liberation struggle of the African continent and their role in Africa's development', Resolution on the World Women Conference, CM/Res.985(XLI), preamble. Geisler notes that during the fights for independence, 'as combatants, many women experienced equality with men for the first time', G. Geisler, 'Troubled Sisterhood: Women and Politics in Southern Africa: Case Studies from Zambia, Zimbabwe and Botswana', *African Affairs* 95 (1995) 545–78, at 551.

[5] In 1975 the Council of Ministers adopted a resolution on African NGOs in which it noted the Pan-African Youth Movement and the All Africa Women's Committee,

> considering the great importance of these organisations and the eminently positive role that they play in the building and consolidating of African unity; bearing in mind the obvious concern of the Founding fathers of our inter-governmental organisation to associate all the active forces of our continent closely with the noble mission of the OAU with a view to achieving the objectives it has set itself and the noble aspirations of the African peoples to political, economic and cultural independence.

It requested those organisations to contact the General Secretary of the OAU to indicate ways of cooperating with it, Resolution on African Non-Governmental Organisations, CM/Res.355(XXIII).

[6] S. Tamale, 'Towards Legitimate Governance in Africa: The Case of Affirmative Action and Parliamentary Politics in Uganda', in Quashigah and Okafor (eds.), *Legitimate Governance in Africa* 235–62, at 235 and 236. See also M. Russell and C. O'Cinneide, 'Positive Action to Promote Women in Politics. Some European Comparisons', *ICLQ* 52 (2003) 587–614.

[7] UN Human Rights Committee General Comment No. 18(37), 10 November 1989.

balanced against the requirement that such measures are proportionate and necessary to achieve that aim.[8]

The OAU/AU has consistently stressed the need for increased participation of women at all levels of decision making, and this seems to have been where its attention has been focused in terms of action that has to be taken to improve the position of women. The OAU has thus urged the 'Secretary General as well as Member States, to take all appropriate measures to ensure that women are appropriately represented in decision making processes in the OAU'.[9] The Council of Ministers, for example, has called for increased participation of women in its proceedings, through membership of the delegations[10] and has noted the Secretary General's efforts to recruit women into the Secretariat.[11]

Concrete action has been taken to ensure that this has been achieved, particularly in the transition to the AU, with it being recognised that 'the objectives of the African Union cannot be achieved without the full involvement and participation of women at all levels and structures of the Union'.[12] Thus, there was a recognition that there should be 'the effective and equitable participation of women in all stages leading to the establishment and functioning of the African Union'.[13] As a consequence, the Constitutive Act provides for one of the Principles of the Union to be 'promotion of gender equality'.[14]

The Statutes and Protocols of the various AU organs also provide expressly for a specific number of women to sit on such bodies.[15] Thus,

---

[8] See CEDAW, Articles 4(1) and 7 CEDAW. See also Russell and Cinneide, 'Positive Action'.

[9] Decision on Women and Gender.

[10] Report of the Seventy-Third Ordinary Session of the Council of Ministers, CM/Rpt (LXXIII), para. 74.

[11] Ibid., paras. 74–5.

[12] Durban Declaration in Tribute of the Organization of African Unity and on the Launching of the African Union, ASS/AU/Decl.2(I), para. 18.

[13] Introductory Note of the Secretary General to the Seventy-Fourth Ordinary Session of the Council of Ministers, at 64.

[14] Constitutive Act, Article 4(1).

[15] The Protocol on the Peace and Security Council requires that members of the Council should be elected on the basis of 'equal rights', Article 5(1). The Protocol on the African Court of Justice provides that 'due consideration shall be given to adequate gender representation in the nomination process', Article 5(3) and 'in the election of judges the Assembly shall ensure that there is equal gender representation', Article 7(3). The Draft Statutes of the Economic, Social and Cultural Council provide that it will be composed of civil society organisations which should include women's organisations and that a 50 per cent gender equality principle applies in terms of membership as a whole, Draft Statutes of the Economic, Social and Cultural Council, Exp/Draft/ECOSOCC Statutes/Rev.2, Articles 2(2)(a) and 4(6).

the Protocol on the Pan-African Parliament requires there to be at least one woman in the five members from each state that sit on the Parliament.[16] Although this is clearly a start, it has been criticised by women's organisations as inadequate and they have lobbied for the quota in the Parliament to be increased to two.[17] Consideration has also been given to ensuring gender balance in the AU Commission;[18] this was achieved to some extent with the appointment of five women to the eight-member Commission.[19]

The African organs have also called for increased participation of women in other international fora, for example, recommending in one instance 'the participation of women in the World Food Summit, as they play a vital role in food production in Africa'.[20]

One of the reasons given for the exclusion of women from international decision making, where the institutions are composed of ministers from various departments of member states,[21] has been the lack of involvement of women in political institutions at the national level.[22] International institutions and decision making have therefore tended to be dominated by men.[23] The OAU/AU has recognised this and that there should be

---

[16] Protocol to the Treaty Establishing the African Economic Community Relating to the Pan-African Parliament, CM/2198(LXXIII), Annex I, Article 4(2).

[17] See Maputo Declaration on Gender Mainstreaming and the Effective Participation of Women in the African Union, no reference.

[18] Decision on Mainstreaming Gender and Women's Issues in the African Union, CM/Dec.683.

[19] The Statutes of the Commission require that for the post of Commissioner, each region should nominate two candidates, one of whom should be a woman and in terms of election, at least one Commissioner from each region should be a woman, Statutes of the Commission ASS/AU/2(I)-d, Articles 13 and 6 respectively.

[20] Resolution on the African Common Position on Food Security and the Preparations for the World Food Summit, AHG/Res.248(XXXII) 1996, para. 6.

[21] The Beijing Platform for Action, A/CONF.177/20, chap.1, resolution 1, Annex II, para. 28, www.un.org/ecosocdev/geninfo/women/women96.htm.

[22] According to the UN, www.un.org/ecosocdev/geninfo/women/women96.htm, only twenty-eight women have been elected heads of state or government in the last hundred years, and women hold only 11.7 per cent of the seats in national parliaments across the world. In addition, although the percentage of women cabinet ministers has risen in the last decade, they still constitute only 6.8 per cent of the total.

[23] The UN has recognised the need to improve the status of women in its Secretariat, see General Assembly Resolution A/RES/53/119, 5 February 1999, Resolution on Improvement of the Status of Women in the Secretariat, 53rd session, which aims to increase the number of women participating at all levels of the Secretariat. See also Press Release, ECOSOC/5769, 9 July 1998, Gender Initiatives at the United Nations Fall Short due to Lack of Commitment at the Management Level, Economic and Social Council Told. For discussion of this issue, see United Nations Office at Vienna Centre for Social Development and Humanitarian

a role for women in decision making at all levels, calling upon states 'to establish mechanisms for tripartism and social dialogue with all civil society groups, including women and youth, and to demonstrate their political will, commitment and positive attitude to social dialogue'.[24] In addition, states should

> take special measures to promote the participation of women in political decision-making, particularly in governments, Inter-African organisations, in national delegations participating in African meetings including meetings relating to peace and development process; enhance the status of women and build human and financial capacities of departments in charge of the promotion of women at all levels to enable them ensure the implementation and follow-up of the African and Global Platforms for Action.[25]

Participation in decision making on conflicts

The need to increase the participation of women has been most notable in respect of decision making on conflict situations.[26] Despite their differing experiences, women are rarely involved in determining any of the decisions about war, security or peace, participating little in political decision making and rarely taking part in the fighting and the conflict in a physical sense.[27] The OAU has also recognised this on several

Affairs, *Women in Politics and Decision-Making in the Late Twentieth Century* (Dordrecht: Martinus Nijhoff, 1992).

[24] Decision on the Report of the Secretary General on the Twenty-Third Ordinary Session of the OAU Labour and Social Affairs Commission (CM/2174(LXXII)), CM/Dec.535 (LXXII), para. 3.

[25] Decision on the Progress Report of the Secretary General on the Efforts Deployed Towards Mainstreaming African Women's Concerns into Peace and Sustainable Development Processes Doc.CM/2117(LXX)), CM/Dec.469(LXX).

[26] Mikell notes that conflict in 1980s and 1990s led to greater debate on women's rights in general as a result of the impact on their rights, G. Mikell, 'African Women's Rights in the Context of Systemic Conflict', *ASIL Proceedings* 89 (1995) 490–500, at 490–91.

[27] 'Women's Role in the Peace Process: An African Perspective', Working paper ECA/OAU/AH.EGM/WLFP/96/2 in *Women and the Peace Process: Perspectives from Africa Women Leadership Forum on Peace, Ad-hoc Expert Group Meeting, Johannesburg, South Africa, 4–8 November 1996* (Addis Ababa: UNECA/African Centre for Women, 1996); Press Release GA/SHC/3525, 13 October 1999, Armed Conflict Worsens Plight of Women say Third Committee; Press Release GA/SHC/3475, 15 October 1998, Plight of Women in Armed Conflict and Foreign Occupation Stressed as Third Committee Continues Debate on Advancement of Women; United Nations General Assembly Declaration on Protection of Women and Children in Emergencies and Armed Conflict, Resolution 3318(XXIX), 14 December 1974. See also C. Niarchos, 'Women, War and Rape: Challenges Facing the International Tribunal for the Former Yugoslavia', *HRQ* 17 (1995) 659–90; T. A. Northrup, 'Personal Security, Political Security: The Relationship among Conceptions of Gender, War and Peace', *Research in Social Movements, Conflict and Change*, 12 (1990) 267–99;

occasions.[28] Even where they have been involved, most decisions relating to conflict not only do not involve women but also, and perhaps as a result of this, take no account of gender issues.[29] Others have attributed the neglect to the public–private divide that underlies international law as well as cultural and religious traditions within society.[30]

The OAU itself has adopted a number of solutions to this paucity of women in decision making regarding conflicts, the majority of which relate to the need to increase women's participation through an increase in the numbers of women in its own organs and mechanisms. It has thus recommended that more women should be included in the observer teams sent to study conflict situations; there should be more women special envoys; more women should be involved in election-monitoring missions; and women 'should form at least half of all peace negotiations panels'.[31]

It has also recommended that women should be 'encouraged to participate in decision-making processes at all levels as well as on military issues, with special accent on participation in decision-making at the

J. H. Stiehm, 'Men and Women and Peacekeeping: A Research Note', *International Peacekeeping* 2(4) (1995) 564–9; M. Barron, 'When the Soldiers Come Home: A Gender Analysis of the Reintegration of Demobilised Soldiers, Mozambique 1994–6' (MA thesis, University of East Anglia, 1996); see also A. Ager, W. Ager and L. Long, 'The Differential Experience of Mozambican Refugee Women and Men', *Journal of Refugee Studies* 8 (1995) 265–87.

[28] See Report of the Secretary General on the Twenty-Second Ordinary Session of the OAU Labour and Social Affairs Commission, CM/2112(LXX), considering the Report of the Secretary General on the Role and Contribution of Women to Peace-Making, Peace-Building and Socio-Economic Development in Africa (Doc.LSC/8(XXII)), para. 83. See also Lessons from a Decade of Conflicts: Prospects of Peace and Security by the Year 2000. A Presentation by His Excellency Salim Ahmed Salim, Secretary General, Conference of African Ministers of Planning and UNDP Resident Representatives, 31 January–2 February, Ouagadougou, at 24: 'The major victims of conflicts in Africa are women and children.'

[29] See E. Z. Berg, 'Gendering Conflict Resolution', *Peace and Change* 19(4) (1994) 325–48; B. Byrne, 'Towards a Gendered Understanding of Conflict', *IDS Bulletin*, 27(3) (1996) 31–40; S. R. Dunbar, 'Role of Women in Decision-Making in the Peace Process', in S. Wölte (ed.), *Human Rights Violations against Women during War and Conflict* (Geneva: Women's International League for Peace and Freedom, 1997) 12–18; J. Gardam, 'The Law of Armed Conflict: A Gendered Regime?', in D. Dallmeyer (ed.), *Reconceiving Reality: Women and International Law* (Washington, DC: American Society of International Law, 1993) 171–93; S. Wali, 'Women in Conditions of War and Peace: Challenges and Dilemmas', in M. Schuler (ed.), *From Basic Needs to Basic Rights: Women's Claim to Human Rights* (Washington, DC: Institute for Women, Law and Development, 1995).

[30] See CEDAW Committee, General Recommendation No. 23, Political and Private Life, Sixteenth Session, 13 January 1997, paras. 8–9; Press Release WOM/961, 12 March 1997, Status of Women Commission Focus on Women in Power and Decision-Making.

[31] Report of the Secretary General on the Twenty-Second Ordinary Session of the OAU Labour and Social Affairs Commission, para. 87.

highest levels' and that 'military contingents dispatched by member states include women'.[32] In addition, there should be a boost to women's political decision-making power by 'governments, political parties, trade unions, private sector, women's groups and all other actors' who should adopt measures to increase their proportion in decision making, promote qualified women to power at all levels, integrate women's concerns into actions on conflict prevention and preventive diplomacy, and increase the number of women in leadership.[33] Further, there should be support for the 'significant role of women in conflict resolution and peace-making'.[34] Women should 'get critical mass in ministries and other offices and be represented at that level in other organisations';[35] there should be incorporation of women in peace education;[36] and states should promote legal literacy underscoring women's plight as victims and peacemakers.[37] African First Ladies have also undertaken some role.[38]

As a further consequence of the impact of conflicts on women, the OAU has also looked at the position of women as refugees. It has, for example, recognised the experiences of women as refugees and internally displaced persons that may bring a different perspective to resolving conflict situations: 'As refugees and internally displaced persons, women can play a very important role in conflict resolution, rehabilitation and peace-building.'[39] Thus, the approach of the OAU would also seem to suggest that the inclusion of women is necessary for peace and cannot be achieved without them. As was stated in the Beijing Declaration: 'we are convinced that women's empowerment and their full participation on the basis of equality in all spheres of society, including participation in the decision-making process and access to power, are fundamental for the achievement of equality, development and peace'; and 'local, national, regional and global peace is attainable and is inextricably linked with the advancement of women, who are a fundamental force for

---

[32] Ibid.   [33] Ibid.   [34] Ibid.   [35] Ibid.   [36] Ibid.   [37] Ibid.
[38] Report of the Sixth Ordinary Session of the Committee of Ambassadors and Other Plenipotentiaries, Amb/Cttee/Rpt(VI) notes among items proposed by states at the Second Meeting of the African First Ladies, proposed by Sudan (Doc.CM/2022(LXVII) Add.2), that the Sudanese representative 'emphasised the important role African First Ladies took upon themselves to play in search of peace and political stability in the continent and the need for them to be supported', para. 144. Then 'after the presentation some delegations explained that they were not against such concern by First Ladies which they found commendable, but their fear was that it should not be institutionalised at the level of the OAU', para. 145. The item was withdrawn from the agenda of the Council of Ministers.
[39] Report of the Secretary General on the Twenty-Second Ordinary Session of the OAU Labour and Social Affairs Commission, para. 11.

leadership, conflict resolution and the promotion of lasting peace at all levels'.[40]

Participation in decision making on development

The other area where the OAU/AU has focused on increasing women's participation is in respect of development. The OAU has called on states to ensure that not only are women involved in the development process but that they are central to the development of Africa as a whole.[41] In this respect it has said that 'the role of women in development must be taken seriously into account in development planning and in the disbursement of resources, both as contributors to and beneficiaries of development efforts'.[42] States have been required to promote 'the integration of women in development, as an integral part of their national development programmes',[43] through the adoption of instruments from the ILO and 'other international conventions and recommendations pertaining to the promotion of socio-economic development of women'.[44] States are also called on to set up national mechanisms 'in the form of ministries or other institutions charged with implementing the different strategies on the advancement of women adopted by the supreme bodies of the OAU, if they have not already done so', ratify CEDAW and 'to intensify the training programmes, through the introduction of new techniques and appropriate technology concerning women as well as their functional

---

[40] Beijing Declaration, paras. 13 and 18 respectively. It was therefore essential 'to increase the participation of women in conflict resolution at decision-making levels . . . and integrate a gender perspective in the resolution of armed or other conflicts . . . and ensure that bodies are able to address gender issues properly', UN, Report of the Fourth World Conference on Women, Beijing, 4–15 September 1995, Doc.A/CONF.177/20, at 61.

[41] Introductory Note of the Secretary General to the Seventy-Fourth Ordinary Session of the Council of Ministers, at 95–6. Further, in a 1995 African Plan of Action on Women the AHSG noted Articles 13(3) and 19 of the ACHPR and that 'women's empowerment is the key to development', and reaffirmed 'that there is both economic value and social justice in investing in the improvement of the health of African women', Declaration on the African Plan of Action Concerning the Situation of Women in Africa in the Context of Family Health, AHG/Dec.1(XXXI).

[42] Africa's Priority Programme for Economic Recovery 1986–1990, includes the Lagos Plan of Action and the Final Act of Lagos: Evaluation and Measures for Accelerated Implementation, para. 49.

[43] Resolution on Integration of Women in Development in Africa, CM/Res.714(XXXII), para. 4.

[44] Ibid., paras. 6–7.

literacy; take the necessary steps to prepare the participation of women in the decision-making process on all levels'.[45]

NEPAD pays some attention to women in its provisions. It thus commits itself to 'promoting the role of women in social and economic development by reinforcing their capacity in the domains of education and training; by developing revenue-generating activities through access to credit; and by assuring their participation in the political and economic life of African countries'.[46] In addition, one of its long-term aims is to 'promote the role of women in all activities'.[47] Benchmarks include 'to make progress towards gender equality and empowering women by eliminating gender disparities in the enrolment in primary and secondary education by 2005';[48] and 'to give special attention to the reduction of poverty among women'[49] through establishing 'a gender task team to ensure that the specific issues faced by poor women are addressed in the poverty reduction strategies of the New Partnership for Africa's Development'.[50] In terms of agriculture it aimed to 'improve the productivity of agriculture, with particular attention to small-scale and women farmers; . . . Enhance agricultural credit and financing schemes, and improve access to credit by small-scale and women farmers'.[51] It also intended to 'strengthen and encourage the growth of micro-, small and medium-scale industries through appropriate technical support from service institutions and civil society, and improve access to capital by

---

[45] Resolution on the Integration of Women in Development, CM/Res.1215(L), paras. 1–4. States should

> promote the integration of women in the economic development process by facilitating their autonomy and their access to resources (land, capital) and technology by making economic, social and cultural policy conducive to sustainable development . . . provide women with access to education, health and all the services which would enable them to maximize their capacities to attain full integration in development processes, eliminate all forms of violence against women, increase the participation of women in conflict resolution and protect them in international armed conflicts, mobilise all media resources to promote awareness amongst men and women of their responsibilities with regard to the establishment of equality, development and peace, and develop mechanisms at all levels to monitor the promotion of women and their integration in development.

> Resolution on the Preparation of the Fourth World Conference on Women (Beijing 1995), CM/Res.1550(LX).

See also Resolution on the Fifth African Regional Conference on Women and the African Platform for Action, CM/Res.1602(LXII).
[46] New Partnership for Africa's Development, October 2001, para. 49.
[47] Ibid., para. 67.   [48] Ibid., para. 68.   [49] Ibid., para. 115.   [50] Ibid., para. 116.
[51] Ibid., para. 154.

strengthening microfinancing schemes, with particular attention to women entrepreneurs'.[52]

The Declaration on Democracy, Political and Economic Corporate Governance under NEPAD[53] reaffirms states' commitment to various international documents including CEDAW and recognises the particular impact of conflicts on women, among others.[54] It also reiterated that women had a central role to play in democracy, good governance and economic reconstruction and therefore 'we accept it as a binding obligation to ensure that women have every opportunity to contribute on terms of full equality to political and socio-economic development in all our countries'.[55] It also committed to 'work with renewed vigour to ensure gender equality and ensure their full and effective integration of women in political and socioeconomic development'.[56]

However, the real extent of the OAU/AU's commitment in this regard is questionable when one considers the lack of involvement of women in the actual process of developing NEPAD.[57]

> No formal role has been reserved for women in the emerging implementation framework for NEPAD. The reference to women, albeit, eight times in very general terms in the latest version of the document are mainly linked to NEPAD's limited plans for women. Women should not only be recipients of NEPAD's generosity but active participants in its development and decision making, the gender factor should be [the] cross cutting theme for this and any other such initiative. The structure and language of NEPAD is a reflection of the patriarchal nature of African society that encourages little or no female participation in its evolution.[58]

Further, the lack of real attention to the position of rural women,[59] for example, suggests that any commitment may not be as strong as had been hoped. It is debatable, therefore, whether the OAU/AU in general has

---

[52] Ibid., para. 164.

[53] Declaration on Democracy, Political and Economic Corporate Governance, AHG/235 (XXXVIII), Annex I.

[54] Ibid., paras. 3 and 10.   [55] Ibid., para. 11.   [56] Ibid., para. 22.

[57] On the other hand, however, NEPAD has been criticised from all angles for its top-down approach and the AU is at present trying to rectify this by calling on states to ensure popularisation at the domestic and local levels.

[58] T. Ige, 'NEPAD and African Women: Mechanism for Engagement Input and Ownership', http://www.unesco.org/women/NEPAD/tokunbo.htm.

[59] C. I. Nyamu, 'Rural Women in Kenya and the Legitimacy of Human Rights Discourse and Institutions', in Quashigah and Okafor (eds.), Legitimate Governance in Africa 263–308, at 303.

spent sufficient time on the most vulnerable and neglected women, in particular those living rurally.[60] While the OAU/AU has recognised the link between poverty and rural areas,[61] 'the essential role played by women in African economies and in food production'[62] and the importance of their participation in this respect,[63] the attention to these women has been very limited.[64]

Reasons for focusing on participation

There are several reasons given by the OAU for the need to increase the participation of women and these have been indicated as follows:

[60] As Nyamu notes, 'rural women in sub-Saharan Africa are twice removed from the international human rights system. They are alienated from the system, first, on account of their sex, and second, on account of their poverty and diminished political power,' and further that 'we have to admit the exclusionary nature of rights discourse', Ibid., at 263–4.

[61] 'Reiterating in this context its commitment to working to create conditions in which rural women can develop their full potential and thus foster more equitable balanced and viable development', Resolution on the Summit on the Economic Promotion of Rural Women Presented by Senegal, AHG/Res.208(XXVIII), preamble.

[62] Resolution on the World Conference to Review and Appraise the Achievements of the United Nations Decade for Women: Equality, Development and Peace, CM/Res.1045 (XLIV), preamble. 'In view of the importance accorded to food self-sufficiency and the acknowledged role of women in food production in the continent, the pivotal role of women in this sector must be recognised and encouraged', Africa's Priority Programme for Economic Recovery 1986–1990, includes the Lagos Plan of Action and the Final Act of Lagos: Evaluation and Measures for Accelerated Implementation, para. 49. See also Resolution on the Implementation of Strategies Adopted in the Wake of the Symposium on African Women, Food Self-Sufficiency and the Economic Recovery of Africa, CM/Res.1358(LIV).

[63] Report of the Sixty-Fourth Ordinary Session of the Council of Ministers, CM/Rpt(LXIV), para. 103: with regard to the World Food Security Summit, the Council of Ministers 'further encouraged the participation of women in the World Food Summit in view of the vital role they play in food production in Africa'. See also Resolution on the Fourth World Conference on Women and the Global Platform for Action, CM/Res.1669(LXIV), preamble.

[64] In the Nairobi Forward-Looking Strategies for the Advancement of Women in 1990 it was noted that 'women are no more prominent among those making decisions on conflict than in the past' and that the issue should be monitored, at 3. The Beijing Platform for Action, at para. 15, itself admits that 'popular participation of women in key decision-making as full and equal partners with men . . . has not yet been achieved'. See also, 'United Nations, Women in Power and Decision-Making. Regional Preparatory Meeting on 2000 Review of Implementation of the Beijing Platform for Action, 19–21 January 2000', paper prepared for the Economic Commission for Europe, J. Lovenduski and J. Regulska, IPU/FEM/EUR/2000.2; D. K. Conroy, The Global and Regional Situation of Women Top Civil Servants (Vienna: UNDAW, 1989) EGM/EPPDM/1989/WP.3.

Women have a legitimate demand to participate in the process of growth and development, especially given the fact that women are part of societies that are largely dominated by men and often working on their own agenda separate from the women . . . Increasing women's participation and improving their share in resources, land, employment and income relative to men should, indeed, be considered both necessary to effect dramatic change in their economic and social development and therefore as one way of preventing conflicts. Improving women's role in development has the immediate effect of conflict prevention as it promotes gender equality. Moreover it has also the effect of accelerating the process of agriculture development, increasing the level of national production and the supply of food at the national levels. This process, therefore, has the effect of making development more responsive to human needs. But a more active role of women in development is only possible in a condition of peace, security and stability at the national, sub-regional and regional levels.[65]

This statement and others indicate certain presumptions apparent in the OAU/AU's stance. Firstly, there is a presumption that involving women will promote peace rather than conflict. The OAU has on various occasions linked the role of women in conflict with their role in development more generally, arguing, for example, that 'empowering' women in development processes will assist in preventing conflicts:

Considering that women belong to the most vulnerable group in situations of conflict [it] is logical that women should also be given special focus in all efforts towards conflict prevention, management or resolution. It is often said that one of the basic conditions for the realisation of a self-reliant approach is the self-identification of the development role of women. In this regard, it is clear that the role of women in development should be defined largely in the first place by women themselves, both through their more intensive general social and political involvement and through proper organisation. Similarly, in a situation of conflict women should also be allowed to define their specific role in preventing, managing or resolving a specific conflict situation. Indeed to underestimate the role of women in this process is tantamount to ignoring a very important variable in conflict prevention, management and resolution.[66]

[65] Lessons from a Decade of Conflicts, at 24.
[66] 'The major victims of conflicts in Africa are women and children.' Furthermore, 'Women should also be at the centre of building [a] culture of tolerance and in supporting the democratisation process in Africa. Indeed, the empowering of women is a conflict-reducing factor which must be seen both in political and socio-economic terms,' ibid.

The OAU therefore seems to consider the role of women, in theory at least, as essential to ensuring peace: 'We believe that youth and women's commitment and participation can contribute towards creating an enabling environment which conduces towards a culture of peace and tolerance.'[67] Thus, when it was establishing its Women's Committee on Peace and Development the OAU noted that this was to recognise 'the importance of the role and contribution of women in the promotion of the culture of peace'.[68]

There is also a perception that certain attitudes will result from the inclusion of women; for example, states have been called on to cut military spending and channel this to humanitarian needs and development, with women identifying areas of greatest need.[69] The benefits of collective action are also something that the OAU seems to envisage women providing when it notes that 'because of women's ability to rally together to solve common problems, it is important to build upon their collective action by helping them and their organisations translate their acquired knowledge into action, using their resource base and capitalising on their social networking'.[70] The peaceful resolution of disputes and the attainment of non-violent solutions are also associated with the contribution of women. The OAU has thus called on states to 'revise education curricula to shift emphasis from war to peace, tolerance and non-violence . . . and for women and men in the media to recommit themselves to peace education'.[71]

Various international bodies have stressed the importance of involving women at the international level[72] on the basis that effective debate on

[67] Algiers Declaration, AHG/Decl.1(XXXV).
[68] Decisions Adopted by the Sixty-Sixth Ordinary Session of the Council of Ministers, CM/Dec.330–363(LXVI), Dec.337 on Report of Secretary General on the Implementation of the African Platform of Action: Women, Peace and Development.
[69] Report of the Secretary General on the Twenty-Second Ordinary Session of the OAU Labour and Social Affairs Commission.
[70] Ibid., para. 38.   [71] Ibid., para. 40.
[72] See Commission on the Status of Women, Follow-Up to the Fourth World Conference on Women: Implementation of Strategic Objectives and Action in the Critical Areas of Concern. Women and Conflict, Forty-Second Session, March 1998, CRP.4, which notes that governments should

> promote a gender balance and gender expertise in all relevant international bodies, at all times . . .; mainstream a gender perspective into humanitarian responses to crises and armed conflicts and into post-conflict reconstruction activities; increase the participation of women in peace-keeping, peace-building, pre and post-conflict decision-making, preventing conflict, post-conflict resolution and reconstruction. Further, international and regional intergovernmental institutions should also 'increase . . . women's participation and leadership in decision-making and in preventing conflict . . . encourage . . . of the participation of more female personnel at all levels, in particular at senior or high levels of field missions . . . ; . . . develop and implement innovative strategies

conflict can only be achieved with the involvement of all actors in society and a consideration of their roles: 'Policies developed and decisions made by men alone reflect only part of human experience and potential. The just and effective organization of society demands the inclusion and participation of all its members.'[73] This is not only necessary for effective analysis of conflicts but is also an essential requirement for democracy[74] and for ensuring that the international bodies themselves are not discriminatory in terms of employment.[75]

Yet the OAU/AU's reasons for wanting women to participate seem less to do with this than with a belief that the inclusion of women will add something different, stressing that they will reflect notions such as peace, non-violence and collectivity. Thus, implicit within its approach are certain presumptions about women and what they are and how they act.

to increase the participation of women in peace-keeping operations'. Note also the role of other UN bodies: UN ECOSOC, Peace: Women and the Peace Process, Report of the Secretary-General, Doc.E/CN.6/1993/4, 28 December 1993; UNESCO, Peace: Women in International Decision-Making. Report of the Secretary-General, Doc.E/CN.6/1995/12, 21 February 1995.

[73] CEDAW Committee, General Recommendation No. 23, at para. 13. See also E. Kasmann and M. Korner, Gender-Aware Approaches to Relief and Rehabilitation: Guidelines (Bonn: InterAktion, 1996); R. Mabeza-Chimedza, 'Gender and Environmentally Induced Conflict in Sub-Saharan Africa', in Swiss Peace Foundation, War against Women: The Impact of Violence on Gender Relations: Report of the Sixth Annual Conference, 16–17 September 1994 (Bern: Swiss Peace Foundation, 1995) 27–32; A. Mama, 'The Need for Gender Analysis: A Component on the Prospects for Peace, Recovery and Development in the Horn of Africa', in M. Doornbos et al. (eds.), Beyond Conflict in the Horn (The Hague: Institute of Social Studies, 1992) 72–7; S. McKay, 'Women's Voices in Peace Psychology: A Feminist Agenda', Peace and Conflict: Journal of Peace Psychology 1(1) (1995) 67–84; S. McKay, 'Gendering Peace Psychology', Peace and Conflict: Journal of Peace Psychology 2(2) (1996) 93–107; J. Mutero (ed.), Looking at Peace through Women's Eyes (Nairobi: UNIFEM/AFWIC, 1996).

[74] See in general, CEDAW Committee, General Recommendation No. 23; also R. Jacobson, 'Women's Political Participation: Mozambique's Democratic Transition', Gender and Development 3(3) (1995) 29–35.

[75] See H. Charlesworth, 'Transforming the United Nations Men's Club: Feminist Futures for the United Nations', Transnational Law and Contemporary Problems 4 (1994) 422–54, at 438–49. See also O. R. Holsti and J. N. Rosenau, 'The Foreign Policy Beliefs of Women in Leadership Positions', Journal of Politics 43 (1981) 326–40; M. Leijenaar, How to Create a Gender Balance in Political Decision-Making: A Guide to Implementing Policies for Increasing Participation of Women in Political Decision-Making (Brussels: European Union, 1997); R. Kumari, Women in Decision-Making (London: Vikas Publishing House, 1997); J. C. Beilstein, 'Women in Political Decision-Making. Progress Towards a "Critical Mass"' paper for SADC Regional Parliamentary Seminar, in co-operation with UNDP, Women in Decision-Making: Empowerment for Action, Cape Town, 5 September 1996.

What is also interesting from the OAU/AU's approach is that there seems to be a suggestion inherent in its statements that the approach likely to be adopted by women is an 'African way'. For example: 'The OAU can draw from its pool of Eminent Women who have commutative experience and in-depth knowledge of African socio-economic and cultural conditions, for purposes of helping in the resolution of differences between warring factions, in the African way.'[76] Similarly, in the creation of the Women's Committee on Peace and Development it was argued that, in the light of the 'traditional African way of conciliation', African women, in particular, may have an alternative perspective to offer in relation to dealing with conflicts.[77] This is never fully developed or explained by the OAU/AU, and certainly, the idea that women are synonymous with peace is not one that is applied just to the African situation.[78]

Other rights

It is clearly not sufficient merely to increase the numbers of women in particular situations, and the OAU/AU has tried to adopt a wider approach by looking at structures of society and empowerment issues generally, for example, noting the need to promote the education of girls and their empowerment in terms of employment: 'guided by the Charter of the UN and the UDHR, the African Charter on Human and Peoples; Rights and the African Charter for Popular Participation in Development, 1990; . . . commends the Ugandan government for the initiative in the conference and calls on all states to be involved in it. Calls on states to ensure policy reforms to implement the various OAU and other resolutions 'on the promotion of girls' education, empowerment of women and gender equity', calling further on states to ratify the African Charter on the Rights of the Child, UN Convention on the Child and ILO Convention 138 on Minimum Age of Admission to Employment.[79] It also called on states to adopt the Charter on Fundamental Social Rights and Duties of

[76] Report of the Secretary General on the Twenty-Second Ordinary Session of the OAU Labour and Social Affairs Commission, para. 87. Welch notes the portrayal in the ACHPR of women's rights as linked to traditional and African values, C. E. Welch, 'Human Rights and African Women: A Comparison of Protection under Two Major Treaties', HRQ 15 (1993) 549–74, at 554–5.

[77] Working Paper, at 1.

[78] See F. Banda, 'Global Standards: Local Values', International Journal of Law Policy and Family (2003) 1–27.

[79] Draft Resolutions, CM/Draft/Res.1–30(LXIII) Rev.1; Draft Resolution on the African Conference on the Empowerment of Women through Functional Literacy and the Education

African and Arab Migrant Workers in Europe.[80] The OAU/AU has also consistently called on African states to ratify CEDAW.[81]

It has also spent some time looking at literacy of women and girls in general, convening conferences on the issue, for example.[82] Thus it has recognised the education of the girl child 'as one of the critical issues requiring policy intervention at all levels, and prerequisite for the achievement of such goals', expressly linking this with rights under the ACHPR, CEDAW and being 'guided by' the UN Charter, UDHR and the African Charter on Popular Participation in Development. The Secretary General has also assisted states to draw up 'joint regional gender responsive programmes'.[83]

The health of women has also had some attention.[84] The OAU has required states to adopt legislative and administrative measures to protect the rights of women[85] as well as adopting strategies to consider gender issues.[86] In the process of considering a Convention on Harmful and Traditional Practices,[87] the OAU also 'urged Member States to re-commit themselves to constantly improve women's conditions, eradicate all traditional practices that are detrimental to their health and progress, and to give greater importance to gender balance in all sectors of development, in conformity with the African and Global Platforms for Action'.[88] It would

of the Girl Child, DM/Draft/Res.19(LXIII) Rev.1; Resolution on the Thirteenth Ordinary Session of the OAU Labour Commission, CM/Res.1298(LII).

[80] Report of the Secretary General on the Twenty-First Session of the OAU Labour and Social Affairs Commission Doc.CM/2975(LXVIII), CM/Dec.419(LXVIII), para. 10.

[81] Resolution on the Preparation Meeting of the World Conference to Review and Appraise the Achievements of the UN Decade for Women, CM/Res.991(XLII).

[82] African Conference on the Empowerment of Women through Functional Literacy and the Education of the Girl Child in 1996, Resolution on the African Conference on the Empowerment of Women through Functional Literacy and the Education of the Girl Child, CM/Res.1641(LXIII).

[83] Introductory Note of the Secretary General to the Seventy-Fourth Ordinary Session of the Council of Ministers, at 78.

[84] African Forum on Adolescent Reproductive Health (Doc.CM/1999(LXVI) ADD.3), CM/Res.339(LXVI), paras. (d) and (e).

[85] For example, the Council of Ministers has asked states to 'consider as crime the issue of trafficking in children and women and to this end take appropriate legislative and administrative measures', CM/OAU/AEC/REGL.1(IX).

[86] For example, the Council of Ministers has also called on states to 'adopt strategies to extend social security and protection based on [the] economic, social and political context of each country and respect gender equality in social security issues', ibid.

[87] See below.

[88] Report of the Secretary General on the Twenty-First Session of the OAU Labour and Social Affairs Commission Doc.CM/2975(LXVIII), CM/Dec.419(LXVIII), paras. 4 and 5.

be useful, however, to stress this aspect further, particularly when some courts have applied human rights standards in cases involving women, upholding their internationally recognised rights above customary law.[89] There has been some attention to the impact of HIV/AIDS on women, for example, stressing the need to ensure that information was given about the disease; education on family planning, particularly to women; that a care plan is drawn up; and that ministers of health, labour, education and social affairs should play a role.[90]

In a 1995 African Plan of Action on Women the AHSG stressed the need to 'mobilize political will and commitment to ensure compliance with the UN Convention on the Rights of the Child and the African Charter on the Rights and Welfare of the Child', noting discrimination in education, access to food and health, and suggesting compulsory education or affirmative action policies in schools. It also noted 'labour saving devices to reduce workload of women and their daughters', legislation to prohibit female genital mutilation and promote education, legislation to protect against child labour and child abuse, setting a minimum age for marriage, compulsory and free schooling for girls, sex education, measures to deal with early and unwanted pregnancy and STDs, measures to deal with AIDS including education, measures on maternal mortality, safe motherhood, pregnancy issues, health in general, menopause, mental health, malaria and violence. In relation to the latter, states should adopt laws prohibiting it, ensure the punishment of the perpetrators, carry out campaigns and provide treatment for victims and legal support. The document also noted occupational and environmental hazards, and called for an increase in the number of women in decision-making positions.[91] In the same session in 1995 it adopted the Addis Ababa Declaration on the Dakar African Platform for Action for Women.[92] In this the AHSG noted that it had critically reviewed the Dakar Platform of Action, noting its commitment to the UN Charter, UDHR, ICCPR, ICESCR, CEDAW, ACHPR, Vienna Declaration, UNCRC and African Charter on the Rights and Welfare of the Child, Declaration on the Right to Development, and Declaration on the Elimination of Violence against women. The Assembly was also 'conscious that the total commitment to promote popular

---

[89] For example, see the Tanzanian case of *Ephraim* v. *Pastory*, [1990] LRC 757.

[90] Declaration on AIDS Epidemic in Africa, AHG/Decl.1(XXVIII).

[91] Plan of Action on Women, AHSG, 1995.

[92] Addis Ababa Declaration on the Dakar African Platform for Action for Women, AHG/Dec.2(XXXI).

participation cannot be realised without the total and active participation of women who actually make up over half the population', and 'appreciative of the vital and crucial role of women in an interdependent world'. It also affirmed its conviction that freedoms 'are legitimate aspirations of the African women in their right to be effective partners in all spheres of human endeavour'. The document noted critical areas of concern such as poverty, access to education and training, role in culture and family, health, relationship to the environment, involvement in the peace process, political empowerment, legal and human rights, mainstreaming gender, communication and arts and girl-child.

Protocol on the Rights of Women in Africa

In July 2003 the Assembly of the AU adopted the Protocol on the Rights of Women in Africa.[93] This document was the result of an extended process of drafting which took place mostly under the auspices of the African Commission on Human and Peoples' Rights. The ACHPR was seen as providing inadequate protection for women and its Commission as failing to consider their position.[94] As a result, the involvement of the OAU/AU organs in its development was largely limited to organisation of the experts' meetings and approval of the final document. So detached from the process of creation of this important document was the OAU that a parallel process took place under its Women's Unit to draft a Convention on Harmful and Traditional Practices with the Inter-African Committee on Harmful and Traditional Practices. When the African Commission on Human and Peoples' Rights came to forward its draft Protocol to the OAU for its consideration and adoption in 1999 the document was sent back to the Commission along with a request to incorporate the provisions on harmful and traditional practices. This evidenced the lack of involvement of the OAU organs in its development and the lack of awareness of what each was doing.

The Protocol is an interesting document which goes further than CEDAW in terms of its content. It contains provisions relating to the elimination of harmful practices including the 'prohibition, through legislative measures backed by sanctions, of all forms of female genital

---

[93] Assembly/AU/Dec.14(II), Draft Decision on the Draft Protocol to the African Charter on Human and Peoples' Rights Relating to the Rights of Women.

[94] Article 18(3) of the ACHPR, however, is broad enough to allow for a more dynamic use of the Charter to promote and protect the rights of women.

mutilation';[95] marriage;[96] the right to participation in political and decision-making processes;[97] and protection for women in armed conflicts,[98] as well as rights to education,[99] health,[100] employment,[101] food security[102] and housing.[103] It is innovative and adds to international standards in a number of its provisions, for example, on violence, its attention to armed conflict and female genital mutilation. It is clearly trying to address specific problems facing women in Africa.

Its enforcement is to take place under the ACHPR organs, the Commission and the Court, once established,[104] thus further isolating the role of the AU. It is important that the AU organs go beyond simply the attention they have so far shown to the document – namely, ensuring that states ratify it – to a more meaningful engagement with its provisions.

Mainstreaming

Although the focus of the OAU's approach to the position of women has been on the specific areas of conflict, participation and development, there is some more recent evidence of attempts 'to mainstream women's effective participation and vision within the OAU'.[105] Thus, at its 73rd

---

[95] Protocol on the Rights of Women in Africa, Article 5(b).

[96] Including that 'monogamy is encouraged as the preferred form of marriage and that the rights of women in marriage and family, including in polygamous marital relationships are promoted and protected', ibid., Article 6(c).

[97] Article 9.   [98] Article 11.   [99] Article 12.   [100] Article 14.

[101] Article 13.   [102] Article 15.   [103] Article 16.

[104] Article 26 provides that '(1) States parties shall ensure the implementation of this Protocol at national level, and in their periodic reports submitted in accordance with Article 62 of the African Charter, indicate the legislative and other measures undertaken for the full realisation of the rights herein recognised'. Article 27 states: 'The African Court on Human and Peoples' Rights shall be seized with matters of interpretation arising from the application or implementation of this Protocol.' Article 32 states: 'Pending the establishment of the African Court on Human and Peoples' Rights, the African Commission on Human and Peoples' Rights shall be seized with matters of interpretation arising from the application and implementation of this Protocol.'

[105] Decision on Women and Gender. The OAU has called for the participation of women in decision making at the level of the OAU itself, with the Council of Ministers, for example, urging increased participation of women in its proceedings and the Secretary General noting efforts he had made to recruit women into the Secretariat, Report of the Seventy-Third Ordinary Session of the Council of Ministers, paras. 74–5. There is also a recognition that there should be 'the effective and equitable participation of women in all stages leading to the establishment and functioning of the African Union', Introductory Note of the Secretary General to the Seventy-Fourth Ordinary Session of the Council of Ministers, at 64. In its Decision, the Council of Ministers appealed to states 'to undertake concrete actions . . . to promote the economic empowerment of women by adopting

Ordinary Session the Council of Ministers noted: 'Commenting on the issue of women, gender and development, delegations stressed the need for programmes to focus specifically on women rather than treat the subject as an appendage to other subjects.'[106] In this respect the Council recommended that the OAU's Secretary General 'in co-operation with the Executive Secretary of the ECA and other interested international organisations . . . ensure the convening, on a regular basis, of a Pan-African Conference of Ministers responsible for Women Matters, aimed at co-ordinating and mainstreaming women issues into development on the continent, for a successful implementation of the African and Global platforms for Action'.[107] The OAU has also participated in other conferences aiming to integrate the issue of gender.[108]

Further again, at the 74th Session of the Council of Ministers the Secretary General stated:

> We know that gender equality is not an issue of women's rights but a developmental issue – because Africa will not develop unless and until all its human resource potential is unleashed to serve the Continent and this will not happen unless and until women have assumed their rightful place alongside men. In this regard, we have increasingly realised that the task of correcting gender imbalances and the associated systematic distortions is not an isolated project based task. It is an overarching undertaking that impinges on all sectors. It therefore requires a coherent strategy of mainstreaming into all activities. The notion of mainstreaming does not justify an ad hoc approach to addressing Women's issues. As we embark into the African Union there is a need for a more coherent strategic planning and programming at all levels on issues of gender in our societies.[109]

context-specific micro-credit systems', see Council of Ministers Decision on the Report of the Secretary General on the Implementation of the African Platform of Action: Women, Peace and Development (Doc.CM/2016(LXVI)), CM/Dec.337(LXVI), at para. f. In the same Decision it also called for the Secretary General of the OAU and his equivalent in the ECA to convene regularly a Pan-African Conference of Ministers Responsible for Women Matters, 'aimed at coordinating and mainstreaming women issues into development on the continent'. In addition, the calls for reducing military spending in place of increasing attention to social security have been called for, see Working Paper, at i.

[106] Report of the Seventy-Third Ordinary Session of the Council of Ministers, paras. 74–5.

[107] Decisions Adopted by the Sixty-Sixth Ordinary Session of the Council of Ministers, CM/Dec.330–363(LXVI), Dec.337.

[108] Report of the Secretary General on the Activities of the General Secretariat, CM/2058 (LXVIII), part I.

[109] Introductory Note of the Secretary General to the Seventy-Fourth Ordinary Session of the Council of Ministers, at 95–96. Further, in a 1995 African Plan of Action on Women the AHSG noted Articles 13(3) and 19 of the ACHPR and that 'women's empowerment

Similar attempts at mainstreaming have been made at the level of the UN,[110] and has been seen as an important aim of the feminist movement.[111]

The OAU thus aimed to do this through strengthening the capacity of the Women's Unit within the Secretariat of the OAU 'in terms of . . . resources to enable it to carry out the strategies, programmes and other activities directed towards mainstreaming women's concerns and gender issues into the policies, programmes and activities of the General

is the key to development', and reaffirmed 'that there is both economic value and social justice in investing in the improvement of the health of African women', Declaration on the African Plan of Action Concerning the Situation of Women in Africa in the Context of Family Health, AHG/Dec.1(XXXI).

[110] See A. Gallagher, 'Ending the Marginalization: Strategies for Incorporating Women into the United Nations Human Rights System', *HRQ* 19 (1997) 283–333; in general, 'Symposium. Women's Rights are Human Rights: Selected Articles Dedicated to Women in the International Human Rights Arena', Special edition of *Brooklyn Journal of International Law* 21 (1996); A. Byrnes, 'Women, Feminism and International Human Rights Law – Methodological Myopia, Fundamental Flaws or Meaningful Marginalization? Some Current Issues', *Australian Yearbook of International Law* 12 (1992) 216–23.

[111] In its Resolution Follow-up to the Fourth World Conference on Women and Full Implementation of the Beijing Declaration and the Platform for Action, Resolution A/RES/53/120, 10 February 1999, Fifty-Third Session, para. 3, the General Assembly called on states, the UN and other actors to implement the Platform for Action, particularly 'by promoting an active and visible policy of mainstreaming a gender perspective at all levels'. At para. 7 it 'directs all its committees and bodies, and draws the attention of other bodies of the UN system to the need to mainstream a gender perspective systematically into all areas of their work, in particular in such areas as . . . human rights, humanitarian assistance . . . disarmament, peace and security'. This is also recognised by several instruments, including the UNHCR, Policy on Refugee Women, UN Doc.A/AC.96/754, 20 August 1990, at 1–7; FAO, *Peoples' Participation in Rural Development. The FAO Plan of Action* (Rome: Food and Agriculture Organization, 1992) part 2; Promotion of Equality in Education and Training. Women and Discrimination based on Race and Exploitation of the Prostitution of Others and Traffic in Persons, Report of the World Conference of the United Nations Decade for Women: Equality, Development and Peace, Copenhagen, 14–30 July 1980, UN Doc.A/CONF.94/35; Declaration of Mexico on the Equality of Women and their Contribution to Development and Peace, E/CONF.66/34 (76.IV.1), 1976; Nairobi Forward-Looking Strategies on the Advancement of Women, ECOSOCC Resolution 1990/15, 24 May 1990, Annex, para. 84; Vienna Declaration and Programme of Action, A/CONF.157/23, 12 July 1993, paras. 36–7; Protection of the Rights of Women in Africa, Resolution AFRM/13 of Regional Meeting for Africa of the World Conference on Human Rights, Tunis, 2–6 November 1992; Report of the Regional Meeting for Africa of the World Conference on Human Rights, UN Doc.A/CONF.157/AFRM/14, A/CONF.157/PC/57 of 24 November 1992, 18–19, para. 4 of preamble.

Secretariat and the OAU member states'.[112] There has also been some
attempt to screen existing OAU treaties for gender sensitiveness, the Secretary General noting, for example, in respect of the ACHPR that it 'does
not incorporate the gender component', hoping that the Draft Additional
Protocol on the Rights of Women would rectify this.[113] This has had
some success. For example, the OAU Convention on Terrorism preamble
notes: 'Concerned that the lives of innocent women and children are most
adversely affected by terrorism . . .'.[114]

In July 2002 the Council of Ministers adopted its important Decision
on Mainstreaming Gender and Women's Issues in the African Union.
In this it stressed that the Secretary General should continue to ensure
mainstreaming and 'reaffirms that the gender issue cuts across all the
portfolios of the Commission and welcomes the establishment of a special
unit in the Office of the Chairperson of the Commission to coordinate
all activities and programmes of the Commission relating to gender'.[115]
The results of these deliberations have been that the statutes of all the AU
organs have provisions on gender equality and the need for women to be
nominated and appointed to them,[116] which has already achieved some
success.

Yet this tension between mainstreaming and providing women with
specific attention has been reflected in discussions on how best to deal
with gender issues in the structure of the African Commission of the
AU. During discussion of the Rules of Procedure of the Assembly, for

[112] A Council of Ministers' Decision, for example, noted a previous resolution 'setting out
measures needed to bring about gender equity and create a more egalitarian society',
Decision on the Progress Report of the Secretary General on the Efforts Deployed Towards
Mainstreaming African Women's Concerns into Peace and Sustainable Development
Processes, Doc.CM/2117(LXX)), CM/Dec.469(LXX).

[113] Introductory Note of the Secretary General to the Seventy-Fourth Ordinary Session of
the Council of Ministers, at 79. The OAU Convention on Refugees is not gender specific
and does not recognise the impact on women specifically. It is also argued that the UN
Convention and Protocol are 'especially prejudiced against women from non-Western
countries' as it neglects economic, social and cultural rights and focuses on public aspects
only, and that a well-founded fear of persecution could be said to apply to women in
respect of violation of their economic, social and cultural rights, J. Oloka-Onyango, 'The
Plight of the Larger Half: Human Rights, Gender Violence and the Legal Status of the
Refugee and Internally Displaced Women in Africa', *Denver Journal of International Law*
24 (1996) 349–94, at 350 and 364–5.

[114] OAU Convention on the Prevention and Combating of Terrorism, 21 August 2002,
www.africa-union.org/en/commarchive.asp?Page=2&ID=141.

[115] Decision on Mainstreaming Gender.   [116] See above.

example, 'while some delegations called for the establishment of a portfolio specifically on gender, other delegations were of the opinion that this
would undermine the delicately crafted compromise regarding the number of portfolios'.[117] It was agreed by the meeting that the Unit responsible
for gender be placed in the Office of the AU Commission's Chairperson
and that 'all the Commissioners would be responsible for promoting
gender equality in areas falling within their competence; and secondly, that
the primary and ultimate responsibility for promoting gender equality in
the activities of the African Union would rest with the Chairperson
of the Commission who would take all the necessary structural measures
to that effect'.[118]

It was decided that placing the Directorate under the Chairperson
would ensure that gender issues were mainstreamed across the AU
structures.[119]

In the first AU ministerial meeting on human rights special attention
was also paid to the issue of women's rights. Recommendations adopted by
the meeting included that the Protocol on Women's Rights be adopted and
ratified, the Gender Directorate be strengthened, a Specialised Technical
Committee on Gender be set up and the Draft Protocol be included 'as
an integral part of the African human rights' framework'.[120]

Thus, whilst mainstreaming has helped to ensure that there may have
been increased participation of women in the organs of the AU, beyond
this it is difficult to see what is has achieved in practice.

Case study: the Women's Committee on Peace and Development

Such ideas on the role of women in decision making on development
and conflict have fed directly into the establishment of the Women's
Committee on Peace and Development. This Committee at first seemed

---

[117] Report of the Special Session of the Council of Ministers on the African Union, 29 July
2002, SP/CM/AU/RPT, at paras. 55–7.

[118] Ibid.

[119] Article 12(3) of the Statutes of the Commission states: 'Considering that gender issues
are cross-cutting through all the portfolios of the Commission, a special unit shall be
established in the Office of the Chairperson to coordinate all activities and programmes
of the Commission related to gender issues'.

[120] Report of the Meeting of Experts of the First AU Ministerial Conference on Human Rights
in Africa, Kigali, 5–6 May 2003, EXP/CONF/HRA/RPT.(II), para. 59.

to provide a real opportunity for women to be included in OAU high-level decision making on conflicts. On closer consideration, however, its creation may continue to contribute to the marginalisation of women, and its mandate is so wide as to risk it being little more than a promotional body.

As a result of conferences held in Kampala in 1993[121] and Johannesburg in 1996[122] and of lobbying by organisations in 1997 the OAU created the Women's Committee on Peace and Development,[123] under the auspices of the OAU and the UN's Economic Commission for Africa (ECA).[124] Its stated objectives reflected the themes of the preparatory meetings, namely to 'ensure and enhance the participation of women in the decision-making processes relating to peace and development'[125] and to reflect 'the importance of the role and contribution of women in the promotion of the culture of peace'.[126] Rule 2 of its Terms of Reference emphasises that the Committee is independent but will work closely with the OAU Secretary General and the Executive Secretary of the ECA. The aim of the Committee was to bring 'women into the mainstream of the Continent's efforts aimed at preventing, managing and resolving conflicts while ensuring the full and active participation of women in decision-making for sustainable development'.[127]

The opportunity for women to be directly involved in the decisions of the OAU's Central Organ appeared, on the one hand, to have been realised by the creation and stated aims of the Women's Committee. Several of the features of the Committee bode well for its achieving this objective. Its clear advisory role to the OAU and ECA on gender and peace and

---

[121] Kampala Action Plan. Regional Conference on Women and Peace, 22–25 November 1993, Kampala.

[122] Resolution Calling on the OAU to Formalise the African Women's Committee on Peace, ECA/OAU/AH.EGM/wlfP/96/8, at 30.

[123] Report of the Secretary General on the Implementation of the African Platform of Action: Women, Peace and Development. This was announced at the fortieth anniversary celebrations of the Economic Commission for Africa, April 1998, endorsed by the AHSG, 30th Ordinary Session, in May 1997. It was here in Harare that the Committee adopted its Terms of Reference and Rules of Procedure.

[124] The ECA is a regional arm of the UN, set up in 1958, to deal with cooperation and integration in Africa. An African Centre for Women has been set up under the ECA.

[125] Rule 1, Terms of Reference and Rules of Procedure, OAU/ECA/AF/WM/PD/6(1).

[126] Council of Ministers' Decision.   [127] See Press Release No. 28/98.

the inclusion of six women from senior government positions[128] in its Sixteen members,[129] including five from NGOs[130] and five individuals elected on their personal capacity,[131] suggested that its views were to be taken seriously.

This Committee arguably enabled women to be involved immediately in high-level decision making on conflicts. On the other hand, however, a more than cursory glance at the Committee's Terms of Reference and its activities so far would appear to suggest that this practical involvement in the Central Organ is not actually as central to its work as one may have hoped.

The Committee's Terms of Reference state that it has a number of 'missions', including 'bringing women and a gender perspective into the mainstream of decision-making in preventing, managing and resolving conflicts',[132] as well as a number of 'functions', such as advising the Secretary General of the OAU and Executive Secretary of the ECA, maintaining close relations with the OAU's Conflict Management Centre and the ECA's African Centre for Women and defining strategies for and ensuring the participation of women in all decision making. While these appear to be focused towards integrating women into OAU decision making itself, the Committee has been mandated with a series of other tasks as well. These are: development;[133] capacity building;[134] resource mobilisation;

---

[128] These individuals are nominated by states: Mme Diallo-Da (Burkina Faso), Mrs Kachingwe (Zimbabwe), Mme Aslaoui (Algeria), Dr Gadzama (Nigeria), Dr Kazibwe (Uganda), Mme Missambo (Gabon).

[129] This is the same number of states as sit on the OAU Central Organ and was a deliberate attempt to reflect this. They are appointed by the Secretary General for a period of three years, although there are slight variations in this term of office for the initial appointments. Members of the Committee should represent the five regions of Africa, with four from West Africa and three each from Central Africa, East Africa, southern Africa and the north.

[130] Mrs Nzambazamariya, Pro-Femmes (Rwanda), Hon Lewanika, Federation of African Women for Peace (Zambia), Mrs Diop, FAS (Africa-Wide), Ms Ashenafi, Ethiopian Women's Lawyers' Association (Ethiopia), Ms Elmi, Save Somali Women and Children (Somalia).

[131] Mrs Perry (Liberia), Mrs Mongella (Tanzania), Ms Pashe (South Africa), Mrs Agrebi (Tunisia), Mme Avemeka (Central Africa).

[132] Rule 3(2)a.

[133] '. . . harnessing the continent's human and material resources away from financing conflicts towards development', Rule 3(2)(b).

[134] '. . . preventing conflicts and promoting a culture of peace and tolerance, justice, human rights, peaceful resolution of disputes and reconciliation', Rule 3(2)(c).

advocacy;[135] monitoring;[136] and networking, as well as creating strategies for dealing with the debt burden; lobbying to reduce military expenditure; working with refugee agencies and international bodies; networking; lobbying for gender equality; and mobilising resources for the Women's Unit at the OAU.[137] Furthermore, the Committee has recently identified as its priorities: field missions to areas of conflict; the need to include women in all negotiations; and the need to take concrete action on poverty reduction and humanitarian issues.[138]

This wide mandate could suggest that the OAU is, through the Committee, in fact displaying a holistic approach to conflict which should be encouraged. This relationship between conflict and development will be discussed further below and is something the OAU has also stressed in other areas. As the name of the Committee ('Peace and Development') and the fact that it is a joint venture between the UN and the ECA suggest, the OAU has affirmed that conflict must be viewed within the context of a wide variety of issues including development, economics and equality in general: 'Peace is not only the absence of war, violence and hostilities at the national and international levels, but also the enjoyment of economic and social justice, equality and the entire range of human rights and fundamental freedoms within societies.'[139] As has been argued, 'gender is a particularly well-suited point of reference for the reconstruction of the flawed, monocular scheme precisely because it encompasses vital and often ignored issues . . . It affords a sharp focus . . . Sex inequality is a global reality.'[140]

The Committee's mandate for wider issues and its actual involvement in the Central Organ need not be mutually exclusive, but there is a danger of the former risks marginalising the latter. Indeed, the practice of the

---

[135] '. . . aimed at giving women a voice at all levels in peace and development issues, and centred around creating strategies for effecting gender justice', Rule 3(2)(e).

[136] '. . . keeping track of the performance level of governments, institutions and organizations vis-à-vis including women's concerns, a gender perspective as well as the empowerment of women in all their operations', Rule 3(2)(f).

[137] Rule 4.

[138] See interview with Dr Abdelatif at Headquarters of the OAU, September 1999, on file with author.

[139] Nairobi Forward-Looking Strategies, para. 13. See also B. Byrne, *Gender, Conflict and Development*, vols. I and II, Bridge Report Nos. 34–5 (Brighton: Institute of Development Studies, 1996).

[140] B. E. Hernández-Truyol, 'Women's Rights as Human Rights, Realities and the Role of Culture: A Formula for Reform', *Brooklyn Journal of International Law* 21 (1996) 605–77, at 613.

Committee so far in its short history[141] suggests that its focus has been on the wider aspects of its mandate rather than its role within the Central Organ. For example, the relationship with the PSC is not yet settled and although the Committee is to be funded by the OAU Peace Fund which finances the Conflict Mechanism as a whole,[142] lack of financial resources for the Committee is already perceived to be a problem.[143] The OAU has sponsored several missions by NGOs, which have included some members of the Committee, to monitor elections in Burundi, Liberia, South Africa and Nigeria, and the Committee itself issued a press release in February 1999 on the situation in Sierra Leone; but these do not appear to have been done in conjunction with the Central Organ. The fact that NGOs can attend its sessions[144] and that there is provision for a type of 'complaints mechanism'[145] add to this danger of the Committee becoming more detached from the Central Organ, not integral to its decisions. It seems that only a small part of its activities is directed towards involving women in the OAU's Central Organ itself.

It was promising that despite the secretive and introspective nature of the Central Organ, it did appear to have opened itself up to this Women's Committee. The Committee itself made a presentation at one

---

[141] Meetings have so far been focused on procedural matters such as adopting the Terms of Reference and Work Programme and electing its Board. See Report of the Secretary General on the Efforts Made to Take into Account the Concerns of Women and Gender Issue in the Peace and Sustainable Development Process, CM/2117(LXX). See A. Ngu, 'Inauguration of African Women's Committee on Peace and Development', *Resolving Conflicts: OAUConflict Management Bulletin* 2(6) (July–August 1998) 29–30. The Committee elected to their Bureau: Dr Kazibwe as Chair, Ms Perry as First Vice-Chair, Mrs Mongella as Second Vice-Chair, Mme Diallo-Da as Third Vice-Chair and Mrs Diop as Secretary. It met again in February, July and November 1999, see 'Pan-African Conference for a Culture of Peace', *Resolving Conflicts, OAU Conflict Management Bulletin* (Addis Ababa: Special Edition, May–August, 1999).

[142] $100,000 has been given into its own Special Trust Fund and the Committee is in the process of opening bank accounts in this respect, see Introductory Note to the Report of the Secretary General, Council of Ministers Seventy-First Ordinary Session, Addis Ababa, 6–10 March 2000, paras. 268–9. The Committee is financially autonomous.

[143] Although some donations have been received, including from non-African sources, see Interview with Mrs Teriba at Headquarters of the OAU, September 1999, on file with author. See also African Women's Committee on Peace and Development Project Document, February 2000, part II: 'AWCPD's Budget for Three Years'.

[144] Committee's Terms of Reference, Rule 8, although the Committee will usually meet in private, Rule 19.

[145] Ibid., Rule 41, enables a member of the Committee or NGO 'which has relations of co-operation with the Committee or observer status with the Committee' to approach the Committee if the complainant has 'good reason to believe that a situation justifying intervention by the Committee exists or is about to occur'.

of the Organ's meetings and organised or contributed to a number of meetings.[146] The Committee has also gone on peace missions with the OAU[147] and developed some databases[148] and programmes.[149]

During the existence of the OAU this Committee could have played a key role in enhancing and coordinating the position of women in the Organization. However, it seemed that it was marginalised and did not play an active or central role. Now with the establishment of the AU and its increasing attention to a gender perspective in the statutes and remits of its organs, the existence of this Committee and its place in the new Union are open to question.

Under the AU it is intended that the Committee will be revamped under the Gender Directorate, thus bringing it in from the periphery of the AU structures at the ECA. There has, however, been no clear indication of how this will be achieved as yet.

Conclusion

The efforts that the OAU/AU has made with regard to highlighting the position of women should not be dismissed lightly, and have had some success in ensuring that women actually sit on their various organs. There are still, however, some ongoing concerns. These were highlighted in

---

[146] The AWCPD organised, with the African Leadership Forum, a Third Africa Women's Forum, Tunis, 22–24 January 2001, to review the role of women in conflict management and to develop a strategy for their role in peace building. It also held a Consultative Conference on the Unification of Africa, Tripoli, 19–22 April 2001. The Secretariat of the Committee has made inputs into the African Development Forum (III) (ADF III) organised in March 2002 by UNECA, e-mail from Elise Attafuah, AWCPD Secretariat, 4 July 2002.

[147] E-mail from Elise Attafuah, AWCPD Secretariat, 4 July 2002.

[148] The Committee has developed some databases: African and non-African women's organisations working for peace in Africa; and one on major conflicts in Africa, 'to highlight best practices and specific efforts by women in peacemaking and peace building at local, regional, national and international levels. The aim is to draw on these experiences to establish the proposition that women have and can constructively influence peace processes when they are given greater decision-making roles at all levels of peace processes,' 'Most Recent Activities', document attached to e-mail from Elise Attafuah, AWCPD Secretariat, 4 July 2002.

[149] It also developed some programmes on capacity building, 'in recognition of the Beijing and Dakar Platforms of Action and United Nations Resolution 1325 and the Nairobi Forward Looking Strategies for the Advancement of Women which call for the participation of women in decision-making and peace processes; the protection of women; and gender mainstreaming into peace initiatives and implementation mechanisms, among other things', 'ibid.

particular by a meeting in Maputo prior to the AU Summit in July 2003 of women's organisations and others, including UNIFEM and SADC, which resulted in the adoption of the Maputo Declaration on Gender Mainstreaming and the Effective Participation of Women in the African Union. The Declaration noted various concerns including that the mainstreaming process needed to be speeded up; there was no Specialised Technical Committee on Gender; the Directorate on Women had very few resources; there was no mechanism for women's organisations and organs of the AU to cooperate; the provision in the Pan-African Parliament Protocol for one representative in five to be a woman was not enough; and there were insufficient women ambassadors and others accredited to the AU. In addition not enough was being done to tackle maternal mortality; harmful and discriminatory practices increased risk of death during pregnancy and birth, and increased the risk of HIV/AIDS among women; some places in Africa had had to have GM food dumped on them; there were many difficulties facing women in agriculture, and women often lacked access to land; and war and conflict impacted on women.

Participants stressed the need to create an African Union Gender Policy Declaration and to clarify the status of the African Women's Committee on Peace and Development and recommended setting up a mechanism for high-level discussion between organisations and organs of the AU.

Overall it is clear that the OAU/AU has taken various initiatives. These have centred around ensuring participation of women at the international and national level, particularly in political structures, and in developing, through its African Commission on Human and Peoples' Rights, the Protocol to the African Charter on the Rights of Women in Africa. The attention to the former by the Addis Ababa organs could suggest that it sees participation as a panacea for gender equality. This is based on various presumptions of the role of women and what their participation can bring to society. The OAU/AU has so far failed to take a wider view on the position of women beyond this. The development of the Protocol offers hope for a more comprehensive approach to the situation of women and their rights in the continent. However, this has been developed largely on the periphery of the OAU/AU structures and its enforcement is seen as falling within the Banjul organs, not those in Addis Ababa. In the process, therefore, rather than actually contributing to the mainstreaming of women's rights and concerns into the AU, the Protocol could be seen as further ghettoising them.

One body needs to take responsibility to ensure that the AU organs will take the Protocol on board in their work.

6

Children's rights in the OAU/AU

On paper, it seems that considerable attention has been paid to the position of children and protection of their rights by the OAU/AU, culminating in the adoption and eventually coming into force of its own African Charter on the Rights and Welfare of the Child (ACRWC). This Charter has been said to have been an attempt to instil some element of 'African' characteristics into the international standards created by the UN Convention on the Rights of the Child (UNCRC).[1] However, whilst many OAU states ratified the UNCRC, an insufficient number of ratifications delayed the coming into force of the OAU Charter. Even when this had been achieved, the appointment of its Committee was delayed. This suggests that the commitment to such African values has not been accompanied by adequate enforcement. In addition, standards and values formulated outside the Charter framework by the OAU/AU organs do not appear to have been consolidated into a coherent plan for dealing with the rights of the child in Africa. Further, the overall approach of the OAU/AU has been criticised for focusing more on the situation of children and their position in the context of development, rather than their rights.

Although the OAU organs paid some attention to children, their rights remained neglected for many years as they were generally not seen to be within the scope of the African Commission on Human and Peoples' Rights in Banjul while it awaited the adoption of the additional Charter on the Child and the appointment of its Committee. Even with the advent of these new structures the difficulty of funding this new Committee and the time it is likely to take to ensure full state ratification, and development of the experience of the Committee, raises questions about the desirability of creating new organs on human rights and the OAU's real commitment to them. There is some hope that the AU organs created under the

---

[1] See B. Thompson, 'Africa's Charter on Children's Rights: A Normative Break with Cultural Traditionalism', *ICLQ* 41 (1992) 432–45.

Constitutive Act, in particular the ACJ, the PSC and ECOSOCC, will have some remit over children.

Influences on the OAU with respect to the rights of the child

Although the OAU devoted considerable attention to urging states to ratify the ACRWC[2] or the UNCRC, the decision to adopt the former document and give attention to children comes from a variety of factors.

International conferences and other international initiatives

It is clear that the decision to look at the position of children was prompted in part by international conferences on the subject in which the OAU was involved. Various conferences on children's rights were often followed, therefore, by OAU resolutions on issues that were raised during the debates.[3]

Thus, in 1979 for the first time the Council of Ministers referred to children, following on from the UN Declaration on the International Year of the Child adopted by the UN General Assembly[4] and recommended for adoption by the AHSG a Declaration on the Rights and Welfare of the African Child, and for the OAU to ensure full implementation of its provisions.[5] The work of the ILO also had an impact on the decision of the OAU organs to look at the issue of children. The OAU reminded states of their obligations under ILO instruments and called on them to ratify those, for example, on child labour.[6] This helped to develop OAU standards on this area and child employment in general.[7] The OAU/AU was also involved in developing and supporting the African Common Position on Children.[8]

---

[2] Status of OAU Treaties, Doc.CM/2095(LXIX), CM/Dec.443(LXIX): The OAU urges states to ratify all treaties, with special attention to the ACRWC and Protocol on the African Court of Human and Peoples' Rights.

[3] See, for example, Resolution on the World Summit on Children, AHG/Res.192(XXVI).

[4] UN General Assembly Resolution A/31/169. See also Resolution on the International Conference on Assistance to African Children, CM/Res.1408(LVI), preamble.

[5] Resolution on the International Year of the Child, CM/Res.737(XXXIII) Rev.1; Declaration on the Rights and Welfare of the African Child, AHG/ST.4(XVI) Rev.1.

[6] Decision on the Report of the Secretary General on the Twenty-Fifth Ordinary Session of the OAU Labour and Social Affairs Commission/Ministerial Conference on Employment and Poverty Reduction in Africa, Doc. CM/2262(LXXVI), CM/Dec.671, paras. 4 and 5.

[7] See further below.

[8] This resulted from the Pan-African Forum on the Future of Children in Cairo, 28–31 May 2001, Decision on the Pan-African Forum on the Future of Children, CM/Dec.584(LXXIV). See Child Trafficking: Africa–Europe Programme. Joint Plan of Action to Combat

Increase in conflicts

The OAU's decision to look at children's rights also came about with increased recognition of the impact of conflict situations on the continent. In this regard, it has adopted a number of resolutions relating to children and conflict[9] and in its consideration of conflicts in various African states noted the vulnerability of children. As a consequence of this, it has also considered the position of children as refugees.[10]

Observer status

The OAU has also been clearly influenced by the activities of NGOs working in this area. Although it only granted observer status to one such organisation, the African Network for the Prevention and Protection Against Child Abuse and Neglect (ANPPCAN) in 1990,[11] the impact of NGOs on its attention to children's issues should not be underestimated. As the drafting of the Charter on the Rights and Welfare of the Child indicated, and the subsequent work of its Committee so far, NGOs have prompted the OAU/AU organs to take action, facilitated progress and have maintained the pressure on them to implement their ideas.

The African Charter on the Rights and Welfare of the Child

In a 1979 AHSG Declaration on the Rights and Welfare of the Child,[12] the OAU noted the need to consider children's rights. This was precipitated further with the 1990 UN conference.[13] While developments were taking

Trafficking in Human Beings, Especially Women and Children, drafted September 2002, adopted November 2002, Burkina Faso and endorsed April 2003; see also African Common Position on Child Labour.

[9] For example, Resolution on Peace for Children: Reducing the Effects of Armed Conflicts on Children and Women in Africa, CM/Res.1292(LII).

[10] Decision on the Report of the Secretary General on the Situation of Refugees, Returnees and Displaced Persons, Doc. CM/2256 (LXXVI), CM/Dec.667, paras. 1 and 2. The Council of Ministers, for example, has noted 'the serious violations of human rights of which refugee populations particularly children are victims', and further 'denounces and condemns sexual violence and exploitation of refugee children and demands that the perpetrators of such acts be brought to justice and punished'. See also ICRC, Continental Conference on Children in Situations of Armed Conflict, Addis Ababa, 1997.

[11] Resolution on Granting OAU Observer Status to the African Network for the Prevention and Protection Against Child Abuse and Neglect (ANPPCAN), CM/Res.1293(LII).

[12] Sixteenth session, Monrovia.

[13] A. Lloyd, 'Regional Developments on the Rights and Welfare of Children in Africa: A General Report on the African Charter on the Rights and Welfare of the Child and the African Committee of Experts', http://www.uwe.ac.uk/law/research/acr/report.htm.

place at the level of the UN to draft a treaty on the rights of the child, lawyers in Africa were considering ways of adapting these proposals to the African context as a way of promoting the UN Convention on the continent. A conference was organised by the NGO ANPPCAN in collaboration with UNICEF to look at children in situations of armed conflict in Africa in 1987, during which the draft UN Convention was discussed.[14] Given the lack of participation of African states in the UN process, a further meeting was organised in May 1988 and a number of issues were considered which were deemed to be particularly relevant to the African context. These included children and apartheid; living conditions; female genital mutilation and unequal treatment of the girl child; lack of participation of children in local communities; refugee children; responsibilities of the child; the children of imprisoned mothers; adoption and fostering by relatives; discrimination; and the definition of the child.[15] A Committee of Experts was appointed between the OAU and ANPPCAN to draft a document for an African Charter on the Rights and Welfare of the Child. This draft was then submitted to the OAU which adopted it unanimously, without real debate.[16] The consequences of this are that states did not debate its provisions in full; indeed, many states on viewing the document seem to have seen little difference (without analysing it in depth) between the African instrument and the UNCRC. They thus may well have seen no reason to adopt the African instrument, or even been aware of its existence. This may help to explain the difference in ratification success of both, despite the ACRWC being held up as the African interpretation on the issue. It took nine years before it came into force,[17] after obtaining the fifteen states' ratifications necessary to do so.[18]

As Lloyd notes, 'the African Children's Charter prides itself on its African perspective on rights, yet was inspired by the trends evident in the UN system. It was intended to be a complementary mechanism to that of the UN in order to enhance the enjoyment of the rights of children in Africa.'[19] Yet while it seemed to have been primarily a promotional vehicle

---

[14] Ibid.   [15] Information from Amanda Lloyd, December 2003.
[16] Twenty-Sixth Session AHSG, OAU Doc. CAB/LEG/24.9/49 (1990).
[17] A. Lloyd, 'Evolution of the African Charter on the Rights and Welfare of the Child and the African Committee of Experts. Raising the Gauntlet', *International Journal of Children's Rights* 10 (2002) 179–98, at 181.
[18] ACRWC, Article 47(3).
[19] Lloyd, 'Evolution of the African Charter', at 182. See also Draft Resolution on the Signature and Ratification of the African Charter on the Rights and Welfare of the Child, CM/Draft/Res.13(LXIII) Rev.1.

for the UNCRC in Africa, the Charter did attempt to add an 'African' perspective to be defined or accepted.[20]

A child is defined in the Charter as anyone under the age of eighteen.[21] The Charter adopts a similar, but slightly higher, standard than that found elsewhere, in requiring that 'in all actions concerning the child undertaken by any person or authority the best interests of the child shall be the primary consideration'.[22] The Charter is also very clear and with fewer limitations than can be found elsewhere on the age issue.[23] However, it has been noted that this does not seem to fit with African culture and tradition, where childhood is determined not on the basis of years but other factors.[24]

The ACRWC lays out rights of the child including the right to life, which is broader than that provided for under the UNCRC;[25] to a name and nationality;[26] freedom of expression, association and thought; conscience and religion;[27] to privacy;[28] to education;[29] rights relating to leisure, recreation and cultural activities;[30] health;[31] issues on child labour;[32] protection against abuse and torture;[33] provisions on juvenile justice;[34] and maintenance.[35] There are provisions on the enjoyment of parental care and protection;[36] protection against harmful social and cultural practices;[37] rights during times of armed conflict which provide greater protection than the UNCRC;[38] and rights of refugees.[39] Other rights relate to adoption and separation from parents;[40] protection against apartheid and discrimination;[41] sexual exploitation; drug abuse; trafficking; and abduction.[42] There are specific provisions in the Charter for 'handicapped children'[43] and those of imprisoned mothers.[44] Overall, therefore,

---

[20] 'Emphasis must clearly be placed on the treaties adopted under the aegis of the OAU, which, by definition, are Africa-specific', Report of the Secretary General on the Status of OAU Treaties, CM/2122(LXX).

[21] ACRWC, Article 2.

[22] Ibid., Article 4. The UNCRC requires only the best interests to be 'a consideration', Lloyd, 'Evolution of the African Charter', at 183.

[23] M. Gose, 'The African Charter on the Rights and Welfare of the Child: An Assessment of the Legal Value of its Substantive Provisions by Means of a Direct Comparison to the Convention on the Rights of the Child', Community Law Centre (2002), http://www.communitylawcentre.org.za/children/publications/african_charter.pdf, at 27.

[24] Ibid., at 27–8.   [25] Article 5; see also Lloyd, 'Evolution of the African Charter'.

[26] Article 6.   [27] Articles 7–9.   [28] Article 10.   [29] Article 11.   [30] Article 12.

[31] Article 14.   [32] Article 15.   [33] Article 16.   [34] Article 17.   [35] Article 18(3).

[36] Article 19.   [37] Article 21.   [38] Article 22.   [39] Article 23.

[40] Articles 24 and 25.   [41] Article 26.   [42] Articles 27–9.   [43] Article 13.

[44] Article 30.

the Charter in some important respects does build upon international standards. [45]

Enforcement of the Charter

The Charter establishes an eleven-member Committee to 'promote and protect the rights and welfare of the child'.[46] The members of the Committee are supposed to be independent and are appointed by the AHSG on the nomination of states.[47] They sit for five years.[48] The first members were appointed in July 2001.[49] Four individuals were appointed to fill vacated places at the July 2003 Summit.[50] Unlike the African Commission on Human and Peoples' Rights, the issue of independence and incompatibility of the members of the Committee appears to have been taken seriously by the AU, due in part to the fact that the provisions in the Rules of Procedure were much clearer on this point.[51] Two members of the Committee were thus requested by the AU to leave when they changed positions in their home states which rendered their position as Committee members incompatible.[52]

---

[45] See Amnesty International, *The African Charter on the Rights and Welfare of the Child,* AI Index: IOR 63/006/1998, 1 December 1998.

[46] Article 32(1).

[47] Articles 33–6. See also Rules of Procedure of the African Committee on the Rights and Welfare of the Child, Article 11(2).

[48] Although this differs slightly in the first round, Article 37.

[49] Mr Rodolphe Soh – Cameroon (four-year term), Mr Dirus Diale Dore – Guinea (two-year term), Hon. Lady Justice Joyce Aluoch – Kenya (four-year term), Mr Karabo Karabo Mohau – Lesotho (two-year term), Mr Straton Nsanzabaganwa – Rwanda (four-year term), Mrs Dior Fall Sow – Senegal (five-year term), Prof. Lullu Tshiwula – South Africa (four-year term), Mrs Nanitom Motoyam – Chad (four year term), Mrs Suzanne Aho – Togo (two-year term), Dr Rebecca M. Nyonyintono – Uganda (two-year term) and Mr Louis Pierre Robert Ahnee – Mauritius (four-year term).

[50] Assembly AU/Dec.19(II), Draft Decision on Appointment of Members of the African Committee of Experts on the Rights and Welfare of the Child – Doc./EX/CL/58(III). They were Prof. Peter Onyekwere Ebigbo (Nigeria), Dr Asseffa Bequele (Ethiopia), Mr Jean Baptiste Zougrana (Burkina Faso) and Ms Nakpa Polo (Togo). There are still two positions vacant on the Committee, and Chad and Senegal must nominate individuals to finish the terms left by the previous members.

[51] The Charter requires that 'the Committee shall consist of 11 members of high moral standing, integrity, impartiality and competence in matters of the rights and welfare of the child. The members of the Committee shall serve in their personal capacity,' Articles 33(1) and (2).

[52] Mrs Nanitom Motoyam from Chad, when she started work for UNICEF; Mrs Dior Fall Sow of Senegal, when she became a member of the International Criminal Tribunal for Rwanda. Mrs Suzanne Aho from Togo resigned when she was appointed to a ministerial

Although the Chair of the AU Commission is to appoint staff to the Committee[53] and the AU is to be its primary source of funding, it has already faced financial and logistical constraints in its short history, causing it to obtain the help of a representative from UNICEF to apply for funding from outside the AU.[54] The OAU/AU has so far only provided temporary staff to the Committee and no full-time secretary has yet been appointed,[55] despite calls for adequate resources to be provided to the Committee.[56] To support implementation of the Charter, it has been suggested, in addition, that national commissions for child protection be set up.[57]

It is now clear that the Committee has been officially incorporated under the AU.[58] The same procedures as occurred under the OAU appear to have been followed under the AU, although the Charter has not been amended to reflect the new organs. The Committee sits under the Social Affairs Directorate and the relationship between its Director, Grace Kalimugogo, and the Chair of the Committee appears to be positive and AU staff have attended meetings of the Committee. The Committee reports to the Assembly and Executive Council on an annual basis and can submit other reports to them.[59] The Chair of the AU

position, although her term was due to expire shortly anyway. The Rules of Procedure rather disappointingly require that the state of which the resigned member is a national should appoint another person in their place, Article 14(4) Rules of Procedure of the African Committee on the Rights and Welfare of the Child.

[53] Rules of Procedure of the African Committee on the Rights and Welfare of the Child, Article 22.

[54] Lloyd, 'Regional Developments'.

[55] Rules of Procedure of the African Committee on the Rights and Welfare of the Child, Article 22. Under the OAU it was the Secretary General who appointed the Secretary, ACRWC, Article 40; Decision on the Report of the African Committee on the Rights and Welfare of the Child, AHG/Dec.172(XXXVIII).

[56] Kigali Declaration, MIN/CONF/HRA/Decl.1(I), para. 18. The NGO Save the Children has offered support to establish a website and the African Child Forum has also offered to assist in research activities, although it is not clear whether these offers have been taken up.

[57] Re OAU Civil Society Conference recommendations, see Introductory Note of the Secretary General to the Seventy-Fourth. Ordinary Session of the Council of Ministers, at 64; Report of the Meeting of Experts of the First AU Ministerial Conference on Human Rights in Africa, Kigali, 5–6 May 2003, EXP/CONF/HRA/RPT.(II), para. 30.

[58] 'The African Commission on Human and Peoples' Rights and the African Committee of Experts on Rights and Welfare of the Child shall henceforth operate within the framework of the African Union', Decision on the Interim Period, ASS/AU/Dec.1(I), para. xi.

[59] Rules of Procedure of the African Committee on the Rights and Welfare of the Child, Article 64.

Commission has a duty to inform the Committee of any matters of interest to it.[60]

The Committee has various functions under Article 41 of the ACRWC, namely:

> To promote and protect the rights enshrined in this Charter and in particular to:
>
> (i) collect and document information, commission inter-disciplinary assessment of situations on African problems in the fields of the rights and welfare of the child, organize meetings, encourage national and local institutions concerned with the rights and welfare of the child, and where necessary give its views and make recommendations to Governments;
>
> (ii) formulate and lay down principles and rules aimed at protecting the rights and welfare of children in Africa;
>
> (iii) cooperate with other African, international and regional Institutions and organizations concerned with the promotion and protection of the rights and welfare of the child.
>
> (b) To monitor the implementation and ensure protection of the rights enshrined in this Charter.
>
> (c) To interpret the provisions of the present Charter at the request of a State Party, an Institution of the Organization of African Unity or any other person or Institution recognized by the Organization of African Unity, or any State Party.
>
> (d) Perform such other task as may be entrusted to it by the Assembly of Heads of State and Government, Secretary-General of the OAU and any other organs of the OAU or the United Nations.

In its work the Committee can draw inspiration from other international and regional documents.[61]

Article 43(1) of the ACRWC requires that states submit reports to the Committee, through the Chairperson of the AU, on 'measures they have adopted which give effect to the provisions of this Children's Charter and on the progress made in the enjoyment of these rights' within two years of entry into force and then every three years. The Guidelines for Initial Reports of State Parties of the Committee note that the Committee sees this process as a way of 'conducting a comprehensive review of the various measures undertaken to harmonise national law and policy with the Children's Charter and to monitor progress', as well as encouraging

[60] Ibid., Article 25.   [61] Ibid., Article 46.

and facilitating 'popular participation and public scrutiny of government polices, private sector policies and generally the practices of all the sectors of society towards children'. It is also 'an ongoing reaffirmation by states parties of their commitment to respect and ensure observance of the rights' in the Charter and 'the essential vehicle for the establishment of a meaningful dialogue between the states parties and the African Committee'.[62] Reports should include copies of legislation and texts, statistics and other material, but there will be no translation or reproduction for general distribution.[63] The Guidelines on reporting are separated into a number of areas including general measures; definition of the child; general principles; civil rights and freedoms; family environment and alternative care; health and welfare; education, leisure and cultural activities; special protection measures; responsibilities of the child; and specific provisions for the reporting process.[64] States that have already submitted reports to the UN Committee on the Rights of the Child with regard to their obligations under the UN Convention 'may use elements of that report for the report that it submits to the [African] Committee as required by the [African] Children's Charter. The report shall, in particular, highlight the areas of rights that are specific to the children's Charter.'[65] Further, 'the report must specify the action taken by the state party in response to any recommendations made to it by the Committee and/or the UN Committee on the Rights of the Child'.[66]

This may avoid the possibility of states failing to submit reports in adequate time. No states so far have submitted their reports to the Committee. The Committee must carefully consider the procedure in advance and it is to be hoped that a timetable for submission proposed by an NGO, the Institute for Human Rights and Development in Africa, will be used and followed up by the Committee.

The Committee also has the power to receive communications from individuals, NGOs, states or other organisations alleging violations of the provisions of the Charter.[67] There is a wide power of investigation on 'any matter falling within the ambit' of the Charter.[68] The Committee on the Rights of the Child, however, has yet to consider its procedure. It is essential in this regard that a clear working relationship is established with

---

[62] Guidelines for Initial Reports of State Parties of the Committee, on file with author, paras. 3 and 4.

[63] It is not clear if this relates to the reports themselves or the additional documentation, Guidelines for Initial Reports of State Parties of the Committee, para. 6.

[64] Ibid.   [65] Ibid., Guideline 24.   [66] Ibid., Guideline 25.   [67] ACRWC, Article 44.

[68] Ibid., Article 45(1).

the African Commission on Human and Peoples' Rights with respect to its communication procedure. Although the latter has not received any cases dealing specifically with the rights of the child, some of its decisions have touched upon violations committed against children.[69]

The Committee also has the power to issue general comments and to undertake investigations and studies.[70] It reports to the Assembly every two years, with the report being published after the Assembly has considered it.[71]

The Committee adopts a similar approach to the African Commission on Human and Peoples' Rights on many aspects of its functioning and mandate; indeed, the latter served as a guide for the Committee when it was formulating its Rules of Procedure.[72] Sessions of the Committee should be held twice a year for two weeks with the power to hold extraordinary sessions if necessary, at the Headquarters of the AU, although they can be held elsewhere and indeed have been.[73]

The Committee has so far held only three meetings, the first taking place from 29 April to 3 May 2002 in Addis Ababa, Lloyd noting that this was delayed due to lack of nominations to the Committee by states, other work of the OAU and 'documentation and translation problems'.[74] At the meeting the officers were elected[75] and the Rules of Procedure were considered. The meeting also identified as priorities a number of issues including armed conflicts, trafficking, child labour, sexual abuse, orphans and HIV/AIDS, the right to education and the creation of a national plan for children,[76] although it resolved initially to concentrate on increasing the number of ratifications to the Charter.[77] The Committee also decided to use the Day of the African Child, 16 June, to raise awareness on the

---

[69] For example, Communication No. 207/97, *Africa Legal Aid* v. *The Gambia*, Fourteenth Annual Activity Report of the African Commission on Human and Peoples' Rights, 2000–2001, AHG/222(XXXVI), Addendum.

[70] Rules of Procedure of the African Committee on the Rights and Welfare of the Child, Articles 73, 74 and 77.

[71] Ibid., Article 45(2) and (3). The first report of the Committee was submitted in Durban at the Summit in July 2002 and discussed by the Assembly, AHG/Dec 172(XXXVIII).

[72] Rules of Procedure of the African Committee. See Lloyd, 'Regional Developments'.

[73] Articles 2, 3 and 4. The second session was held in Nairobi, for example.

[74] Lloyd, 'Regional Developments'. See also A. Lloyd, 'Recent Developments: The First Meeting of the African Committee of Experts on the Rights and Welfare of the Child', *African Human Rights Law Journal* 2(2) (2002) 13–22.

[75] The Chair of the Committee is Lady Justice Joyce Aluoch and the Deputy Chair is Mr Rodolphe Soh

[76] Lloyd, 'Regional Developments'.   [77] Ibid.

Charter. The Committee agreed to do several things including contacting relevant ministries, issuing press statements and addressing AU officials and participating in events.[78]

The second meeting of the Committee took place from 17 to 21 February 2003 in Nairobi, again having been postponed from November the previous year due to other commitments of the members and other meetings of the OAU.[79] The meeting considered the Rules of Procedure and also the guidelines for state reporting, as well as reporting on the activities that had taken place in the inter-sessional period.[80] The Committee also considered its priorities for the 2003–4 period and it was agreed that a meeting be held with interested partners prior to the next session of the Committee.[81] Issues were distributed among different members of the Committee. It was agreed that the Chairperson of the Committee would write to states reminding them of their obligations on reporting under the Charter and with the guidelines for their information.[82] The third meeting of the Committee took place in November 2003 and discussed, among other matters, the impact of HIV/AIDS on children, armed conflict and the eradication of polio.[83]

NGOs can attend the Committee's meetings, although as yet there are no formal requirements for applying for observer status.[84] At the most recent meeting of the Committee it stressed the need to be open and transparent and that it would look to the African Commission on Human and Peoples' Rights and its practice to assist in formulating guidelines. A handful of NGOs have so far attended the meetings, including Amnesty International, Save the Children, UNICEF, the International Red Cross and the Institute for Human Rights and Development in Africa.

Themes from the work of the OAU/AU

There is little apparent awareness of various initiatives undertaken by the OAU organs outside the debate around the Charter on the Rights of the Child. However, over the years they have adopted a number of

---

[78] Ibid.

[79] Ibid. See also A. Lloyd, 'Recent Developments: The Second Ordinary Session of the African Committee of Experts', *African Human Rights Law Journal* 3(2) (2003) 31–48.

[80] Lloyd, 'Regional Developments'.   [81] Ibid.   [82] Ibid.

[83] Press Release No.094/2003, African Committee on Rights and Welfare of the Child.

[84] The Charter simply requires that the Committee 'cooperate with other African, international and regional Institutions and organizations concerned with the promotion and protection of the rights and welfare of the child', Article 42(a)(iii).

Resolutions and Decisions in this area which are useful and would be worth building upon by the Committee on the Rights of the Child. Some of these have appeared already to feed into the Committee's choice of priorities so far. They clearly indicate a focus on development and health matters.[85]

Link with development

The OAU/AU clearly sees the issue of children from the perspective of development.[86] While this is a positive approach, enabling a holistic attitude to be taken to children, in practice the attention has been more on their welfare and their situation, rather than their rights per se. Thus, the focus is often on the development of the continent, rather than the rights of child: 'mindful of the fact that in order to ensure the future development of the continent, African countries should provide the necessary resources to promote equitable growth of the African child'.[87] Recommendations for measures to be taken by states are made with the aim of ensuring that children can participate and contribute to development of the African continent: 'convinced of the need to ensure the welfare of mothers and children through effective and less expensive actions, with long lasting effects, so as to guarantee their active participation in the economic development efforts of African States'.[88] Conversely, the OAU/AU has recognised the impact of lack of development or negative development policies on the rights of the child:

> cognizant of the fact that food health constitutes a vital factor in African development, concerned about the negative impact of structural adjustment programmes on vulnerable groups such as women and children . . .
> fully aware of the need to strengthen child survival, protection and development interventions including immunization and safe motherhood

[85] See also opening speech of AU Commissioner for Social Affairs to the 3rd meeting of the African Committee on the Rights and Welfare of the Child, on file with the author.

[86] Resolution on the World Summit on Children.

[87] Resolution on Universal Immunization in Africa, AHG/Res.163(XXIII). Further, 'aware that well being, in general and good health in particular constitute vital factors in the socio economic development of Africa; convinced of the need to protect children who are the future of the continent', Resolution on the World Summit on Children.

[88] Resolution on the Programme of Essential Medicines for Children and their Mothers, CM/Res.1164(XLVIII). See also Report of the Secretary General on Activities in the Field of Youth in Africa, OAU/CONF/YOUTH/Doc.2(I). The establishment of the Pan-African Youth Movement had as its main objective 'to initiate youth to participate fully in the development of their continent as future responsible citizens'.

programmes for the sake of both mothers and their children in Africa, aware
of the interaction between child survival, protection and development and
formal as well as informal education and the role of functional literacy in
development.[89]

There has been no real discussion on the relationship between NEPAD
and the ACRWC, other than its inclusion on the agenda of the next Committee's meeting. This is despite reference in NEPAD's Declaration on
Democracy, Political, Economic and Corporate Governance to the African
Charter on the Rights and Welfare of the Child, a recognition of the impact
of conflicts on children[90] and that states should enrol all children of school
age in primary schools by 2015[91] and reduce infant and child mortality
by two-thirds between 1990 and 2015.[92] Similarly, despite some, albeit
limited, reference in the CSSDCA process to children,[93] there has been no
apparent attempt to link this with the other developments in this area.

Health

The OAU/AU has called on states to protect the health of children: 'There
can be no socioeconomic development on the continent without the provision of sound health facilities for our peoples, aware of the fact that this
phenomenon is a result of a very high infant mortality rate, malnutrition,
pre-matured death, chronic health problems and inability to work during
years of active life.'[94] In this regard it has spent some time convincing states
of the need to improve primary health-care facilities[95] and also to establish
immunisation programmes and 'progress made towards in the universal
vaccination of children'.[96] It set states some quite specific benchmarks

---

[89] Resolution on the Strategies for the African Child (1990–2000), CM/Res.1230(L),
preamble.
[90] AHG/235(XXXVIII), Annex I, paras. 3(a) and 10.
[91] The New Partnership for Africa's Development (NEPAD), October 2001,
http://www.au2002.gov.za/docs/key_oau/nepad 1.htm.
[92] Ibid.
[93] The CSSDCA Solemn Declaration states that governments should address the phenomenon of child soldiers, ensure enactment of national laws to 'extend equal opportunities with respect to health, education, employment and other civic rights to all citizens,
especially women and the girl child', CSSDCA Solemn Declaration, AHG/Decl.4(XXXVI),
'Development', para. n.
[94] Resolution on the Immunization of Children in Africa, CM/Res.1301(LII), preamble.
[95] Resolution on the Implementation of the African Decade for Child Survival, Protection
and Development, CM/Res.1360(LIV), preamble and paras. 1–4.
[96] Resolution on the Adoption of the African Charter on the Rights and Welfare of the African
Child, AHG/Res.197(XXVI).

including ensuring universal immunisation against six diseases by 1990, reduction of child and maternal mortality rates by 50 per cent at least by 2000 and also primary health care for women and children by the mid-1990s.[97] In addition, services should be made 'universally accessible to all children within the shortest possible time'.[98] These services should include 'medical care, nutrition, education and other basic services'.[99] Unfortunately, it would appear that these targets have not been met.

There has been some attention to the 'need to drastically reduce the rate of infant mortality in Africa through an adequate health policy'.[100] Considerable attention has also been paid to the impact of HIV/AIDS on children and their rights. In this regard the OAU/AU has stressed prevention as the key issue and called on states to create national policy frameworks.[101] States should also take measures to advise pregnant HIV-infected women.[102] There is a recognition of the impact of AIDS on development and long-term health problems for the child:

> realising that the child is the future of the continent but that AIDS will limit the countries' efforts to ensure child survival, protect the rights of the child and provide for an educated cohort particularly with regard to moral and ethical values, to ensure Africa's development, recognising that the AIDS epidemic as well as accompanying opportunistic illness such as tuberculosis which continues to seriously undermine health and development efforts in Africa poses immediate and long terms problems for the child in Africa, exhorts states to take efforts to eradicate the disease.[103]

States have been asked 'to consider the implementation of sex education programmes with special emphasis on AIDS in the curricula of pre-teen schools as an essential part of the AIDS Prevention Education programme'.[104] The OAU has also recognised that children and those suffering from HIV/AIDS can be isolated.[105] In this regard it has recommended that the

[97] Resolution on African Child Survival and Development and Universal Immunization in Africa, CM/Res.1163(XLVIII), para. 9.

[98] Ibid., preamble.   [99] Ibid.

[100] Resolution on the Adoption of the African Charter.

[101] Tunis Declaration on AIDS and the Child in Africa, AHG/Decl.1(XXX) 1994; Decision on the Report of the Secretary General on the Twenty-Second Ordinary Session of the OAU Labour and Social Affairs Commission (Doc.CM/2112(LXX)), CM/Dec.465(LXX).

[102] Tunis Declaration on AIDS. It did not make any specific mention of human rights per se.

[103] Resolution on AIDS and the Child in Africa Call for Action, CM/Res.1542(LX).

[104] Ibid.

[105] Report of the Seventy-Third Ordinary Session of the Council of Ministers, CM/Rpt (LXXIII), para. 77.

situation of HIV/AIDS should be an agenda item in all relevant meetings regarding social and economic affairs; the problems of child labour and impact of HIV/AIDS need to be strongly linked and programmes to address these issues coordinated within governments; the problems faced by children, families and communities are linked to underlying causes that need to be made explicit in all formal analyses, among them widespread poverty and armed conflict.[106]

Infant mortality is also a specific concern, with the OAU/AU being 'deeply concerned at the persistent high rate of infant mortality in a number of African countries and at the growing population of children under five suffering from malnutrition on the continent'.[107] States have thus been required to set up 'national regional and local follow up mechanisms for the achievement of the mid-decade goals', celebrate 16 June as African Child Day and evaluate the progress made.[108]

Work and child labour

Referring expressly to ILO standards, the OAU/AU has spent some time considering the issue of child labour.[109] Thus, it has called upon states 'to include social protection and work safety areas in their national development priorities and facilitate the development of self employment strategies, in collaboration with social partners', also calling on states that had not yet done so to ratify the ACRWC as well as the ILO Convention 182 on the Elimination of the Worst Forms of Child Labour.[110] It further required states to 'include compulsory education, the elimination of child labour as

---

[106] Report of the Secretary General on the Twenty-Second Ordinary Session of the OAU Labour and Social Affairs Commission, CM/2112(LXX), noted Strategies for Assistance to Children Isolated by AIDS (Doc.LSC/6b(XXII)), para. 77.

[107] Resolution on Setting up Follow-Up Mechanisms for the Achievement of the Mid-Decade Goals Emanating from the Consensus of Dakar as well as the Goals set for the Year 2000 Emanating from the World Declaration on Child Survival, Protection and Development in the 1990s, CM/Res.1533(LX).

[108] Ibid. Resolution on the Follow-Up of the International Conference on Assistance to African Children (ICAAC), CM/Res.1532(LX), preamble.

[109] Introductory Note to the Report of the Secretary General to the Sixty-Eighth Ordinary Session of the AHSG and the Thirty-Fourth Ordinary Session of the Council of Ministers, June 1998, paras. 175 and 177.

[110] Decision on the Report of the Secretary General on the Twenty-Fifth Ordinary Session of the OAU Labour and Social Affairs Commission/Ministerial Conference on Employment and Poverty Reduction in Africa, Doc. CM/2262(LXXVI), CM/Dec.671, at paras. 4 and 5.

well as children in conflict situations and child trafficking in their priority programmes on children'.[111]

It has been recommended that the 'OAU should collaborate with other bodies such as IOM, ILO to implement the Programme of Action adopted by the First African Seminar on Intra-African Migration and the Charter on the Fundamental Duties and Social Rights of African and Arab Migrant Workers'.[112]

The OAU has endorsed[113] the need for an in-depth study on the problems of child protection and elimination of child labour at national, sub-regional, regional and continental levels.[114]

It has given the impression, on some occasions, however, that child labour is not prohibited per se, suggesting that a distinction should be made in the case of those children helping in domestic situations. This reflects the reality in many African countries where children may head households. In this regard, however, the OAU/AU has stressed the responsibilities of the child within the family, over and above the potential for exploitation in terms of performing those tasks:

> The issue of child labour should be situated in the social and economic context of the African continent. Children helping the family in domestic situations and activities which are part of the socialisation process and which could be characterised as child work are not the problem. Child labour is work, paid or unpaid, which deprives the child of an education and threatens safety, health or morals which is considered as exploitation of the child, even when employed in family enterprises.[115]

---

[111] Ibid., para. 6. In a resolution in 1995 on the OAU Labour Commission the Council of Ministers called on states to ratify the ACRWC as well as the UNCRC and the ILO Convention on minimum age for admission to employment, Resolution on the Proceedings of the Eighteenth Ordinary Session of the OAU Labour Commission, CM/Res.1598(LXII), para. 8. See also Decision on the Report of the Secretary General on the Twenty-Third Ordinary Session of the OAU Labour and Social Affairs Commission (CM/2174(LXXII)), CM/Dec.535(LXXII), para. 8. Other ILO Conventions that the OAU/AU has encouraged states to ratify include the Convention on Minimum age for Employment, Resolution on the Proceedings of the Seventeenth Ordinary Session of the OAU Labour Commission, CM/Res.1536(LX). See also Regulation, EC/AU/AEC/Regl.(I), paras. 5(d) and (e).

[112] Report of the Secretary General on the Twenty-Second Ordinary Session, at 1–11.

[113] Recommendations of Arusha Seminar on Protection of Child and Elimination of Child Labour.

[114] Decision on the Report of the Secretary General on the Twentieth Session of the Labour and Social Affairs Commission, CM/Dec.335(LXVI).

[115] Report of the Secretary General on the Activities of the General Secretariat, CM/2058(LXVIII) part I, para. 106.

On other occasions, outside the family context, however, it has called on states to implement the ILO Convention banning child labour.[116]

There is also a discrepancy with international standards. The ACRWC defines a child as anyone below the age of eighteen, and the ILO Convention of 1999 on the Worst Forms of Child Labour calls for its elimination for those under eighteen, yet the ILO Minimum Age Convention 138 defined child labour as that done by children under fifteen years and which was hazardous to health or schooling, etc.[117] It would seem that UNICEF and others see access to education as a way of resolving the child labour problem.[118]

Children and conflict

The OAU has recognised the impact conflict can have on the rights of a child:

> noting with concern that as a result of these continuing conflicts, African children and women continue to suffer and die in disturbingly large numbers from causes directly or indirectly related to conflicts; considering the effects of the widespread externally-supported destabilization of countries continued practices of forced removal of peoples, and the consequences of apartheid and Bantustan policies for child survival, health and well being within the region, concerned about the use of children for military purposes wherever this may occur, aware of the fact that children and women make up more than 80% of the victims of these armed conflicts throughout the African continent, reaffirming the legal and moral obligations of African governments to put an end to the current suffering and deaths among children and women due to armed conflicts affecting these respective countries; . . . denounces the use of children for military purposes, wherever such practices occur.[119]

Conflicts are thus said to negatively impact on the 'survival and development of African children and hence the future of the continent'.[120]

---

[116] Decision on the Report of the Secretary General on the Twenty-Second Ordinary Session of the OAU Labour and Social Affairs Commission (Doc.CM/2112(LXX)), CM/Dec.465(LXX); Decision on the ILO Convention on the Banning of the Worst Forms of Child Labour and Immediate Action for their Elimination, AHG/Dec.139(XXXV).

[117] Note also UNCRC, Article 32.

[118] S. F. Arat, 'Analysing Child Labour as a Human Rights Issue: Its Causes, Aggravating Policies and Alternative Proposals', HRQ 24 (2002) 177–204, at 201.

[119] Resolution on Peace for Children.

[120] Resolution on the Plight of African Children in Situation of Armed Conflicts, CM/Res.1659(LXIV), Rev.1, preamble.

Conflicts as the cause of refugee flows has also been recognised in relation to the impact on children.

But the OAU/AU has also recognised the impact of conflict on children not only as civilians, but also as combatants.[121] The ACRWC requires states to respect humanitarian law rules that apply during armed conflicts.[122] In this respect the OAU has called on all warring parties, governments and others to 'release child combatants from the army and give them adequate education and training, rehabilitate them and reintegrate them in civil society so as to make them once more productive and responsible citizens of their respective countries, reaffirms that the use of children in armed conflicts constitutes a violation of their rights and should be considered as war crimes'.[123] It has asked the Secretary General, NGOs and others to organise training for members of the armed forces on human rights and international humanitarian law and for 'warring parties to pay special attention to the protection of girls and women'.[124] While the Charter, therefore, provides a higher degree of protection than under the UNCRC for child soldiers, it fails to adequately consider those affected by indirect hostilities.

In 1999 the Council of Ministers decided to set up a Special Committee on the Situation of Children in Armed Conflicts to consider the conclusions of a conference on the issue.[125] This Special Committee[126] ceased functioning when the African Charter Committee on the Rights of the Child was created, and handed over its remaining tasks to it.[127]

The OAU had previously called on African states 'to keep children out of war situations and to refrain from recruiting children under the age of

---

[121] C. Jesseman, 'The Protection and Participation Rights of the Child Soldier: An African and Global Perspective', *African Human Rights Law Journal* 1(1) (2001) 140–54, at 140. Report of the Seventy-Third Ordinary Session of the Council of Ministers, para. 76.
[122] Article 22(1).
[123] Resolution on the Plight of African Children in Situation of Armed Conflicts, paras. 5–7.
[124] Ibid., paras. 8 and 10.
[125] Introductory Note of the Secretary General to the Seventy-Fourth Ordinary Session of the Council of Ministers, at 76.
[126] The Committee was composed of representatives from Burkina Faso, South Africa, Togo, Uganda and Zimbabwe, and worked with Save the Children and ANPPCAN.
[127] Introductory Note of the Secretary General to the Seventy-Fourth Ordinary Session, at 76. The OAU recommended the establishment of a Special Committee on the Situation of Children in Armed Conflicts and for the Secretary General to 'put in place the appropriate mechanisms in order to set in motion the process of combating this phenomenon in anticipation of the elaboration of an International Convention on this issue', Decision on the Report on the African Conference on the Use of Children as Soldiers, CM/Dec.482(LXX). See also Lloyd, 'Evolution of the African Charter', at 189.

19 in armed conflict or violent activities of any kind whatsoever'.[128] The OAU/AU has been consistent with international humanitarian law standards which prohibit recruitment of children under fifteen years old into the armed forces,[129] indeed urging states to 'adopt and promote norms in respective countries prohibiting recruitment and use as soldiers, children under 18 years of age',[130] noting the ACRWC.[131] Articles 2 and 22(2) of the ACRWC provide further that no one under eighteen (definition of a child) can take a direct part in hostilities or be recruited.[132] It has recognised that this is not respected in practice:

> The Secretary General is of the view that laxism on the part of member states is due, among other things, to negligence and that in a not too distant future people will mobilise themselves to discharge their duty vis-à-vis the millions of children of this continent who constitute the active force of tomorrow and whose conditions should be improved to ensure a better future.[133]

The impact of trafficking in light weapons on the increased involvement of child soldiers has been recognised, and the OAU/AU has appealed to states and the international community 'to assist in the psycho-social rehabilitation of children who have been affected by the trafficking, circulation and the proliferation of light weapons'.[134]

Conclusions on the work of the OAU/AU

While it cannot be said that the OAU/AU has ignored the position of children, its approach does not evidence a coherent philosophy and its rhetoric has not been matched by concrete actions. It would seem that while the Charter provides that it is the child that holds the right, and takes

---

[128] Resolution on the Plight of African Children in Situation of Armed Conflicts, paras. 5–7.

[129] Geneva Convention IV, Article 68(4); Geneva Protocol I, Article 77(5); Geneva Protocol II, Article 6(4).

[130] Decision on the Report on the African Conference on the Use of Children as Soldiers.

[131] Ibid.

[132] Jesseman, 'Protection and Participation Rights', at 146.

[133] Progress Report of the Secretary General on the Ratification of the African Charter on the Rights of the Child, CM/2116(LXX), para. 14.

[134] Decision on the Illicit Proliferation, Circulation and Trafficking of Small Arms and Light Weapons, AHG/ Dec.137(LXX).

an individualist approach to some issues,[135] which has been commended by many,[136] it also refers to the child as a 'physically and mentally immature person who is therefore in need of special safeguards'.[137] Related to this is the central place of the family which is so often raised in the African context. The ACRWC makes it clear that 'the family shall be the natural unit and basis of society. It shall enjoy the protection and support of the State for its establishment and development.'[138]

The Charter's provisions on parental responsibility note that

> Parents or other persons responsible for the child shall have the primary responsibility of the upbringing and development of the child and shall have the duty: (a) to ensure that the best interests of the child are their basic concern at all times; (b) to secure, within their abilities and financial capacities, conditions of living necessary to the child's development; and (c) to ensure that domestic discipline is administered with humanity and in a manner consistent with the inherent dignity of the child.[139]

In this regard there are also duties on the state.[140] Thus, whereas the UNCRC seems more rooted in the rights of the child, the African

---

[135] For Example, the right to be heard in judicial and other proceedings:
> In all judicial or administrative proceedings affecting a child who is capable of communicating his/her own views, an opportunity shall be provided for the views of the child to be heard either directly or through an impartial representative as a party to the proceedings. And those views shall be taken into consideration by the relevant authority in accordance with the provisions of appropriate law.
>
> ACRWC, Article 4(2)

[136] This
> is significant considering the fact that children in Africa are not perceived as autonomous. Children are normally considered to be deficient in their decision-making capabilities and deserving of protection. Decisions concerning children are often made by a group of male elders. At most, children are heard indirectly, *e.g.*, through aunties, uncles or grand parents. Specific guarantees for children's participation and their right to privacy are therefore commendable.
>
> D. M. Chirwa, 'The Merits and Demerits of the African Charter on the Rights and Welfare of the Child', *International Journal of Children's Rights* 10 (2002) 157–77, at 160

[137] Gose, 'The African Charter', at 23–4.   [138] Article 18(1).   [139] Article 20(1).
[140] Article 20(2) reads:
> States Parties to the present Charter shall in accordance with their means and national conditions take all appropriate measures: (a) to assist parents and other persons responsible for the child and in case of need provide material assistance and support programmes particularly with regard to nutrition, health, education, clothing and housing; (b) to assist parents and others responsible for the child in the performance of child-rearing and ensure the development of institutions responsible for providing care of children; and (c) to ensure that the children of working parents are provided with care services and facilities.

instrument and OAU/AU Resolutions focus more on the welfare of the extended family.[141]

The OAU/AU has therefore tended not to look at individual rights of the child or to see them as justiciable, but is more interested in improving the situation at the institutional level and in focusing on external factors. This welfare-oriented approach is preferred within the context of the family.[142]

While the ACRWC seemed primarily to have been an attempt to promote the UN Convention in Africa, and although some of the Charter's provisions give greater protection,[143] the adoption of standards such as 'the best interests of the child' have been criticised by some as sitting uncomfortably in the African context. The focus on parental responsibility and, therefore, authority over the child, makes it 'difficult to discern how effect can be given to the specific rights of the child guaranteed by the Charter and premised on the notion of "the best interests of the child"'.[144] Whereas the Charter envisages the 'best interests' principle as being primary, the OAU/AU appears to have focused on other matters around development and welfare, moving the focus away from the individual rights of the child.[145]

As a result, the approach to the rights of the child has been, as we have seen, rather ad hoc. Any standards that have been set by the OAU/AU organs have not yet been linked with the Charter to develop a coherent whole. This must surely be the task of the new AU. While it seems logical that this coordination should take place under the newly established African Committee on the Rights and Welfare of the Child, this Committee must now consolidate what has been achieved by the previous OAU organs to develop a consistent approach to policies towards children in the future. Although the political rhetoric supporting children having rights may be apparent at the level of the AU, it would appear that the

---

[141] Lloyd, 'Evolution of the African Charter'. The 'welfare of the African child is inextricably bound up with that of its parents and other members of the family, especially the mother', Declaration on the Rights and Welfare of the African Child, preamble.

[142] Interview with Amanda Lloyd, November 2003.

[143] For example on armed conflict, refugees and marriage, F. Viljoen, 'Why South Africa Should Ratify the African Charter on the Rights and Welfare of the Child', *South African Law Journal* 11(6) (1999) 660–4, at 661. There are various provisions in the ACRWC which stress that inconsistent customs and traditions must give way to the provisions of the Charter, for example, Article 1(3) reads: 'Any custom, tradition, cultural or religious practice that is inconsistent with the rights, duties and obligations contained in the present Charter shall to the extent of such inconsistency be discouraged.'

[144] Thompson, 'Africa's Charter on Children's Rights', at 439. See also Gose, 'The African Charter', at 26.

[145] Interview with Amanda Lloyd, November 2003.

Committee and the AU's Social Affairs Directorate in particular are going to have to work very hard to elaborate on the fundamental issues underlying their resolutions and decisions to appeal to the domestic resistance that may be faced:

> At present it is fair to assert that there is no general culture of children's rights in Africa, particularly due to the embryonic nature of the African Children's Charter. For some Africans the very idea of children having rights is threatening, and there is much misunderstanding about what children's rights actually mean. There is, however, eager willingness to promote the fulfilment of children's needs. There needs to be a better understanding of the societal views of children, the idea that children have rights should no longer be deemed as 'un-African.'[146]

---

[146] A. Lloyd, 'A Theoretical Analysis of the Reality of Children's Rights in Africa: An Introduction to the African Charter on the Rights and Welfare of the Child', *African Human Rights Law Journal* 2 (2002) 11–32, at 32.

7

Refugees and human rights

The relationship between human rights and refugee law

Although human rights law generally applies to all individuals, regardless of nationality or citizenship, refugees have traditionally been dealt with via humanitarian law.[1] Yet the continued separation of the two disciplines seems untenable: 'It is no longer possible to interpret or apply the Refugee Convention without drawing on the text and jurisprudence of other human rights treaties. Conversely it is not possible to monitor the implementation of other human rights treaties, where refugees are concerned, without drawing on the text of the Refugee Convention and related interpretive conclusions of the UNHCR Executive Committee.'[2] In addition, there is an increased awareness that perhaps more permanent protection of refugees, returnees and internally displaced persons is needed, and this is accompanied by increasing reference to human rights standards.[3]

---

[1] G. Goodwin-Gill, *The Refugee in International Law*, 2nd edition (Oxford: Oxford University Press, 1996), at 268. It has been suggested that there may be benefits in avoiding a non-human rights approach, see B. Gorlick, 'Human Rights and Refugees: Enhancing Protection through International Human Rights Law', Working Paper No. 30, *New Issues in Refugee Research* (New York: UNHCR, October 2000) www.unhcr.ch, at 10 and 52.

[2] T. Clark and F. Crépeau, 'Mainstreaming Refugee Rights. The 1951 Refugee Convention and International Human Rights Law', *NQHR* 17(4) (1999) 389–410, at 389.

[3] Lawyers' Committee for Human Rights, *African Exodus. Refugee Crisis, Human Rights and the 1969 OAU Convention* (New York: Lawyers' Committee for Human Rights, 1995), at 39. See also B. Harrell-Bond, *Towards the Economic and Social 'Integration' of Refugee Populations in Host Countries in Africa* (Muscatine, IA: Stanley Foundation, 2002), http://reports.stanleyfoundation.org/hrp/HRP02B.pdf, at 4; G. Goodwin-Gill, 'International Law and Human Rights: Trends Concerning International Migrants and Refugees', *International Migration Review* 23(3) (1989) 526–46, at 526; see also Goodwin-Gill, *The Refugee in International Law*, at 8; Gorlick, 'Human Rights and Refugees', at 16; J. Mertus, 'The State and the Post Cold War Refugee Regime: New Models, New Questions', *International Journal of Refugee Law* 10(3) (1998) 321–48, at 335–6; G. Noll and J. Vedsted-Hansen, 'Non-Communitarians: Refugee and Asylum Policies', in Alston (ed.), *The EU and Human Rights* 359–410, at 364; C. J. Harvey, 'Dissident Voices: Refugees, Human Rights and Asylum

However, even where human rights laws may provide protection, their applicability to refugees may not occur in practice as, it is argued, 'a disproportionate amount of energy and resources tends to be focused on determining *who* is a refugee'.[4] Further, ensuring that human rights standards are actually enforced for the benefit of refugees is problematic and in this regard the mechanisms available under the human rights treaties could be used.[5] Unfortunately the success of the various international and regional human rights bodies in dealing with refugee issues has been limited,[6] and their approach has been cautious.[7] The African Commission on Human and Peoples' Rights, for example, has only recently started to pay attention to the issue in its work, despite calls over many years for greater involvement.[8] It has been important, therefore, that bodies such as the UNHCR take a human rights perspective in their work.[9] In the same regard, it is therefore essential that the OAU/AU organs dealing with refugee issues also consider human rights to be integral to their mandate.

Although the OAU/AU has paid some attention to the rights of refugees, this has been prompted more by other considerations than by the need to protect the refugees themselves. This has meant a rather ad hoc approach to their human rights. There are, however, some promising developments with increased coordination between the UNHCR and the African Commission on Human and Peoples' Rights. The extent to which the Addis Ababa organs will be involved in such collaboration is still to be seen.

The legal basis

The creation of the OAU Refugee Convention and reasons for its adoption

In 1964 the then Commission of Ten on Refugees of the OAU was mandated to draft a convention on refugees.[10] The decision to draft an

---

in Europe', *Social and Legal Studies* 9(3) (2000) 367–96, at 380. See also UN GA resolution 40/144, December 1985 on the human rights of non-nationals.

[4] Gorlick, 'Human Rights and Refugees', at 6.

[5] See Harvey, 'Dissident Voices', at 379.

[6] For discussion see Gorlick, 'Human Rights and Refugees'. The right to seek and gain asylum has been recognised, for example, by Inter-American Commission on Human Rights: *Joseph v. Canada*, No. 27/93, Case 11//092, Annual Report 1993, OEA/Ser.L/V/II.85, Doc.9; and *Haitian Interdiction v. US*, Report No. 51/96, Case No. 10.675, 13 March 1997, Annual Report 1996, at 598.

[7] Clark and Crépeau, 'Mainstreaming Refugee Rights', at 403–4.

[8] Oloka-Onyango, 'The Plight of the Larger Half', at 390–391.

[9] See, for example, UNHCR Executive Committee 1995 and its policy paper, 'UNHCR and Human Rights'.

[10] AHG/Res.26(II). See also CM/Res.36(III).

Africa-specific treaty on refugees was said to have been due to various factors.[11] It was argued that the 1951 UN Convention on Refugees was European in focus and not suitable for the African situation,[12] particularly as many refugees were seen at that stage as being the result of the fight for independence. Thus, 'the African attitude was not so much to broaden the scope of the Convention but rather to draft a document that would "cover all aspects of the problems" in Africa'.[13] A regional High Commissioner for Refugees was also contemplated, although this was resisted by the UNHCR, which felt that this would unnecessarily duplicate its programmes and that the UNHCR should continue to be universal.[14] The UNHCR did assist, however, in drafting the OAU Refugee Convention.[15]

The OAU Convention Governing the Specific Aspects of the Refugee Problem in Africa was finally adopted in 1969,[16] entering into force in 1974. Given the lack of *travaux préparatoires* it has been argued that the origins of the Convention discussion rely on some articles written shortly after it was adopted:

> This situation has allowed a number of perceptions to ossify about the Convention that are not correct. Mainly, purposes and motives that it never pretended to have been attributed to the Convention, and are routinely affirmed and repeated today as incontrovertible truth. The impression of an abiding dissatisfaction with the scope of the application of the 1951 Convention as the reason why the Convention came to be elaborated has taken root in this manner.[17]

Definition of refugee in the OAU Convention

Despite its background, there was a disparity between what the OAU Convention could have been, namely a comprehensive document dealing with all the gaps in refugee protection in Africa, and trying to ensure that it did not conflict with the UN Convention. The latter model left gaps that needed to be dealt with by the OAU.[18]

---

[11] G. Okoth-Obbo, 'Thirty Years On: A Legal Review of the 1969 OAU Refugee Convention', *African Yearbook of International Law* 8 (2000) 3–70, at 14.

[12] P. Weiss, 'The Convention of the Organization of African Unity Governing the Specific Aspects of Refugee Problems in Africa', *Human Rights Journal* 3(3) (1970) 449–61.

[13] S. A. Aiboni, *Protection of Refugees in Africa* (Uppsala: Svenska Institutet för Internaionell Rätt, 1978), at 33. See also G. Loescher, *The UNHCR and World Politics. A Perilous Path* (Oxford: Oxford University Press, 2001), at 124–5.

[14] Loescher, *The UNHCR*, at 125.   [15] Ibid.

[16] 10 September 1969, AHSG, CAB/LEG/24.3.

[17] Okoth-Obbo, 'Thirty Years On', at 11.   [18] Ibid., at 24.

It has been argued that the concept of refugee as defined in the Statute of the UNHCR[19] and UN Convention of 1951[20] 'is not universal and creates certain problems when it comes to its application to new refugees from new areas and notably in the Third World'.[21] One would therefore have hoped that the OAU Convention would expand and improve on the existing definitions. From one angle, it has been said that this was achieved. Article 1 provides that

> the term 'refugee' shall mean every person who, owing to well-founded fear of being persecuted for reasons of race, religion, nationality, membership of a particular social group or political opinion, is outside the country of his nationality and is unable or, owing to such fear, is unwilling to avail himself of the protection of that country, or who, not having a nationality and being outside the country of his former habitual residence as a result of such events, is unable or, owing to such fear, is unwilling to return to it. The term 'refugee' shall also apply to every person who, owing to external aggression, occupation, foreign domination or events seriously disturbing public order in either part or the whole of his country of origin or nationality, is compelled to leave his place of habitual residence in order to seek refuge in another place outside his country of origin or nationality.

It is therefore clear that 'individuals and large numbers of people fleeing public disorder' are afforded protection under the OAU instrument when they might not have been under the UN Convention.[22] In this way it has been used to cover those fleeing natural disasters, despite this perhaps having not been the original intention.[23]

---

[19] Statute of UNHCR, Article 6, para. B: the UNHCR can deal with any
       person who is outside the country of his nationality, or if he has no nationality, the country of his former habitual residence, because he has or had a well-founded fear of persecution by reason of his race, religion, nationality or political opinion and is unable or, because of such fear, is unwilling to avail himself of the protection of the government of the country of his nationality, or, if he has no nationality to return to the country of his former habitual residence.
[20] UN Convention of 1951, Article 1(a):
       As a result of events occurring before 1st January 1951 and owing to well-founded fear of being persecuted for reasons of race, religion, nationality, membership of a particular social group or political opinion, is outside the country of his nationality and is unable or, owing to such fear, is unwilling to avail himself of the protection of that country or who not having a nationality and being outside the country of his former habitual residence as a result of such events, is unable or owing to such fear, is unwilling to return to it.
[21] Aiboni, *Protection of Refugees*, at 30. See also M. J. Schultheis, 'Refugees in Africa: The Geopolitics of Forced Displacement', *African Studies Review* 32(1) (1989) 3–29, at 8–10.
[22] Aiboni, *Protection of Refugees*, at 35.   [23] Naldi, *An Analysis*, at 83.

This expanded definition was prompted by the need to protect freedom fighters and those who were fleeing places under colonial domination.[24] The OAU Convention was innovative for a number of other reasons as well.[25] Firstly, it referred to the need for states to consider the grant of asylum, although it could not really be said to amount to a right as such.[26] Further, the non-refoulement principle appears to be absolute, Article 2(2) reading: 'No person shall be subjected by a Member State to measures such as rejection at the frontier, return or expulsion, which would compel him to return to or remain in a territory where his life, physical integrity or liberty would be threatened for the reasons set out in Article I, paragraphs 1 and 2.' The OAU Refugee Convention also expressly includes reference to voluntary repatriation, in Article 5.[27]

However, the definition of a refugee in the OAU Refugee Convention, it is argued, does not go far enough: it is 'entirely silent' on issues of mass influx[28] and the procedure for determining who is a refugee is largely left to states' discretion.[29] In addition, there is a suggestion that the principle of non-refoulement can be limited if the individual acts contrary to the principles of the Convention.[30] This is also reinforced by Article 3 of the OAU Convention and Articles 12(4) and (5) of the ACHPR.[31]

The OAU Convention on Refugees does not take a strong human rights approach.[32] There is no real mention of the rights of refugees beyond those discussed above, it does not deal with women and restricts freedom of movement and rights of expression and association.[33] Although

---

[24] Okoth-Obbo, 'Thirty Years On', at 38.   [25] Naldi, *An Analysis*, at 82.

[26] Article 2(1) reads: 'Member States of the OAU shall use their best endeavours consistent with their respective legislation to receive refugees and to secure the settlement of those refugees who, for well-founded reasons, are unable or unwilling to return to their country of origin or nationality.'

[27] 'Although the subject of numerous UN General Assembly resolutions this principle has not featured in internationally binding instruments although the OAU Convention is an exception', Naldi, *An Analysis*, at 86.

[28] Okoth-Obbo, 'Thirty Years On', at 25.

[29] A. C. Helton, *The Price of Indifference. Refugees and Humanitarian Action in the New Century* (Oxford: Oxford University Press, 2002), at 164.

[30] Article 1(4)(g) states: 'This Convention shall cease to apply to any refugee if: . . . he has seriously infringed the purposes and objectives of this Convention.' See also Oloka-Onyango, 'The Plight of the Larger Half', at 374.

[31] Article 12(4) states: 'A non-national legally admitted in a territory of a State Party to the present Charter, may only be expelled from it by virtue of a decision taken in accordance with the law'. Article 12(5) reads: 'The mass expulsion of non-nationals shall be prohibited. Mass expulsion shall be that which is aimed at national, racial, ethnic or religious groups'. See Naldi, *An Analysis*, at 82.

[32] Oloka-Onyango, 'The Plight of the Larger Half', at 375.   [33] Ibid.

provisions relating to the quality of life of refugees were found in earlier drafts of the Convention, they were omitted from the final version.[34]

Finally, there may well have been a perception that the UNHCR would provide the enforcement mechanism to the OAU Convention, but the silence on this issue in the Convention itself perhaps explains why issues of refugee protection have been left to other bodies to deal with on an ad hoc basis.

Later development of concepts

As will be seen below, various important statements and development of standards can be gleaned from the work of the various OAU and now AU organs. The OAU Convention on Refugees in this regard has always been referred to, yet so have other international and regional documents. It cannot be said that there has been any real consistent and comprehensive attempt to provide an authoritative interpretation of its provisions, and following on from this, no serious attempt to review the OAU Convention in the light of present-day realities. Various reasons for this have been suggested:

> Conceived in the womb of the anti-colonial, anti-imperialist zest of the immediate post-independence period, the Convention has mandated to generate an aura of home-grown African authenticity which few other instruments on the continent have been able to match. When it was adopted, here at last was Africa's own regulatory framework for its refugees, conceived and brought to life by Africans themselves. It was, moreover, also being hailed globally as the example to be followed elsewhere . . .
>
> Hallowed ideologically in the aplomb of a sacred African symbol, the Convention has essentially been sheltered from the kind of rigorous inquiry which for instance, the 1951 Convention has had to endure . . .
>
> It is little surprising then, that there has really been no reform-oriented groundswell around the Convention, even if reform itself is episodically pointed to.[35]

Thus, although used rhetorically, and due in part to the lack of integral enforcement mechanism under the Convention, developments have taken place outside the Convention framework: 'It is striking to note the limited extent to which the OAU Convention has actually and concretely provided the anchor for refugee dialogue and action in Africa.'[36]

---

[34] Okoth-Obbo, 'Thirty Years On', at 29.   [35] Ibid., at 31.   [36] Ibid., at 32.

A significant conference took place in Arusha in May 1979.[37] Recommendations adopted by the Conference were subsequently adopted
and endorsed by the OAU[38] and UN.[39] These included highlighting that
although there was no right to asylum in international law, states should
be encouraged to incorporate this and the principle of non-refoulement
in their national laws. It also affirmed the principles of burden sharing and
voluntary repatriation, although it did stress that amnesty was important
and should be examined further. The Conference considered that refugees
should not be classified as illegal immigrants and expressed concern about
detention and imprisonment measures relating to refugees and the fact
that they are not subject to review and that the basic rights of refugees
should be protected. States should facilitate the movement of refugees,
and refugees should have rights to employment and access to education,
although they in turn have an obligation not to engage in subversive
activities. States were also encouraged to incorporate into national laws
the OAU and UN Conventions and to place them in the wider context of
human rights.

The International Conferences on Assistance to Refugees in Africa,
ICARA I and ICARA II, expressly linked the refugee problem with human
rights violations[40] and the International Conference on the Plight of
Refugees, Returnees and Displaced Persons in Southern Africa, SARRED,
held in August 1988 by the UN and OAU, resulted in a Declaration and
Plan of Action noting that the refugee situation was a global responsibility
and that asylum should be an international obligation. The conference in
1994 organised by the OAU and UNHCR resulted in the Addis Ababa Recommendations which further helped to develop standards in this area,[41]
and 'reaffirmed its belief in the continuing validity of the 1969 OAU Convention as the cornerstone of refugee protection and solutions in Africa'.[42]

Increased reference to the human rights of refugees was made in the
important seminar in Guinea in March 2000. Held in conjunction with

---

[37] The Pan African Conference on the Situation of Refugees in Africa.
[38] CM/Res.727(XXXIII).   [39] GA Resolution 34/61 (1979).
[40] Naldi, *An Analysis*, at 91–2.
[41] Recommendations of the OAU/UNHCR Symposium on Refugees and Forced Population Displacements in Africa, adopted by the OAU/UNHCR Symposium on Refugees
and Forced Population Displacements in Africa, 8–10 September 1994, Addis Ababa. The
Addis Ababa Document is said to carry significant authority as there was a high level of
participation from African states and organisations, G. Okoth-Obbo, 'The OAU/UNHCR
Symposium on Refugees and Forced Displacements in Africa – A Review Article', *International Journal of Refugee Law* (special issue, 1995) 274–99.
[42] Recommendations of the OAU/UNHCR Symposium, Recommendation No. 5.

the UNHCR this consolidated the OAU's approach and directed the way in which it would operate in the future.[43] This conference resulted in a number of key issues under a Comprehensive Action Plan.[44] Various recommendations related to the human rights of refugees, including that the OAU request its member states to ratify the various conventions on refugees as well as human rights treaties such as the ACHPR, its Protocol on the Court and the ACRWC.[45] It was recommended that the OAU and UNHCR create a working group to examine changes to the OAU Refugee Convention, including considering provisions for the oversight of the Convention,[46] with the possibility of adopting an additional protocol to make the necessary changes.[47] The conference also recommended that the OAU and UNHCR should 'request asylum countries, which have not yet done so, to issue refugee identity and travel documents to all refugees, including refugee women and unaccompanied minors', including the issuing of provisional documentation to those awaiting asylum decisions, and identification documents for refugees and asylum seekers.[48] There is a specific requirement for non-party states to comply with customary international law and human rights obligations, in particular the principle of non-refoulement, 'the duty to ensure that every refugee or asylum seeker enjoys basic human rights',[49] and to 'observe any principles found in human rights and humanitarian instruments, which provide additional protection'.[50] It was at this meeting that the UNHCR was directed to conclude a Memorandum of Understanding with the African Commission on Human and Peoples' Rights 'with the aim, inter alia, of strengthening its monitoring capacity and programme of work with respect to the human rights of refugees and asylum seekers'.[51]

The CSSDCA process also pays some attention to the rights of refugees,[52] noting among the 'core values' that the 'plight of African

---

[43] Report. Special OAU/UNHCR Meeting of Government and Non-Government Technical Experts on the Thirtieth Anniversary of the 1969 OAU Refugee Convention, Conakry, 27–29 March 2000.

[44] Comprehensive Action Plan, adopted by the Special OAU/UNHCR Meeting of Government and Non-Government Technical Experts on the Thirtieth Anniversary of the 1969 OAU Refugee Convention, Conakry, 27–29 March 2000, CONF.P/OAU30th/CORE/4-Rev.1. This has been endorsed by the 72nd Council of Ministers Meeting and the AHSG 37th Summit and is seen as guiding refugee protection on the continent.

[45] Action 1.   [46] Action 4.   [47] Action 2.   [48] Action 6.   [49] Action 9.

[50] Action 10.   [51] Action 15.

[52] 'The problem of refugees and displaced persons constitutes a threat to peace and security of the continent and its root causes must be addressed', CSSDCA Solemn Declaration, AHG/Decl.4(XXXVI), para. 10(g).

refugees and internally displaced persons constitutes a scar on the conscience of African governments and people',[53] and giving an undertaking to strengthen protection for refugees.[54] Among the key performance indicators were that all AU states should ratify the OAU Convention on Refugees and ensure legislative and other measures to implement its provisions by 2003, and for the AU to review the scope of the Convention by 2005, ensuring strengthening of its oversight mechanisms. In this context states will be required to provide information on 'the condition of refugees, the protection of their human rights and mechanisms for mitigating the situation of refugees'.[55]

Perhaps the most hopeful developments for a more integrated approach to refugees and human rights have come with two recent events. The first was at the AU Ministerial Conference on Human Rights in Kigali in May 2003, where it was recommended that there be 'inclusion of human rights and humanitarian principles, as well as other legal protection measures in peace agreements in order to facilitate the safe return to, and reintegration of refugees, returnees and former combatants in their countries of origin'.[56] The conference called for mechanisms to be set up to address the root causes of refugees in Africa, 'identification, documentation and dissemination of the best practices regarding refugees, such as allowing refugees to be integrated into local societies'.[57] It was also recommended that there be collaboration of civil society organisations in promoting and protecting the rights of refugees,[58] 'ensuring that the assistance given to refugees is directed at making them free and independent',[59] 'promotion of local capacities of member states hosting refugees',[60] 'encouraging the host countries and countries of origin to cooperate with the UNHCR in the establishment of tripartite commissions to facilitate the repatriation of refugees'.[61]

The resulting Kigali Declaration also stressed that AU organs 'in the exercise of their peace building and conflict resolution functions, ensure the inclusion of human rights, humanitarian principles and other legal

---

[53] Draft Memorandum of Understanding, Ministerial Review Meeting on the Calabashes of the Conference on Security, Stability, Development and Cooperation in Africa (CSSDCA), July 2002, Durban, OAU/Civil Society.3(II), Annex, para. I(e).

[54] Ibid., para. II(m).

[55] Ibid., para. 3.A.11. These issues are dealt with under the 'security' element.

[56] Report of the Meeting of Experts of the First AU Ministerial Conference on Human Rights in Africa, Kigali, 5–6 May 2003, EXP/CONF/HRA/RPT.(II), para. 40(1).

[57] Ibid., para. 40(5).   [58] Ibid., para. 40(6).   [59] Ibid., para. 40(7).

[60] Ibid., para. 40(8).   [61] Ibid., para. 40(9).

protection measures in peace agreements, in order to facilitate the voluntary repatriation and reintegration of refugees, returnees and former combatants in their countries of origin'.[62]

However, for the first time the AU identified a body which should have responsibility to enforce the OAU Refugee Convention, recommending that the African Commission on Human and Peoples' Rights have oversight on the OAU Convention on refugees and monitor compliance with it.[63] This places the issue firmly within a human rights field.

This has been consolidated further with the recent development of relationships between the UNHCR and the African Commission on Human and Peoples' Rights. As a result of a series of meetings, one in Harare in February 1994, another workshop in Dakar in December 1998 organised by the UNHCR, and the Commission's 26th Session in Rwanda in November 1999, attended by the UNHCR, an item was added to the agenda of the African Commission on Human and Peoples' Rights on refugees.[64] A Consultative Meeting was organised between the two organisations on 20–21 March 2003 in Ethiopia. Present at this meeting were members of the Commission, the UNHCR and the AU's Head of Division of Humanitarian Affairs, Refugees and Internally Displaced Persons in its African Commission. The meeting concluded that 'refugees are endowed with the same rights and responsibilities as all other human beings. The specific rights of refugees are an integral part of human rights and are universal, indivisible, inter-dependent and inter-related. Where national laws on refugees are inadequate or non-existent, general human rights law should therefore be invoked to protect refugees.'[65]

Among the recommendations from the meeting were that they should both develop a Memorandum of Understanding and that the Commission should monitor implementation of the OAU Refugee Convention.[66] Further, the African Commission should encourage states to implement rights domestically; they should focus on both women and children; and they should promote the Guiding Principles on Internal Displacement of the UN Secretary General's Representative on this issue. The Coordinating Committee on Assistance and Protection to Refugees and

[62] Kigali Declaration, MIN/CONF/HRA/Decl.1(I), paras. 12–14.

[63] Report of the Meeting of Experts of the First AU Ministerial Conference on Human Rights in Africa, para. 40(2). See also Draft Report of the Consultative Meeting between the African Commission on Human and Peoples' Rights and the United Nations High Commissioner for Refugees, 20–21 March 2003, Addis Ababa (no reference, on file with author), Conclusions and Recommendations, Annex I, para. 7.

[64] Ibid., at 1.   [65] Ibid., at Annex I, para. 7.   [66] Ibid., at Annex I.

Internally Displaced Persons under the AU should see how the OAU Convention could be improved to deal with the situation and 'should examine the possibility of promoting the adoption of an annual Decision by the Summit of Heads of State and Government, dealing with one specific refugee-related issue of concern to member states of the African Union', and should 'examine the feasibility of promoting the adoption of a Protocol to the 1969 OAU Refugee Convention which would expand its scope to cover issues not adequately addressed therein'.[67] It also recommended that the African Commission on Human and Peoples' Rights become a member of the Coordinating Committee on Assistance and Protection to Refugees and Internally Displaced Persons; the UNHCR and African Commission build partnerships with the UNHCHR and NGOs; and that the links between the Conflict Mechanism under the AU and the African Commission and Court on Human and Peoples' Rights should be explored.[68]

This Memorandum of Understanding has recently been concluded and states that the two organisations should cooperate in a number of ways including in the exchange of information, awareness raising, research and publications, application and using mechanisms under the Commission, setting up joint mechanisms for encouraging domestic implementation and maintaining contact with other organisations.[69] They agreed that each should participate in the meetings of the other, and the secretariats of each were charged with coordination.[70]

OAU mechanisms for dealing with refugees

Up until these developments, however, the OAU had several bodies to deal with refugee issues, although, as noted above, none of them were created under the Convention.

Commission on Refugees

In 1964 the Council of Ministers, having been informed that Rwandan refugees were becoming 'a very heavy charge on the countries adjacent

---

[67] Ibid.   [68] Ibid.

[69] Memorandum of Understanding between the African Commission on Human and Peoples' Rights and the UN High Commissioner for Refugees, no reference, on file with author, Article 2.

[70] Ibid., Article 3.

to Rwanda', set up a committee to visit the countries in question.[71] This became the Commission of Ten.[72] The Commission was mandated to consider how to deal with this situation and 'ways and means of maintaining refugees in their country of asylum'[73] and it visited about twenty-five refugee camps in Burundi, Uganda and Tanzania.[74] At the Council of Ministers' July 1964 meeting it was recommended that the Commission become a permanent body of the OAU.[75] The Commission was later expanded to fifteen,[76] and then twenty members.[77]

The Commission thus became the main policy-making body of the OAU on refugee issues. It held yearly sessions and the Bureau reported to its meetings. The Commission has taken missions to states,[78] given advice to governments and could provide emergency financial help to states.[79]

Given its central position one may have assumed that it would be the primary enforcement mechanism for the Convention, despite not being referred to in the Treaty. However, the Commission failed to make an impact, being criticised for being too politically influenced and for its lack of action: 'The extent of the impact of the C15 is clearly limited by considerations of realpolitik, as well as by the very real constraint of the "non-interference" clause that still holds considerable sway in Africa despite the recent examples of interventions.'[80]

It is perhaps unfortunate, therefore, that this body has survived the OAU/AU transition under the Directorate of Humanitarian Affairs. It has already carried out visits to a number of states.[81] The Council at the July

---

[71] Commission on the Problem of Refugees in Africa, CM/Res.36(II).
[72] Problem of Refugees in Africa, CM/Res.19(II).
[73] Ibid.   [74] Amate, *Inside the OAU*, at 462.   [75] Ibid., at 463.
[76] At the 35th Session of the Council of Ministers in 1980, Resolution on the Situation of Refugees in Africa, CM/Res.814(XXXV). The members were Angola, Cameroon, Mali, Niger, Nigeria, Senegal, Sudan, Swaziland, Tanzania, Uganda, Zaire, Zambia and Zimbabwe and two others to be chosen by North African states, Amate, *Inside the OAU*, at 472–3.
[77] Resolution on Refugees, Returnees and Displaced Persons in Africa, CM/Res.1521(LX), para. 10.
[78] See, for example, Resolution CM/Res.774(XXXIV) 1980. The Commission was asked by the Council of Ministers to go to some states to promote burden sharing and see how serious the problems were there and make recommendations: Resolution on the Situation of Refugees in Africa, CM/Res.829(XXXVI).
[79] Lawyers' Committee for Human Rights, *African Exodus*, at 146–7.
[80] Ibid., at 148. See also J. Oloka-Onyango, 'The Place and Role of the OAU Bureau for Refugees in the African Refugee Crisis', *International Journal of Refugee Law* 6 (1994) 34–52, at 39.
[81] Draft Report of the Executive Council, EX/CL/Draft/Rpt(III), para. 78.

2003 Summit called for attention to be paid to 'returnees'.[82] It was also suggested that consideration be given to setting up a national disasters committee in the Political Department,[83] although Ambassador Djinnit suggested that it would be better placed under humanitarian affairs.[84] The UNHCR hope that with improvements to the Coordinating Committee on Assistance to Refugees (CCAR), the effectiveness of the Commission can be improved.[85]

Bureau[86]

One of the conferences held, and co-sponsored with the UNHCR, ECA and others in 1967, on the Legal, Economic and Social Aspects of African Refugees, led to the setting up of the Bureau for Placement and Education of African Refugees in 1 March 1968.[87] Initially it was independent, but in 1971 was placed under the direction of the Assistant Secretary General for Political Affairs,[88] and in 1974 under the Political Department of the OAU. That same year the Bureau became the Secretariat to the Commission and to the Coordinating Committee on Assistance to Refugees.[89] The UNHCR has had staff seconded to the Bureau. In the early 1990s the Bureau was renamed the Bureau for Refugees, Displaced Persons and Humanitarian Assistance: 'Conceptually, the successive changes in the nomenclature of the bureau may reflect a metamorphosing mandate, and are in part reflective of the role that the bureau was supposed to play in the ever-changing refugee situation on the continent. However, in practical terms the operations of the office have remained largely the same since its inception.'[90] The tasks of the Bureau were to look for educational opportunities for refugees; give them resources to deal with their situation; mediate with host countries to ensure their rights are not violated; cooperate with the UNHCR and others; and provide information to states on

---

[82] Ibid., para. 82.   [83] Ibid., para. 83.   [84] Ibid., para. 85.

[85] See discussion on CCAR below.

[86] See Oloka-Onyango's summary of the Bureau which sums up its failures at that stage, Oloka-Onyango, 'The Place and Role of the OAU Bureau', at 47–52.

[87] Resolution of OAU Conference on Legal, Economic and Social Aspects of the Refugee Crisis in Africa.

[88] Bureau for the Placement and Education of African Refugees, CM/Res.244(XVII).

[89] Resolution on the OAU Bureau for the Placement and Education of Refugees, CM/Res.346(XXIII); Amate, *Inside the OAU*, at 467. See also Oloka-Onyango, 'The Place and Role of the OAU Bureau', at 42.

[90] Lawyers' Committee for Human Rights, *African Exodus*, at 140.

the causes of refugee crisis in Africa. Thus, at the early stages of its history it was intended 'primarily to be a "clearing house" of implementing resettlement operations in countries that host refugees, and to give refugees an opportunity for education and training in a bid to help them in the acquisition of skills that would assist them'.[91] The Bureau was 'expected to become actively involved in helping states to reconcile and harmonise their relations with other states, to enact amnesty laws to ensure the safety of returning refugees, to declare general amnesty to their nationals in exile and to help the refugees who decided to return home to do so in safety'.[92] This reflected the situation at the time, where most refugees came from states under colonial domination and the refugee issue was seen mainly as temporary.[93]

Over the years the Bureau shifted the focus of its attention to encouraging refugees to gain income for themselves. Through the Bureau, the OAU has funded various projects, and women and children were given particular consideration.[94] The ILO has also provided some financial assistance. Unfortunately it would appear these projects were not particularly successful as there was lack of evaluation of the programmes, the projects chosen were said to reinforce stereotypes – for example, of the role of women – and they did not actually receive a lot of money.[95] Further, despite its focus on education the Bureau appeared to be biased against rural refugees; only a very small number of individuals were ever supported; there was no provision for further education; and it had a limited budget.[96] There was also the problem of what happened when studies were over, 'the reality has been that there are serious obstacles to the employment of refugees in their host countries'.[97] In the end the impact of the Bureau on the refugee situation has been very limited.[98]

It is notable that at an early stage the Bureau was given a specific role in respect of refugee protection. This was later widened to include, for example, protecting refugees against arbitrary arrest and expulsion.[99] This could have enabled it to pay more attention to a human rights perspective. Unfortunately, this became secondary to its educational functions for various reasons, including the manner in which the Bureau was

---

[91] Ibid., at 142; see also Oloka-Onyango, 'The Place and Role of the OAU Bureau'.
[92] Amate, *Inside the OAU*, at 473.
[93] Lawyers' Committee for Human Rights, *African Exodus*, at 142–3.
[94] Ibid., at 157–8.   [95] Ibid., at 158.   [96] Ibid., at 155–6.   [97] Ibid., at 156.
[98] P. Ladouceur, 'Seminar on African Refugee Problems', *Journal of Modern African Studies* 8(2) (1970) 298–301, at 301.
[99] Amate, *Inside the OAU*, at 472–3.

set up under the direction of the political organs of the OAU:

> There is a loss [of] autonomy of action or decision-making insofar as the
> operations of the bureau are concerned. This severely [affects] the operation
> of the bureau and its ability to effectively respond to the refugee situation
> in Africa, since the question of [refugees] is often intrinsically a political
> matter. This perhaps explains the consistent emphasis on the question of
> education, training and placement, and the lesser emphasis given to issues of
> protection. Indeed today, the Bureau merely pays lip service to the question
> of protection.[100]

Further, 'the Bureau cannot issue public criticisms of member states, and
is constrained to urge, encourage or persuade them to adhere to their
obligations under the OAU Convention. Bureau officials assert that they
are involved in a good deal of quiet diplomacy, but the results of such
activity are not apparent.'[101]

   The lack of protective function has also been attributed to the failure of
the system of national correspondents.[102] It had initially been envisaged
that the OAU organs would be complemented and assisted in their work
by a network of national correspondents in countries across the continent.
However, few of these correspondents were appointed and of those that
were, few sent documentation and reports to the Bureau or attended meetings, and there were allegations of financial mismanagement.[103] Further,
no individual was appointed at the Bureau to be responsible for protection.[104] The Bureau also seemed to operate without reference to the
ACHPR or the work of its Commission.[105]

   These were not the only difficulties facing the Bureau. It also suffered
from a failure to publicise its activities outside the OAU; a limited number
of professionals; and its passive approach to its work in terms of the OAU
Convention:

> For one thing, the bureau could play a more assertive role in promoting
> the adoption of the principles of the OAU Convention . . . [Ratification]
> is clearly insufficient, unless accompanied by a serious process of incorpo-
> ration of the convention into domestic legislation, or (at a minimum) the

---

[100] Lawyers' Committee for Human Rights, *African Exodus*, at 152; Oloka-Onyango, 'The
      Place and Role of the OAU Bureau', at 41–2.
[101] Lawyers' Committee for Human Rights, *African Exodus*, at 161.
[102] Oloka-Onyango, 'The Place and Role of the OAU Bureau', at 42.
[103] Amate, *Inside the OAU*, at 42.
[104] Lawyers' Committee for Human Rights, *African Exodus*, at 153.
[105] Amnesty International, *Organization of African Unity*, at 27.

amendment of such legislation to reflect the convention's basic tenets. The bureau has been virtually silent on this crucial aspect of ensuring refugee protection.[106]

There were difficulties in funding the Bureau even from its early years, with special funds being set up, for example, in 1977 for southern African refugees.[107] Contribution to the funds was eventually made compulsory,[108] although this produced little result.[109] A Refugee Contingency Fund was set up in 1990–1 and provided the main funding for the Bureau, in theory obtaining 2 per cent of the budget of the OAU, although the amount was very small due to the OAU's overall financial problems. The CCAR was also supposed also to provide financial support, but this has been limited.[110]

The Bureau was in a position, with its protective mandate, to carry out a key role in the development of human rights of refugees; yet its impact was limited.[111] It has not survived the transition to the AU, although scholarship funds are still provided, on advice of the UNHCR, by the Humanitarian Division of the Political Affairs Directorate of the AU Commission.

Coordinating Committee on Assistance to Refugees (CCAR)

A Standing Committee of the OAU, ECA, ILO, UNESCO and UNDP was set up to advise the Bureau at first and a Consultative Board set up from representatives of other agencies to advise on general policy. These two committees then joined to make the Coordinating Committee[112] and this later included the OAU Liberation Committee and other liberation movements recognised by the OAU. The Committee was thus composed of NGOs and inter-governmental bodies. Therefore, although the Committee was initially created to assist the Secretary General in the organisation of conferences on African refugees (ICARA), it became more like a committee, giving advice to the Commission and assisting the OAU to work externally.[113]

---

[106] Lawyers' Committee for Human Rights, *African Exodus*, at 152–3.
[107] CM/Res.547(XXIX).		[108] Amate, *Inside the OAU*, at 468.		[109] Ibid., at 469.
[110] Lawyers' Committee for Human Rights, *African Exodus*, at 158–60.		[111] Ibid., at 6.
[112] At the 35th Session of the Council of Ministers the Coordinating Committee was also renamed Coordinating Committee on Assistance to Refugees and its mandate widened to implementation and advice on such, Amate, *Inside the OAU*, at 472–3.
[113] Lawyers' Committee for Human Rights, *African Exodus*, at 149.

Although initially it was felt to be a dynamic organisation in the face of liberation and apartheid, with the change in circumstances this impetus seemed to have waned. Although it offered the hope of involvement of a wide number of outside organisations in the refugee work of the OAU, unfortunately, it appeared to make little positive impact in reality:

> Even in the admission of members of the CCAR, it is clear that the Committee has not done as much as it could have, particularly in terms of meeting financial commitments made to Bureau programmes. At present, this body is largely inactive, in part because of the relative malaise of the Bureau, but also because the members of the Committee do not fully believe in its effectiveness, or in the capacity of the OAU to tackle the refugee question in a forthright, non-political fashion. One encounters a high level of skepticism – indeed cynicism – about the Bureau among most CCAR members.[114]

The Lawyers' Committee suggests that this may be a result of donor fatigue in general, although some members of the CCAR have been more enthusiastic than others.[115]

At present the UNHCR is compiling proposals with the AU to reinvigorate the CCAR by revamping its membership to include organisations working in the field who will actively contribute to the process at this level. It is hoped that the African Commission on Human and Peoples' Rights will be requested to act as an ex-officio member of the Committee. This Committee could then make recommendations to the Commission on Refugees and guide it in its policy making. In this way it could help determine when missions to states are required in view of a wide range of factors.

OAU attention to the issue of refugees: summary of trends

The OAU's approach to the refugee situation and human rights has gone through various changes over the years.

Generosity and settlement

Decolonisation and the number of conflicts in the 1960s increased the number of refugees within Africa.[116] Initially it is clear that the OAU saw

---

[114] Ibid., at 149–50.   [115] Ibid., at 150–1.

[116] A Resolution in 1975 linked refugees expressly to decolonisation: 'considering the progress realised in the field of decolonisation in Africa and the repercussions on refugee problems in Africa', Resolution on Africa Refugee Day, CM/Res.398(XXIV).

the refugee situation in Africa as resulting from the impact of colonisation and the moves towards independence.[117] Its OAU Liberation Committee was alerted to the issue of refugees at the 2nd Session in Dar es Salaam, in December 1963, with refugees being forced to leave colonial regimes in Mozambique, Angola, Namibia and others as a result of difficult conditions in those countries.[118] Sub-Committees set up to look into the matter further proposed that a commission on refugees actually be established under the Liberation Committee, clearly indicating how much this was seen as a decolonisation issue.[119]

As a result of this perception refugees were seen as another consequence of the fight against colonialism and for independence,[120] and the approach of the OAU to refugees in the early years of its existence, reflecting that adopted by African countries, was generous:

> In spite of some of the recent expulsions which have occurred, the record in Africa of a willingness to accommodate strangers, whether the cause of their movement was voluntary or involuntary, has generally been exemplary. The idea of large numbers of people, labelled refugees, who have not been incorporated into the host society in Africa is relatively new.[121]

In the course of this, the human rights of the refugees themselves were often mentioned and given favourable treatment.[122] This included recommending, for example, that children of refugees should be integrated into schools of host states and that the refugees all be given travel and identity

---

[117] For example, in its 1985 Resolution on the Root Causes of the African Refugee Problem the Council of Ministers noted that 'the oppressive systems of apartheid, colonialism and racism constitute major causes for the exodus of refugees in South Africa', Resolution on the Root Causes of the African Refugee Problem, CM/Res 987(XLII). See also International Conference on the Plight of Refugees, Returnees and Displaced Persons in Southern Africa, CM/Res.1181(XLIX). See Aiboni, *Protection of Refugees*, at 32.

[118] Amate, *Inside the OAU*, at 459.   [119] Ibid., at 460.

[120] It may also have been due to the relative prosperity of African states in their early independent years and the fact that international aid was provided, J. Crisp, 'Africa's Refugees: Patterns, Problems and Policy Challenges', Working Paper No. 28, *New Issues in Refugee Research* (New York: UNHCR, August 2000), www.unhcr.ch, at 5.

[121] B. E. Harrell-Bond, 'Repatriation: Under What Conditions is it the Most Desirable Solution for Refugees? An Agenda for Research', *African Studies Review* 32(1) (1989) 41–69, at 59. See also J. Fitzpatrick, 'Temporary Protection of Refugees: Elements of a Formalized Regime', *AJIL* 94(2) (2000) 279–306, at 284.

[122] B. Rutinwa, 'The End of Asylum? The Changing Nature of Refugee Policies in Africa', Working Paper No. 5, *New Issues in Refugee Research* (New York: UNHCR, 1999) www.unhcr.ch, at 7.

documents.[123] Solutions generally preferred at this time were resettlement in the host state and perhaps for more permanent solutions.[124] The OAU therefore looked at the position from the point of view of the refugee: 'recognising the essentially humanitarian nature of the problem and anxious to adopt measures to improve the living conditions of refugees and help them to lead a normal life'.[125]

Recognition of refugees beyond the colonial context

Towards the beginning of the 1980s, however, there was a shift as fights for independence became less relevant across the continent; yet the conflicts within these new African states continued to occur and the number of refugees continued to increase. At this stage the OAU started to recognise that the refugee situation may now be caused by African states themselves and that refugees could originate from territories that were not under colonial or white minority regimes. Thus, in a conference in Arusha in May 1979 held by the OAU, UNHCR and ECA and other voluntary organisations, it was stated:

> We must boldly accept and recognise that independent African states have only themselves to blame for the ever-increasing number of refugees originating from independent Africa, because we cannot anymore continue to invoke the administrative and exploitative methods of our former colonial rulers to explain why asylum-seeking is becoming one of the permanent features of the political and social situation in Africa.[126]

The conference made a number of important recommendations on human rights. These included the need for African states to

> make every effort to fully implement the basic instruments relating to human rights . . . to include the provision of international instruments dealing with human rights and refugee problems in their national

---

[123] Amate, *Inside the OAU*, at 460; Resolution on the Problem of Refugees in Africa, CM/Res.103(IX).

[124] B. S. Chimni, 'From Resettlement to Involuntary Repatriation: Towards a Critical History of Durable Solutions to Refugee Problems', Working Paper No. 2, *New Issues in Refugee Research* (New York: UNHCR, 1999), www.unhcr.ch.

[125] Resolution on the Problem of Refugees in Africa, CM/Res.149 (XI); see also Resolution on the Activities of the Bureau of Placement and Education of Refugees, CM/Res.202(XIII).

[126] ECA Executive Secretary Adebayo Adedeji, as cited by Amate, *Inside the OAU*, at 470. The OAU Assistant Secretary General, Peter Onu, also stated: 'We all know too well that the largest number of refugees in Africa have fled from independent and sovereign states.'

legislations . . . to launch, possibly with the aid of modern communications techniques, an educational campaign to instill the respect for human
rights and tolerance of differences into all the people of the various nation-
alities in African countries, whatever socio-cultural, economic or political
differences may exist between them . . . to consider making official public
declarations of amnesty to their respective nationals currently in exile, so
as to encourage their voluntary repatriation.[127]

These were adopted by the Council of Ministers and AHSG in July 1979,
who in turn urged for the full implementation of amnesty laws and for
respect for OAU and UN charters on human rights: 'This was about
the first time that one heard African delegates express open concern in
an OAU forum about the violation of human rights by OAU member
governments.'[128] As a result of the conference, increased funding came
from international bodies to the OAU.[129] There was a clear recognition, as
stated in 1982, by the OAU that 'the refugee situation currently obtaining
in Africa is fundamentally different from that which was prevailing when
the OAU refugee serving organs were first set up more than a decade
ago'.[130]

Despite this and the rhetoric on human rights, however, the recognition marked the start of moves towards less generous policies towards
refugees.[131] Besides the increasing irrelevance of the colonial situation,
other factors also had a part to play, including the sheer number of refugees
and their impact on host states; restrictive policies by the western states;
and increasing public awareness, accompanied by xenophobia.[132]

By the 1990s the new perspective on refugees was reflected in the
Khartoum Declaration on Africa's Refugee Crisis.[133] This 1990 Declaration expressed the themes important to the OAU at that stage, including
a focus on root causes, and a recognition that refugees are the responsibility of Africans themselves, but that there was a need for international
assistance.[134] By the end of the 1990s, the 1998 Khartoum Declaration

---

[127] Amate, *Inside the OAU*, at 471.   [128] Ibid., at 472.
[129] Ibid., at 474. See also Resolution on the Situation of Refugees in Africa on the OAU Bureau
for Refugees and Other OAU Refugee Organs, CM/Res.915(XXXVIII).
[130] Ibid., preamble.   [131] Rutinwa, 'The End of Asylum?', at 1.
[132] Ibid., at 1–2. See also Mertus, 'The State and the Post Cold War Refugee Regime', at 334.
[133] Adopted by the 17th Ordinary Session of the Commission of Fifteen on Refugees, Khartoum, 22–24 September 1990.
[134] 'Africa fully realizes that the major root causes of the refugee problem are situated within
Africa, and that the total eradication of these causes is the primary responsibility of the
Africans themselves', but then further, given the economic situation in Africa, 'Africa's
capacity to handle the problem is limited especially considering that the majority of

added to this the need to enhance the capacity of the OAU's role in resolving conflicts; for states to accede to the UN and OAU Conventions on refugees as well as the ACHPR;[135] concern about internally displaced persons, and for states to take action to protect humanitarian workers;[136] the hardships of refugees in their countries of asylum and for these countries 'to protect their human rights and safeguard their welfare';[137] and to ensure 'the full participation of refugees, returnee and internally displaced women and children in rehabilitation, reintegration, reconstruction and peace building programmes'.[138] The Recommendations stressed that 'voluntary repatriation and reintegration remain the most durable solution to the problem of refugees', requiring states 'to strengthen democratic institutions and other mechanisms for resolving disputes', noting the role of women and youth, 'conventional reintegration programmes should be complemented with activities which are more specifically designed to promote democracy, reconciliation and justice, including consensus building on notions of responsibility and justice and the promotion of human rights and majority rights'.[139]

The present approach

The approach of the OAU/AU to the refugee situation and the rights of refugees is marked, therefore, by a number of themes.

Refugees seen as threat to the state

One of the consequences of this shift in approach to refugees was that the refugee situation was viewed less as a threat to the individual refugee rights and more in terms of refugees being a potential threat to the state and a security issue:

> The problem of refugees and displaced persons continues to threaten peace, security and stability which as a result has hampered the economic and social development process in most of the member states. The factors that

the World's Least Developed Countries are situated in Africa', Khartoum Declaration on Africa's Refugee Crisis, September 1990, adopted by the 17th Ordinary Session of the Commission of Fifteen on Refugees, Khartoum, 22–24 September 1990, para. 2.
[135] Paras. 3 and 4.   [136] Paras. 10 and 11.   [137] Para. 13.   [138] Para. 16.
[139] Khartoum Recommendations of the OAU Ministerial Meeting on Refugees, Returnees and Internally Displaced Persons in Africa, adopted at the OAU Ministerial Meeting on Refugees, Returnees and Internally Displaced Persons in Africa, 13–14 December 1998, Khartoum, para. 16.

generate refugees and displaced persons have generally remained the same; they have varied only in terms of intensity as the continent is witnessing continuous causes for refugee movements such as incidents of civil strife; persistent conflicts as well as violations of human rights.[140]

Although there was some (limited) recognition of the impact, for example, of attacks on refugees themselves, the focus was often on the impact on the state: 'These attacks, apart from the human and material losses they cause, constitute a grave violation of the national sovereignty and territorial integrity [of] recipient states.'[141]

The ACHPR[142] and the OAU Refugee Convention's mention of subversive activities in Article 3 comes to the fore in this regard, despite this having been associated with colonialism.[143]

This approach therefore saw in the 1990s 'a marked decline in the standards of protection . . . Perhaps the most disregarded rights are those relating to security . . . The large size of modern refugee camps and the way refugee settlements are maintained has also resulted in significant erosion of basic rights to human dignity, as well as self-sufficiency rights.'[144]

Addressing root causes

Since the end of the Cold War international support for the refugee situation in Africa has declined and left Africa to deal more with its own problems,[145] and the OAU has focused on the need to address the 'root causes' of the refugee problem.[146] However, this perspective has not been

---

[140] Report of the OAU Commission of Twenty on the Situation of Refugees, Returnees and Displaced Persons in Africa, CM/1985(LXV) Rev.1, para. 75.

[141] Resolution on the Situation of Refugees in Africa, CM/Res.1117(XLVI), para. 5.

[142] Article 12; Article 23(2)(a) reads: 'Any individual enjoying the right of asylum under Article 12 of the present Charter shall not engage in subversive activities against his country of origin or any other State Party to the present Charter.'

[143] Lawyers' Committee for Human Rights, *African Exodus*, at 32. See also Declaration on the Problem of Subversion, AHG/Res.27(II); The Problem of Refugees in Africa, AHG/Res.26(II).

[144] Rutinwa, 'The End of Asylum?', at 14.

[145] Lawyers' Committee for Human Rights, *African Exodus*, at 140.

[146] See for example, 'Council therefore, underscored the imperative need to put an end to this situation by addressing the root causes', Report of the Seventy-Third Ordinary Session of the Council of Ministers, February 2001, CM/Rpt.(LXXIII), paras. 58–9. Report of the Secretary General on the Thirtieth Ordinary Session of the OAU Commission on Refugees, on the Situation of Refugees, Returnees and Displaced Persons in Africa, CM/2105(LXX) Rev.1 notes a series of meetings held by the OAU and the activities of the

particularly helpful:

> Root causes discussions contribute little to the search for durable solutions.
> The root causes are well known . . . Rarely do refugees seem to be a prime
> factor in the end of a crisis . . . The root causes are largely beyond redress or
> elimination by the refugee assistance system, but the system can sometimes
> deal with immediate causes, can moderate and discourage outflows, or can
> encourage and facilitate return.[147]

This attention to root causes was attributed in part to the organisation
of the Political Department of the OAU: 'This led to the creation of
a division concerned exclusively with conflict management among
member states. The Bureau for Refugees is an integral part of the Political
Department of the OAU Secretariat, significantly impacting on the
character of the response as well as the nature of the operations of the
office.'[148]

The 1994 Addis Ababa Recommendations noted that the OAU should
develop a Comprehensive Plan of Action for tackling root causes, noting in particular the need for states to 'rise up to the challenges of
practicing politics of inclusion and popular participation in national
affairs; creating a firm foundation for responsible and accountable
governance; and promoting social progress, economic development and
a just and fair society'.[149] In this context it also noted conflict resolution
and prevention and the need to respect humanitarian law during such
times.[150]

Among the root causes highlighted by the OAU are: 'natural disasters,
violation of human rights, armed conflicts and racist South Africa's
destabilisation activities [which] give rise to refugee problems in some
member states'.[151] Further recognition of the abuse of human rights,
refusal to respect democracy or free and fair election results, as well as

---

Commission itself including missions to various countries. It constantly mentions the
need to tackle the 'root causes' of refugees and IDP. Further, 'the imperative need to put an
end to this situation by resolutely addressing its causes', Decision on Refugees, CM/Dec.
574(LXXIII).

[147] B. N. Stein, 'Durable Solutions for Developing Country Refugees', *International
Migration Review* 20(2) (1986) 264–82, at 267–8. See also Harrell-Bond, 'Repatriation',
at 46.

[148] Lawyers' Committee for Human Rights, *African Exodus*, at 140–1.

[149] Recommendations of the OAU/UNHCR Symposium, Recommendation No. 2.

[150] Ibid., Recommendation No. 4.

[151] Resolution on the Situation of Refugees in Africa, CM/Res.1117(XLVI), preamble.

external factors, including 'international economic forces', have also been recognised.[152]

The solutions therefore suggested have included reference to states' commitments to human rights:

> noting with satisfaction the outgoing efforts on the part of some Member States to address the root causes of the refugee problem and most notably the coming into force in October 1986 of the African Charter of Human and People's Rights and the measures being taken in order to bring about the establishment of the African Human Rights Commission, which will greatly contribute to the eradication of one of the causes of the African Refugee problem.[153]

The OAU itself should also contribute by 'elaborating and expanding its activities in the fields of human rights monitoring, the promotion of human rights and humanitarian law, election monitoring, the management of political transitions, and the development of early warning systems at national, sub-regional and continental levels'.[154]

States in this regard have been called upon to ratify and adhere to the various human rights treaties and set up national commissions to coordinate refugee issues.[155] They have also been required to 'create the propitious conditions to spare their populations forced movements and asylum drive, by establishing a climate of peace and stability as well as the necessary democratic institutions'.[156] It seems that the OAU sees human rights protection as providing the framework 'towards the creation of an enabling environment which guarantees respect for human rights, accountability and the observance of the rule of law for the purpose of reversing, or, at least, reducing the incidence of asylum seeking',[157] and an

---

[152] Addis Ababa Document on Refugees and Forced Population Displacements in Africa, adopted by the OAU/UNHCR Symposium on Refugees and Forced Population Displacements in Africa, 8–10 September 1994, Addis Ababa, Special Issue, *IJRL* (1995) 303–19.

[153] Resolution on the Situation of Refugees in Africa, preamble.

[154] Addis Ababa Document on Refugees and Forced Population Displacements, at 317.

[155] Resolution on the Root Causes of the African Refugee Problem, CM/Res.1274(LII), paras. 4–6; Resolution on Refugees and Displaced Persons in Africa, CM/Res.1370 (LV).

[156] Report on the OAU Commission on the Situation of Refugees, Returnees and Displaced Persons in Africa (Doc.CM.2067(LXVIII), CM/Dec.412(LXVIII), para. 2.

[157] Resolution on Refugees and Displaced Persons in Africa, CM/Res.1370(LV), para. 4. See also Report of the Secretary General on the Thirtieth Ordinary Session of the OAU Commission on Refugees, on the Situation of Refugees, Returnees and Displaced Persons in Africa, CM/2105(LXX) Rev.1, para. 130; Decision on the Report of the Secretary General on the Thirtieth Ordinary Session of the OAU Commission on Refugees, on the Situation of Refugees, Returnees and Displaced Persons (Doc.CM/2105(LXX)), CM/Dec.459(LXX).

'African society characterised by the rule of law, tolerance, democracy and economic and social development'.[158] Root causes in this regard clearly include dealing with conflicts,[159] and have also been extended to cover 'persecution'[160] as well as a requirement more generally 'to promote the democratic culture'.[161]

Refugees as a temporary issue

The shift from seeing refugees as the result of colonisation to an acknowledgement that the refugee situation was being caused by African states themselves led to more temporary solutions being preferred. This reflected a similar approach by the international community in general.[162]

There are various elements to this. Temporary protection can offer some assistance to those who do not satisfy the full status under the UN and OAU Conventions and has certain benefits.[163] Those given 'prima facie' status often live in camps and are not accorded basic Convention refugee rights.[164] This has led many to argue that such individuals should be accorded a right of temporary asylum in some circumstances. Unlike the right to non-refoulement, however, it is unlikely that this has reached the status of legally binding rule.[165] Article 1(2) of the OAU Convention has been said to make the link between prima facie determination and procedures for determining full status, and it has been argued that Article 2(5) provides for temporary asylum and when linked with the right of

---

[158] Tunis Declaration on the 1969 Convention Governing the Specific Aspects of Refugee Problems, 13–15 June 1994, Tunis, AHG/DECL.6(XXX).

[159] Resolution on Refugees, Returnees and Displaced Persons in Africa, CM/Res.1433(LVII). Decision on the Report of the Commission of the Twenty on the Situation of Refugees, CM/Dec.362(LXVI); Introductory Note of the Secretary General to the Seventy-Fourth Ordinary Session of the Council of Ministers, on file with the author, at 30.

[160] Decision on the Fiftieth Anniversary of the Adoption of the 1951 Convention on the Status of Refugees, AHG/Dec.165(XXXVII).

[161] Draft Decisions of the Sixty-Seventh Ordinary Session of the Council of Ministers, CM/DRAFT/DECISIONS(LXVII) REV.1, in the Decision of the OAU Council of Ministers on the Report of the Commission of Twenty on the Situation of Refugees, Returnees and Displaced Persons in Africa, CM/Draft/Dec.22(LXVII) Rev.2.

[162] Helton, *The Price of Indifference*, at 185.

[163] It 'serves as an interim response to mass influx, providing safety while a durable solution is sought'; is 'often associated with effective responsibility sharing'; 'states weary of their obligations under refugee law may look upon a TP regime as a strategy to shift refugee protection from the realm of law to that of politics and voluntary humanitarian assistance', Fitzpatrick, 'Temporary Protection', at 4.

[164] J. Hyndman and B. V. Nylund, 'UNHCR and the Status of Prima Facie Refugees in Kenya', *International Journal of Refugee Law* 10(1) (1998) 21–48, at 35.

[165] Ibid., at 35–6.

non-refoulement in Article 2(3) 'this might provide some sort of safe haven until a more durable solution has been found'.[166]

Further, it is suggested that because standards applicable to the treatment of refugees have historically developed under the remit of humanitarian laws and in response to conflicts, any solutions to them are seen as temporary, rather than relating to the long term. Moving refugees into the area of human rights law does bring with it some suggestion of permanent obligations. For those who are unable to return to their home states, it is important that their rights are considered on a long-term basis:

> While there is no right to asylum as such, there are standards to be respected once it has been granted. Recognition must also be given to the fact that there may be circumstances under which refugees are not contemplating returning to their country of origin, and therefore must be able to enjoy their human rights in the place that they have taken refuge.[167]

In order for refugees to be able to become self-sufficient in their host states, they must be able to enjoy their rights to freedom of movement, work and education, for example.[168]

However, this more permanent approach brings obvious concerns for states.[169] Thus,

> refugee law challenges traditional notions of state sovereignty and requires states to tolerate the presence of certain non-national[s]. The remedial obligations of refugee law fall on states that bear no direct responsibility for the human rights violations or uncontrolled violence that provoked the victim's flight. Moreover, these duties arise from the fortuitous arrival of the claimants. Compliance with refugee law can thus entail significant political costs.[170]

The OAU has tended, therefore, to stress the 'civilian and humanitarian nature of asylum'.[171] This has had two consequences.

Voluntary repatriation rather than settlement

In its early years voluntary repatriation had not been promoted by the OAU due to the anti-colonial wars from which individuals had

---

[166] Ibid., at 36.   [167] Ibid., at 43.   [168] Ibid., at 39.
[169] Mertus, 'The State and the Post Cold War Refugee Regime', at 343.
[170] Fitzpatrick, 'Temporary Protection', at 3.
[171] Decision on the Report of the Secretary General on the Situation of Refugees, Returnees and Displaced Persons, Doc.CM/2256(LXXVI), CM/Dec.667, paras. 4–6.

fled.[172] Instead, the OAU promoted local integration and settlement in the host state as the preferred solution,[173] something also preferred by Western states. The activities of the Bureau on Refugees in finding education and employment opportunities reflected this approach.[174]

However, in more recent years after the colonial legacy became less important, the OAU has advocated voluntary repatriation as the ideal solution, rather than the permanent settlement of the refugees in the host states.[175] This reflects a similar approach by the UN.[176] Article 5(1) of the Convention notes that 'the essentially voluntary character of repatriation shall be respected in all cases and no refugee shall be repatriated against his will', although it is not advocated in the Convention itself as the primary solution.[177] This is also supported by the fact that the principle of non-refoulement is expressly laid out in the Convention.[178] In addition Article 2(3) states that 'no person shall be subjected by a Member State to measures such as rejection at the frontier, return or expulsion, which would compel him to return to or remain in a territory where his life, physical integrity or liberty would be threatened for the reasons set out in Article I, paragraphs 1 and 2'.

---

[172] Resolution on Voluntary Repatriation of African Refugees, CM/Res.399(XXIV).

[173] Resolution on the Refugee Situation in Africa, CM/Res.1241(L), paras. 5 and 6. See J. R. Rogge and J. O. Akol, 'Repatriation: Its Role in Resolving Africa's Refugee Dilemma', *International Migration Review* 23(2) (1989) 184–200, at 187.

[174] Resolution on the Bureau for the Placement and Education of Refugees, CM/Res.266 (XIX). The Council of Ministers, for example, called consistently for the BREAR to be strengthened and enlarged to cover 'resettlement of rural refugees', Resolution on Commission of Ten on Refugees, CM/Res.296(XX).

[175] Resolution on the Root Causes of the African Refugee Problem, CM/Res.1274(LII), preamble. The solutions advocated by the Addis Ababa document of 1995 are: voluntary repatriation as the 'best solution'; and that 'every opportunity for the voluntary repatriation of refugees should be seized upon', stressing that 'the principle of voluntariness should be respected at all times', Addis Ababa Document on Refugees and Forced Population Displacements in Africa. Goodwin-Gill notes that the UNHCR seem to see this as the option of last resort, Resettlement as an Instrument of Protection, Sub-Committee of the Whole on International Protection, UN Doc.EC/SCP/65, 9 July 1991; Goodwin-Gill, *The Refugee in International Law*, at 277. See also Chimni, 'From Resettlement to Involuntary Repatriation'.

[176] Harrell-Bond, 'Repatriation', at 41; Statute of UNHCR, para. 1 as detailed in UNGA Resolution 428(V); Mertus, 'The State and the Post Cold War Refugee Regime', at 342.

[177] With Article 5(2) simply stating: 'The country of asylum, in collaboration with the country of origin, shall make adequate arrangements for the safe return of refugees *who request repatriation.*'

[178] M. Barutciski, 'Involuntary Repatriation when Refugee Protection is no Longer Necessary: Moving Forward after the 48th Session of the Executive Committee', *International Journal of Refugee Law* 10(2) (1998) 236–55, at 247.

The Addis Ababa Conference in 1994 underscored the principle of voluntary repatriation as the best solution – noting, however, constraints to its implementation given the security situation prevailing in some countries. It deplored attempts to return refugees against their will but recommended that 'every opportunity for voluntary repatriation of refugees should be seized upon', stressing the principle of voluntariness.[179] States are required in this regard to allow refugees to 'participate in decisions affecting their repatriation', including that 'they should be provided with all the relevant information necessary for informed judgments. The government of the country of origin, the government of the country of asylum, the United Nations High Commissioner for Refugees should cooperate in providing refugees with the necessary information.'[180] It was, however, willing to consider that on some occasions 'inter-African resettlement' may be the only solution: 'there is a need for African countries to reinvigorate inter-African resettlement of refugees'. It recommended that African states offer places for resettlement in their territories; and that the UNHCR provide the necessary facilities for this.[181]

Thus, it has urged states to find 'durable solutions to refugee problems most importantly by facilitating voluntary repatriation, while endeavouring to create conducive conditions to that effect, and concomitantly to taking preventative measures to peacefully resolve conflicts, to avoid forced displacement of populations'.[182] This should be done 'in conformity with the international legal instruments on refugees'.[183]

States of refugees' origin, however, have certain obligations which have human rights implications in this regard. The OAU has said that they should 'create conducive conditions in order to promote the voluntary repatriation of refugees who wish to return home, in conformity with the relevant provisions of the 1951 UN Convention with its 1967 Protocol and the 1969 OAU Convention on Specific Aspects of Refugee Problems

---

[179] Recommendations of the OAU/UNHCR Symposium, Recommendation Nos. 16–18.

[180] Ibid., Recommendation No. 19.   [181] Ibid., Recommendation Nos. 22–4.

[182] Decision on the Fiftieth Anniversary of the Adoption of the 1951 Convention on the Status of Refugees, AHG/Dec.165(XXXVII). See also Resolution on Refugees, Returnees and Displaced Persons in Africa, CM/Res.1433(LVII).

[183] Report of the OAU Commission on Refugees, Returnees and Displaced Persons in Africa, CM/2171(LXXII), Rev.2. See also Decision on the Report of the OAU Commission on Refugees, Regarding the Situation of Refugees, Returnees and Displaced Persons in Africa, CM/Dec.531(LXXII); Draft Resolutions, CM/Draft/Res.1–30(LXIII) Rev.1, Draft Resolution on Refugees, Returnees and Displaced Persons, CM/Draft/Res.5(LXIII) Rev.1. See Rogge and Akol, 'Repatriation', at 186; Chimni, 'From Resettlement to Involuntary Repatriation', at 13; and Rutinwa, 'The End of Asylum?', at 9.

in Africa'.[184] Further, 'governments should not resort to the forcible repatriation of refugees for any reason. Furthermore, refugees should not be returned to conditions where they may be endangered.'[185] In this regard it has stressed the democratic nature of society: 'appeals to all member states concerned to consider creating the necessary conducive political atmosphere in order to enable the voluntary repatriation of refugees to their countries of origin to take place ... to give special attention to the plight of vulnerable categories of refugees, namely, women, children, the aged and the disabled'.[186] While there may be benefits of voluntary repatriation, it raises certain difficulties. Refugees who have been away from their home state, or children born outside their parents' home state, have to readjust to society elsewhere, with the skills that they may have acquired.[187] They may have set up a new life in the host state,[188] and 'the emphasis upon promoting repatriation may have the effect of reducing the importance of integration as a durable solution; even successful UNHCR assistance programs in host countries are thus endangered'.[189] Home states are also not always ready to readmit refugees, who may be seen as a financial burden or as a security threat.[190]

Despite the obvious stress in the OAU Convention on repatriation as voluntary,[191] the whole issue of the definition of a voluntary act needs to be considered, particularly where, as has occurred in the African context, repatriation can now take place back to states which may not be free from conflict.[192] The OAU/AU has made some slight concession to the fact that 'while voluntary reparation means the best solution to refugee problems, resettlement to another country is sometimes the only way to guarantee the protection of refugees ... There is a need for African countries to reinvigorate inter-African resettlement of refugees', appealing to African states 'to offer additional places for the resettlement in their territories of refugees from other African countries', and that UNHCR should 'provide the necessary resources to facilitate their reintegration

---

[184] Report of the OAU Commission of Twenty on the Situation of Refugees, Returnees and Displaced Persons in Africa, CM/2038(LXVII) Rev.1.

[185] Addis Ababa Document on Refugees and Forced Population Displacements in Africa, at 317.

[186] Ibid.   [187] Rogge and Akol, 'Repatriation', at 193 and 194–5.

[188] Ibid., at 194.   [189] Harrell-Bond, 'Repatriation', at 44.   [190] Ibid., at 45.

[191] Rogge and Akol, 'Repatriation', at 197. On voluntary repatriation, see Executive Committee of UNHCR, Conclusion No. 18(XXXI) and Conclusion No. 40(XXXVI), 1980 and 1985 respectively; Harrell-Bond, 'Repatriation', at 47.

[192] Harrell-Bond, 'Repatriation', at 55; Goodwin-Gill, *The Refugee in International Law*, at 276; Helton, *The Price of Indifference*, at 179.

into their new society. In cooperation with the OAU it should also help in developing resettlement criteria to ensure that inter-African resettlement is implemented in a way which is compatible with the integration capacity of the accepting countries.'[193] The main focus of its approach, however, is voluntary repatriation.

It is interesting to consider to what extent, therefore, the OAU is 'promoting' or 'facilitating' voluntary repatriation.[194] Further,

> from the point of view of most African refugees, the *promotion* of voluntary repatriation would seem to be a contradiction in terms. Most refugees do want to go home and, as the scanty evidence available suggests . . . refugees who return when conditions at home permit it do so *with or without transport or material assistance*. And in some cases, certain groups of refugees . . . do return 'spontaneously' even before conditions are conducive.[195]

The OAU Convention envisages organised repatriation, 'return under the terms of a plan worked out well in advance and has the support of both the home and asylum governments as well as that of UNHCR and refugees themselves', although many refugees will often return home without assistance.[196]

Repatriation imposes huge burdens on the UNHCR and the OAU, both of whom, it has been argued, 'lack the capacity to superintend the social and economic reintegration of returnees into their home society, and [have] no power to ensure their protection'.[197] But voluntary repatriation carries with it human rights obligations:

> Both the facilitation and the promotion of voluntary repatriation fall within the province of the UNHCR, while the right to return to one's own country locates such efforts squarely in a human rights context. To ignore this dimension and the legal implications arising from the concept of nationality would be to condone exile at the expense of human rights. Voluntary repatriation also involves a dimension of responsibility, namely, the responsibility of the international community to find solutions without 'institutionalising' exile to such a degree that it disregards the interests of individuals and communities.[198]

---

[193] Addis Ababa Document on Refugees and Forced Population Displacements in Africa, at 318.
[194] Goodwin-Gill, *The Refugee in International Law*, at 273.
[195] Harrell-Bond, 'Repatriation', at 58.   [196] Okoth-Obbo, 'Thirty Years On', at 53.
[197] Harrell-Bond, 'Repatriation', at 45.
[198] Goodwin-Gill, *The Refugee in International Law*, at 271.

In addition, the idea of group eligibility in Article 1(2) of the OAU Convention suggests a temporary approach:

> At the time the convention was adopted, it was thought that group eligibility would be mitigated by two factors – namely burden sharing and the temporary character of the African refugee problem. This explains the convention's provisions on burden-sharing and voluntary repatriation. In other words, the notion of group eligibility under the OAU Convention was based on the premise of legally institutionalised temporary protection coexistent with individual status determination procedures.[199]

But states have obligations. Firstly, the OAU has required 'Member states to create, insofar as possible, with the assistance of the Bureau, OAU, HCR, of countries of asylum or any other party, the conditions which will favour such repatriation.'[200] This was accompanied by the need 'to create an atmosphere conducive to the return of these refugees to their countries of origin' and for assistance to home states through raising 'funds and collect[ing] materials to help the new states to create conditions, congenial for the return of the refugees', and 'facilitat[ing] the full transfer of the refugees savings and property especially working tools and personal effects; allow[ing] couples of mixed marriages to decide freely on their repatriation; prevent[ing] the formation on their territories of subversive groups, which would hinder the tasks of rehabilitation and reconstruction of the newly independent countries and which would be inimical to the efforts of reconciliation'.[201] Furthermore, it appealed 'to the governments concerned to solemnly declare a long lasting general amnesty in order to facilitate the tasks or reconciliation and the return of their refugees'.[202]

This has human rights implications. As has been noted:

> The notion of safe return has come to occupy an interim position between the refugee deciding voluntarily to go back home and any other non national who, having no claim to international protection, faces deportation or is otherwise required to leave . . . although the state remains bound by such provisions as prohibit torture or cruel and inhuman treatment, no rule of international law appears formally to require that a state proposing to

---

[199] Lawyers' Committee for Human Rights, *African Exodus*, at 29–30.
[200] Resolution on Commission of Ten on Refugees, CM/Res.296(XX), para. 9.
[201] Resolution on Voluntary Repatriation of African Refugees, CM/Res.399(XXIV).
[202] Ibid.

implement returns take into account and act on assessments of both 'legal' safety and safety in fact, including basic issues like conflict, de-mining and a working police and justice system.[203]

Emergency relief rather than development

The way in which refugees have been treated, as falling under humanitarian/conflict and temporary emergency responses, has meant that budgets for development have not tended to include reference to refugees, despite the huge impact this can have on a state.[204] As a result any funding and support provided for host states has tended to focus on relief rather than development, again stressing the temporary nature of the situation.[205]

However, there has been a shift, with the end of the Cold War, to considering the development implications of the refugee situation. This has still been accompanied by repatriation of refugees as the preferred solution[206] but is based on the idea that the root causes of refugee problems are internal factors, so that 'developing' the home state will make an exodus of refugees less likely. In this sense, giving development assistance is essential.[207]

Recently the OAU/AU has recognised the link between the rights of refugees and development, although not because the rights of the individual refugees themselves may be affected. Indeed, beyond the colonial context, in recent years, the OAU/AU has seemed to see the need to focus on refugees primarily because of the impact on African states' development, 'conscious of the fact that the continuation of such a situation may have direct and very adverse effects on the economic and social development of these countries which have so far borne the heavy burden along', but then 'considering the extremely critical situation of the displaced people of Chad who have been displaced by the civil wars'.[208] Conversely, it also

---

[203] Goodwin-Gill, *The Refugee in International Law*, at 275–6.

[204] Harrell-Bond, *Towards the Economic and Social 'Integration'*, at 3.

[205] Chimni, 'From Resettlement to Involuntary Repatriation', at 15. See also Harrell-Bond, 'Repatriation', at 51.

[206] J. Macrae, 'Aiding Peace . . . and War: UNHCR, Returnee Reintegration, and the Relief-Development Debate', Working Paper No. 14, *New Issues in Refugee Research* (New York. UNHCR, 1999), www.unhcr.ch, at 8–9.

[207] Ibid., at 10; Harrell-Bond, *Towards the Economic and Social 'Integration'*, at 9.

[208] Resolution on the Assistance of the Organization of African Unity to the Chadian Refugees and the Displaced Persons, CM/Res.818(XXXV), preamble. For example, in the 1984 ICARA II, held in Geneva, 9–11 July 1984, it seemed to focus more on development

saw the 'the serious nature of the refugee phenomenon in Africa which is being further aggravated by the deplorable state of global economy'.[209]

As a result, however, the OAU/AU has stated that relief and assistance in the context of refugees should

> be conceived and delivered within the context of the long-term development goals of the concerned countries and with a view to preventing the recurrence of conflict and/or displacement. Relief and humanitarian assistance should therefore be designed in such a way that their short-term nature paves the way for medium- to long-term solutions, namely rehabilitation, reconstruction and development with transformation as the ultimate and most durable goal.[210]

Thus,

> in relation to repatriation, particularly of refugees of an agricultural background, they should be provided [with] seeds, tools and other agricultural implements, and livestock so that they may be able to regain a normal way of life. There should also be major investments in health, education, shelter and sanitation and in the recovery and rehabilitation of the social and economic infrastructures.[211]

In this regard, with Africa's Priority Programme for Economic Recovery 1986–90, the OAU called on states to take measures to prevent the impact of refugees and internally displaced persons and prevent population exodus. Included within the short-term measures at the national level are 'promotion and respect for human rights', and, long term, 'enacting national legislation to define and guarantee the rights of the individual and the community, and also those of refugees, displaced persons and victims of natural disasters'.[212]

Thus, there is a desire to improve the human rights of refugees because this is necessary for Africa's development.

---

assistance to states, R. F. Gorman, 'Beyond ICARA II: Implementing Refugee-Related Development Assistance', *International Migration Review* 20(2) (1986) 283–98.

[209] Resolution on the Refugees Situation, CM/Res.1247(LI), preamble.

[210] Recommendations of the OAU/UNHCR Symposium on Refugees and Forced Population Displacements in Africa, Recommendation No. 29.

[211] Ibid., Recommendation No. 30.

[212] In addition, the Council of Ministers, for example, has called on states to 'incorporate as much as possible in their national and regional development plans, the specific problems of refugees especially since they constitute an important human potential which is able to contribute fully in the socio economic development of their countries', Decision on the Report of the Secretary General on the Situation of Refugees, Returnees and Displaced Persons, Doc.CM/2256(LXXVI), CM/Dec.667, para. 8.

recognising the problems of refugees, because of their adverse effects on
individual human beings and the economies of the countries affected
require urgent and lasting solutions, including efforts to prevent the causes
of refugee flows as well as efforts to facilitate the voluntary return of the
refugee; . . . stresses that in order to facilitate lasting solutions, assistance for
refugees and returnees must be development oriented, taking into account
the needs of the countries of asylum as well as those of the countries of
origin; stresses further the need for more assistance to the countries of
asylum to enable them to properly shoulder their increased responsibilities
and assume the additional burden caused by the presence of refugees on
their economies.[213]

This is consolidated further through NEPAD. While the Declaration on
Democracy and the Peace and Security Initiatives makes no mention
of refugees and their situation, in respect of the African Peer Review
Mechanism the position is much clearer. The Objectives, Standards, Criteria and Indicators for the APRM[214] include among their 'key objectives for
democracy and political governance' the 'promotion and protection of the
rights of vulnerable groups including displaced persons and refugees', and
Objective 9 deals specifically with refugees and the internally displaced.
It cites as the relevant standards both the UN and OAU Conventions on
Refugees and states as indicative criteria: 'Are the constitutional provisions
guaranteeing the protection [of] vulnerable groups adequate? Has the
country acceded and ratified the relevant African Union and United
Nations instruments protecting the rights of vulnerable groups?'[215]
Examples of indicators mentioned include adequacy of constitutional
protection; ratification of international instruments; and enactment of
legislation against human trafficking. While these are rather vague, they
do at least indicate that the position of refugees will be given some
consideration in the peer-review process.

From refugees as humanitarian concern to human rights

Because there was a recognition that refugees were the result of conflicts,[216]
the situation was treated as a humanitarian rather than a human rights

---

[213] Resolution on the Second International Conference on Assistance to Refugees in Africa
(ICARA) II, CM/Res.937(XL), preamble and paras. 3 and 4.

[214] Objectives, Standards, Criteria and Indicators for the African Peer Review Mechanism,
NEPAD/HSGIC-03-2003/APRM/Guideline/OSCI, 9 March 2003, para. 2.2(i)

[215] Ibid., para. 2.11.

[216] For example, in its Decision on the Fiftieth Anniversary of the Adoption of the 1951
Convention on the Status of Refugees the AHSG noted that it was 'deeply concerned
by the recurrent cycles of armed conflicts and persecution which generate displacement

concern.[217] Thus, various resolutions of the OAU refer to humanitarian law but not human rights law.[218]

The duty of states was therefore to provide humanitarian assistance to refugees and emergency supplies.[219] This suggests that what was to be given was outside the norm, also enabling a focus to be placed on the role of non-state actors rather than the responsibility of states themselves: 'commends all international organisations and non-governmental organisations involved in refugee work . . . for the humanitarian assistance they have continued to render to refugees and displaced persons as well as the countries of asylum and urges them to continue providing assistance to refugees and displaced persons'.[220] In this respect there was a presumption that humanitarian standards provided sufficient protection.[221]

However, in more recent years there has been increased attention to the need for greater integration between refugees' and human rights, as will now be considered.

Rights of refugees, returnees and internally displaced persons

Although the OAU has paid considerable attention to the position of refugees over the years, the manner in which it has done so does not necessarily evidence a coherent and comprehensive rights-based approach.[222] Yet there has been some evidence, and increasingly so, of recognition of the rights of refugees.

---

often on a massive scale, as well as by the absence of safe and timely solutions for millions of displaced persons in Africa', AHG/Dec.165(XXXVII).

[217] Amnesty International, *Organization of African Unity*, at 24.

[218] For example, Resolution on Respect for International Humanitarian Law and Support for Humanitarian Action in Armed Conflicts, CM/Res.1526(LX); Resolution on Burundi, CM/Res.1560(LXI), para. 8.

[219] Draft Decisions of the Sixty-Seventh Ordinary Session of the Council of Ministers, CM/DRAFT/DECISIONS(LXVII) REV.1, in the Decision of the OAU Council of Ministers on the Report of the Commission of Twenty on the Situation of Refugees, Returnees and Displaced Persons in Africa, CM/Draft/Dec.22(LXVII) Rev.2.

[220] Report of the OAU Commission of Twenty on the Situation of Refugees, Returnees and Displaced Persons in Africa, CM/2038(LXVII) Rev.1.

[221] Resolution on Refugees, Returnees and Displaced Persons in Africa, CM/Res.1588(LXII), preamble. See H. Storey and R. Wallace, 'War and Peace in Refugee Law Jurisprudence', *AJIL* 95(2) (2001) 349–66, at 359. Decision on the Report of the Secretary General on the Thirtieth Ordinary Session of the OAU Commission on Refugees, on the Situation of Refugees, Returnees and Displaced Persons (Doc.CM/2105(LXX)), CM/Dec.459(LXX).

[222] M. K. Juma, 'Migration, Security and Refugee Protection: A Reflection', prepared for discussion at Stabley Foundation Conference, Refugee Protection in Africa: How to Ensure Stability and Development for Refugees and Hosts, Entebbe, 10–14 November 2002, http://reports.stanleyfoundation.org/HRP02A.pdf.

In general, the OAU has called on states to recognise their commitments with respect to refugees under international human rights instruments such as the ACHPR and the ACRWC.[223] The following are some of the main areas in which the OAU organs have themselves recognised the human rights of refugees.

Principle of non-refoulement and the right to asylum

The ACHPR states that 'every individual shall have the right, when persecuted, to seek and obtain asylum in other countries in accordance with the law of those countries and international conventions'. The link between the principle of non-refoulement and human rights is clear and has been recognised by the UN itself[224] and various human rights bodies.[225] The OAU Refugee Convention's principle of non-refoulement in Article 2(3) is said to go much further than the UN Convention in that it seems to allow no exceptions and also prohibits rejection at the border. Whether this amounts to a right to asylum has been questioned,[226] with some arguing, for example, that

> Despite the encouraging tone of the OAU Convention, neither this instrument nor any other permits the conclusion that states have accepted an international obligation to grant asylum to refugees in the sense of admission to residence and lasting protection against persecution and/or the exercise of jurisdiction by another state. The period under review, however, is replete with examples of asylum given; the humanitarian practice exists, but the sense of obligation is missing.[227]

---

[223] Resolution on Refugees, Returnees and Displaced Persons in Africa, CM/Res.1521(LX), para. 5. See also Resolution on Refugees, Returnees and Displaced Persons in Africa, CM/Res.1489(LIX); Tunis Declaration on the 1969 Convention Governing the Specific Aspects of Refugee Problems. Resolution on the Situation of Migrants in Africa, CM/Res.1413(LVI), preamble and para. 1.

[224] Principles on the Effective Prevention and Investigation of Extra-Legal, Arbitrary and Summary executions: 'No one shall be involuntary returned or extradited to a country where there are substantial grounds for believing that he or she may become a victim of extra-legal, arbitrary or summary execution in that country', UNGA Res.44/162, 15 December 1989, para. 5.

[225] For example, *Soering* v. *UK*, ECHR; *Chahal* v. *UK*, 15 November 1996, Reports of Judgments and Decisions 1996-V); *Moustaquim* v. *Belgium*, Series A No. 193, 18 November 1991, right of appeal.

[226] Okoth-Obbo, 'Thirty Years On', at 12–13.

[227] Goodwin-Gill, *The Refugee in International Law*, at 178.

Asylum is referred to in various human rights documents,[228] and the OAU Convention in Article 2 requires that states 'use their best endeavours ... to receive refugees and secure [their] settlement', 'recalling that one of the basic principles of assistance to African refugees, as defined in the OAU Convention, is that of "granting of asylum as a peaceful and humanitarian act"'.[229] The OAU has suggested that there is a right to asylum, noting in its 1995 Plan of Action that 'the granting of asylum should not be seen as an unfriendly or hostile act, but rather should be seen as a responsibility and an obligation under international law'.[230]

This is subject, however, to a number of limitations – for example, that the reception of refugees is still subject to national laws. Awuku notes, as do others,[231] that

> the term subversive has in the past given rise to different interpretations and that the clause which prohibits any activity likely to cause tension between member states is rather vague in its wording. The danger therefore exists that this clause may lead to undue restrictions on the freedom of expression and of association of refugees and to the excessive use of the exclusion and cessation clauses concerning refugees who have seriously infringed the principles of the OAU or the purposes and objectives of the OAU Convention on Refugees.[232]

The ability or right to be granted asylum, however, is essential for the protection of human rights. As Nathwani notes,

> the purpose of the institution of asylum is to serve as a backup system. Individuals whose human rights cannot be guaranteed in their country of origin are granted asylum; thus, their human rights are protected abroad by the institution of asylum ... However, this approach copes poorly with two major challenges: the lack of motivation of states granting asylum and the need to create a hierarchy of human rights for the purpose of asylum policy.[233]

---

[228] For example, UDHR, Article 14(1).

[229] Resolution on the Conference on the Situation of Refugees in Africa, CM/Res.621(XXXI), preamble.

[230] Plan of Action of the OAU/UNHCR Regional Conference on Assistance to Refugees, Returnees and Displaced Persons in the Great Lakes Region, adopted by the OAU/UNHCR Regional Conference on Assistance to Refugees, Returnees and Displaced Persons in the Great Lakes Region, 12–17 February, 1995, Bujumbura, para. 25.

[231] See, for example, Weiss, 'The Convention of the OAU', at 457.

[232] E. O. Awuku, 'Refugee Movements in Africa and the OAU Convention on Refugees', *JAL* 39 (1995) 79–86, at 83–4.

[233] N. Nathwani, 'The Purpose of Asylum', *International Journal of Refugee Law* 12(3) (2000) 353–79, at 364–5.

Position of internally displaced persons

There has been increased recent international attention paid to the position of internally displaced persons.[234] This has been prompted by moves at the international level,[235] as well as calls from civil society.[236] There has been a recent decline in the number of refugees in Africa, but at the same time an increase in internally displaced persons.[237]

Those who are internally displaced raise particular questions, as they have not left their home state so cannot claim refugee law protection, and at the same time face particular difficulties in their own countries.[238] In this regard human rights law is particularly important but also suffers often from limitations where states can derogate from certain rights during times of war or other public emergency, situations which are likely to face many internally displaced persons.[239] Yet the responsibility for their protection must rest with the home state.[240]

The OAU Convention was not designed to deal with the massive problem of internally displaced persons that was later to face the African continent.[241] The OAU/AU more recently has, however, recognised the

---

[234] The 1998 Guiding Principles on Internal Displacement define internally displaced persons as 'persons or groups of persons who have been forced or obliged to flee or to leave their homes or places of habitual residence, in particular as a result of or in order to avoid the effects of armed conflict, situations of generalised violence, violations of human rights or natural or human-made disasters, and who have not crossed an internationally recognised state border', http://www.reliefweb.int/ocha_ol/pub/idp_gp/idp.html. See N. Geissler, 'The International Protection of Internally Displaced Persons', *International Journal of Refugee Law* 11(3) (1999) 451–78.

[235] See ECOSOC Resolution 1655(LII), 1 June 1972; UNGA Resolution 2958(XXVII), 12 December 1972. The UN also has a Special Coordinator on Internal Displacement, Dennis McNamara, and the UN Secretary General set up within the Office for the Coordination of Humanitarian Affairs (OCHA) a Unit on Internal Displacement in January 2002. See Helton, *The Price of Indifference*, at 129–30. The Special Representative on Internally Displaced Persons and the ILA Committee have adopted a Declaration on Principles of International Law on Internally Displaced Persons, 25–29 July 2000, *International Law Association. Conference Report*, 69 (2000) 794, see *International Journal of Refugee Law* 12(4) (2001) 672–9.

[236] The Secretary General noted that the conclusions of the OAU Civil Society Conference included 'the need for CSOs to provide the OAU on a regular basis early warning information that could be used to avert situations of crises in Africa. The participants further called for the creation of an institution to cater for the needs of internally displaced persons and an additional African Protocol to reinforce the implementation of international humanitarian law', Introductory Note of the Secretary General to the Seventy-Fourth Ordinary Session of the Council of Ministers, at 64.

[237] Crisp, 'Africa's Refugees', at 3–4.   [238] Geissler, 'International Protection', at 457–8.

[239] Ibid., at 462–7.   [240] Goodwin-Gill, *The Refugee in International Law*, at 264.

[241] Oloka-Onyango, 'The Plight of the Larger Half', at 376.

REFUGEES AND HUMAN RIGHTS

existence of and difficulties faced by the internally displaced,[242] and many resolutions relating to refugees now refer to internally displaced persons as well. There are also provisions in the Addis Ababa Recommendations of 1994 on Internally Displaced Persons, noting that the 'prime responsibility to ensure the protection of all its nationals belongs to the state . . . States should uphold the rights provided for under international and national law in favour of internally displaced persons', and also calling on all parties to conflicts where internally displaced persons are, to cooperate with agencies involved 'to gain access to the displaced so as to cater to their needs'.[243] Further, the moves towards examining the situation as part of the development of the continent is therefore to be welcomed in that it can encompass protection for the internally displaced as well as refugees.[244]

In 1998 the OAU held an important conference with the Brookings Institute and the UNHCR on internal displacement. The recommendations from this meeting reaffirmed the prominence of the UN's Guiding Principles on Internal Displacement, noting their basis in human rights law, humanitarian law and refugee law. The workshop also recommended the prevention of internal displacement, and the protection of those who found themselves internally displaced, noting that states bear the primary responsibility in both regards. In this respect, it stressed that this should be through state sovereignty which 'should be perceived in terms of the duty of all states to protect and respect the rights of their citizens and to promote international peace and security'.[245] Some attention was also paid to the role of non-state actors in the protection of the internally displaced.[246] The workshop also argued for the strengthening of the African Commission on Human and Peoples' Rights in this regard and for it to take a more active role in internally displaced issues including sending joint field missions with the OAU's Commission on Refugees.[247]

The workshop made specific recommendations with regard to the rights of the internally displaced, including that their human rights be

---

[242] Resolution on the Holding of a Conference on the Situation of Refugees and Displaced Persons, AHG/Res.237(XXXI).

[243] Recommendations of the OAU/UNHCR Symposium on Refugees and Forced Population Displacements in Africa, para. 41.

[244] Goodwin-Gill, *The Refugee in International Law*, at 265.

[245] Recommendations of the Brookings Institute/UNHCR/OAU Workshop on Internal Displacement in Africa, adopted at the Brookings Institute/UNHCR/OAU Workshop on Internal Displacement in Africa, 19–20 October 1998, Addis Ababa, para. 21.

[246] Ibid., para. 22.   [247] Ibid., para. 31.

observed and that development and relief programmes involving them should include a human rights protection element.[248] It specifically recommended to international agencies that they should be undertaking monitoring and data protection of international programmes and their human rights impact, training of staff in human rights, ensuring links with local organisations, and supporting local groups to ensure that perpetrators of abuses were brought to justice. There should also be increased cooperation between humanitarian and human rights agencies, and all human rights operations should have a focal point for internally displaced persons.[249] The resulting Guiding Principles on Internal Displacement defined such persons as those 'persons or groups of persons who have been forced or obliged to flee or to leave their homes or places of habitual residence, in particular as a result of or in order to avoid the effects of armed conflict, situations of generalised violence, violations of human rights or natural or man-made disasters, and who have not crossed an internationally recognised state border'.[250]

The principles are said to be consistent with international human rights and humanitarian law and stress that internally displaced persons 'shall enjoy, in full equality, the same rights and freedoms under international and domestic law, as do other persons in their country. They shall not be discriminated against in the enjoyment of any rights and freedoms on the ground that they are internally displaced.'[251] This is, however, without prejudice to individual criminal responsibility under international law.[252] The primary responsibility is on the national authorities to provide them with protection, and there is a right of such persons to request and receive such protection from them.[253] There are also provisions on non-discrimination; protection against arbitrary displacement from home or habitual residence;[254] that authorities ensure 'all feasible alternatives' to avoid displacement, and if this is not possible, then the effects of such be minimised. In this regard they should also provide 'proper accommodation . . . that such displacements are effected in satisfactory conditions of safety, nutrition, health and hygiene and that members of the same family are not separated'.[255] Where displacement occurs other than during

---

[248] Ibid., para. 33.   [249] Ibid., paras. 34 and 35.
[250] Guiding Principles on Internal Displacement, Recommendations of the Brookings Institute/UNHCR/OAU Workshop on Internal Displacement in Africa, adopted at the Brookings Institute/UNHCR/OAU Workshop on Internal Displacement in Africa, 19–20 October 1998, Addis Ababa, Annex, para. 2.
[251] Ibid., Principle 1(1).   [252] Ibid.   [253] Ibid., Principle 3.
[254] Ibid., Principle 6. What amounts to displacement is defined further by the provision.
[255] Ibid., Principle 7.

emergency situations there are a number of guarantees laid down, including that this be authorised by a specific decision of a state authority with the power under law to do so; measures be taken to provide full information on the reasons for the displacement; free and full informed consent of those to be displaced; involvement of those affected, particularly women, in planning their relocation; law enforcement should be carried out by competent authorities; and the right to an effective remedy.[256] Further, the displacement 'should not be carried out in a manner that violates the right to life, dignity, liberty and security of those affected', and states should protect against displacement of particular groups including indigenous peoples, minorities, peasants, pastoralists and 'other groups with a special dependency on and attachment to their lands'.[257]

There are also principles relating to protection during displacement, including the right to life; protection against direct or indiscriminate attacks or other acts of violence; the use of anti-personnel mines; the right to dignity and integrity; the right to liberty and security of the person; for children not to be recruited or take part in hostilities; liberty of movement and freedom to choose residence; the right to know the fate and whereabouts of relatives; and respect for family life. Other clauses provide for an adequate standard of living; particular protection for those wounded, sick or with disabilities; recognition before the law; protection for property; the right to education; and protection against discrimination. There are also principles relating to humanitarian assistance and to return, resettlement and reintegration.

Freedom of expression and association

The OAU Convention does not provide expressly for a right to free expression and association. Indeed, it has been argued that Article 3 of the Convention 'establishes explicit limitations on the political rights of refugees', namely in respect of 'subversive activities', it being argued that these violate Article 2 of the ACHPR, as they refer to citizenship not individuals, and Articles 19 and 22 of the ICCPR.[258]

Economic, social and cultural rights

The OAU has spent more time considering the economic, social and cultural rights of refugees than their civil and political ones. Besides some

---

[256] Ibid., Principle 7(3).   [257] Ibid., Principles 8 and 9.
[258] Lawyers' Committee for Human Rights, *African Exodus*, at 93.

important decisions by the African Commission on Human and Peoples' Rights on mass expulsions,[259] one can find very little reference among the Addis Ababa organs to issues such as the right to fair trial, arbitrary detention and torture or inhuman treatment.

As the remit of its Bureau indicated,[260] the education of refugees was clearly seen as an important consideration in its early years, and later for development as a whole. Educational support has also been seen as way of protecting the refugees' own security.[261] This is clearly an important consideration in the African context where most refugees are from rural areas where there are few educational facilities.[262] One of the most important issues for refugees may be their ability to obtain work, but often nationals of the host state will have priority over them in terms of access to paid employment.[263]

Thus, states have been asked, if they have the means, to 'offer, insofar as possible, greater employment possibilities, and access to scholastic establishment, for the refugees; in this connection, requests the Bureau to periodically collect from member states a list of their needs and to assess their employment opportunities'.[264] The OAU has also called on states, for example, to 'construct more classrooms which should also include higher education'[265] and to 'make more vacancies, bursaries and scholarships available to those refugees in their educational institutions'[266] and 'make a special effort to help refugees wishing to undertake studies'.[267]

---

[259] See, for example, Communication No. 159/96, *Union Interafricaine des Droits de l'Homme, Féderation Internationale des Ligues des Droits de l'Homme, Rencontre Africaine des Droits de l'Homme, Organisation Nationale des Droits de l'Homme au Sénégal, and Association Malienne des Droits de l'Homme* v. *Angola*, Eleventh Annual Activity Report of the African Commission on Human and Peoples' Rights, Annex II.
[260] Resolution on Refugees, Returnees and Displaced Persons in Africa, CM/Res.1489(LIX), paras. 4 and 11.
[261] 'Considering that the placement of these young refugees in African Educational Institutions is one of the most urgent and friendly aspects of the problem both for the safety and the training of the refugees', Resolution on Special Assistance to Southern African Refugees, CM/Res.547(XXIX), preamble.
[262] J. B. Kabera, 'Education of Refugees and their Expectations in Africa: The Case of Returnees with Special Reference to Uganda', *African Studies Review* 32(1) (1989) 31–9, at 31.
[263] Lawyers' Committee for Human Rights, *African Exodus*, at 100.
[264] Resolution on Commission of Ten on Refugees, CM/Res.296(XX), para. 12.
[265] Report of the Secretary General on the Thirtieth Ordinary Session of the OAU Commission on Refugees, on the Situation of Refugees, Returnees and Displaced Persons in Africa, CM/2105(LXX) Rev.1, para. 30.
[266] Resolution on Special Assistance to Southern African Refugees, CM/Res.547(XXIX), para. 5.
[267] Resolution on Refugees, Returnees and Displaced Persons, CM/Res.1627(LXIII), para. 5.

In addition, the OAU has also spent some time recognising the right to health of refugees, requesting, for example, that the IOM promote projects in relation to, among others, 'health and legal protection of the rights of migrants in their capacity as vulnerable persons especially in conflict and transit areas and set up, in collaboration with member states, research networks.'[268] African states have also been called upon to provide better facilities such as water: 'this affects the well being of refugees, particularly the children. The Commission recommends that the OAU seriously consider contributing some funds to construct some shallow wells which would help to meet the demand by both the refugees and nationals as well as cattle.'[269]

This is particularly important in relation to facilities provided to camps and in this regard requests have been made to the OAU, rather than the state, to assist. For example, in relation to Djibouti: 'Concerning the country's population, the refugees, including migrant workers, exert tremendous pressure on the country, the mission requests the OAU to consider giving some assistance to both camps to buy the much needed blankets and assist in constructing simple delivery rooms for the expectant mothers.'[270] There has also been some recognition by the OAU of the living conditions of refugees, but this tends to be in general terms: 'cognizant of the fact that the living conditions of refugees in Africa, especially those of the aged, women, children and the disabled is steadily deteriorating every year', and calling on states to ratify the ACHPR among other instruments.[271]

Whose responsibility?

One of the main reasons why the approach to refugees and their rights has been incoherent in the OAU/AU could relate to the lack of clarity as to whose responsibility they are.[272] The OAU has consistently expressed

---

[268] CM/OAU/AEC/REGL.1(IX).

[269] Report of the Secretary General on the Thirtieth Ordinary Session of the OAU Commission on Refugees, on the Situation of Refugees, Returnees and Displaced Persons in Africa, CM/2105(LXX) Rev.1, para. 30.

[270] In relation to Sudan the Commission 'requests the OAU to consider buying essential items such as blankets, jerrycans, plastic sheets and cooking utensils to benefit the internally displaced persons', Ibid., para. 47.

[271] Resolution on the Situation of Refugees in Africa, CM/Res.939(XL), preamble and para. 3. See also Resolution on the Situation of Refugees in Africa and on Prospective Solutions to their Problems in the 1980s, CM/Res.727(XXXIII), Rev.1, paras. 3–5.

[272] The OAU has on a few occasions stressed that refugees themselves have responsibilities, Decision on the Progress Report of the Secretary General on the Efforts Deployed Towards Mainstreaming African Women's Concerns into Peace and Sustainable Development

gratitude to host states[273] and recognised the 'heavy burden' imposed on them,[274] in spite of their limited resources,[275] and sometimes difficult home conditions,[276] noting this is done 'in a humanitarian spirit, as well as in the spirit of African solidarity and brotherhood'.[277] The OAU has praised countries for giving asylum to refugees from conflicts.[278] Although host states have an obligation to comply with the various international standards on refugees and human rights,[279] the granting of asylum still seems to be treated as an optional act. The OAU has stated that 'refugees should be allowed to participate in decisions concerning their repatriation. In this connection, they should be provided with all the relevant

Processes, Doc.CM/2117(LXX): 'calls upon all stakeholders, returnees and internally displaced persons to support and implement the Plan of Action'.

[273] Resolution on Special Assistance to Southern African Refugees, CM/Res.547(XXIX), paras. 1 and 2.

[274] Report of the Secretary General on the Thirtieth Ordinary Session of the OAU Commission on Refugees, on the Situation of Refugees, Returnees and Displaced Persons in Africa, CM/2105(LXX) Rev.1.

[275] 'Pays tribute to member states who continue to receive and cater for the needs of refugees and displaced persons in spite of their limited resources', Resolution on Refugees, Returnees and Displaced Persons in Africa, CM/Res.1433(LVII).

[276] Congratulates 'host countries that continue to receive and assist refugees in spite of the socio-economic difficulties which are recently compounded by complex situations and new challenges and currently aggravated by the floods and drought', Report of the OAU Commission on Refugees, Returnees and Displaced Persons in Africa, CM/2171(LXXII), Rev.2.

[277] Decision on the Report of the Secretary General on the Thirtieth Ordinary Session of the OAU Commission on Refugees, on the Situation of Refugees, Returnees and Displaced Persons (Doc.CM/2105(LXX)), CM/Dec.459(LXX).

[278] For example, it 'expresses its appreciation to the people and Government of Guinea for the generous hospitality they have always accorded the populations of the neighbouring countries in distress and hails its commitment to continue to give asylum to these populations, in accordance with the relevant provisions of the OAU Convention on Refugees', Decision on the Situation in the Mano River Sub-Region, CM/Dec.572 (LXXIII).

[279] Decision of the OAU Council of Ministers on the Report of the Commission of Twenty on the Situation of Refugees, Returnees and Displaced Persons in Africa, CM/Dec.22(LXVII) Rev.2. See also Report of the OAU Commission of Twenty on the Situation of Refugees, Returnees and Displaced Persons in Africa, CM/2038(LXVII) Rev.1, Draft Resolutions, CM/Draft/Res.1–30(LXIII) Rev.1, Draft Resolution on Refugees, Returnees and Displaced Persons, CM/Draft/Res.5(LXIII) Rev.1, Draft Rapporteur's Report of the Sixty-Seventh Ordinary Session of the Council of Ministers, CM/Plen/Draft/Rapt/Rpt(LXVII), considering the Report of the Commission of Twenty on the Situation of Refugees, Returnees and Displaced Persons in Africa, at 50, para. 192; Decision on the Report of the OAU Commission on Refugees, Regarding the Situation of Refugees, Returnees and Displaced Persons in Africa (CM/2171(LXXII), CM/Dec.531(LXXII).

information necessary for informed judgments.'[280] In addition, 'the international community should provide assistance for the rehabilitation or reconstruction of the social and economic infrastructures, services and distribution systems in the areas of return in order that the conditions for successful repatriation are thereby created'.[281]

States of origin, in turn, are urged to 'promote conditions conducive to the return and sustainable reintegration of refugees and displaced persons in their countries of origin'.[282] Further, 'it is the responsibility of African leaders to find political solutions to the on-going crises which produce refugees and internally displaced persons and as a result, threaten peace, security and stability which slows down the socio-economic development in Africa'.[283] This fudge has resulted in human rights obligations being kept off the agenda and a coherent approach to them in the context of refugees avoided.

Further, considerable attention has been paid to the notion of burden sharing. The widespread practice and attention paid to this concept by the OAU suggests that it is a legally binding norm.[284] The OAU Convention provides in this regard that 'where a Member State finds difficulty in continuing to grant asylum to refugees, such Member State may appeal directly to other Member States and through the OAU, and such other Member States shall in the spirit of African solidarity and international co-operation take appropriate measures to lighten the burden of the Member State granting asylum'.[285]

---

[280] Addis Ababa Document on Refugees and Forced Population Displacements in Africa, at 318.

[281] Ibid.

[282] Decision on the Report of the Commission of Twenty on the Situation of Refugees, CM/Dec.362(LXVI). Addis Ababa Document on Refugees and Forced Population Displacements in Africa.

[283] Report of the Secretary General on the Thirtieth Ordinary Session of the OAU Commission on Refugees, on the Situation of Refugees, Returnees and Displaced Persons in Africa, CM/2105(LXX) Rev.1. Further, 'it is the responsibility of Africans themselves to resolve the problem of refugees and displaced persons. There is no substitute to the continent's political will to tackle the root causes of this problem. In this regard, there is an enormous task to be fulfilled by the governments of Africa towards attaining this goal', Report of the OAU Commission of Twenty on the Situation of Refugees, Returnees and Displaced Persons in Africa, CM/1985(LXV) Rev.1.

[284] Noll and Vedsted-Hansen, 'Non-Communitarians', at 388–9. See also J. P. Fonteyne, 'Burden Sharing: An Analysis of the Nature and Function of International Solidarity in Cases of Mass Influx of Refugees', Australian Yearbook of International Law 8 (1983) 162–88.

[285] OAU Refugee Convention, Article 2(4).

This has been considerably elaborated on by the OAU in subsequent resolutions and decisions. Burden sharing has thus been directed at African
states who do not host refugees, for example, with the OAU inviting:
'member states of the OAU which are not directly confronted with the
problem of refugees to foresee the possibility of sharing the burden of
the countries of first and second asylum of these refugees, in accepting
every year a number of refugees which they will be free to determine'[286]
and 'countries not sheltering refugees or accommodating only a limited
number of refugees to take necessary measures with a view to sharing the
burden with countries sheltering refugees'.[287] The OAU has stressed consistently the need to ensure 'responsibility sharing' among states for dealing with refugees: 'the problem of refugees is social and humanitarian
in nature and should therefore not become a cause of tension between
states', and given the heavy burden of asylum, the solution could only be
achieved through 'responsibility sharing'.[288]

In this regard, therefore, Africans have the 'primary responsibility'.[289]
As the Secretary General of the OAU noted:

> I would like to stress that the solution to this problem lies primarily in
> our own hands. As Africans, we should endeavour, in a serious and prac-
> tical way to address root causes of the problem. Genuine efforts on the
> part of the African peoples to seek solutions to the conflict situations,
> to eradicate poverty and ensure greater participation of our people in the
> political and economic processes, to build democratic institutions and pro-
> mote a culture of tolerance and national reconciliation will go a long way
> towards addressing the problem of refugees and displaced persons in our
> Continent.[290]

Despite this, burden sharing is also perceived as being borne by the
international community.[291] This is of course an issue recognised by the

---

[286] Resolution on Commission of Ten on Refugees, CM/Res.296(XX).
[287] Resolution on the Situation of Refugees in Africa, CM/Res.774(XXXIV), para. 6.
[288] AHG/Dec.165(XXXVII).   [289] Decision on Refugees, CM/Dec. 574(LXXIII).
[290] Introductory Note to the Report of the Secretary General on the Sixty-Ninth Ordi-
    nary Session of the Council of Ministers, Addis Ababa, 19–23 March 1999, para. 287.
    See also Report of the Seventy-Third Ordinary Session of the Council of Ministers,
    February 2001, CM/Rpt.(LXXIII), paras. 58–9; Resolution on Refugee Problems in Africa,
    CM/Res.620(XXXI), preamble.
[291] Resolution on the International Conference on Assistance to Refugees in Africa (ICARA)
    and on its Follow-up, CM/Res.868(XXXVII). Report of the Sixth Ordinary Session of the
    Committee of Ambassadors and Other Plenipotentiaries, Amb/Cttee/Rpt(VI).

international community itself through the UN Charter[292] and 'reflects recognition of the inherently *international* dimension to the movements of persons across borders'.[293] Thus, the OAU, in the 1994 Addis Ababa Recommendations, noted:

> It is now evident that African countries cannot sustain the burdens of host-ing refugees on their own. Yet because of 'compassion fatigue' or 'donor fatigue', financial and material resources for refugee programmes in Africa from the developed countries are declining. In recent emergency situa-tions, the response of the international community has been hesitant and characterised by poor preparedness and limited resources.[294]

It made recommendations that 'donor countries, relevant intergovern-mental and non-governmental organisations should provide financial, material and technical assistance to the African asylum countries hosting refugee populations . . . The Symposium recommends that this problem be addressed in a global and comprehensive manner'. It further appealed for 'genuine international solidarity and burden sharing to be brought back to the centre of the refugee problem . . . In particular, a truly inter-national system embracing global standards and principles on preven-tion, refugee protection, assistance and solutions should be reinvigorated. The steady slide towards restrictive, deterrent, laws, policies and prac-tices at a global level must be halted and reversed'.[295] In order to do this Africa should define modalities on a regional or sub-regional basis, where appropriate.[296]

Indeed, the international community has been criticised for 'focusing on the plight of refugees elsewhere, at a time when the African Continent is experiencing a complex refugee crisis',[297] noting 'the treatment of refugees in Africa who do not receive the necessary attention and resources, com-pared to the assistance granted to refugees in other regions of the world'. The international community has been urged to provide support and

---

[292] Articles 1, 13(1)(b), 55 and 56; Goodwin-Gill, *The Refugee in International Law*, at 291. The UNHCR has said that 'there is a need for continuing international cooperation in finding durable solutions . . . and for the provision of support and assistance to first countries of asylum', 1984 UN International Conference on Population, Recommendation 47, UN Doc.A/AC.96/INF.170, 3 September 1984.

[293] Goodwin-Gill, *The Refugee in International Law*, at 292.

[294] Recommendations of the OAU/UNHCR Symposium on Refugees and Forced Population Displacements in Africa, at para. 8.

[295] Ibid., Recommendation Nos. 9–11.   [296] Ibid., Recommendation No. 12.

[297] Press Release 34/99, 28 April 1999 (mission to Angola, DRC, Tanzania and Zambia).

assistance 'comparable to the quantum of resources available to refugees in other parts of the world'.[298]

The OAU has stated that what burden sharing entails is not only humanitarian and emergency assistance,[299] but also more long-term measures, 'especially in some areas which affect both the refugees and the host countries. These areas include education, environmental degradation and water resources, food and non-food items, health services as well as in reintegration and rehabilitation programmes.'[300] This does appear to recognise, therefore, that international assistance must go further than financial or technical assistance.[301]

As a consequence of this, emphasis has been placed on the role of the UNHCR. As seen above, no organ was established under the OAU Refugee Convention to monitor implementation of its provisions. Indeed, considerable focus has been placed by the OAU on the role of the UNHCR in this regard. This began early on in its history with a cooperation agreement being signed between the OAU and UNHCR in June 1969 which provided for regular consultation, exchange of documents and information, going to each other's meetings, etc.[302] As has been noted:

> UNHCR has slipped easily into the role of guarantor of the OAU Convention, with its broader definition of refugee, since 1969. In part, the expansion of UNHCR's role in Africa reflects the complete ineffectiveness of the OAU Bureau of Refugees in performing any of the protective functions contained in the Convention. The OAU Bureau has been a major actor in none of the refugee crises since its inception. In practice, it is the UNHCR that has become the inter-governmental body with primary responsibility for policing the 1969 OAU Convention.[303]

Despite the recognition above that African states themselves had 'primary responsibility', and the existence of OAU organs which had some remit over refugee issues, the UNHCR was thus seen by the OAU as the primary body for dealing with refugees.[304] Apart from detracting from

---

[298] Decision on the Report of the OAU Commission on Refugees, Regarding the Situation of Refugees, Returnees and Displaced Persons in Africa, (CM/2171(LXXII), CM/Dec.531 (LXXII).

[299] Ibid.

[300] Report of the Secretary General on the Thirtieth Ordinary Session of the OAU Commission on Refugees, on the Situation of Refugees, Returnees and Displaced Persons in Africa, CM/2105(LXX) Rev.1.

[301] Fonteyne, 'Burden Sharing', at 175–6.   [302] Amate, Inside the OAU, at 466.

[303] Lawyers' Committee for Human Rights, African Exodus, at 168–9.

[304] Resolution on Cooperation between OAU and UNHCR, CM/Res.622(XXXI), preamble.

the responsibilities of African states, it has been questioned whether the UNHCR can fulfil this role, particularly with regard to human rights protection.[305]

Conclusion

The overall perception of the treatment of refugees and internally displaced persons in Africa by the OAU/AU is therefore mixed. While there clearly has been some attention to their rights, and the OAU Convention offered some progressive developments on international standards, the OAU/AU has failed to develop a coherent human rights integrated policy towards the treatment of refugees across the continent. One of the main reasons for this must be the lack of clear mechanisms to deal with the issue of refugees as a whole. The matter has been separated amongst various bodies over the years, none of which has taken the initiative or acted in anything other than a passive way, certainly with respect to human rights.

Along with a desire to see the refugee situation as part of the development process as a whole, there has been recent attention to a more integrated approach to human rights and refugees in the OAU/AU. Presently, therefore, the Humanitarian Affairs Refugee and Displaced Persons Division of the Political Affairs Directorate at the AU Commission coordinates the AU's approach to refugees, although some aspects of migration are dealt with under the Social Affairs Directorate. The UNHCR is closely involved in supporting the development of the AU in this regard, and its relationship with the African Commission on Human and Peoples' Rights is a positive step in this direction. It is also apparent that the rights of refugees have been integrated into the CSSDCA process and NEPAD.

---

[305] In recent years there has been staunch criticism from many circles regarding UNHCR's inability to take a strong stance towards governments on issues of the rights of refugees and, hence, its inability to perform an effective monitoring role ... UNHCR's increasing emphasis on the provision of humanitarian aid has made the organisation incapable of maintaining a strong stance towards governments. UNHCR's priorities currently lie in retaining presence in countries of asylum, and running large scale, expensive aid operations. Speaking out and criticising a country's refugee policies, often seems to take a back seat to these aid operations, which are less controversial for all and which, being far more high profile, also attract large amounts of funding.

S. Takahashi, 'Recourse to Human Rights Treaty Bodies for Monitoring of the Refugee Convention', NQHR 20(1) (2002) 53–74, at 58–60

It is clear, however, that the AU now needs to consolidate the numerous resolutions, agencies and standards that it has created over the years and produce a comprehensive and coherent approach to this area in the future. In doing so it needs to match its rhetoric on the refugee and internally displaced persons situation as the primary responsibility of Africans with mechanisms and procedures at the level of the AU to consolidate this. As Amate noted in 1986, but which is perhaps even more relevant today:

> The OAU cannot any longer pretend that the problem of refugees in Africa can be solved by merely adopting resolutions which none of its member-governments is willing to implement. What is required now is for the OAU to set up machinery that will follow up its resolutions and to do its best to persuade its member-governments to implement the resolutions they have themselves adopted.[306]

The closer relationship between the African Commission on Human and Peoples' Rights and the UNHCR has largely taken place outside the main AU structures. What is needed now is for these initiatives to be accompanied by involvement from the AU organs with remit in this area. The references in the main instruments such as the Constitutive Act, NEPAD, CSSDCA, provide the potential for AU organs to ensure that the human rights of refugees are integrated in their mandates.

---

[306] Amate, *Inside the OAU*, at 474–5.

8

Development, NEPAD and human rights

OAU historical view of development

While in its early years the OAU was preoccupied with decolonisation and ending apartheid in southern Africa, from fairly early on – and certainly central to its deliberations now – was an awareness of the need for Africa's development. This has encompassed focusing on the impact of globalisation on Africa,[1] the OAU/AU's role in international fora and international financial institutions,[2] its work with Western states through the G77 and ACP–Lomé agreements,[3] the relationship with the ECA,[4] and the contributions it has made at the level of the UN and elsewhere to the development of a New International Economic Order.[5] Thus, the

---

[1] Decision on the Convening of an Extraordinary Session of the OAU Assembly of Heads of State and Government in accordance with Art.33(5) of its Rules of Procedure, AHG/Dec.140(XXXV): suggestions by Qadhafi on collective security and conflicts and ways to make the OAU effective 'so as to keep pace with political and economic development taking place in the world and the preparation required of Africa within the context of globalisation so as to preserve its social, economic and political potentials'. See also Draft Rapporteur's Report of the Sixty-Seventh Ordinary Session of the Council of Ministers, CM/Plen/Draft/Rapt/Rpt(LXVII) para. 210, which notes the meetings of the OAU and that the Minister of Foreign Affairs of Burkina Faso noted that the next session 'should be one with a difference centred on the effective implementation of the decisions in the face of challenges posed by globalisation'.

[2] Resolution on Africa and the International Financial Institutions, CM/Res.213(XIV), focusing on the need to make 'the participation of African representatives more effective in these organisations'.

[3] Resolutions on the OECD, CM/Res.215(XIV); Resolution on UN Conference on Trade and Development, CM/Res.43(III); Resolution on UNCTAD, CM/Res.122(IX).

[4] E. K. Kouassi, 'OAU–UN Interaction over the Last Decade', in El-Ayouty (ed.), *OAU after Thirty Years* 139–46, at 144.

[5] With regard to the development of the NIEO in the UN, it is noted that 'although members of the OAU actively participated in all these conferences, the Organization's role was marginal. It restricted itself to the support of African initiative led by the ECA and of the ECA's "African Plan for the Implementation of the Programme of Action on the Establishment of a New International Economic Order"', Z. Cervenka, *The Unfinished Quest for Unity. Africa and the OAU* (London: Friedmann, 1977), at 184. More generally, as Western states started to

need for African unity in the face of decolonisation has been replaced by the need for Africa to unite in the face of globalisation.[6] As the Algiers Declaration noted:

> Despite the hopes generated by the end of the Cold War and the attendant prospects of peace, development and integration in the world economy, we note that the post-Cold War era is fraught with new and grave uncertainties, serious risks of marginalisation and new challenges that pose numerous threats to our continent . . . Globalisation is undoubtedly the most widespread of these challenges . . . it has aroused fears in that it poses serious threats to our sovereignty, cultural and historical identities as well as gravely undermining our development prospects. We believe that globalisation should be placed within the framework of a democratically conceived dynamics, and implemented collectively to make it an institution capable of fulfilling the hope for a concerted development of mankind and prosperity shared by all peoples . . . We, for our part, strongly believe that the promotion of economic co-operation and integration for the establishment of the African Economic Community as provided for under the Abuja Treaty will help consolidate the efforts being deployed . . . and to address the major problems facing Africa, notably problems of refugees and poverty, illiteracy and pandemics including the scourge of AIDS, as well as environmental problems, namely water and desertification related issues and threats to bio-diversity.[7]

It is in recent years that the initiative for a more integrated approach to development has become apparent through the adoption of the New Partnership for Africa's Development (NEPAD). This merged the Millennium Partnership for Africa's Recovery Programme (MAP) and the Omega Plan. This merger was approved by the AHSG on 11 July 2001 and its policy framework, NEPAD, was finalised on 23 October 2001. Its aims are to deal with poverty and sustainable development, and it has been formulated by African leaders themselves. Human rights appear to play an important role in NEPAD. Its Declaration on Democracy, Political,

---

link aid flows with democratic conditions and reference to human rights, the OAU may have been prompted to look at development in this context as well, G. R. Olsen, 'Western Europe's Relations with Africa since the End of the Cold War', *Journal of Modern African Studies* 35(2) (1997) 299–319, at 306.

[6] Decision, CM/Dec.334(LXVI), the Council 'expresses the firm determination of African countries to achieve at [the Tokyo International Conference on African Development] action-orientated results, with concrete plan of action, to further promote African development in the spirit of African ownership and global partnership'.

[7] Algiers Declaration, AHG/Decl.1(XXXV).

Economic and Corporate Governance,[8] for example, stresses support for the ACHPR and the UN High Commission for Human Rights. Further, concrete obligations are set out for states in its Objectives, Standards, Criteria and Indicators which include 'promotion and protection of economic, social, cultural, civil and political rights as enshrined in all African and international human rights instruments'.[9] While these commitments only have to be undertaken voluntarily at present, the CSSDCA process also suggests a more integrated approach to human rights and development and has the further benefit of being compulsory.

Human rights-based approach to development?

Human rights and development have been increasingly linked.[10] The influence of the Western aid donors, international financial and institutions and the UN,[11] and the increased attention to good governance and democratisation in development debates,[12] has led to an increasing acceptance that development is not possible without protection of human rights: 'The relationship between human rights and development has occupied a prominent place in the international discourse of rights.'[13]

Over the years the OAU/AU has also begun to look at development and human rights as inseparable. For example, in its involvement with the EC through the ACP–Lomé agreements, there were discussions over the reference that should be made in the various documents to human rights.[14] The ACHPR in this context 'represented an attempt to respond to foreign criticisms concerning the ACP position during the renegotiation

---

[8] Declaration on Democracy, Political, Economic and Corporate Governance, AHG/235 (XXXVIII), Annex I, para. 15.

[9] Objectives, Standards, Criteria and Indicators for the African Peer Review Mechanism, NEPAD/HSGIC-03-2003/APRM/Guideline/OSCI, 9 March 2003, para. 2.5.

[10] M. Haile, 'Human Rights, Stability and Development in Africa: Some Observations on Concept and Reality', *Virginia Journal of International Law* 24(3) (1984) 575–615, at 600–1.

[11] UNGA Res.1710(XVI) (1961); UN Report on Development, UN Doc/E/3347/Rev.1 (1960); GA Declaration on Social Progress and Development in 1969, GA Res.2542(XXIV), 1969.

[12] H.-O. Sano, 'Development and Human Rights: The Necessary, but Partial Integration of Human Rights and Development', *HRQ* 22 (2000) 734–52, at 735–6.

[13] N. J. Udombana, 'The Third World and the Right to Development: Agenda for the Next Millennium', *HRQ* 22 (2000) 753–87, at 765.

[14] R. I. Meltzer, 'International Human Rights and Development: Evolving Conceptions and their Application to Relations between the European Community and the Africa–Caribbean–Pacific States', in Welch and Meltzer (eds.), *Human Rights and Development* 208–25, at 215.

period and, more important, to insulate future economic agreements from similar EC human rights initiatives'.[15]

One way in which the OAU/AU has linked development and human rights is through the concept of sustainable development.[16] In 1999, for example, the Council of Ministers considered the possibility of setting up a regional African Commission on Sustainable Development;[17] the OAU was also involved in the World Summit on Sustainable Development,[18] and the Secretary General stressed that such issues must be consolidated in the African Common Position.

> [This] must address poverty and debt issues in Africa, trade and environment, infrastructure and health, financing of development and promoting peace building and governance as well as other relevant environment and sustainable development issues that may come up during the national and sub-regional consultative processes. The issue of land degradation, desertification and drought must take centre stage in the Common Position. Member states must be urged to undertake a common assessment of implementation of Agenda 21 . . . and to propose adequate policy and development plans for the further implementation of this global blueprint for sustainable development.[19]

Within this, sustainable development has been interpreted as including human rights protection. For example, in the 1995 Cairo Agenda for Action, the AHSG noted the commitment to self-sustaining development, and stressed in this context the importance of democracy for development, noting that states should

---

[15] Ibid., at 219.

[16] See for example, Draft Declaration on Africa's Industrialisation, AHG/Draft/Decl.4 (XXXIII) Rev.2. See D. Lang, *Sustainable Development and International Law* (London: Kluwer Law International, 1995); P. Sands, 'International Law in the Field of Sustainable Development', *BYIL* 65 (1994) 303–81, at 303; D. McGoldrick, 'Sustainable Development and Human Rights: An Integrated Conception', *ICLQ* 45 (1996) 796–835; A. Boyle and D. Freestone (eds.), *International Law and Sustainable Development. Past Achievements and Future Challenges* (Oxford: Oxford University Press, 1999).

[17] Decision on the Report on the Conference on an African Process for the Development and Protection of the Coastal and Marine Environment (Doc.CM/2097(LXX) Add.1), CM/Dec.479(LXX).

[18] Introductory Note of the Secretary General to the Seventy-Fourth Ordinary Session of the Council of Ministers, on file with the author, at 81.

[19] Ibid., at 81–2. See also Resolution on Africa's Preparation for the United Nations Conference on Environment and Development, CM/Res.1361(LIV), preamble; Draft Decisions of the Sixty-Seventh Ordinary Session of the Council of Ministers, CM/DRAFT/ DECISIONS(LXVII) REV.1, at 27.

launch programmes to promote national unity especially through the politics of inclusion and a culture of tolerance among the various segments of our people and among the countries of Africa, based on the principles of respect of human rights and dignity, free and fair elections, as well as respect of the freedom of the press, speech, association and conscience . . . ; ensure the speedy promotion of good governance, characterised by accountability, probity, transparency, equal application of the rule of law, and clear separation of powers . . . ; take measures for the eradication of the root causes of refugees and displaced persons.[20]

A further way in which a human rights approach to development has been taken is through the use of the right to self-determination. Here the OAU/AU has said that self-determination requires economic independence:

> The current wave of democratisation and its undeniable links with structural adjustment programs and donor conditionality raise serious questions regarding the extent to which African states and for that matter their citizens, may be said to be in control of the determination of their collective political and economic destinies. From the standpoint of constitutional political economy, external 'ownership' or political and economic programmes and policies impact directly and adversely on the right to self-determination and diminish its force as one of the pillars of the right to democratic governance. Indeed, such external control may be said to constitute a violation of the right to self-determination and, to an extent, the emerging right to democratic governance.[21]

Thus, the OAU's Algiers Declaration noted that issues previously characterised by colonisation were now related to 'universal principles of the rights of peoples to be the architect of their own destiny, the right to self-determination and independence, as well as the principle of the sovereign equality of states and their right to development'. In this respect, self-determination has also been defined by the OAU/AU as encompassing a right to the use and control of natural resources. In the African Declaration

---

[20] Relaunching Africa's Socio and Economic Development: The Cairo Agenda for Action, AHG/Res.236(XXXI), Annex, paras. 10(b)–(e).

[21] D. M. Ayine, 'Ballots or Bullets?: Compliance with Rules and Norms Providing for the Right to Democratic Governance. An African Perspective', *RADIC* 10 (1998) 709–33, at 717. The Report and Decisions of the Eighth Ordinary Session of the Conference of African Ministers of Information noted that in the past attention in Africa was focused on political independence, 'the task of attaining economic independence and promoting sustainable development would be even more difficult', 17–19 June 1997, Cairo, CIM/8 RPT.(VIII), para. 8.

on Co-operation, Development and Economic Independence,[22] the AHSG said that one must review the resources and 'defend vigorously, continually and jointly the African countries' inalienable sovereign rights and control over their natural resources'.[23]

The OAU/AU have, however, gone further, to argue for a right to development. The existence of such a right in international law has been questioned by many,[24] although UN organs have taken various initiatives in this regard, noting on several occasions a 'right to development as a human right'.[25] Whether this is a legally binding right,[26] whether it is simply a manifestation of other (already accepted) rights,[27] and to whom the right belongs[28] are issues that have not been settled by international law. The OAU/AU has been willing to refer, however, to a right to development per se. The ACHPR has led the way in this area by including expressly within its provisions the right to development.[29] Unfortunately, little use has been made of it by its Commission despite the OAU organs noting,

[22] Tenth Ordinary Session AHSG, 25 May 1973, para. A.8 ff.

[23] Draft Resolution on the Question of Palestine, CM/Draft/Res.23(LXIII) Rev.1.

[24] See, for example, S. R. Chowdhury, E. M. G. Denters and P. J. I. M. de Waart (eds.), *The Right to Development in International Law* (Dordrecht: Martinus Nijhoff, 1992); Donnelly argues that the right to development 'is both conceptually and practically misguided', J. Donnelly, 'The "Right to Development": How Not to Link Human Rights and Development', in Welch and Meltzer (eds.), *Human Rights and Development* 261–83, at 261; P. Alston, 'Making Space for New Human Rights: The Case of the Right to Development', *Harvard Human Rights Yearbook* 1 (1988) 1–38, at 21; R. Rich, 'The Right to Development: A Right of Peoples?', in J. Crawford (ed.), *The Right of Peoples* (Oxford: Oxford University Press, 1988) 17–38.

[25] The UN Commission on Human Rights adopted a resolution CHR/Res/4(XXIII), UN Doc.E/CN.4/1257 (1977). In 1986 the UN General Assembly adopted the Declaration on the Right to Development, GA Res.41/128, UN Doc.A/41/153, which stated that this right was inalienable to all human beings, includes the right to self-determination, and provides responsibility of human beings for development.

[26] Udombana, 'The Third World', at 755–7.

[27]   The right to development flows from the right to self-determination and has the same nature. There is little sense in recognising self-determination as a superior and inviolable principle if one does not recognise at the same time a 'right to development' for the peoples that have achieved self-determination. This right to development must be an 'inherent' and 'built-in' right forming an inseparable part of the right to self-determination. This makes the right to development much more a right of the state or of the people, than a right of the individual. According to this view, therefore, the primary responsibility for development and determination rests with nations themselves.

ibid., at 769–70

[28] Declaration on Right to Development, but note 1979 Human Rights Commission resolution that equality of opportunity was for nations as well, CHR/Res./5(XXXV).

[29] ACHPR, Article 22.

for example, 'with satisfaction that the African Charter is the first Treaty that sanctions the right to development as a Human Right'.[30]

The OAU/AU has stated that the right to development is the right of an individual 'as an inalienable human right by virtue of which every human being is entitled to participate in, contribute to and enjoy the economic, social and cultural and political development of the society'.[31] It has thus stressed the 'focal role of man, as objective and supreme beneficiary of development, and that there is a need to entrench the human dimension in all policies seeking the economic development of our countries'.[32]

It does also suggest, however, that the right to development is a combination of the range of human rights: 'convinced that human rights are an indivisible whole encompassing political, economic, social, cultural and environmental dimensions', and also notes the importance of the democratic process to this.[33] In particular it has stressed the importance of economic, social and cultural rights:

> stressing the importance that African peoples have always attached to the respect for human dignity and the fundamental human rights bearing in mind that human and peoples' rights are not confined to civil and political rights but cover economic, social and cultural problems and that the distinction between these two categories of rights does not have any hierarchical implications but that it is nevertheless essential to give special attention to economic, social and cultural rights in future; . . . considering that economic and social development is a human right.[34]

This position was consolidated at the Ministerial Conference on Human Rights held under the auspices of the OAU in Mauritius in 1999,[35] and more recently at the Kigali Ministerial Meeting on Human Rights of the AU. The African Commission on Human and Peoples' Rights at this meeting stated that 'the right to development has been so far considered as

---

[30] Resolution on the African Commission on Human and Peoples' Rights, Twenty-Ninth Ordinary Session of the Assembly of Heads of State and Government of the Organization of African Unity, 28–30 June 1993, Cairo, http://www1.umn.edu/humanrts/africa/resafchar29th.html.

[31] Ibid.   [32] Declaration on Social Development, AHG/Decl.5(XXX), preamble.

[33] Ibid.

[34] Decision on Human and Peoples' Rights in Africa, AHG/Dec.(XVI) Rev.1 1979, preamble.

[35] 'The Conference also affirms that the right to development, the right to a generally satisfactory healthy environment and the right to national and international peace and security are universal and inalienable rights which form an integral part of fundamental human rights', Grand Bay Mauritius Declaration and Plan of Action, CONF/HRA/DECL.(I), para. 2.

a "Directive Principle" and requested all member states to give effect to this right and adopt adequate strategies'.[36] The resulting Kigali Declaration reaffirmed 'the right to development and calls upon the international community to support Member States in their continuing efforts to realize this right'.[37]

Elements of a human rights approach to development as evidenced by the OAU/AU

The OAU/AU has clearly taken a view of development that is wider than just encompassing economic issues. Political factors are therefore seen as essential features in the development of African states and the continent as a whole.

Importance of democracy for development

The OAU/AU has seen a clear link between democracy and development,[38] recognising that 'the reconstruction of the state in Africa is an essential first, if not the most, important step in the transition to sustainable development'.[39] Thus, in its Cairo Agenda for Action the AHSG noted that 'we recognise and resolve that democracy, good governance, peace, security, stability and justice are among the most essential factors in African socio-economic development', recommending that states promote national unity 'based on principles of respect for human rights and dignity, free and fair elections, as well as respect for the freedom of the press, speech, association and conscience', together with good governance, the rule of law, the separation of powers, full participation of all people, and tackling root causes of refugees and displaced persons.[40] Human rights protection is thus necessary for development:

> Democracy and human rights are prerequisites for peace and sustainable development in Africa. There is no doubt that non-respect for human rights impedes socio-economic development. In other words, violations of human rights constrains efforts of the African people aimed at building

---

[36] Report of the Meeting of Experts of the First AU Ministerial Conference on Human Rights in Africa, Kigali, 5–6 May 2003, EXP/CONF/HRA/RPT.(II), para. 42.

[37] Kigali Declaration, MIN/CONF/HRA/Decl.1(I), para. 3.

[38] See further chapter 3, on democracy.

[39] H. W. O. Okoth-Ogendo, 'Governance and Sustainable Development in Africa', in K. Ginther, E. Denters and P. J. I. M. de Waart (eds.), *Sustainable Development and Good Governance* (Dordrecht: Martinus Nijhoff, 1995) 105–10, at 109–10.

[40] Relaunching Africa's Economic and Social Development, Annex, para. (a).

peace and sustainable development. Inversely, low levels of economic performance may lead to violation of economic, social and cultural rights and the proliferation of conflicts. The hypothesis here is that low level macro economic performance may lead to conflicts, conflicts may lead to human rights violations and human rights violations may also lead to conflict... In other words, what is intrinsic in this new vicious cycle is that the higher proliferation of conflicts, the higher the degree and levels of human rights violations and the lower the level of macro economic performance and socio-economic development.[41]

The concept of 'good governance' in this regard has consistently been stressed as an important element in development.[42] NEPAD itself supports this approach.[43]

Right to participation

An important element of development is the ability of individuals and peoples to participate in the decision making affecting them.[44] In addition, previous OAU organs also stressed that 'people have a fundamental right to participate fully in the making of policy decisions that affect their lives at all levels'[45] and that 'there is a need to consolidate democracy founded on participation encouraging initiatives and organization patterns that would enable our societies to influence development and rely on their own capacities so as to shield themselves against all forms

[41] Addressing the Challenges of Peace and Security in Africa, Conflict Management Center, Occasional Paper Series No. 1/1999 has a separate section on 'Good governance, human rights and conflict management', 14 ff., at 21.

[42]   Good governance means the management of relations between government and its populace within a given constitutional order. Good governance is the opposite of poor or bad governance, which reaches from denial of political and civil as well as economic, social and cultural rights, administrative inefficiency and corruption, to deficient legal protection and political repression, and ultimately to mass violations of human rights and tyranny. It entails waste of human power and natural resources; it leads to environmental degradation and prevents sustainable development.

          K. Ginther, 'Sustainable Development and Good Governance: Development and Evolution of Constitutional Orders', in Ginther et al. (eds.), *Sustainable Development and Good Governance* 150–77, at 157.

[43] 'It is now generally acknowledged that development is impossible in the absence of true democracy, respect for human rights, peace and good governance', New Partnership for Africa's Development (NEPAD), October 2001, para. 79. See also Objectives, Standards, Criteria and Indicators, paras. 2.1 and 2.4.

[44] A. S. Tolentino, 'Good Governance through Popular Participation in Sustainable Development', in Ginther et al. (eds.), *Sustainable Development and Good Governance* 137–49.

[45] CM/Res.1286(LII).

of violence, extremism and discrimination'.[46] NGOs have a role to play.[47] A particularly important contribution in this regard has been the adoption under the OAU of the African Charter on Popular Participation in Development and Transformation. This provided that 'nations cannot be built without the popular support and full participation of the people'.[48] It defines 'popular participation' as 'the empowerment of the people to effectively involve themselves in creating the structures and designing the policies and programmes that serve the interests of all as well as to effectively contribute to the development process and share equitably in its benefits'.[49] This requires 'an opening up of political process to accommodate freedom of opinions, tolerate differences, accept consensus on issues as well as ensure the effective participation of the people and their organisations and associations'; and 'that the political system evolve to allow for democracy and full participation by all sections of our societies'.[50] Particular attention is also paid to the position of women, who should be 'given the highest priority by society as a whole and African governments in particular',[51] and biases against women should be eliminated.[52] Governments should 'set themselves targets for the appointment of women in senior policy and management posts in all sectors of government',[53] and the UN should implement its decision to have at least 30 per cent women in senior positions and ensure that African women are adequately represented at this level.[54] The Charter states that this is not only the responsibility of African governments to ensure freedom of expression and basic human rights and ending conflicts,[55] but also of the people themselves.[56] The UN is also called upon to 'promote the application of justice in international economic relations, the defence of human rights, the maintenance of peace and achievement of disarmament and to assist African countries and peoples' organisations with the development of human and economic resources'.[57] Other recommendations are also made to NGOs,[58] the media,[59] women's organisations,[60]

---

[46] Declaration on Social Development, AHG/Decl.5(XXX), para. 4.
[47] 'Desirous of making African Non-Governmental Organizations play their role in favour of the economic and social development of OAU Member States, without interfering in the internal affairs of the member states, and/or projecting extra continental interests not in conformity with OAU objectives', Resolution on the Conference of African Non-Governmental Organizations, CM/Res.712(XXXII), preamble.
[48] African Charter for Popular Participation in Development and Transformation, Arusha, 1990, para. 7.
[49] Ibid., para. 11.   [50] Ibid.   [51] Ibid., para. 12.   [52] Ibid., para. 14.
[53] Ibid., para. 16.   [54] Ibid., para. 22.   [55] Ibid., paras. 17–19.   [56] Ibid., para. 13.
[57] Ibid., para. 22.   [58] Ibid., para. 23.D.   [59] Ibid., para. 23.E.   [60] Ibid., para. 23.F.

trade unions[61] and youth and student organisations.[62] Popular participation is to be monitored on the basis of the literacy rate, freedom of
association, representation of the people in national bodies, the rule of
law and social and economic justice, protection of the environment, freedom of the press and media, implementation of the Abuja Declaration
on women, political accountability of leadership and decentralisation in
decision making.[63]

The establishment of the Pan-African Parliament has a great potential to increase participation on issues under the AU which relate to
development, and it has been emphasised that this should be part of
its role: 'in order to ensure that the peoples of Africa are fully involved
in the economic development and integration of the Continent'.[64] The
creation of ECOSOCC may assist in ensuring some degree of popular participation in the work of the AU in development; certainly that
was one of the intentions behind it. The CSSDCA Solemn Declaration also affirms 'the principles of popular participation'.[65] Unfortunately, NEPAD has already been criticised for its top-down approach
and failure of states to popularise it domestically despite its reference
to the need for participation[66] and objectives and indicators in this
regard.[67]

Socio-economic rights

Central to the issue of development is the protection of economic and
social rights. The OAU/AU has stressed the importance of these rights,
in particular when compared with civil and political rights, in achieving
development on the continent. NEPAD and the CSSDCA also contain
specific obligations.[68]

---

[61] Ibid., para. 23.G.   [62] Ibid., para. 23.H.   [63] Ibid., para. 32.
[64] Treaty Establishing the African Economic Community, Article 14(1).
[65] CSSDCA Solemn Declaration, AHG/Decl.4(XXXVI), para. 12(e).
[66] 'Promote political representation, thus providing for all citizens to participate in the
political process in a free and fair political environment', Declaration on Democracy,
Political, Economic and Corporate Governance, para. 13.
[67] For example, 'what measures has government taken to provide opportunities for participation in development by key stakeholders in civil society, the private sector, communities
and their organisations', Objectives, Standards, Criteria and indicators, para. 5.6.2.
[68] See, for example, NEPAD, paras. 123, 126; CSSDCA Solemn Declaration, para. 12(n):
'ensure the enactment of appropriate national laws to extend equal opportunities with
respect to health, education, employment and other civic rights to all citizens, especially
women and the girl child'.

Corruption

Some attention has been paid to developing principles on corruption and linking these with the violation of economic and social rights. The AHSG has suggested that the Secretary General of the OAU convene a high-level meeting of experts with the African Commission on Human and Peoples' Rights to examine 'obstacles to the enjoyment of economic and social rights including corruption'.[69] NEPAD requires a mechanism to be established to deal with corruption, and it is clear that the AU sees the adoption of its Convention on Preventing and Combating Corruption as fulfilling this role. Certainly, among the Objectives and Principles of the Convention are the promotion of 'socio-economic development by removing obstacles to the enjoyment of economic, social and cultural rights as well as civil and political rights' and 'respect for human and peoples' rights in accordance with the African Charter on Human and Peoples Rights and other relevant human rights Instruments'.[70]

Unfortunately the Convention does not provide for particularly strong enforcement. Its independent Advisory Board on Corruption has a promotional and advisory capacity, and states are required to report to the Board on the progress they have made in implementing its provisions.[71]

Education

The issue of education has been a theme of the OAU's approach to development: 'convinced that basic education constitutes the cornerstone for development; . . . determined to ensure the effective participation of communities and partners in education in defining and implementing educational policies in order to guarantee social integration and individual fulfillment'.[72] What standard of education is required to be provided, however, is not entirely clear.[73] On some occasions the OAU/AU refers to the importance of 'basic education'[74] without necessarily defining what it is. The UN Committee on Economic, Social and Cultural Rights has

[69] Annual Activities of the African Commission on Human and Peoples' Rights, AHG/Dec 126(XXXIV) 1997.
[70] Convention on Preventing and Combating Corruption, Articles 2(4) and 3(2).
[71] Ibid., Article 22.
[72] Resolution on the Declaration of 1996 Year of Education in Africa, CM/Res.1603(LXII), preamble.
[73] See Committee on Economic, Social and Cultural Rights, 'The Right to Education (Art.13)', General Comment, 8 December 1999, E/C.12/1999/10.
[74] Report of the Secretary General on the Conference of African Ministers of Education (COMEDAF) and the Implementation of the Programme of Action of the Decade of Education in Africa (Addendum), CM/2113(LXX) Add., at 12.

stated that although 'primary education is not synonymous with basic education, there is a close correspondence between the two', endorsing UNICEF's approach that 'primary education is the most important component of basic education'.[75] The OAU has said, however, that the right to education is a 'basic human right'[76] and that education should be made available to all.[77] States have been asked to 'provide free and universal primary education',[78] which is similar to the approach adopted under the ICESCR.[79] With regard to higher education,[80] it would appear that the OAU/AU has stated that there is not necessarily a right to such, but that states should be encouraged to provide it. Therefore, the OAU has stressed the important 'role of universities and institutions of higher learning in the promotion of socio-economic, scientific and cultural development on the one hand and freedom, dignity and democracy on the other'.[81] Further, if states are to provide higher education, then the OAU/AU has suggested that fees should be kept to a minimum.[82] The right to education

---

[75] Committee on Economic, Social and Cultural Rights, 'The Right to Education (Art.13)', para. 9.

[76] Introductory Note to the Report of the Secretary General on the Sixty-Ninth Ordinary Session of the Council of Ministers, Addis Ababa, 19–23 March 1999, para. 81; Introductory Note of the Secretary General to the Seventy-Fourth Ordinary Session, at 73 ff.; Resolution on the Formation of a Panel of Experts to Propose Possible Innovations in Curricula Reforms and Methods of Teaching in Primary and Secondary Schools, CM/Res.368(XXIII); Resolution on the Formation of a Panel of Experts to Study and Report on the Progress of Adult Continuing Education in Member States, CM/Res.369(XXIII); Resolution on the Launching of the Decade of Education in Africa (1997–2006), AHG/Res. 251(XXXII) 1996.

[77] Report of the Seventh Ordinary Session of the Committee of Ambassadors and Other Plenipotentiaries, Amb/Cttee/Rpt(VII).

[78] Report of the Secretary General on the Twenty-Second Ordinary Session of the OAU Labour and Social Affairs Commission, CM/2112(LXX), para. 45.

[79] Committee on Economic, Social and Cultural Rights, 'The Right to Education (Art.13)', para. 10.

[80] The OAU/AU has said very little about secondary education. Under the UN ICESCR, Article 13(2)(b), the Committee has clarified that '"generally available" signifies, firstly that secondary education is not dependent on a student's apparent capacity or ability and, secondly, that secondary education will be distributed throughout the state in such a way that it is available on the same basis to all', Committee on Economic, Social and Cultural Rights, 'The Right to Education (Art.13)', para. 13.

[81] Resolution on the Role of African Universities and Institutions of Higher Learning in the Development of the Continent, CM/Res.1601(LXII), preamble. See also Resolution on Strengthening the Role of African Higher Educational Institutions and Universities in the Development of Africa, AHG/Res.215(XXVIII); African Declaration on Cooperation, Development and Economic Independence, CM/St.12(XXI), paras. A2–A7.

[82] 'Noting with concern that some member states despite several OAU resolutions continue to charge "Economic" fees in their educational institutions', Resolution on the Situation of Refugees in Africa, CM/Res.1084(XLV), preamble.

also encompasses the development of adult education as 'one of the fundamental aspects of the promotion of the right to education and democratization of education, as well as the effective introduction of continuing education for all'.[83] In this regard, the Council of Ministers has stated that 'eradication of illiteracy is necessary for ensuring the exercise of the right to education, enshrined in the Universal Declaration of Human Rights and the African Charter on Human and Peoples' Rights'.[84]

Beyond these statements, however, it would appear that there is a certain amount of discretion allowed to states as to what level of facilities they provide. So states should 'guarantee to the entire population the right to education and training based on African realities and provided in a form suited to Africa's needs and development objectives and take all necessary measures to respect this right'.[85] This could suggest that African relativities will be taken into account, a more progressive approach which moves away from the immediacy of the obligations in the African Charter.[86] Further, where the OAU/AU has called on states to give priority to education in their development plans, this has been more from an economic point of view, in terms of developing the economy, than from a human rights perspective.[87]

Health

Among the economic and social rights considered important for development is the right to 'sustainable preservation and protection of health

---

[83] Resolution on International Literacy Year, CM/Res.1295(LII).
[84] Resolution on the World Conference on Education for All, CM/Res.1294(LII), preamble. See also Resolution on Adult/Continuing Education in Africa, CM/Res.800(XXXV); Resolution on the Meeting of Experts on the Objectives of Primary and Secondary Education in Africa, CM/Res.799(XXXV); Resolution on Africa and the International Literacy Year (1990), CM/Res.1237(L).
[85] African Declaration on Co-operation, Development and Economic Independence, Tenth Ordinary Session AHSG, 25 May 1973, para. A.2.
[86] Even the ICESCR has been interpreted by its Committee as providing for immediate obligations. These include that the right be guaranteed without discrimination and that states take steps towards its full realisation, see Committee on Economic, Social and Cultural Rights, 'The Right to Education (Art.13)'.
[87] Decision on the Report of the Secretary General on the Conference of African Ministers of Education (COMEDAF I) and the Implementation of the Programme of Action of the Decade of Education in Africa, AHG/Dec.136(XXXV). See also Report of the Secretary General on the Conference of African Ministers of Education (COMEDAF) and the Implementation of the Programme of Action on the Decade of Education in Africa, CM/2113(LXX); Resolution on Conference of African Ministers of Education, AHG/Res.183(XXV), paras. 2 and 5.

as a basic necessity of the individual, an inalienable right and an international public good'.[88] The OAU has therefore called on states 'to consider health as an indicator and integral part of their economic development', recommending that they 'set out policies, strategies and programmes for the promotion and improvement of the health of the populations in disadvantaged urban and rural areas, . . . improve the efficacy of non-western medicine, . . . pay particular attention to and consider as a matter of priority the health of the most vulnerable group especially children, women and the elderly'.[89]

What standard of health is required is not clear, however. On some occasions the OAU/AU has referred to 'a level of health which will permit them to lead a socially and economically productive life, through primary health care programmes'.[90] On other occasions it has referred to the right 'to enjoy the best attainable state of physical and mental health'.[91] The latter is the standard as set out in the ACHPR,[92] although this differs slightly from that provided under the UN ICESCR.[93] The UN Committee on Economic, Social and Cultural Rights has stated that the right to health includes not only health care, but also 'embraces a wide range of socio-economic factors that promote conditions in which people can lead a health life, and extends to the underlying determinants of health, such as food and nutrition, housing, access to safe and potable water and adequate sanitation, safe and healthy working conditions and a healthy environment'.[94] The OAU/AU has similarly adopted a broad approach.

In this regard, states have various obligations, including the requirement that they 'strengthen primary health care systems . . . ; strengthen all public education policies by establishing nutrition education in curricula

---

[88] Decision on the Control of Arterial Hypertension in Africa, AHG/Dec.179(XXXVIII).

[89] Resolution on Health and Development Policies, CM/Res.1549(LX). See also Declaration of Health as a Foundation for Development, AHG/Decl.1(XXIII).

[90] Resolution on Health as a Component of Development, CM/Res.1104(XLVI).

[91] Draft Resolution on the Report of the Secretary General on the Control of Micronutrient Deficiencies, CM/Draft/Res.15(LXIII) Rev.1.

[92] Article 16 ACHPR reads: '(1) Every individual shall have the right to enjoy the best attainable state of physical and mental health. (2) States Parties to the present Charter shall take the necessary measures to protect the health of their people and to ensure that they receive medical attention when they are sick.'

[93] Article 12(1) of the ICESCR provides that states should recognise 'the right of everyone to the enjoyment of the highest attainable standard of physical or mental health'.

[94] Committee on Economic, Social and Cultural Rights, 'The Right to the Highest Attainable Standard of Health', General Comment, 11 August 2000, E/C.12/2000/4, para. 4.

at all levels of schooling; ... strengthen a public information system which can help individuals and communities to be self-sufficient in controlling Vitamin A and iron deficiencies'.[95] They should also ensure 'access to health care for all, inviolability of the human body and of the genetic heritage of the human species' and 'the right of everyone, especially children, to protection from all forms of trade and exploitation'.[96]

It has paid some attention to the protection of individuals from scientific exploitation,[97] stressing 'the right of the individual to the benefits of scientific progress as well as application thereof ... to ensure that scientific progress benefit the individual human being and is achieved under condition of respect for fundamental human rights'.[98]

Eradication of disease is central among the OAU/AU's considerations,[99] in particular polio[100] and malaria, the latter being seen as 'a barrier to sustainable social and economic development'.[101] States should thus 'implement well planned and coordinated malaria control programmes involving individuals, families, communities, institutions, relevant government ministries, and other public and private sectors', allocate sufficient resources and get resources from external sources. It calls on states to give political support to such action, and for organisations such as WHO to assist states.[102]

There has been recognition of the impact of drug abuse on development[103] and on political stability.[104] A model Preventive Drug Abuse Education curriculum for Africa is being developed, as is a study on the

---

[95] Draft Resolution on the Report of the Secretary General on the Control of Micronutrient Deficiencies, CM/Draft/Res.15(LXIII) Rev.1.

[96] Resolution on Bioethics, AHG/Res 254(XXXII) 1996, paras. 3 and 4.

[97] Ibid., paras. 2–4.   [98] Ibid., preamble.

[99] See, for example, Decision on the Holding of an African Summit on HIV/AIDS, Tuberculosis and Other Related Infectious Diseases, AHG/Dec.154(XXXVI); Decision on the Report of African Summit on Roll Back Malaria, AHG/Dec.155(XXXVI); Decision on Proposal for the Eradication of Tsetse Flies in the African Continent, AHG/Dec.156(XXXVI).

[100] Yaounde Declaration on Polio Eradication in Africa, AHG/Decl.1(XXXII).

[101] Harare Declaration on Malaria Prevention and Control in the Context of African Economic Recovery and Development, AHG/Decl.1(XXXIII).

[102] Draft Harare Declaration on Malaria Prevention and Control in the Context of African Economic Recovery and Development, AHG/Draft/Decl.I(XXXIII) Rev.2.

[103] Introductory Note of the Secretary General to the Seventy-Fourth Ordinary Session, at 76.

[104] Declaration and Plan of Action on Drug Abuse Control and Illicit Drug Trafficking in Africa, AHG/Decl.2(XXXII): 'recognising that illicit drug traffic undermines civil authorities and governments and poses a threat to political stability; ... concerned about the socio-economic consequences of drug abuse because of their particular burden on national development, productivity and social services as drug abuse affects the society,

link between drug abuse and trafficking.[105] There has been a decision to establish a Drug Control Fund,[106] and a Drug Control and Crime Prevention Unit has been set up under the Social Affairs Directorate of the AU.[107]

There has been less attention, in general, to reproductive health, although states have been required to 'provide political support and commitment to adolescent health programmes' by 'involving the youth and adolescents in the formulation and implementation of reproductive health programmes as well as allocating the necessary material and financial resources'.[108] However, this has been placed within the context of social and cultural norms, the OAU/AU recognising 'that the implementation of this recommendation shall not prejudice the specificity of each society, its religious beliefs, social and cultural traditions'.[109] This removes some of the original force of the resolution.

Despite the occasional reference to HIV/AIDS,[110] the OAU/AU did not really start considering the issue seriously until the late 1990s.[111] A clear link has been made between AIDS and its impact on development.[112] In June 2001 a Summit on HIV/AIDS was held in Abuja, resulting in the Abuja Framework and Abuja Declaration for Action for the Fight against HIV/AIDS, Tuberculosis and Other Related Infectious Diseases in Africa.[113] The OAU has also concluded a Cooperation Agreement with

---

family and individual', Report of the Secretary General on the Activities of the General Secretariat, CM/2058(LXVIII), para. 185.

[105] Introductory Note of the Secretary General to the Seventy-Fourth Ordinary Session, at 77.

[106] Ibid.   [107] CM/OAU/AEC/REGL.1(IX).

[108] Decision on the African Forum on Adolescent Reproductive Health, CM/Dec.339(LXVI). See also Declaration on the African Plan of Action Concerning the Situation of Women in Africa in the Context of Family Health, AHG/Decl.1(XXXI).

[109] Decision on the African Forum on Adolescent Reproductive Health.

[110] For example, in a 1991 resolution, Declaration on the Current African Health Crisis, AHG/Dec.3(XXVII).

[111] Resolution on Regular Reporting of the Implementation Status of OAU Declarations on HIV/AIDS in Africa, AHG/Res 247(XXXII) 1996; Report of the Secretary General on the Activities of the General Secretariat, CM/2058(LXVIII) part I; Resolution on the AIDS Epidemic in Africa: Progress Report and Guidelines for Action, AHG/Res. 223(XXIX) 1993; Lomé Declaration on HIV/AIDS in Africa, AHG/Decl.3(XXXVI). See also Decision on the African Summit on HIV/AIDS, Tuberculosis and Other Related Infectious Diseases, AHG/Dec.161(XXXVII); Declaration AHG/Decl.(XXIII) on Health, as a Foundation for Socio-Economic Development, endorsed in 1987 in Addis Ababa, as well as in the Dakar (1992) and Tunis (1994) Declarations on HIV/AIDS in Africa.

[112] Resolution on the Prevention and Control of AIDS in Africa, CM/Res.1302(LII). Introductory Note of the Secretary General to the Seventy-Fourth Ordinary Session, at 96.

[113] Abuja Framework for Action for the Fight against HIV/AIDS, Tuberculosis and Other Related Infectious Diseases in Africa, OAU/SPS/ABUJA/4.

UNAIDS which is 'an innovative framework to mobilise, urgently, governments and civil societies to redirect national and international policies and resources so as to address the evolving HIV/AIDS epidemic in Africa and its many compelling implications'.[114]

Various issues have been covered. Firstly, it has been stressed that those with HIV/AIDS should not be discriminated against, in line with statements by UN bodies.[115] States have thus been asked to make 'full political commitment to making AIDS prevention a matter of highest priority, ... to fight against all discriminatory practices and stigmatization against people with AIDS and actively protect vulnerable groups including women and children'.[116] Those with HIV/AIDS should be ensured 'equal rights'[117] and states should 'protect the rights and dignity of nationals with HIV infection or suffering from AIDS'.[118] Particular attention has been paid to women in this regard, recognising that 'biologically, women and girls are particularly vulnerable to HIV infection. In addition, economic and social inequalities and traditionally accepted gender roles leave them in a subordinate position to men.'[119]

It has recognised that 'the transmission of AIDS can be controlled through education and information to the public to effect change of

---

[114] Decision on the Report of the Secretary General on the Draft Co-operation Agreement between the OAU and UNAIDS (Doc.CM/2124(LXX)-e), CM.Dec.478(LXX). See also Decision on the Report of the Secretary General on Co-operation between the General Secretariat and UNAIDS within the Framework of the International partnership to Control HIV/AIDS in Africa (Doc.CM/2115(LXX)), CM/Dec.467(LXX); also, more recently, Draft Maputo Declaration on HIV/AIDS, Tuberculosis, Malaria and Other Related Infectious Diseases, Assembly/AU/Decl.3(II).

[115] For example, UN Commission on Human Rights, Discrimination Against HIV-Infected People or Peoples with AIDS, 8 December 1993, E/CN.4/1994/37.

[116] Resolution on AIDS and Africa: Agenda for Action, AHG/Res.216(XXVIII). In the Abuja Declaration it recognised: 'We are aware that stigma, silence, denial and discrimination against people living with HIV/AIDS (PLWA) increase the impact of the epidemic and constitute a major barrier to an effective response to it. We recognize the importance of greater involvement of People Living with HIV/AIDS.', para. 12.

[117] Abuja Declaration, para. 24.

[118] Resolution on the Prevention and Control of AIDS in Africa, CM/Res.1302(LII), para. 2(e). See also Progress Report of the Secretary General on the Follow-Up on the Abuja Declaration and Framework Plan of Action on HIV/AIDS, Tuberculosis, and Other Related Infectious Diseases in Africa, Doc.CM/2249(LXXVI)-d, Report of the Fifteenth Ordinary Session of the Committee of Ambassadors and Other Plenipotentiaries, 6 July 2002, Cttee/AMB/Rpt(XV), para. 70.

[119] Abuja Declaration, para. 7. Note that the UN CEDAW Committee has recognised the impact of HIV/AIDS on women in particular, 'Women and Health', General Recommendation No. 24, 2 February 1999.

their behavioral patterns and life styles'.[120] This includes developing pro-grammes to ensure sensitivity to the negative impact on such people, enacting legislation to protect the rights of those infected; strengthening existing legislation relating to human rights, gender inequalities and respecting the rights of those infected; harmonising approaches to human rights across countries; and assisting women in protecting themselves against HIV/AIDS. States should also provide access to treatment and support and affordable drugs and technology; strengthen health systems;[121] and provide counselling on AIDS.[122] States have a responsibility to deal with primary health care and to provide a sustainable way of treating those with HIV/AIDS.[123]

Besides the duty of the state in providing access to affordable medicine, the OAU/AU has recognised that this is an international problem and has therefore called on the international community to ensure that Africa has access to medicines[124] and 'to adequately consider Africa in the global resources available for HIV/AIDS in order to facilitate prevention and wider accessibility to current research findings, especially on drugs and other medicines necessary in the overall responses to this infection'. Thus pharmaceutical companies 'manufacturing anti-retroviral and other drugs necessary in the management of HIV/AIDS patients [are to be urged] to consider wider accessibility to those drugs by lowering their retail price'.[125] The OAU has also recommended a special fund to meet the cost of treating African AIDS victims.[126]

Food, water and housing

Nutrition and access to food has been raised in UN bodies as a relevant issue in development,[127] as it has been before the OAU/AU. The reasons

---

[120] Resolution on AIDS Prevention in Africa, CM/Res.1165(XLVIII).
[121] Abuja Declaration, para. 31.   [122] Resolution on AIDS Prevention in Africa.
[123] Abuja Declaration.
[124] Report of the Seventh Ordinary Session of the Committee of Ambassadors and Other Plenipotentiaries, Amb/Cttee/Rpt(VII), para. 97.
[125] Establishment of an African Fund for AIDS Control, AHG/Dec.125(XXXIV), paras. 2 and 3. See also Report of the Secretary General on the Follow-Up of OAU Declarations on HIV/AIDS in Africa – Doc.CM/2079(LXVIII), CM/Dec.423(LXVIII), paras. 2–6.
[126] Report of the Seventh Ordinary Session of the Committee of Ambassadors and Other Plenipotentiaries, Amb/Cttee/Rpt(VII), noting the Report of the Secretary General on the Follow-Up to the OAU Resolutions and Declarations on HIV/AIDS in Africa (Doc.CM/2079(LXVIII)), para. 97.
[127] See UN Committee on Economic, Social and Cultural Rights, 'The Right to the Highest Attainable Standard of Health', General Comment, 11 August 2000, E/C.12/2000/4;

behind issues of food insecurity are attributed by the OAU/AU to a number of causes including 'drought, . . . inadequate or absence of storage facilities and transport infrastructure as well as of conflicts'.[128] The need for African self-sufficiency has been stressed in this regard[129] and the wider responsibility of the international community is also recognised.[130] The AU has, for example, stressed the need to protect domestic producers: 'urges member states to develop mechanisms of support and protection of domestic food producers on the Continent, individually or collectively; further urges member states to devise and implement policies that can increase public awareness for the production and consumption of indigenous and traditional foods which are rich in micronutrients'.[131] There has also been a recognition of the wider importance of nutrition, including the impact of vitamin deficiencies on individuals' health. States are therefore required to improve their primary health-care systems and to 'strengthen all public education policies'.[132]

The impact of safe water on development has also been noted by the OAU/AU[133] and reaffirmed by commitments in NEPAD.[134] Within the context of one's 'living environment', the OAU/AU organs have paid some attention to housing needs, reflecting the approach of the UN,[135] noting 'due to, inter alia, the pressure of population growth and urbanisation and because the financial resource requirements for human settlement

UN Committee on Economic, Social and Cultural Rights, 'The Right to Adequate Food (Art.11)', 12 May 1999, E/C.12/1999/5.

[128] Introductory Note of the Secretary General to the Seventy-Fourth Ordinary Session, at 73.

[129] Draft Resolution on the World Food Summit, the Need of an Active African Involvement and Participation, CM/Draft/Res.26(LXIII) Rev.1. See also AHG/Res.244(XXXI) on Food and Security and Agricultural Development in Africa.

[130] Message to the G8 Summit of Genoa, 20–22 July 2001, AHG/ST 3(XXXVII).

[131] Decision on the Progress Report of the Secretary General on the Status of Implementation of the African Regional Nutrition Strategy 1993–2003 on Nutrition (Doc.CM/2119(LXX)), CM/Dec.471(LXX).

[132] Draft Resolution on the Report of the Secretary General on the Control of Micronutrient Deficiencies, CM/Draft/Res.15(LXIII) Rev.1. See also Report of Secretary General on the control of Vitamin A and Iron Deficiencies (Doc.CM/1928(LXIII)).

[133] Report of the Seventh Ordinary Session of the Committee of Ambassadors and Other Plenipotentiaries, Amb/Cttee/Rpt(VII), noting Background Documents to the OAU Resolution on Water Supply and Sanitation in Africa Item proposed by Nigeria, CM/2057 Add 3, Doc.CM/2057.

[134] 'To ensure sustainable access to safe and adequate clean water supply and sanitation, especially for the poor', NEPAD, para. 116.

[135] See UN Committee on Economic, Social and Cultural Rights, 'The Right to Adequate Housing (Art.11(1))', General Comment No. 4, 13 December 1991.

programmes far exceed the availability of resources in these countries'.[136] In this regard attention should be paid to 'securing renewed political and financial commitment by the international community to the provision of shelter for the homeless particularly in Africa as a matter of priority'.[137] This appears more limited than the UN ICESCR definition that 'the right to housing should not be interpreted in a narrow or restrictive sense which equates it with, for example, the shelter provided by merely having a roof over one's head or views shelter exclusively as a commodity. Rather, it should be seen as the right to live somewhere in security, peace and dignity.'[138]

Employment and social security

One of the early reasons the OAU seems to have looked at the issue of employment in the context of rights arose in relation to the treatment of African workers abroad. Some early resolutions noted the 'conditions of life and work of African and Arab migrant workers in the European Union' and recommendations had been made to draw up a charter to protect their rights.[139] Over the years, more generally, particular attention has been paid to trade union-related rights, including tripartism and 'the role it can play in bringing about balanced socio-economic development, industrial peace and democracy in Africa'.[140] If states created 'opportunities for productive and gainful employment of the youth in development',[141] this would assist development. Much of this has been influenced by ILO Conventions, which states have also been called upon to ratify.[142]

---

[136] Draft Resolution on the Second United Nations Conference on Human Settlements (HABITAT II) Implementation and Follow-Up Mechanism, CM/Draft/Res.12(LXIII) Rev.1.

[137] Resolution on the International Year of Shelter for the Homeless, AHG/Res.117(XIX).

[138] UN Committee on Economic, Social and Cultural Rights, 'The Right to Adequate Housing (Art.11(1))', para. 7.

[139] Report of the Secretary General on the Activities of the General Secretariat, CM/2058 (LXVIII) part I, paras. 155 and 158.

[140] Resolution on the Proceedings of the Fifteenth Ordinary Session of the OAU Labour Commission, CM/Res.1410(LVI), preamble. See also Report of the Secretary General on the Twenty-Second Ordinary Session of the OAU Labour and Social Affairs Commission, CM/2112(LXX), noting the Report of the Secretary General of the Organization of African Trade Union Unity (Doc.LSC/10a(XXII)), para. 110.

[141] Resolution on the Participation of Youth in Development in Africa, CM/Res.1236(L), preamble.

[142] Report of the Secretary General on the Twenty-Second Ordinary Session of the OAU Labour and Social Affairs Commission, CM/2112(LXX). See also Decision on the Report of the Secretary General on the Twenty-Third Ordinary Session of the OAU Labour and

The OAU Labour and Social Affairs Commission plays an important role in this regard. It is a tripartite composed of states' ministers, delegates from employers and delegates from employees, and this Commission has charge over 'all matters . . . in the field of labour, economic and related social matters', including 'promoting tripartite and trade union freedom in Africa and working for tripartite consensus on the right to collective negotiations on labour and related social and economic issues'.[143] Under the AU this Commission now falls under the Social Affairs Directorate.[144]

Beyond work, the OAU/AU has called on states to 'revamp, increase and extend the coverage of their social security schemes',[145] with extension being 'based on economic, social and political context of each country and respect gender equality in social security issues'.[146]

Protection of the environment

The idea of sustainable development in international law has clearly included protection for the environment.[147] In the same vein, the OAU/AU has paid considerable attention in its development policies to environmental issues, for example: 'conscious of the need to sensitise the African populace on the relevance of and link between social and economic development and rational management of the environment'.[148] In terms of environmental protection, this has encompassed a wide range of issues:

> providing of clean food and water for human beings and livestock; preservation and utilisation of Africa's natural resources and in the environmental interests of the continent; transfer of technologies from industrialised countries to developing regions which should henceforth take into consideration new environmental norms; incidence of environment on trade patterns and development; threats to human environment in southern African introduced by apartheid, racist and colonial practices.[149]

Social Affairs Commission (CM/2174(LXXII)), CM/Dec.535(LXXII), para. 6; Decision on the Report of the Secretary General on the Twenty-Second Ordinary Session of the OAU Labour and Social Affairs Commission (Doc.CM/2112(LXX)), CM/Dec.465(LXX).

[143] Rules of Procedure of Labour and Social Affairs Commission, LSC/7(XXI) Rev.2, Annex, Rule 3.

[144] The Commission will eventually be replaced by a Specialised Technical Committee under Article 14 of the Constitutive Act.

[145] Decision on the Report of the Secretary General on the Twenty-Third Ordinary Session of the OAU Labour and Social Affairs Commission (CM/2174(LXXII)), CM/Dec.535(LXXII), para. 6.

[146] CM/OAU/AEC/REGL.1(IX).   [147] See above.

[148] CM/Res.1299(LII). See also Resolution on Environment, AHG/Res.245(XXXI).

[149] Resolution on Environment, CM/Res.262(XVIII).

States in this context have a right to exploit their natural resources. This has been apparent not only from the colonial legacy but also from a recognition of the impact of globalisation:

> In the face of increasing marginalisation in the context of the globalisation of the world economy, the Prime Minister urged member states to quicken the pace towards regional integration and cooperation. He observed that the Continent had abundant natural and human resources and there was no reason for Africa to continue to suffer a widespread prevalence of poverty and economic destitution.[150]

Yet the right of African states to exploit natural resources must be 'for the economic benefit of African people'[151] and although there is a right of the state 'to manage its resources pursuant to its environmental policies', it does have 'an obligation in the prevention and control of pollution of the marine environment'.[152] It must thus recognise 'the principles of the Common Heritage of Mankind which principle should in no way be limited in its scope or restrictive interpretation'.[153] The right encompasses protection from international interference.[154] Environmental concerns have also included reference to industrialisation and the need for Africa to explore 'alternative sources of energy such as hydro-power, petroleum and natural gas. The exploitation of these resources should be done in such judicious and coordinated manner as to allow those member states who are less endowed to benefit from others through a negotiated marketing distribution and pricing strategy'.[155]

Even though this has been held to be a right of the state, the OAU/AU has recognised that individuals have rights in this respect as well. Thus, one of the main reasons for protection of the environment seems to be protection of the health of individuals.[156] Beyond this, other issues covered by environmental concerns are the need to guard against natural disasters[157] and

---

[150] Report of the Sixty-Fourth Ordinary Session of the Council of Ministers, CM/Rpt(LXVI), para. 5.

[151] OAU Declaration on the Issues of the Law of the Sea, CM/St.11(XXI).

[152] Ibid., paras. 16–17.   [153] Ibid., para. 20.

[154] See African Declaration on Cooperation, Development and Economic Independence, CM/St.12(XXI), paras. A8–A15.

[155] Introductory Note of the Secretary General to the Seventy-Fourth Ordinary Session, at 80–1. See also Resolution on World Charter for Nature, CM/Res.852(XXXVII).

[156] See Introductory Note of the Secretary General to the Seventy-Fourth Ordinary Session, at 82.

[157] Decision on Natural Disasters in Africa, CM/Dec. 576(LXXIII).

to deal with deforestation, desertification,[158] drought and famine.[159] The OAU has therefore expressed its support for the UN to establish a panel of experts on the 'illegal exploitation of natural resources and other forms of wealth'.[160] An African Energy Commission has been established[161] which would facilitate cooperation with various stakeholders.[162] States have been asked to 'take concrete measures towards the preparation and implementation of an African Solar Programme'.[163]

Considerable attention has also been paid to pollution and dumping of toxic and other waste in Africa,[164] calling this a 'crime against Africa and the African people' and demanding that multinational corporations 'clean up the areas that have already been contaminated by them'.[165] There

---

[158] Report of the Seventh Ordinary Session of the Committee of Ambassadors and Other Plenipotentiaries, Amb/Cttee/Rpt (VII), noting the Report of the Secretary General on the Draft Cooperation Agreement between the OAU and the Secretariat of the UN Convention to Combat Desertification (CCD) (Doc.CM/2082(LXVIII)). See also Draft Resolution on the International Convention on the Control of Desertification, CM/Draft/Res.30(LXIII) Rev.1; Resolution on the International Convention to Combat Desertification in those Countries Experiencing Serious Drought and/or Desertification, Particularly in Africa. The Establishment of a High-Level Commission on Sustainable Development, CM/Res.1438(LVII); Report of the Secretary General on the Conference on Environment and Development, CM/Dec.336(LXVI).

[159] Decision on the Effective Implementation of the UN Convention to Combat Desertification (UNCCD) in Countries Seriously Affected by Drought and/or Desertification, Particularly in Africa, and its Consideration During Deliberations of the World Summit on Sustainable Development, CM/Dec.677; Resolution on the Special Emergency Assistance Fund for Drought and Famine in Africa, CM/Res.1436(LVII); Resolution on Cooperation in the Field of Environment, CM/Res.1261(LI).

[160] Decision on Democratic Republic of Congo (CM/2164(LXXII)-d), CM/Dec.524(LXXII), para. 6.

[161] Decision on the Report of the Secretary General on the Establishment of the African Energy Commission (Doc CM/2193(LXXIII)-c), CM/Dec.559(LXXIII). See also Draft Resolution on African Energy Commission, CM/Draft/Res.9(LXIII) Rev.1.

[162] A Conference of African Ministers of Energy took place to consider the establishment of the African Energy Commission in Algiers on 23–24 April 2001.

[163] CM/Dec.480(LXX).

[164] Decision on the Report on the Conference on an African Process for the Development and Protection of the Coastal and Marine Environment (Doc.CM/2097(LXX) Add.1), CM/Dec.479(LXX); Resolution on Control of Transboundary Movements of Hazardous Wastes and the Unanimous Adoption of the Bamako Convention, CM/Res.1225(L); Resolution on Nuclear and Industrial Wastes in Africa, CM/Res.1153(XLVIII); Decision on the Report of the Secretary General on the Outcome of the Second and Third Seminars on Nuclear Science and Technology (Doc.CM/2114(LXX)), CM/Dec.466(LXX).

[165] Resolution on Dumping Nuclear and Industrial Waste in Africa, CM/Res/1153/28; reprinted in 28 ILM (1989) 567. See also Resolution on Basel Convention on the Control of Transboundary Movements of Dangerous Wastes, CM/Res.119(XLIX).

is therefore some recognition of the impact of waste on human health, albeit not necessarily in human rights terms.[166] Unfortunately, very limited attention has been paid to the need to ensure rural development.[167]

More recently, the OAU/AU considered the revision of the 1968 Convention on the Conservation of Nature and Natural Resources.[168] The initial text paid little attention to a human rights perspective. The AU collaborated with the UNEP and IUCN to revise the Convention, and this was finally adopted in July 2003.[169] The amended Convention makes express reference to the ACHPR and includes among its principles 'the right of all peoples to a satisfactory environment favourable to their development',[170] and the 'duty of states individually and collectively to ensure the enjoyment of the right to development'.[171] Further, with regard to land and soil, states are required to 'develop and implement land tenure policies able to facilitate the above measures, inter alia by taking into account the rights of local communities',[172] and there are substantial provisions on 'procedural rights', including that states disseminate environmental information and that there is participation of the public in decision making on significant environmental issues.[173] Of particular importance is express recognition, in Article 17 of the Convention, of the 'traditional rights of local communities and indigenous knowledge'. Here states are required to protect traditional rights and intellectual property rights, to ensure that access to such information is subject to the consent of the local communities and that they should be able to participate in the planning and management of natural resources. This potentially important contribution, therefore, clearly sees human rights as integral to its provisions.

---

[166] Introductory Note of the Secretary General to the Seventy-Fourth Ordinary Session, at 82. See also Draft Resolution on the Ratification of the Bamako Convention on the Ban of the Import into Africa and the Control of Transboundary Movements and Management of Hazardous Wastes within Africa, CM/Draft/Res.14(LXIII) Rev.1.

[167] See, for example, Resolution on the Payment of Contributions to the Centre on Integrated Rural Development for Africa (CIRDAFRICA) and Invitation to Join the Centre, CM/Res.1441(LVII).

[168] 1001 UNTS 3. See Decision on the Report of the Secretary General on Revision of the 1968 African Convention on the Conservation of Nature and Natural Resources (Algiers Convention) (Doc. CM/2193(LXXIII)-g), CM/Dec.563(LXXIII). Again, in July 2002, Decision on the Revision of the 1968 African Convention on the Conservation of Nature and Natural Resources (Algiers Convention), Doc. CM/2265(LXXVI), CM/Dec.680.

[169] African Convention on the Conservation of Nature and Natural Resources, EX/CL/50(III).

[170] Article 3(1).   [171] Article 3(2).   [172] Article 6(4).   [173] Article 11.

Focus on the most vulnerable

One aspect of the right to development, as defined elsewhere, is the need to pay attention to the most vulnerable members of society.[174] Generally the OAU/AU has referred to protection for a number of 'vulnerable groups' including women, children, youth, the elderly and those with disabilities.[175] Particular attention has been paid to women in the context of development.[176] As NEPAD confirms, African leaders should take responsibility for 'promoting the role of women in social and economic development',[177] and this is stated as a long-term objective.[178] Further, it notes that states 'accept it as a binding obligation to ensure that women have every opportunity to contribute on terms of full equality to political and socio-economic development in all our countries'.[179] With regard to 'indigenous peoples', although the OAU/AU has recognised the importance of 'traditional knowledge and folklore' with respect to traditional medicines,[180] the focus is more on *African* management of resources and information and protection against Western or multinational interference.[181]

The OAU has paid some attention to the position of those with disabilities, prompted in part by the number of persons with disabilities as a result of conflict and disease[182] and, in its early years, tied their situation to the liberation struggle. The UN Year of the Disabled has also prompted the OAU to consider its position,[183] with OAU states being required to help

---

[174] UN Declaration on the Right to Development, Article 6(1) notes that 'all States should co-operate with a view to promoting, encouraging and strengthening universal respect for and observance of all human rights and fundamental freedoms for all without any distinction as to race, sex, language or religion'.

[175] Declaration on Social Development, AHG/Decl.5(XXX) 1994, para. 5.

[176] See further discussion in chapter 5.

[177] NEPAD, para. 49.   [178] NEPAD, para. 67.

[179] NEPAD Declaration on Democracy, Political, Economic and Corporate Governance, para. 11. There are specific objectives set out for the promotion and protection of the rights of women and progress towards gender equality, and indicators include ratification of international instruments, effectiveness of constitutional and legal provisions, steps to ensure their meaningful participation, and measures to increase girl-child enrolment in schools, NEPAD Objectives, Standards, Criteria and Indicators, paras. 2.9 and 5.5.

[180] T. Kongolo, 'WTO Doha Ministerial Declaration and Intellectual Property: African Perspectives', *African Yearbook of International Law* 9 (2001) 185–211, at 185–6.

[181] Report of the Seventh Ordinary Session of the Committee of Ambassadors and Other Plenipotentiaries, Amb/Cttee/Rpt(VII).

[182] African Decade of Disabled Persons 1999–2002, CM/Dec.535(LXXII); Resolution on the International Year of the Disabled, CM/Res.594(XXX), preamble.

[183] Resolution on International Year of the Disabled, CM/Res.724(XXXIII), para. 2.

the disabled towards physical rehabilitation and psychological readjustment to the community; encouraging all efforts exerted at national and international levels for the purpose of providing the necessary assistance, care, training, and guidance to the disabled as well as adequate employment opportunities in addition to ensuring their total integration within the community; promoting study and research projects aimed at easing in practical manner the participation of the disabled in daily life by providing for their use of public buildings and communications facilities fully adapted to their needs; teaching and installing awareness in the public as to the rights of the disabled to participate in the various economic, social and political life as well as contributing to them; favouring the adoption of efficient measures for protecting against total disability and for the rehabilitation of the disabled.[184]

Although the OAU/AU has not attempted to define 'disability',[185] it has consistently stressed the need for their participation in society,[186] including ensuring equal opportunities,[187] and for the needs of such vulnerable groups to be 'mainstreamed' within strategies for employment.[188] These reflect the approach of the UN bodies.[189] Other measures suggested by the OAU include that states should set up national coordinating bodies, encourage exchange of information on disabled persons, and set up a regional institute on the subject. In 1981 the Council of Ministers established an ad hoc ministerial committee to consider the problems of disabled persons in Africa.[190] Such matters now fall under the Social Affairs Directorate of the AU.

---

[184] Resolution on the International Year of the Disabled, CM/Res.594(XXX), preamble.
[185] The Committee under the UN ICESCR relies upon one definition: 'the term "disability" summarises a great number of different functional limitations occurring in any population . . . People may be disabled by physical, intellectual or sensory impairment, medical conditions or mental illness. Such impairments, conditions or illnesses may be permanent or transitory in nature', see UN Committee on Economic, Social and Cultural Rights, 'Persons with Disabilities', General Comment No. 5, 9 December 1994, para. 3.
[186] Resolution on International Year of the Disabled, CM/Res.724(XXXIII), preamble; Decision on the Plan of Action for the African Decade of Disabled Persons, CM/Dec.676, paras. 2 and 3; Regulation, EC/AU/AEC/Regl.(I), para. 7.
[187] Report of the Secretary General on the Twenty-Second Ordinary Session of the OAU Labour and Social Affairs Commission, para. 127.
[188] Declaration of the Twenty-Seventh Ordinary Session of the Assembly of Heads of State and Government on Employment in Africa, AHG/Dec.1(XXVII), paras. 16 and 17.
[189] See, for example, UN Committee on Economic, Social and Cultural Rights, 'Persons with Disabilities'.
[190] Resolution on Disabled Persons, CM/Res.875(XXXVII). See also Resolution on the Problem of Disabled Persons, CM/Res.834(XXXVI).

Some attention has been paid to the position of older persons in Africa, and this has clearly been made in the context of the 'extended family'. As the Secretary General noted:

> The extended family as a critical support system is increasingly under threat. He also pointed out the gender dimensions of ageing especially the feminisation of poverty . . . While older people are both a liability and an asset to their communities, the responsibility of governments for the promotion and protection of the rights and dignity of older people is non-negotiable.[191]

Thus, the human rights of older persons have been stressed, including the requirement that states 'prevent neglect and abuse' and 'enhance social security systems for them and self-reliance of older people, strengthen systems and eliminate all forms of violence and discrimination against elderly people in all countries, paying special attention to the needs of elderly women'.[192] The Council of Ministers has asked the General Secretariat to convene a high-level seminar to consider the Draft OAU Policy Framework and Plan of Action on Ageing, with recommendations to be submitted to the OAU's Labour and Social Affairs Commission.[193] These seem to cover some of the protection as provided for under the UNICESCR.[194]

Whose responsibility?

One of the issues in the context of development and whether there is any right to such is whose duty it is to provide this right. In this regard, the OAU/AU has taken an expansive approach, recognising that responsibility lies with a variety of actors.

Firstly, there has been considerable emphasis on the responsibility of non-African actors regarding the exploitation of the continent's natural resources. It has referred to the colonial legacy and suggested that compensation should be paid, noting the 'ecological consequences of the

---

[191] Report of the Secretary General on the Twenty-Second Ordinary Session of the OAU Labour and Social Affairs Commission, CM/2112(LXX), noting the Report on the Issues and Problems of Ageing in Africa (Doc.LSC/1(XXII) Add 1.), para. 141.

[192] Report of the Secretary General on the Twenty-Second Ordinary Session of the OAU Labour and Social Affairs Commission, CM/2112(LXX), para. 147.

[193] CM/OAU/AEC/REGL.1(IX).

[194] See UN Committee on Economic, Social and Cultural Rights, 'The Economic, Social and Cultural Rights of Older Persons', General Comment No. 6, 8 December 1995.

construction of giant dams in these same territories' under colonial domination and

> the responsibility of the colonial powers and other industrialised countries in the destructive exploitation and dissipation of Africa's natural resources; feeling that this responsibility implies recognition of the right to reparation from the countries whose development has been based or is still based on this exploitation, condemns all forms of degradation and dissipation of human values and resources and requests that the Stockholm declaration on the environment if it has not yet been adopted, unambiguously denounce the crimes committed against humanity and the human environment in Africa in relation to racial and colonial practices.[195]

More generally, the OAU/AU has consistently called on the international community to shoulder some responsibility for Africa's debt.[196] Considerable attention has also been paid to the responsibilities of multinational and private companies to development in Africa. This has included not only Western-based companies, but also the African private sector: 'The private sector in Africa should play a more important part in the industrialisation of African countries and to that effect, governments should provide the private sector with the necessary guidelines, advice and assistance.'[197] The public sector should improve its efficiency.[198]

The OAU/AU has not shied away, however, from some recognition that responsibility must fall within the hands of African states themselves: 'gravely concerned that a further deterioration of the African Environment could lead to catastrophe, recognising that the responsibility for prudent environmental management rests with the African people themselves, recognising further that environmental awareness needs to be buttressed from the grassroots level upwards'.[199] This approach has been particularly reflected recently in the NEPAD and CSSDCA processes.[200]

---

[195] Resolution on Environment, CM/Res.281(XIX).
[196] Declaration of Third Extra Ordinary Session of AHSG of OAU on Africa's External Debt Crisis, EAHG/Decl.1(III); African Common Position on Africa's External Debt Crisis, EAHG/2(III).
[197] Report of the Second Meeting of OAU/AEC/ECOSOC, CM/2072(LXVIII), para. 28.
[198] Ibid., para. 33.
[199] Resolution on the Declaration of the African Year of the Environment 1991, CM/Res.1662(LI), CM/Res.1299(LI), preamble.
[200] 'The New Partnership for Africa's Development is envisaged as a long-term vision of an African-owned and African-led development', NEPAD, para. 60. 'The responsibility for the security, stability and socio-economic development of the Continent lies primarily with African states', CSSDCA Solemn Declaration, para. 9(f).

Conclusion: NEPAD: the way forward for a right to development?

NEPAD is being hailed as the way in which Africa will take responsibility for its own affairs in terms of development,[201] and the UN has accepted NEPAD as the basis on which to work with Africa.[202] On a positive note, NEPAD appears to take not only economic factors into consideration with regard to development, but also political issues.[203] Its attention to good governance, human rights and the rule of law as essential elements in the development process are to be applauded. However, the problems with NEPAD are many, including lack of clear priorities[204] and that many of the standards on which it is based have not been elaborated.[205] There is also very vague language,[206] and while there are 'laudable goals ... they fail to suggest anything but modest incremental change when Africa needs to make radically faster progress than is being made in Asia and Latin America'.[207] Important, however, is the apparent failure of NEPAD so far to engage with African civil society, it adopting a top-down approach.

So far the focus of the OAU/AU has been on setting standards. While this is important, it has not been backed up in practice with a clear enforcement mechanism. NEPAD and the processes established under it offer some indication of moves in this direction. As noted in chapter 1, NEPAD provides for an African Peer Review Mechanism which may actually facilitate a more integrated approach to human rights and development issues.[208]

---

[201] R. Herbert, *Implementing NEPAD: A Critical Assessment* (Pretoria: South African Institute of International Affairs, 24 June 2002), www.iss.co.za, at 1.

[202] See, for example, UN GA Resolution 57/48, Cooperation between the United Nations and the African Union, UN Res.57/48, 20 January 2003.

[203] See Sen, *Development as Freedom*.

[204] Herbert, *Implementing NEPAD*, at 8–9. See also Progress Report of HE Chief Olusegun Obasango, President of the Federal Republic of Nigeria and Chairperson of the NEPAD Heads of State and Government Implementation Committee (HSGIC) to the Second Ordinary Session of the Assembly of Heads of State and Government of the African Union, Assembly/AU/Rpt(II).

[205] Herbert, *Implementing NEPAD*, at 9.

[206] For example, some of the statements on issues such as HIV/AIDS, despite the rhetoric, are also weak: 'We must therefore do everything in our power to bring it under control. As the leaders of our people, we must lead the campaign and ensure that all our people are mobilized', Progress Report of HE Chief Olusegun Obasango.

[207] Herbert, *Implementing NEPAD*, at 9.

[208] 'The HSIC directed the NEPAD Secretariat to develop detailed criteria and indicators for the APRM that should entail, amongst others, popular participation in development, including trade unions, women's groups, the youth, civil society, private sector, rural communities and professional associations', Communiqué issued at the end of the Fifth

So far sixteen states have signed the Memorandum of Understanding of the APRM[209] and the APRM panel has been appointed.[210] It was intended to conduct the first peer reviews in the second half of 2003,[211] although it was not officially launched until November 2003.[212]

At present NEPAD is still on the periphery of the AU structures, with its headquarters in South Africa. Although NEPAD will eventually be subsumed entirely under the AU structure, this will take some time.[213] Until then, 'pending the ultimate integration of the APRM with the African Union, the HSIC recommends that the specialised commissions, units or organs of the AU responsible for democracy, political governance and human rights be tasked to conduct technical assessments for the APRM'.[214] It is still unclear how NEPAD and the APRM will actually fit with other AU structures, in particular the CSSDCA process, which has the advantage of being obligatory. CSSDCA has set out some clear benchmarks and a mechanism for implementation which draws more closely on existing AU institutions.[215] The relationship between NEPAD and this process needs much greater attention. It has recently been explained that the Chairperson of the AU Commission and the Chairperson of NEPAD HSGIC would work together to establish links between the NEPAD Steering Committee and relevant AU organs.[216]

Summit of the Heads of State and Government Implementation Committee (HSGIC) of the New Partnership for Africa's Development, Abuja, Sunday 3 November 2002, para. 17.

[209] Algeria, Burkina Faso, Cameroon, Democratic Republic of Congo, Ethiopia, Gabon, Ghana, Kenya, Mali, Mauritius, Mozambique, Nigeria, Rwanda, Senegal, South Africa and Uganda, as at December 2003.

[210] This was composed of: Professor Adebayo Adedeji of West Africa, Professor Kiplagat of East Africa, Dr Graca Machel of southern Africa, Ms Dorothy Njeuma of Central Africa, Ms Marie-Angelique Savane of West Africa and Mr C. Stals of southern Africa, Communiqué issued at the end of the Seventh Summit of the Heads of State and Government Implementation Committee (HSGIC) of the New Partnership for Africa's Development, Abuja, Wednesday 28 May 2003, para. 22.

[211] Progress Report of HE Chief Olusegun Obasango.

[212] Press Release, 'Launch of the Country Review Process of the African Peer Review Mechanism of NEPAD', 14 November 2003, http://www.touchtech.biz/nepad/files/en.html.

[213] Draft Declaration on the Implementation of the New Partnership for Africa's Development (NEPAD), Assembly/AU/Decl.5(II).

[214] Communiqué issued at the end of the Fifth Summit of the Heads of State and Government Implementation Committee (HSGIC) of the New Partnership for Africa's Development, Abuja, Sunday 3 November 2002, paras. 14–16.

[215] See chapter 1.

[216] Draft Declaration on the Implementation of the New Partnership for Africa's Development (NEPAD), paras. 26–8.

NEPAD offers the potential to bring together the work of the OAU/AU organs which has been elaborated so far on development issues, and to provide a starting point for their implementation. However, two things need to be carried out in order to achieve this. Firstly, the standards and benchmarks in NEPAD need further elaboration, and it is essential here – particularly given the future integration of NEPAD into the AU – that it draw upon the developments and principles elaborated by the OAU/AU, as indicated above, in this regard. Secondly, there needs to be greater consideration of how the APRM will be built upon in the AU proper, and the AU needs to ensure that the implementation mechanisms under its remit, in particular CSSDCA, the ACHPR and others, are brought together into a coherent whole. Any impetus started with the APRM must not be lost in the transition.

9

Conclusion

The transformation of the OAU into the AU has brought with it huge potential for human rights to play a greater part in the political institution. Although human rights have been a concern to the OAU throughout its history, there is little sign of a coherent and comprehensive approach to the elaboration of standards and their implementation.

While the 1990s saw a change with increased political will for the promotion and protection of human rights by African leaders, and an increasing reference to human rights matters throughout the OAU organs, it is unfortunate that the Constitutive Act and the transformation to the Union in more recent years were not used more dynamically. This could have been the ideal time for the OAU to consolidate the standards and bodies in this field and to make changes to ensure a more coherent approach in the future. This has yet to be achieved.

The present position sees the existence of numerous resolutions and decisions from a variety of bodies across the OAU/AU structure which relate to human rights. Their contribution to the development of human rights promotion and protection on the continent has great potential, yet they appear to be little known and little used, even by the OAU/AU organs themselves. There needs to be a consolidation of these standards and a creation of a sense of institutional history, to ensure that the valuable comments and benchmarks that have already been set are built upon rather than ignored. The work of the African Commission and Court on Human and Peoples' Rights should be central to this development and these bodies should, in turn, draw upon the work of the OAU/AU organs. In this way standards on which the OAU/AU seems to build its future hopes, including democracy and good governance, can be further and more clearly elaborated.

Over the years, and consolidated in the Constitutive Act, there has been evidence of a more integrated approach to human rights across the OAU/AU. This reflects some obvious political will for human rights to be an important element in the work of the AU. Unfortunately, the same degree of attention has not been paid to the implementation of these standards in practice. The AU must now exploit the fact that some degree of commitment to such principles has been laid out at least in theory, and ensure that it is followed up with institutional support and enforcement mechanisms.

The development of standards needs, therefore, to be accompanied by a systematic review of existing instruments and bodies with a human rights remit. Over the years the OAU/AU has created numerous bodies and institutions, many of which were subsumed under the new AU structures without apparent thought being given for their usefulness or efficiency. At present under the AU the following bodies have important human rights remits: the African Committee on the Rights and Welfare of the Child, the CSSDCA Unit, NEPAD APRM, the African Commission on Human and Peoples' Rights, the Commission for Refugees, the AU Commission and its various departments, not to mention the proposed African Court on Human and Peoples' Rights and the African Court of Justice. The AU is facing financial difficulties, and the creation of new organs, if they are to function effectively, must be supported by adequate funding and logistical support. Those that are already in existence have failed to be supported effectively so far, leading them to look to outside sources for assistance. This is clearly unacceptable in the long term. One issue the AU must consider when examining the financial implications of its future is that of the large number of separate bodies, and whether their tasks might be better served through streamlining them.

What little coordination of human rights matters that there has been has taken place under the Commission of the AU, particularly the Department for Political Affairs. It makes sense to have some focal point at the Secretariat. Yet this is not straightforward. While Political Affairs formally coordinates issues on human rights, as well as democracy, popular participation, refugees and electoral processes, the African Commission on Human and Peoples' Rights falls under the Office for Legal Affairs. While women's issues are seen as being dealt with by the Directorate for Women and Gender, which is supposed to ensure integration across the AU Commission, in practice this does not appear to have happened, with the important Protocol on the Rights of Women having its main mechanism for implementation under the African Commission on Human and Peoples' Rights. The obvious focal point for the rights of children is the Committee on the Rights and Welfare of the Child, yet the delays in getting this up and running have not helped to clarify how it is to operate – not only within the AU Commission's structure, falling under the

Directorate for Social Affairs, but also with the African Commission on Human and Peoples' Rights and the Court. The Commission for Refugees still exists but now is under the Political Affairs Department, conflict matters fall within the AU's Peace and Security Directorate and the PSC, and development issues fall within NEPAD.

The Protocol on the African Court on Human and Peoples' Rights at the time of writing had obtained the required fifteen ratifications for it to come into force. The Protocol on the African Court of Justice has recently been adopted and is open for ratification. Whilst the AU Summit decided initially that they should remain as two separate institutions, in a sudden change of heart it decided to merge the two.[1] The practical implications have yet to be fully thought through. As noted in chapter 1, the ACJ will have a remit, under the Constitutive Act, for human rights issues, among others. It is essential that greater thought is given at these, albeit early, stages as to how this new combined court will operate. Furthermore, proper discussion had not taken place at the level of the African Commission on Human and Peoples' Rights as to how it would operate with the Court on Human and Peoples' Rights. Moreover, no discussion had been had on this Commission's relationship with the ACJ.

The CSSDCA Unit in the CSSDCA is at least helping to provide some sort of institutional history and a holistic look at issues within the OAU/AU. But how it relates to the other AU structures is not clear. Although many of its functions will be subsumed under other AU organs in due course, it adds another level to an already full playing field. Similarly, NEPAD, although operating at the periphery of the AU at present, is to be fully integrated by 2006. This will bring with it the APRM which, although drawing upon standards as formulated and interpreted by the OAU organs, again adds another dimension of regulation which would have been applied in relation to some countries, but not all. Its voluntary nature may cause considerable confusion when trying to formulate a coherent approach within the AU.

While the result is a confusing array of instruments and mechanisms, with little sense of each other's contribution and little coordination among them, it at least suggests that human rights have infiltrated all parts of the AU. The task of the AU now must be to have a systematic and in-depth

---

[1] Decision on the Seats of the African Union, Assembly/AU/Dec.45(iii). See also 'Open Letter to the Chairman of the African Union (AU) seeking clarifications and assurances that the establishment of an effective African Court on Human and Peoples' Rights will not be delayed or undermined', Amnesty International, IOR 63/008/2004, 5 August 2004.

consideration not only of the standards it has set, but also of the myriad of mechanisms and bodies in existence, an examination of their respective remits, and how they should interact with each other in the future. This is essential not only from a practical point of view in terms of the limited funding that is available, but also to ensure that the bodies that do exist are aware of each other's work and build upon what has gone before, that they feed into and support each other. If the AU is really to match its statements with action, then there must be a coherent and consolidated institutional approach to human rights.

The AU has developed a vision for the continent, something which was lacking in the later years of the OAU. In order to ensure that the opportunity for human rights is not lost at this crucial stage, certain actions need to be taken. The various bodies under the AU are more likely to consider human rights to be of relevance to them if there is a central organ coordinating these activities. If this is to be the African Commission on Human and Peoples' Rights, as the Assembly has suggested this cannot be achieved without ensuring independence of their members, adequate resources, clear mandates and mapping out structural relationships within the AU. The recent coming into force of the Protocol for the African Court on Human and Peoples' Rights and the sudden decision to merge it with the ACJ is but one indicator that now is the time to make these changes.

Appendix I

Charter of the Organization of African Unity

We, the Heads of African States and Governments assembled in the City of Addis Ababa, Ethiopia,

Convinced that it is the inalienable right of all people to control their own destiny,

Conscious of the fact that freedom, equality, justice and dignity are essential objectives for the achievement of the legitimate aspirations of the African peoples,

Conscious of our responsibility to harness the natural and human resources of our continent for the total advancement of our peoples in all spheres of human endeavour,

Inspired by a common determination to promote understanding among our peoples and cooperation among our states in response to the aspirations of our peoples for brother-hood and solidarity, in a larger unity transcending ethnic and national differences,

Convinced that, in order to translate this determination into a dynamic force in the cause of human progress, conditions for peace and security must be established and maintained,

Determined to safeguard and consolidate the hard-won independence as well as the sovereignty and territorial integrity of our states, and to fight against neo-colonialism in all its forms,

Dedicated to the general progress of Africa,

Persuaded that the Charter of the United Nations and the Universal Declaration of Human Rights, to the Principles of which we reaffirm our adherence, provide a solid foundation for peaceful and positive cooperation among States,

Desirous that all African States should henceforth unite so that the welfare and well-being of their peoples can be assured,

Resolved to reinforce the links between our states by establishing and strengthening common institutions,

Have agreed to the present Charter.

Establishment

Article I

1. The High Contracting Parties do by the present Charter establish an Organization to be known as the ORGANIZATION OF AFRICAN UNITY.
2. The Organization shall include the Continental African States, Madagascar and other Islands surrounding Africa.

Purposes

Article II

1. The Organization shall have the following purposes:
   a. To promote the unity and solidarity of the African States;
   b. To coordinate and intensify their cooperation and efforts to achieve a better life for the peoples of Africa;
   c. To defend their sovereignty, their territorial integrity and independence;
   d. To eradicate all forms of colonialism from Africa; and
   e. To promote international cooperation, having due regard to the Charter of the United Nations and the Universal Declaration of Human Rights.
2. To these ends, the Member States shall coordinate and harmonize their general policies, especially in the following fields:
   a. Political and diplomatic cooperation;
   b. Economic cooperation, including transport and communications;
   c. Educational and cultural cooperation;
   d. Health, sanitation and nutritional cooperation;
   e. Scientific and technical cooperation; and
   f. Cooperation for defence and security.

Principles

Article III

The Member States, in pursuit of the purposes stated in Article II, solemnly affirm and declare their adherence to the following principles:

1. The sovereign equality of all Member States.
2. Non-interference in the internal affairs of States.

3. Respect for the sovereignty and territorial integrity of each State and for its inalienable right to independent existence.
4. Peaceful settlement of disputes by negotiation, mediation, conciliation or arbitration.
5. Unreserved condemnation, in all its forms, of political assassination as well as of subversive activities on the part of neighbouring States or any other States.
6. Absolute dedication to the total emancipation of the African territories which are still dependent.
7. Affirmation of a policy of non-alignment with regard to all blocs.

Membership

Article IV

Each independent sovereign African State shall be entitled to become a Member of the Organization.

Rights and Duties of Member States

Article V

All Member States shall enjoy equal rights and have equal duties.

Article VI

The Member States pledge themselves to observe scrupulously the principles enumerated in Article III of the present Charter.

Institutions

Article VII

The Organization shall accomplish its purposes through the following principal institutions:

1. The Assembly of Heads of State and Government.
2. The Council of Ministers.
3. The General Secretariat.
4. The Commission of Mediation, Conciliation and Arbitration.

The Assembly of Heads of State and Government

Article VIII

The Assembly of Heads of State and Government shall be the supreme organ of the Organization. It shall, subject to the provisions of this Charter, discuss matters of common concern to Africa with a view to coordinating and harmonizing the general policy of the Organization. It may in addition review the structure, functions and acts of all the organs and any specialized agencies which may be created in accordance with the present Charter.

Article IX

The Assembly shall be composed of the Heads of State and Government or their duly accredited representatives and it shall meet at least once a year. At the request of any Member State and on approval by a two-thirds majority of the Member States, the Assembly shall meet in extraordinary session.

Article X

1. Each Member State shall have one vote.
2. All resolutions shall be determined by a two-thirds majority of the Members of the Organization.
3. Questions of procedure shall require a simple majority. Whether or not a question is one of procedure shall be determined by a simple majority of all Member States of the Organization.
4. Two-thirds of the total membership of the Organization shall form a quorum at any meeting of the Assembly.

Article XI

The Assembly shall have the power to determine its own rules of procedure.

The Council of Ministers

Article XII

1. The Council of Ministers shall consist of Foreign Ministers or other Ministers as are designated by the Governments of Member States.

2. The Council of Ministers shall meet at least twice a year. When requested by any Member State and approved by two-thirds of all Member States, it shall meet in extraordinary session.

Article XIII

1. The Council of Ministers shall be responsible to the Assembly of Heads of State and Government. It shall be entrusted with the responsibility of preparing conferences of the Assembly.
2. It shall take cognizance of any matter referred to it by the Assembly. It shall be entrusted with the implementation of the decision of the Assembly of Heads of State and Government. It shall coordinate inter-African cooperation in accordance with the instructions of the Assembly in conformity with Article II (2) of the present Charter.

Article XIV

1. Each Member State shall have one vote.
2. All resolutions shall be determined by a simple majority of the members of the Council of Ministers.
3. Two-thirds of the total membership of the Council of Ministers shall form a quorum for any meeting of the Council.

Article XV

The Council shall have the power to determine its own rules of procedure.

General Secretariat

Article XVI

There shall be a Secretary-General of the Organization, who shall be appointed by the Assembly of Heads of State and Government. The Secretary-General shall direct the affairs of the Secretariat.

Article XVII

There shall be one or more Assistant Secretaries-General of the Organization, who shall be appointed by the Assembly of Heads of State and Government.

Article XVIII

The functions and conditions of service of the Secretary-General, of the Assistant Secretaries-General and other employees of the Secretariat shall be governed by the provisions of this Charter and the regulations approved by the Assembly of Heads of State and Government.

1. In the performance of their duties the Secretary-General and the staff shall not seek or receive instructions from any government or from any other authority external to the Organization. They shall refrain from any action which might reflect on their position as international officials responsible only to the Organization.
2. Each member of the Organization undertakes to respect the exclusive character of the responsibilities of the Secretary-General and the staff and not to seek to influence them in the discharge of their responsibilities.

Commission of Mediation, Conciliation and Arbitration

Article XIX

Member States pledge to settle all disputes among themselves by peaceful means and, to this end, decide to establish a Commission of Mediation, Conciliation and Arbitration, the composition of which and conditions of service shall be defined by a separate Protocol to be approved by the Assembly of Heads of State and Government. Said Protocol shall be regarded as forming an integral part of the present Charter.

Specialized Commission

Article XX

The Assembly shall establish such Specialized Commissions as it may deem necessary, including the following:

1. Economic and Social Commission.
2. Educational, Scientific, Cultural and Health Commission.
3. Defence Commission.

Article XXI

Each Specialized Commission referred to in Article XX shall be composed of the Ministers concerned or other Ministers or Plenipotentiaries designated by the Governments of the Member States.

Article XXII

The functions of the Specialized Commissions shall be carried out in accordance with the provisions of the present Charter and of the regulations approved by the Council of Ministers.

The Budget

Article XXIII

The budget of the Organization prepared by the Secretary-General shall be approved by the Council of Ministers. The budget shall be provided by contribution from Member States in accordance with the scale of assessment of the United Nations; provided, however, that no Member State shall be assessed an amount exceeding twenty percent of the yearly regular budget of the Organization. The Member States agree to pay their respective contributions regularly.

Signature and Ratification of Charter

Article XXIV

1. This Charter shall be open for signature to all independent sovereign African States and shall be ratified by the signatory States in accordance with their respective constitutional processes.
2. The original instrument, done, if possible in African languages, in English and French, all texts being equally authentic, shall be deposited with the Government of Ethiopia which shall transmit certified copies thereof to all independent sovereign African States.
3. Instruments of ratification shall be deposited with the Government of Ethiopia, which shall notify all signatories of each such deposit.

Entry into Force

Article XXV

This Charter shall enter into force immediately upon receipt by the Government of Ethiopia of the instruments of ratification from two-thirds of the signatory States.

Registration of Charter

Article XXVI

This Charter shall, after due ratification, be registered with the Secretariat of the United Nations through the Government of Ethiopia in conformity with Article 102 of the Charter of the United Nations.

Interpretation of the Charter

Article XXVII

Any question which may arise concerning the interpretation of this Charter shall be decided by a vote of two-thirds of the Assembly of Heads of State and Government of the Organization.

Adhesion and Accession

Article XXVIII

1. Any independent sovereign African State may at any time notify the Secretary-General of its intention to adhere or accede to this Charter.
2. The Secretary-General shall, on receipt of such notification, communicate a copy of it to all the Member States. Admission shall be decided by a simple majority of the Member States. The decision of each Member State shall be transmitted to the Secretary-General, who shall, upon receipt of the required number of votes, communicate the decision to the State concerned.

Miscellaneous

Article XXIX

The working languages of the Organization and all its institutions shall be, if possible, African languages, English, French, Arabic and Portuguese.

Article XXX

The Secretary-General may accept, on behalf of the Organization, gifts, bequests and other donations made to the Organization, provided that this is approved by the Council of Ministers.

Article XXXI

The Council of Ministers shall decide on the privileges and immunities to be accorded to the personnel of the Secretariat in the respective territories of the Member States.

Cessation of Membership

Article XXXII

Any State which desires to renounce its membership shall forward a written notification to the Secretary-General. At the end of one year from the date of such notification, if not withdrawn, the Charter shall cease to apply with respect to the renouncing State, which shall thereby cease to belong to the Organization.

Amendment of the Charter

Article XXL

This Charter may be amended or revised if any Member State makes a written request to the Secretary-General to that effect; provided, however, that the proposed amendment is not submitted to the Assembly for consideration until all the Member States have been duly notified of it and a period of one year has elapsed. Such an amendment shall not be effective unless approved by at least two-thirds of all the Member States.

IN FAITH WHEREOF, We, the Heads of African States and Governments have signed this Charter.

Done in the City of Addis Ababa, Ethiopia, 25th day of May, 1963.

Appendix II

Constitutive Act of the African Union

We, Heads of State and Government of the Member States of the Organization of African Unity (OAU):

Inspired by the noble ideals which guided the founding fathers of our Continental Organization and generations of Pan-Africanists in their determination to promote unity, solidarity, cohesion and cooperation among the peoples of Africa and African States;

Considering the principles and objectives stated in the Charter of the Organization of African Unity and the Treaty establishing the African Economic Community;

Recalling the heroic struggles waged by our peoples and our countries for political independence, human dignity and economic emancipation;

Considering that since its inception, the Organization of African Unity has played a determining and invaluable role in the liberation of the continent, the affirmation of a common identity and the process of attainment of the unity of our Continent and has provided a unique framework for our collective action in Africa and in our relations with the rest of the world;

Determined to take up the multifaceted challenges that confront our continent and peoples in the light of the social, economic and political changes taking place in the world;

Convinced of the need to accelerate the process of implementing the Treaty establishing the African Economic Community in order to promote the socio-economic development of Africa and to face more effectively the challenges posed by globalization;

Guided by our common vision of a united and strong Africa and by the need to build a partnership between governments and all segments of civil society, in particular women, youth and the private sector in order to strengthen solidarity and cohesion among our peoples;

Conscious of the fact that the scourge of conflicts in Africa constitutes a major impediment to the socio-economic development of the continent and of the need to promote peace, security and stability as a prerequisite for the implementation of our development and integration agenda;

Determined to promote and protect human and peoples' rights, consolidate democratic institutions and culture, and to ensure good governance and the rule of law;

Further determined to take all necessary measures to strengthen our common institutions and provide them with the necessary powers and resources to enable them to discharge their respective mandates effectively;

Recalling the Declaration which we adopted at the Fourth Extraordinary Session of our Assembly in Sirte, the Great Socialist People's Libyan Arab Jamahiriya, on 9.9.99, in which we decided to establish an African Union, in conformity with the ultimate objectives of the Charter of our Continental Organization and the Treaty establishing the African Economic Community;

Have Agreed as Follows:

Article 1

Definitions

In this Constitutive Act:

'Act' means the present Constitutive Act;

'AEC' means the African Economic Community;

'Assembly' means the Assembly of Heads of State and Government of the Union;

'Charter' means the Charter of the OAU;

'Committee' means a Specialized Technical Committee of the Union;

'Council' means the Economic, Social and Cultural Council of the Union;

'Court' means the Court of Justice of the Union;

'Executive Council' means the Executive Council of Ministers of the Union;

'Member State' means a Member State of the Union;

'OAU' means the Organization of African Unity;

'Parliament' means the Pan-African Parliament of the Union;

'Union' means the African Union established by the present Constitutive Act.

Article 2

Establishment

The African Union is hereby established in accordance with the provisions of this Act.

Article 3

Objectives

The objectives of the Union shall be to:

a. Achieve greater unity and solidarity between the African countries and the peoples of Africa;
b. Defend the sovereignty, territorial integrity and independence of its Member States;
c. Accelerate the political and socio-economic integration of the continent;
d. Promote and defend African common positions on issues of interest to the continent and its peoples;
e. Encourage international cooperation, taking due account of the Charter of the United Nations and the Universal Declaration of Human Rights;
f. Promote peace, security, and stability on the continent;
g. Promote democratic principles and institutions, popular participation and good governance;
h. Promote and protect human and peoples' rights in accordance with the African Charter on Human and Peoples' Rights and other relevant human rights instruments;
i. Establish the necessary conditions which enable the continent to play its rightful role in the global economy and in international negotiations;
j. Promote sustainable development at the economic, social and cultural levels as well as the integration of African economies;
k. Promote cooperation in all fields of human activity to raise the living standards of African peoples;
l. Coordinate and harmonize policies between existing and future Regional Economic Communities for the gradual attainment of the objectives of the Union;
m. Advance the development of the continent by promoting research in all fields, in particular in science and technology;

n. Work with relevant international partners in the eradication of preventable diseases and the promotion of good health on the continent.

Article 4

Principles

The Union shall function in accordance with the following principles:

a. Sovereign equality and interdependence among Member States of the Union;
b. Respect of borders existing on achievement of independence;
c. Participation of the African peoples in the activities of the Union;
d. Establishment of a common defence policy for the African Continent;
e. Peaceful resolution of conflicts among Member States of the Union through such appropriate means as may be decided upon by the Assembly;
f. Prohibition of the use of force or threat to use force among Member States of the Union;
g. Non-interference by any Member State in the internal affairs of another;
h. The right of the Union to intervene in a Member State pursuant to a decision of the Assembly in respect of grave circumstances, namely war crimes, genocide and crimes against humanity;
i. Peaceful co-existence of Member States and their right to live in peace and security;
j. The right of Member States to request intervention from the Union in order to restore peace and security;
k. Promotion of self-reliance within the framework of the Union;
l. Promotion of gender equality;
m. Respect for democratic principles, human rights, the rule of law and good governance;
n. Promotion of social justice to ensure balanced economic development;
o. Respect for the sanctity of human life, condemnation and rejection of impunity and political assassination, acts of terrorism and subversive activities;
p. Condemnation and rejection of unconstitutional changes of governments.

Article 5

Organs of the Union

1. The organs of the Union shall be:
   a. The Assembly of the Union;
   b. The Executive Council;
   c. The Pan-African Parliament;
   d. The Court of Justice;
   e. The Commission;
   f. The Permanent Representatives Committee;
   g. The Specialized Technical Committees;
   h. The Economic, Social and Cultural Council;
   i. The Financial Institutions;
2. Other organs that the Assembly may decide to establish.

Article 6

The Assembly

1. The Assembly shall be composed of Heads of States and Government or their duly accredited representatives.
2. The Assembly shall be the supreme organ of the Union.
3. The Assembly shall meet at least once a year in ordinary session. At the request of any Member State and on approval by a two-thirds majority of the Member States, the Assembly shall meet in extraordinary session.
4. The Office of the Chairman of the Assembly shall be held for a period of one year by a Head of State or Government elected after consultations among the Member States.

Article 7

Decisions of the Assembly

1. The Assembly shall take its decisions by consensus or, failing which, by a two-thirds majority of the Member States of the Union. However, procedural matters, including the question of whether a matter is one of procedure or not, shall be decided by a simple majority.

2. Two-thirds of the total membership of the Union shall form a quorum at any meeting of the Assembly.

Article 8

Rules of Procedure of the Assembly

The Assembly shall adopt its own Rules of Procedure.

Article 9

Powers and Functions of the Assembly

1. The functions of the Assembly shall be to:
   a. Determine the common policies of the Union;
   b. Receive, consider and take decisions on reports and recommendations from the other organs of the Union;
   c. Consider requests for Membership of the Union;
   d. Establish any organ of the Union;
   e. Monitor the implementation of policies and decisions of the Union as well as ensure compliance by all Member States;
   f. Adopt the budget of the Union;
   g. Give directives to the Executive Council on the management of conflicts, war and other emergency situations and the restoration of peace;
   h. Appoint and terminate the appointment of the judges of the Court of Justice;
   i. Appoint the Chairman of the Commission and his or her deputy or deputies and Commissioners of the Commission and determine their functions and terms of office.
2. The Assembly may delegate any of its powers and functions to any organ of the Union.

Article 10

The Executive Council

1. The Executive Council shall be composed of the Ministers of Foreign Affairs or such other Ministers or Authorities as are designated by the Governments of Member States.

2. Council shall meet at least twice a year in ordinary session. It shall also meet in an extra-ordinary session at the request of any Member State and upon approval by two-thirds of all Member States.

Article 11

Decisions of the Executive Council

1. The Executive Council shall take its decisions by consensus or, failing which, by a two-thirds majority of the Member States. However, procedural matters, including the question of whether a matter is one of procedure or not, shall be decided by a simple majority.
2. Two-thirds of the total membership of the Union shall form a quorum at any meeting of the Executive Council.

Article 12

Rules of Procedure of the Executive Council

The Executive Council shall adopt its own Rules of Procedure.

Article 13

Functions of the Executive Council

1. The Executive Council shall co-ordinate and take decisions on policies in areas of common interest to the Member States, including the following:
   a. Foreign trade;
   b. Energy, industry and mineral resources;
   c. Food, agricultural and animal resources, livestock production and forestry;
   d. Water resources and irrigation;
   e. Environmental protection, humanitarian action and disaster response and relief;
   f. Transport and communications;
   g. Insurance;
   h. Education, culture, health and human resources development;
   i. Science and technology;
   j. Nationality, residency and immigration matters;
   k. Social security, including the formulation of mother and child care policies, as well as policies relating to the disabled and the handicapped;
   l. Establishment of a system of African awards, medals and prizes.

2. The Executive Council shall be responsible to the Assembly. It shall consider issues referred to it and monitor the implementation of policies formulated by the Assembly.
3. The Executive Council may delegate any of its powers and functions mentioned in paragraph 1 of this Article to the Specialized Technical Committees established under Article 14 of this Act.

Article 14

The Specialized Technical Committees Establishment and Composition

1. There is hereby established the following Specialized Technical Committees, which shall be responsible to the Executive Council:
   a. The Committee on Rural Economy and Agricultural Matters;
   b. The Committee on Monetary and Financial Affairs;
   c. The Committee on Trade, Customs and Immigration Matters;
   d. The Committee on Industry, Science and Technology, Energy, Natural Resources and Environment;
   e. The Committee on Transport, Communications and Tourism;
   f. The Committee on Health, Labour and Social Affairs; and
   g. The Committee on Education, Culture and Human Resources.
2. The Assembly shall, whenever it deems appropriate, restructure the existing Committees or establish other Committees.
3. The Specialized Technical Committees shall be composed of Ministers or senior officials responsible for sectors falling within their respective areas of competence.

Article 15

Functions of the Specialized Technical Committees

Each Committee shall within its field of competence:

a. Prepare projects and programmes of the Union and submit [them] to the Executive Council;
b. Ensure the supervision, follow-up and the evaluation of the implementation of decisions taken by the organs of the Union;
c. Ensure the coordination and harmonization of projects and programmes of the Union;

d. Submit to the Executive Council either on its own initiative or at the request of the Executive Council, reports and recommendations on the implementation of the provision of this Act; and

e. Carry out any other functions assigned to it for the purpose of ensuring the implementation of the provisions of this Act.

Article 16

Meetings

1. Subject to any directives given by the Executive Council, each Committee shall meet as often as necessary and shall prepare its rules of procedure and submit them to the Executive Council for approval.

Article 17

The Pan-African Parliament

1. In order to ensure the full participation of African peoples in the development and economic integration of the continent, a Pan-African Parliament shall be established.

2. The composition, powers, functions and organization of the Pan-African Parliament shall be defined in a protocol relating thereto.

Article 18

The Court of Justice

1. A Court of Justice of the Union shall be established;

2. The statute, composition and functions of the Court of Justice shall be defined in a protocol relating thereto.

Article 19

The Financial Institutions

The Union shall have the following financial institutions, whose rules and regulations shall be defined in protocols relating thereto:

a. The African Central Bank;
b. The African Monetary Fund;
c. The African Investment Bank.

Article 20

The Commission

1. There shall be established a Commission of the Union, which shall be the Secretariat of the Union.
2. The Commission shall be composed of the Chairman, his or her deputy or deputies and the Commissioners. They shall be assisted by the necessary staff for the smooth functioning of the Commission.
3. The structure, functions and regulations of the Commission shall be determined by the Assembly.

Article 21

The Permanent Representatives Committee

1. There shall be established a Permanent Representatives Committee. It shall be composed of Permanent Representatives to the Union and other Plenipotentiaries of Member States.
2. The Permanent Representatives Committee shall be charged with the responsibility of preparing the work of the Executive Council and acting on the Executive Council's instructions. It may set up such sub-committees or working groups as it may deem necessary.

Article 22

The Economic, Social and Cultural Council

1. The Economic, Social and Cultural Council shall be an advisory organ composed of different social and professional groups of the Member States of the Union.
2. The functions, powers, composition and organization of the Economic, Social and Cultural Council shall be determined by the Assembly.

Article 23

Imposition of Sanctions

1. The Assembly shall determine the appropriate sanctions to be imposed on any Member State that defaults in the payment of its contributions to the budget of the Union in the following manner: denial of the right to speak at meetings, to vote, to present candidates for any position or

post within the Union or to benefit from any activity or commitments therefrom.

2. Furthermore, any Member State that fails to comply with the decisions and policies of the Union may be subjected to other sanctions, such as the denial of transport and communications links with other Member States, and other measures of a political and economic nature to be determined by the Assembly.

Article 24

The Headquarters of the Union

1. The Headquarters of the Union shall be in Addis Ababa in the Federal Democratic Republic of Ethiopia.
2. There may be established such other offices of the Union as the Assembly may, on the recommendation of the Executive Council, determine.

Article 25

Working Languages

The working languages of the Union and all its institutions shall be, if possible, African languages, Arabic, English, French and Portuguese.

Article 26

Interpretation

The Court shall be seized with matters of interpretation arising from the application or implementation of this Act. Pending its establishment, such matters shall be submitted to the Assembly of the Union, which shall decide by a two-thirds majority.

Article 27

Signature, Ratification and Accession

1. This Act shall be open to signature, ratification and accession by the Member States of the OAU in accordance with their respective constitutional procedures.
2. The instruments of ratification shall be deposited with the Secretary-General of the OAU.

3. Any Member State of the OAU acceding to this Act after its entry into force shall deposit the instrument of accession with the Chairman of the Commission.

Article 28

Entry into Force

This Act shall enter into force thirty (30) days after the deposit of the instruments of ratification by two-thirds of the Member States of the OAU.

Article 29

Admission to Membership

1. Any African State may, at any time after the entry into force of this Act, notify the Chairman of the Commission of its intention to accede to this Act and to be admitted as a member of the Union.
2. The Chairman of the Commission shall, upon receipt of such notification, transmit copies thereof to all Member States. Admission shall be decided by a simple majority of the Member States. The decision of each Member State shall be transmitted to the Chairman of the Commission who shall, upon receipt of the required number of votes, communicate the decision to the State concerned.

Article 30

Suspension

Governments which shall come to power through unconstitutional means shall not be allowed to participate in the activities of the Union.

Article 31

Cessation of Membership

1. Any State which desires to renounce its membership shall forward a written notification to the Chairman of the Commission, who shall inform Member States thereof. At the end of one year from the date of such notification, if not withdrawn, the Act shall cease to apply with respect to the renouncing State, which shall thereby cease to belong to the Union.

2. During the period of one year referred to in paragraph 1 of this Article, any Member State wishing to withdraw from the Union shall comply with the provisions of this Act and shall be bound to discharge its obligations under this Act up to the date of its withdrawal.

Article 32

Amendment and Revision

1. Any Member State may submit proposals for the amendment or revision of this Act.
2. Proposals for amendment or revision shall be submitted to the Chairman of the Commission who shall transmit same to Member States within thirty (30) days of receipt thereof.
3. The Assembly, upon the advice of the Executive Council, shall examine these proposals within a period of one year following notification of Member States, in accordance with the provisions of paragraph 2 of this Article.
4. Amendments or revisions shall be adopted by the Assembly by consensus or, failing which, by a two-thirds majority and submitted for ratification by all Member States in accordance with their respective constitutional procedures. They shall enter into force thirty (30) days after the deposit of the instruments of ratification with the Chairman of the Commission by a two-thirds majority of the Member States.

Article 33

Transitional Arrangements and Final Provisions

1. This Act shall replace the Charter of the Organization of African Unity. However, the Charter shall remain operative for a transitional period of one year or such further period as may be determined by the Assembly, following the entry into force of the Act, for the purpose of enabling the OAU/AEC to undertake the necessary measures regarding the devolution of its assets and liabilities to the Union and all matters relating thereto.
2. The provisions of this Act shall take precedence over and supersede any inconsistent or contrary provisions of the Treaty establishing the African Economic Community.

3. Upon the entry into force of this Act, all necessary measures shall be undertaken to implement its provisions and to ensure the establishment of the organs provided for under the Act in accordance with any directives or decisions which may be adopted in this regard by the Parties thereto within the transitional period stipulated above.

4. Pending the establishment of the Commission, the OAU General Secretariat shall be the interim Secretariat of the Union.

5. This Act, drawn up in four (4) original texts in the Arabic, English, French and Portuguese languages, all four (4) being equally authentic, shall be deposited with the Secretary-General of the OAU and, after its entry into force, with the Chairman of the Commission who shall transmit a certified true copy of the Act to the Government of each signatory State. The Secretary-General of the OAU and the Chairman of the Commission shall notify all signatory States of the dates of the deposit of the instruments of ratification or accession and shall upon entry into force of this Act register the same with the Secretariat of the United Nations.

IN WITNESS WHEREOF, WE have adopted this Act.
Done at Lomé, Togo, this 11th day of July, 2000.

Appendix III

African Charter on Human and Peoples' Rights

Preamble

The African States members of the Organisation of African Unity, parties to the present Convention entitled 'African Charter on Human and Peoples' Rights

Recalling Decision 115(XVI) of the Assembly of Heads of State and Government at its Sixteenth Ordinary Session held in Monrovia, Liberia, from 17 to 20 July 1979 on the preparation of 'a preliminary draft on an African Charter on Human and Peoples' Rights, providing inter alia for the establishment of bodies to promote and protect human and peoples' rights';

Considering the Charter of the Organisation of African Unity, which stipulates that 'freedom, equality, justice and dignity are essential objectives for the achievement of the legitimate aspirations of the African peoples';

Reaffirming the pledge they solemnly made in Article 2 of the said Charter to eradicate all forms of colonialism from Africa, to coordinate and intensify their cooperation and efforts to achieve a better life for the peoples of Africa and to promote international cooperation having due regard to the Charter of the United Nations and the Universal Declaration of Human Rights;

Taking into consideration the virtues of their historical tradition and the values of African civilisation which should inspire and characterise their reflection on the concept of human and peoples' rights;

Recognising on the one hand, that fundamental human rights stem from the attitudes of human beings, which justifies their international protection and on the other hand that the reality and respect of peoples' rights should necessarily guarantee human rights;

Considering that the enjoyment of rights and freedoms also implies the performance of duties on the part of everyone;

Convinced that it is henceforth essential to pay particular attention to the right to development and that civil and political rights cannot be dissociated from economic, social and cultural rights in their conception as well as universality and that the satisfaction of economic, social and cultural rights is a guarantee for the enjoyment of civil and political rights;

Conscious of their duty to achieve the total liberation of Africa, the peoples of which are still struggling for their dignity and genuine independence, and undertaking to eliminate colonialism, neo-colonialism, apartheid, zionism and to dismantle aggressive foreign military bases and all forms of discrimination, language, religion or political opinions;

Reaffirming their adherence to the principles of human and peoples' rights and freedoms contained in the declarations, conventions and other instruments adopted by the Organisation of African Unity, the Movement of Non-Aligned Countries and the United Nations;

Firmly convinced of their duty to promote and protect human and peoples' rights and freedoms and taking into account the importance traditionally attached to these rights and freedoms in Africa;

HAVE AGREED AS FOLLOWS:

Part 1
Rights and Duties

Chapter I
Human and Peoples' Rights

Article 1

The Member States of the Organisation of African Unity, parties to the present Charter, shall recognise the rights, duties and freedoms enshrined in the Charter and shall undertake to adopt legislative or other measures to give effect to them.

Article 2

Every individual shall be entitled to the enjoyment of the rights and freedoms recognised and guaranteed in the present Charter without distinction of any kind such as race, ethnic group, colour, sex, language, religion, political or any other opinion, national and social origin, fortune, birth or any status.

Article 3

1. Every individual shall be equal before the law.
2. Every individual shall be entitled to equal protection of the law.

Article 4

Human beings are inviolable. Every human being shall be entitled to respect for his life and the integrity of his person. No one may be arbitrarily deprived of this right.

Article 5

Every individual shall have the right to the respect of the dignity inherent in a human being and to the recognition of his legal status. All forms of exploitation and degradation of man, particularly slavery, slave trade, torture, cruel, inhuman or degrading punishment and treatment shall be prohibited.

Article 6

Every individual shall have the right to liberty and to the security of his person. No one may be deprived of his freedom except for reasons and conditions previously laid down by law. In particular, no one may be arbitrarily arrested or detained.

Article 7

1. Every individual shall have the right to have his cause heard. This comprises:
   a) The right to an appeal to competent national organs against acts of violating his fundamental rights as recognised and guaranteed by conventions, laws, regulations and customs in force;
   b) The right to be presumed innocent until proved guilty by a competent court or tribunal;
   c) The right to defence, including the right to be defended by counsel of his choice;
   d) The right to be tried within a reasonable time by an impartial court or tribunal.
2. No one may be condemned for an act or omission which did not constitute a legally punishable offence at the time it was committed. No penalty may be inflicted for an offence for which no provision was made at the time it was committed. Punishment is personal and can be imposed only on the offender.

Article 8

Freedom of conscience, the profession and free practice of religion shall be guaranteed. No one may, subject to law and order, be submitted to measures restricting the exercise of these freedoms.

Article 9

1. Every individual shall have the right to receive information.
2. Every individual shall have the right to express and disseminate his opinions within the law.

Article 10

1. Every individual shall have the right to free association provided that he abides by the law.
2. Subject to the obligation of solidarity provided for in Article 29, no one may be compelled to join an association.

Article 11

Every individual shall have the right to assemble freely with others. The exercise of this right shall be subject only to necessary restrictions provided for by law, in particular those enacted in the interest of national security, the safety, health, ethics and rights and freedoms of others.

Article 12

1. Every individual shall have the right to freedom of movement and residence within the borders of a State provided he abides by the law.
2. Every individual shall have the right to leave any country including his own, and to return to his country.

    This right may only be subject to restrictions provided for by law for the protection of national security, law and order, public health or morality.
3. Every individual shall have the right, when persecuted, to seek and obtain asylum in other countries in accordance with the law of those countries and international conventions.
4. A non-national legally admitted in a territory of a State Party to the present Charter, may only be expelled from it by virtue of a decision taken in accordance with the law.
5. The mass expulsion of non-nationals shall be prohibited. Mass expulsion shall be that which is aimed at national, racial, ethnic or religious groups.

Article 13

1. Every citizen shall have the right to participate freely in the government of his country, either directly or through freely chosen representatives in accordance with the provisions of the law.
2. Every citizen shall have the right of equal access to the public service of the country.
3. Every individual shall have the right of access to public property and services in strict equality of all persons before the law.

Article 14

The right to property shall be guaranteed. It may only be encroached upon in the interest of public need or in the general interest of the community and in accordance with the provisions of appropriate laws.

Article 15

Every individual shall have the right to work under equitable and satisfactory conditions, and shall receive equal pay for equal work.

Article 16

1. Every individual shall have the right to enjoy the best attainable state of physical and mental health.
2. States Parties to the present Charter shall take the necessary measures to protect the health of their people and to ensure that they receive medical attention when they are sick.

Article 17

1. Every individual shall have the right to education.
2. Every individual may freely take part in the cultural life of his community.
3. The promotion and protection of morals and traditional values recognised by the community shall be the duty of the State.

Article 18

1. The family shall be the natural unit and basis of society. It shall be protected by the State which shall take care of its physical health and moral.
2. The State shall have the duty to assist the family which is the custodian of morals and traditional values recognised by the community.

3. The State shall ensure the elimination of every discrimination against women and also ensure the protection of the rights of women and the child as stipulated in international declarations and conventions.
4. The aged and the disabled shall also have the right to special measures of protection in keeping with their physical or moral needs.

Article 19

All peoples shall be equal; they shall enjoy the same respect and shall have the same rights. Nothing shall justify the domination of a people by another.

Article 20

1. All peoples shall have the right to existence. They shall have the unquestionable and inalienable right to self-determination. They shall freely determine their political status and shall pursue their economic and social development according to the policy they have freely chosen.
2. Colonised or oppressed peoples shall have the right to free themselves from the bonds of domination by resorting to any means recognised by the international community.
3. All peoples shall have the right to the assistance of the States Parties to the present Charter in their liberation struggle against foreign domination, be it political, economic or cultural.

Article 21

1. All peoples shall freely dispose of their wealth and natural resources. This right shall be exercised in the exclusive interest of the people. In no case shall a people be deprived of it.
2. In case of spoilation, the dispossessed people shall have the right to the lawful recovery of its property as well as to an adequate compensation.
3. The free disposal of wealth and natural resources shall be exercised without prejudice to the obligation of promoting international economic cooperation based on mutual respect, equitable exchange and the principles of international law.
4. States Parties to the present Charter shall individually and collectively exercise the right to free disposal of their wealth and natural resources with a view to strengthening African Unity and solidarity.
5. States Parties to the present Charter shall undertake to eliminate all forms of foreign exploitation particularly that practised by international monopolies so as to enable their peoples to fully benefit from the advantages derived from their national resources.

Article 22

1. All peoples shall have the right to their economic, social and cultural development with due regard to their freedom and identity and in the equal enjoyment of the common heritage of mankind.
2. States shall have the duty, individually or collectively, to ensure the exercise of the right to development.

Article 23

1. All peoples shall have the right to national and international peace and security. The principles of solidarity and friendly relations implicitly affirmed by the Charter of the United Nations and reaffirmed by that of the Organisation of African Unity shall govern relations between States.
2. For the purpose of strengthening peace, solidarity and friendly relations, State Parties to the present Charter shall ensure that:
   a) any individual enjoying the right of asylum under Article 12 of the present Charter shall not engage in subversive activities against his country of origin or any other State Party to the present Charter;
   b) their territories shall not be used as bases for subversive or terrorist activities against the people of any other State Party to the present Charter.

Article 24

All peoples shall have the right to a general satisfactory environment favourable to their development.

Article 25

States Parties to the present Charter shall have the duty to promote and ensure through teaching, education and publication, the respect of the rights and freedoms contained in the present Charter and to see to it that these freedoms and rights as well as corresponding obligations and duties are understood.

Article 26

States Parties to the present Charter shall have the duty to guarantee the independence of the Courts and shall allow the establishment and improvement of appropriate national institutions entrusted with the promotion and protection of the rights and freedoms guaranteed by the present Charter.

Chapter II
Duties

Article 27

1. Every individual shall have duties towards his family and society, the State and other legally recognised communities and the international community.
2. The rights and freedoms of each individual shall be exercised with due regard to the rights of others, collective security, morality and common interest.

Article 28

Every individual shall have the duty to respect and consider his fellow beings without discrimination, and to maintain relations aimed at promoting, safeguarding and reinforcing mutual respect and tolerance.

Article 29

The individual shall also have the duty:

1. To preserve the harmonious development of the family and to work for the cohesion and respect of the family; to respect his parents at all times, to maintain them in case of need.
2. To serve his national community by placing his physical and intellectual abilities at its service.
3. Not to compromise the security of the State whose national or resident he is.
4. To preserve and strengthen social and national solidarity, particularly when the latter is strengthened.
5. To preserve and strengthen the national independence and the territorial integrity of his country and to contribute to its defence in accordance with the law.
6. To work to the best of his abilities and competence, and to pay taxes imposed by law in the interest of the society.
7. To preserve and strengthen positive African cultural values in his relations with other members of the society, in the spirit of tolerance, dialogue and consultation and, in general, to contribute to the promotion of the moral well being of society.
8. To contribute to the best of his abilities, at all times and at all levels, to the promotion and achievement of African unity.

Part II
Measures of Safeguard

Chapter I
Establishment and Organisation of the
African Commission on Human and Peoples' Rights

Article 30

An African Commission on Human and Peoples' Rights, hereinafter called 'the Commission', shall be established within the Organisation of African Unity to promote human and peoples' rights and ensure their protection in Africa.

Article 31

1. The Commission shall consist of eleven members chosen from amongst African personalities of the highest reputation, known for their high morality, integrity, impartiality and competence in matters of human and peoples' rights; particular consideration being given to persons having legal experience.
2. The members of the Commission shall serve in their personal capacity.

Article 32

The Commission shall not include more than one national of the same State.

Article 33

The members of the Commission shall be elected by secret ballot by the Assembly of Heads of State and Government, from a list of persons nominated by the States Parties to the present Charter.

Article 34

Each State Party to the present Charter may not nominate more than two candidates. The candidates must have the nationality of one of the States Parties to the present Charter. When two candidates are nominated by a State, one of them may not be a national of that State.

Article 35

1. The Secretary General of the Organisation of African Unity shall invite States Parties to the present Charter at least four months before the elections to nominate candidates.
2. The Secretary General of the Organisation of African Unity shall make an alphabetical list of the persons thus nominated and communicate it to the Heads of State and Government at least one month before the elections.

Article 36

The members of the Commission shall be elected for a six year period and shall be eligible for re-election. However, the term of office of four of the members elected at the first election shall terminate after two years and the term of office of three others, at the end of four years.

Article 37

Immediately after the first election, the Chairman of the Assembly of Heads of State and Government of the Organisation of African Unity shall draw lots to decide the names of those members referred to in Article 36.

Article 38

After their election, the members of the Commission shall make a solemn declaration to discharge their duties impartially and faithfully.

Article 39

1. In case of death or resignation of a member of the Commission, the Chairman of the Commission shall immediately inform the Secretary General of the Organisation of African Unity, who shall declare the seat vacant from the date of death or from the date on which the resignation takes effect.
2. If, in the unanimous opinion of other members of the Commission, a member has stopped discharging his duties for any reason other than a temporary absence, the Chairman of the Commission shall inform the Secretary General of the Organisation of African Unity, who shall then declare the seat vacant.
3. In each of the cases anticipated above, the Assembly of Heads of State and Government shall replace the member whose seat became vacant for the remaining period of his term, unless the period is less than six months.

Article 40

Every member of the Commission shall be in office until the date his successor assumes office.

Article 41

The Secretary General of the Organisation of African Unity shall appoint the Secretary of the Commission. He shall provide the staff and services necessary for the effective discharge of the duties of the Commission. The Organisation of African Unity shall bear the cost of the staff and services.

Article 42

1. The Commission shall elect its Chairman and Vice Chairman for a two-year period. They shall be eligible for re-election.
2. The Commission shall lay down its rules of procedure.
3. Seven members shall form the quorum.
4. In case of an equality of votes, the Chairman shall have a casting vote.
5. The Secretary General may attend the meetings of the Commission. He shall neither participate in deliberations nor shall he be entitled to vote. The Chairman of the Commission may, however, invite him to speak.

Article 43

In discharging their duties, members of the Commission shall enjoy diplomatic privileges and immunities provided for in the General Convention on the Privileges and Immunities of the Organisation of African Unity.

Article 44

Provision shall be made for the emoluments and allowances of the members of the Commission in the Regular Budget of the Organisation of African Unity.

Chapter II
Mandate of the Commission

Article 45

The functions of the Commission shall be:

1. To promote human and peoples' rights and in particular:
   a) to collect documents, undertake studies and researches on African problems in the field of human and peoples' rights, organise

seminars, symposia and conferences, disseminate information, encourage national and local institutions concerned with human and peoples' rights and, should the case arise, give its views or make recommendations to Governments;

b) to formulate and lay down principles and rules aimed at solving legal problems relating to human and peoples' rights and funda- mental freedoms upon which African Governments may base their legislation;

c) to cooperate with other African and international institutions con- cerned with the promotion and protection of human and peoples' rights.

2. Ensure the protection of human and peoples' rights under conditions laid down by the present Charter.

3. Interpret all the provisions of the present Charter at the request of a State Party, an institution of the OAU or an African Organisation recognised by the OAU.

4. Perform any other tasks which may be entrusted to it by the Assembly of Heads of State and Government.

Chapter III
Procedure of the Commission

Article 46

The Commission may resort to any appropriate method of investigation; it may hear from the Secretary General of the Organisation of African Unity or any other person capable of enlightening it.

Communication from States

Article 47

If a State Party to the present Charter has good reasons to believe that another State Party to this Charter has violated the provisions of the Charter, it may draw, by written communication, the attention of that State to the matter. This Communication shall also be addressed to the Secretary General of the OAU and to the Chairman of the Commission. Within three months of the receipt of the Communication, the State to which the Communication is addressed shall give the enquiring State writ- ten explanation or statement elucidating the matter. This should include as much as possible, relevant information relating to the laws and rules of procedure applied and applicable and the redress already given or course of action available.

Article 48

If within three months from the date on which the original communication is received by the State to which it is addressed, the issue is not settled to the satisfaction of the two States involved through bilateral negotiation or by any other peaceful procedure, either State shall have the right to submit the matter to the Commission through the Chairman and shall notify the other States involved.

Article 49

Notwithstanding the provisions of Article 47, if a State Party to the present Charter considers that another State Party has violated the provisions of the Charter, it may refer the matter directly to the Commission by addressing a communication to the Chairman, to the Secretary General of the Organisation of African unity and the State concerned.

Article 50

The Commission can only deal with a matter submitted to it after making sure that all local remedies, if they exist, have been exhausted, unless it is obvious to the Commission that the procedure of achieving these remedies would be unduly prolonged.

Article 51

1. The Commission may ask the State concerned to provide it with all relevant information.
2. When the Commission is considering the matter, States concerned may be represented before it and submit written or oral representation.

Article 52

After having obtained from the States concerned and from other sources all the information it deems necessary and after having tried all appropriate means to reach an amicable solution based on the respect of human and peoples' rights, the Commission shall prepare, within a reasonable period of time from the notification referred to in Article 48, a report to the States concerned and communicated to the Assembly of Heads of State and Government.

Article 53

While transmitting its report, the Commission may make to the Assembly of Heads of State and Government such recommendations as it deems useful.

Article 54

The Commission shall submit to each Ordinary Session of the Assembly of Heads of State and Government a report on its activities.

Other Communications

Article 55

1. Before each Session, the Secretary of the Commission shall make a list of the Communications other than those of States Parties to the present Charter and transmit them to Members of the Commission, who shall indicate which Communications should be considered by the Commission.
2. A Communication shall be considered by the Commission if a simple majority of its members so decide.

Article 56

Communications relating to human and peoples' rights referred to in Article 55 received by the Commission shall be considered if they:

1. Indicate their authors even if the latter requests anonymity;
2. Are compatible with the Charter of the Organisation of African Unity or with the present Charter;
3. Are not written in disparaging or insulting language directed against the State concerned and its institutions or to the Organisation of African Unity;
4. Are not based exclusively on news disseminated through the mass media;
5. Are sent after exhausting local remedies, if any, unless it is obvious that this procedure is unduly prolonged;
6. Are submitted within a reasonable period from the time local remedies are exhausted or from the date the Commission is seised with the matter; and
7. Do not deal with cases which have been settled by those States involved in accordance with the principles of the Charter of the United Nations,

or the Charter of the Organisation of African Unity or the provisions of the present Charter.

Article 57

Prior to any substantive consideration, all Communications shall be brought to the knowledge of the State concerned by the Chairman of the Commission.

Article 58

1. When it appears after deliberations of the Commission that one or more Communications apparently relate to special cases which reveal the existence of a series of serious or massive violations of human and peoples' rights, the Commission shall draw the attention of the Assembly of Heads of State and Government to these special cases.
2. The Assembly of Heads of State and Government may then request the Commission to undertake an in-depth study of these cases and make a factual report, accompanied by its finding and recommendations.
3. A case of emergency duly noticed by the Commission shall be submitted by the latter to the Chairman of the Assembly of Heads of State and Government who may request an in-depth study.

Article 59

1. All measures taken within the provisions of the present Chapter shall remain confidential until the Assembly of Heads of State and Government shall otherwise decide.
2. However the report shall be published by the Chairman of the Commission upon the decision of the Assembly of Heads of State and Government.
3. The report on the activities of the Commission shall be published by its Chairman after it has been considered by the Assembly of Heads of State and Government.

Chapter IV
Applicable Principles

Article 60

The Commission shall draw inspiration from international law on human and peoples' rights, particularly from the provisions of various African instruments on Human and Peoples' Rights, the Charter of the United

Nations, the Charter of the Organisation of African Unity, the Universal Declaration of Human Rights, other instruments adopted by the United Nations and by African countries in the field of Human and Peoples' Rights, as well as from the provisions of various instruments adopted within the Specialised Agencies of the United Nations of which the Parties to the present Charter are members.

Article 61

The Commission shall also take into consideration, as subsidiary measures to determine the principles of law, other general or special international conventions, laying down rules expressly recognised by Member States of the Organisation of African Unity, African practices consistent with international norms on Human and Peoples' Rights, customs generally accepted as law, general principles of law recognised by African States as well as legal precedents and doctrine.

Article 62

Each State Party shall undertake to submit every two years, from the date the present Charter comes into force, a report on the legislative or other measures taken, with a view to giving effect to the rights and freedoms recognised and guaranteed by the present Charter.

Article 63

1. The present Charter shall be open to signature, ratification or adherence of the Member States of the Organisation of African Unity.
2. The instruments of ratification or adherence to the present Charter shall be deposited with the Secretary General of the Oganisation of African Unity.
3. The present Charter shall come into force three months after the reception by the Secretary General of the instruments of ratification or adherence of a simple majority of the Member States of the Organisation of African Unity.

Part III
General Provisions

Article 64

1. After the coming into force of the present Charter, members of the Commission shall be elected in accordance with the relevant Articles of the present Charter.

2. The Secretary General of the Organisation of African Unity shall convene the first meeting of the Commission at the Headquarters of the Organisation within three months of the constitution of the Commission. Thereafter, the Commission shall be convened by its Chairman whenever necessary but at least once a year.

Article 65

For each of the States that will ratify or adhere to the present Charter after its coming into force, the Charter shall take effect three months after the date of the deposit by that State of the instrument of ratification or adherence.

Article 66

Special protocols or agreements may, if necessary, supplement the provisions of the present Charter.

Article 67

The Secretary General of the Organisation of African Unity shall inform members of the Organisation of the deposit of each instrument of ratification or adherence.

Article 68

The present Charter may be amended if a State Party makes a written request to that effect to the Secretary General of the Organisation of African Unity. The Assembly of Heads of State and Government may only consider the draft amendment after all the States Parties have been duly informed of it and the Commission has given its opinion on it at the request of the sponsoring State. The amendment shall be approved by a simple majority of the States Parties. It shall come into force for each State which has accepted it in accordance with its constitutional procedure three months after the Secretary General has received notice of the acceptance. *Adopted by the Eighteenth Assembly of Heads of State and Government, June 1981 – Nairobi, Kenya.*

BIBLIOGRAPHY

Abass, A. and M. A. Baderin, 'Towards Effective Collective Security and Human Rights Protection in Africa: Assessment of the Constitutive Act of the African Union', *Netherlands International Law Review* 49 (2002) 1–38

Abbink, J. and G. Hesseling, *Election Observation and Democratization in Africa* (Basingstoke: Macmillan Press, 2000)

Abdullahi, A. N. M., 'Human Rights Protection in Africa: Towards Effective Mechanisms', *East African Journal of Peace and Human Rights* 3(1) (1996) 1–31

Abdul-Razag, M. A., 'The OAU and the Protection of Human Rights in Africa' (Ph.D. thesis, University of Hull, 1988)

Abi-Saab, G., 'The Newly Independent States and the Rules of International Law', *Harvard Law Journal* 8 (1962) 95–101

Addona, A. F., *The Organization of African Unity* (Cleveland and New York: World Publishing Company, 1969)

Adede, A. O., 'Constitutionalism, Culture and Tradition: African Experiences on the Incorporation of Treaties into Domestic Law', *African Yearbook of International Law* 7 (1999) 239–53

Adedeji, A., *Comprehending and Mastering African Conflicts. The Search for Sustainable Peace and Good Governance* (London: Zed Books, 1999)

Adegbite, L. O., 'African Attitudes to the International Protection of Human Rights', in A. Eide and A. Shou (eds.), *International Protection of Human Rights: Proceedings of the Seventh Nobel Symposium, Oslo, September 25–27 1967* (Stockholm: Almquist & Wiksell, 1968) 69–81

Adepoju, A., 'The Dimension of the Refugee Problem in Africa', *African Affairs* 81 (1982) 21–35

Agbakwa, S. C., 'Reclaiming Humanity: Economic, Social and Cultural Rights as the Cornerstone of African Human Rights', *Yale Human Rights and Development Law Journal* 5 (2002) 177–216

Ager, A., W. Ager and L. Long, 'The Differential Experience of Mozambican Refugee Women and Men', *Journal of Refugee Studies* 8 (1995) 265–87

Aginam, O., 'Legitimate Governance under the African Charter on Human and Peoples' Rights', in Quashigah and Okafor (eds.), *Legitimate Governance in Africa* 345–74

Aiboni, S. A., *Protection of Refugees in Africa* (Uppsala: Svenska Institutet för Internaionell Rätt, 1978)

Aidoo, A., 'Africa: Democracy Without Human Rights?', *HRQ* 15 (1993) 703–15

Ait-Ahmed, H., *L'Afro-fascisme: les droits de l'homme dans la Chartre et la pratique de l'OUA* (Paris: Harmattan, 1980)

Akindele, R. A., *The Organization of African Unity, 1963–1988: A Role Analysis and Performance Review* (Ibadan: Vantage Publishers, 1988)

Akindele, R. A. and B. A. Akinterinwa, 'Reform of the United Nations: Towards Greater Effectiveness, Enhanced Legitimacy Profile and Equitable Regionally-Balanced Membership in an Enlarged UN Security Council', in Obiozor and Ajala(eds.), *Africa and the United Nations System* 200–31

Akinola Aguda, T., *Human Rights and the Right to Development in Africa* (Lagos: Nigerian Institute of International Affairs, 1989)

Akinrinade, S. and S. Sesay, *Africa in Post Cold War International System* (London: Pinter, 1998)

Akintan, S. A., *The Law of International Economic Institutions in Africa* (Leiden: A. W. Sijthoff, 1977)

Akintoba, T. O., *African States and Contemporary International Law. A Case Study of the 1982 Law of the Sea Convention and the Exclusive Economic Zone* (The Hague: Martinus Nijhoff, 1996)

Akinyemi, A. B., 'The Organization of African Unity and the Concept of Non-Interference in Internal Affairs of Member States', *BYIL* 46 (1972–3) 393–400

Allain, J., 'The Jus Cogens Nature of Non-Refoulement', *International Journal of Refugee Law* 13(4) (2001) 533–68

Alao, A., 'The Role of African Regional and Sub-Regional Organisations in Conflict Prevention and Resolution', Working Paper No. 23, *New Issues in Refugee Research* (New York: UNHCR, July 2000), www.unhcr.ch

Almond H. H., 'Human Rights, International Humanitarian Law and the Peaceable Adjustment of Differences in Africa', *East African Journal of Peace and Human Rights* 1(2) (1993) 137–63

Alston, P. (ed.), *The EU and Human Rights* (Oxford: Oxford University Press, 1999)

Alston, P., 'Making Space for New Human Rights: The Case of the Right to Development' *Harvard Human Rights Yearbook* 1 (1988) 1–38

Alston, P., *Peoples' Rights* (Oxford: Oxford University Press, 2001)

Alston, P. and J. H. H. Weiler, 'An "Ever Closer Union" in Need of a Human Rights Policy: The European Union and Human Rights', in Alston (ed.), *The EU and Human Rights* 3–68

Amate, C. O. C., *Inside the OAU: Pan-Africanism in Practice* (New York: St Martin's Press, 1986)

Ambrose, B. P., *Democratization and the Protection of Human Rights in Africa. Problems and Prospects* (Westport, CT: Praeger, 1995)

Ammons, L., 'Consequences of War on African Countries' Social and Economic Development', *African Studies Review* 39(1) (1996) 67–82

Amnesty International, *The African Charter on the Rights and Welfare of the Child* (London: Amnesty International, December 1998) AI Index: IOR 63/006/1998

Amnesty International, *Organization of African Unity: Making Human Rights a Reality for Africans* (London: Amnesty International, August 1998) AI Index: IOR 63/01/98

Amnesty International, *Southern Africa: Policing and Human Rights in the Southern African Development Community* (London: Amnesty International, 1997)

Anand, R. P., 'Attitudes of Asian-African States towards Certain Problems of International Law', *ICLQ* 15 (1966) 1–15

Anand, R. P., 'The Role of the "New" Asian-African Countries in the Present International Legal Order', *AJIL* 56(2) (1962) 383–406

Andemicael, B., 'OAU–UN Relations in a Changing World', in EI-Ayouty (ed.), *OAU after Thirty Years* 119–38

Andemicael, B., *The OAU and the UN. Relations between the Organisation of African Unity and the United Nations* (New York: Africana Publishing Company, 1976)

Andemicael, B., *Peaceful Settlement among African States: Roles of the United Nations and the Organization of African Unity* (New York: UN Institute for Training and Research, 1972)

Ankumah, E., *The African Commission on Human and Peoples' Rights. Practices and Procedures* (The Hague: Martinus Nijhoff, 1996)

An-Na'im, A. (ed.), *Cultural Transformation and Human Rights in Africa* (London: Zed Books, 2002)

An-Na'im, A. and F. M. Deng, *Human rights in Africa: Cross Cultural Perspectives* (Washington, DC: Brookings Institute, 1990)

An-Naim, A., *Universal Rights, Local Remedies, Implementing Human Rights in Legal Systems of Africa* (London: Interights, 1999)

Anthony, C. G., 'Africa's Refugee Crisis: State Building in Historical Perspective', *International Migration Review* 25(3) (1991) 574–91

Anyang'Nyong'o, P., *Popular Struggles for Democracy in Africa* (London: Zed Books, 1987)

Anyangwe, C., 'Obligations of States Parties to the African Charter on Human and Peoples' Rights', *RADIC* 10 (1998) 625–59

Arat, S. F., 'Analysing Child Labour as a Human Rights Issue: Its Causes, Aggravating Policies and Alternative Proposals', *HRQ* 24 (2002) 177–204

Armstrong, K., 'Uncovering Reality: Excavating Women's Rights in African Family Law', *International Journal of Law and the Family* 7 (1993) 314–69

Asante, K. D., 'Election Monitoring's Impact on the Law: Can it be Reconciled with Sovereignty?', *New York University Journal of International Law and Politics* 26 (1994) 269–89

Ault, D., 'The Development of Individual Rights to Property in Tribal Africa', *Journal of Law and Economics* 22(1) (1979) 163–82

Awuku, E. O., 'Refugee Movements in Africa and the OAU Convention on Refugees', *JAL* 39 (1995) 79–86

Ayine, D. M., 'Ballots or Bullets?: Compliance with Rules and Norms Providing for the Right to Democratic Governance. An African Perspective', *RADIC* 10 (1998) 709–33

El-Ayouty, Y., 'An OAU for the Future: An Assessment', in El-Ayouty (ed.), *OAU after Thirty Years*) 179–93

El-Ayouty, Y. (ed.), *The Organization of African Unity after Thirty Years* (Westport, CT: Praeger, 1994)

El-Ayouty, Y. and H. C. Brooks (eds.), *Africa and International Organisations* (The Hague: Martinus Nijhoff, 1974)

Babarinde, O. A., 'Analyzing the Proposed African Economic Community: Lessons from the Experience of the European Union', paper for the Third ECSA-World Conference on The European Union in a Changing World (Brussels: European Commission, D-G X, September 1996), http://www.ecsanet.org/conferences/babarinde.htm

Bakwesegha, C. J., 'The OAU and African Refugees', in El-Ayouty (ed.), *OAU after Thirty Years* 77–96

Bakwesegha, C. J., 'Role of the OAU in Conflict Prevention, Management and Resolution', *International Journal of Refugee Law* 21 (1995) 207–22

Banda, F., 'Global Standards: Local Values', *International journal of Law Policy and Family* (2003) 1–27

Barnett, L., 'Global Governance and the Evolution of the International Refugee Regime', *International Journal of Refugee Law* 14 (2002) 238–62

Barron, M., 'When the Soldiers Come Home: A Gender Analysis of the Reintegration of Demobilised Soldiers, Mozambique 1994–6' (MA thesis, University of East Anglia, 1996)

Barutciski, M., 'Involuntary Repatriation when Refugee Protection is no Longer Necessary: Moving Forward after the 48th Session of the Executive Committee', *International Journal of Refugee Law* 10(2) (1998) 236–55

Bauer, G., 'Namibia in the First Decade of Independence: How Democratic?', *Journal of Southern African Studies* 27(1) (2001) 33–55

Bedjaoui, M., 'The Right to Development and the Jus Cogens', *Lesotho Law Journal* 2(2) (1986) 93–129

Beetham, D., 'Democracy and Human Rights: Civil and Political, Economic, Social and Cultural', in J. Symonides (ed.), *Human Rights: New Dimensions and Challenges* (Dartmouth: Ashgate, 1998) 71–98

Beetham, D., 'Democracy and Human Rights: Contrast and Convergence', Office of the High Commissioner for Human Rights, Seminar on the Interdependence between Democracy and Human Rights (Geneva: OHCHR, 25–26 November 2002)

Beilstein, J. C., 'Women in Political Decision-Making. Progress Towards a "Critical Mass"', paper for SADC Regional Parliamentary Seminar, in co-operation with UNDP, Women in Decision-Making: Empowerment for Action, Cape Town, 5 September 1996

Bello, E. G., 'Human Rights: The Rule of Law in Africa', *ICLQ* 30 (1981) 628–37

Benedek, W., 'The African Charter and Commission on Human and Peoples' Rights: How to Make it More Effective', *NQHR* 1 (1993) 25–40

Benedek, W. E., M. Kisaakye and G. Oberleitner, *Human Rights of Women. International Instruments and African Experiences* (London: Zed Books, 2002)

Berg E. Z., 'Gendering Conflict Resolution', *Peace and Change* 19(4) (1994) 325–48

Betts, T. F., 'Rural Refugees in Africa', *International Migration Review* 15(1/2) (1981) 213–18

Beyani, C., 'International Legal Criteria for the Separation of Members of Armed Forces, Armed Bands and Militia from Refugees in the Territories of Host States', *International Journal of Refugee Law* 12(1) (2000) 251–71

Beyani, C., 'The Needs of Refugee Women: A Human Rights Perspective', *Gender and Development* 3(2) (1995) 29–35

Blavo, E. Q., *The Problems of Refugees in Africa* (Aldershot: Ashgate, 1999)

Blay, S., 'Changing African Perspectives on the Right of Self-Determination in the Wake of the Banjul Charter on Human and Peoples' Rights', *JAL* (1985) 147–59

Boumans, E. and M. Norbart, 'The European Parliament and Human Rights', *NQHR* 7 (1989) 35–56

Boutros-Ghali, B., *L'Organization de Unitè Africaine* (Paris: A. Colin Collection U, Series Institutions Internationales, 1969)

Boyle, A. and D. Freestone (eds.), *International Law and Sustainable Development. Past Achievements and Future Challenges* (Oxford: Oxford University Press, 1999)

Bozeman, A. B., *Conflict in Africa. Concepts and Realities* (Princeton: Princeton University Press, 1976)

Bradley, C. K. St, 'Reflections on the Human Rights Role of the European Parliament', in Alston (ed.), *The EU and Human Rights* 839–58

Bratton, M., *Governance and Politics in Africa* (Boulder: Lynne Reiner, 1991)

Brennan, E. M., 'Irregular Migration: Policy Responses in Africa and Asia', *International Migration Review* 18(3) (1984) 409–25

Busia, N. K. A., 'The Status of Human Rights in Pre-Colonial Africa: Implications for Contemporary Practices', in E. McCarthy-Arnolds, D. R. Penna and D. J. Cruz Sobrepeña (eds.), *Africa, Human Rights, and the Global System. The Political Economy of Human Rights in a changing world* (Westport, CT: Greenwood Press, 1994) 225–50

Buxbaum, D. C., *Traditional and Modern Legal Institutions in Asia and Africa* (Leiden: EJ Brill, 1967)

Byers, M. and S. Chesterman, '"You the People": Pro-Democratic Intervention in International Law', in Fox and Roth (eds.), *Democratic Governance* 259–92

Byrne, B., *Gender, Conflict and Development*, vols. I and II, Bridge Report Nos. 34–5 (Brighton: Institute of Development Studies, 1996)

Byrne, B., 'Towards a Gendered Understanding of Conflict', *IDS Bulletin* 27(3) (1996) 1–10

Byrnes, A., 'Women, Feminism and International Human Rights Law – Methodological Myopia, Fundamental Flaws or Meaningful Marginalization? Some Current Issues', *Australian Yearbook of International Law* 12 (1992) 216–23

Carver, R., 'How African Governments Investigate Human Rights Violations', *Third World Legal Studies* (1988) 161–83

Carver, R. and P. Hunt, *National Human Rights Institutions in Africa* (Banjul: African Centre for Democracy and Human Rights Studies, 1991)

Cassel, D. W., 'Somoza's Revenge: A New Judge for the Inter-American Court of Human Rights', *HRLJ* 13(4) (1992) 137–40

Cervenka, Z., 'Major Policy Shifts in the Organization of African Unity 1963–1973', in K. Ingham (ed.), *Foreign Relations of African States* (London: Butterworths, 1974) 323–44

Cervenka, Z., *The Organization of African Unity and its Charter* (New York: Praeger, 1968)

Cervenka, Z., 'The Role of the OAU in the Peaceful Settlement of Disputes', in E1-Ayouty and Books (eds.), *Africa* 48–68

Cervenka, Z., *The Unfinished Quest for Unity. Africa and the OAU* (New York: Freidman, 1977)

Chabal, P., 'The Quest for Good Government and Development in Africa: Is NEPAD the Answer?', *International Affairs* 78(3) (2002) 447–62

Chanda, A., 'The Organization of African Unity: An Appraisal', *Zambia Law Journal* 21–4 (1989–92) 1–29

Charlesworth, H., 'Transforming the United Nations Men's Club: Feminist Futures for the United Nations', *Transnational Law and Contemporary Problems* 4 (1994) 422–54

Chime, S. C., 'The Organization of African Unity and African Boundaries', in C. G. Widstrand (ed.), *African Boundary Problems* (Uppsala: Scandinavian Institute of Africa Studies, 1969) 74–90

Chimni, B. S., 'From Resettlement to Involuntary Repatriation: Towards a Critical History of Durable Solutions to Refugee Problems', Working Paper No. 2, *New Issues in Refugee Research* (New York: UNHCR, 1999), www.unhcr.ch

Chirwa, D. M., 'The Merits and Demerits of the African Charter on the Rights and Welfare of the Child', *International Journal of Children's Rights* 10 (2002) 157–77

Chowdhury, S. R., E. M. G. Denters and P. J. I. M. de Waart (eds.), *The Right to Development in International Law* (Dordrecht: Martinus Nijhoff, 1992)

Cilliers, J., 'NEPAD's Peer Review Mechanism' (Pretoria: Institute for Security Studies Paper 64, November 2002), www.iss.co.za

Cilliers, J. and G. Mills, *Peacekeeping in Africa* (Pretoria: Institute for International Affairs, 1995)

Cimade, I., M. Inodep and I. Mink, *Africa's Refugee Crisis* (London: Zed Books, 1986)

Clapham, A., 'A Human Rights Policy for the European Community', *Yearbook of European Law* 10 (1990) 309–49

Clapham, A. 'Where is the EU's Human Rights Common Foreign Policy and How is it Manifested in Multilateral Fora?', in Alston (ed.), *The EU and Human Rights* 621–49

Clapham, C., *Africa and the International System. The Politics of State Survival* (Cambridge: Cambridge University Press, 1996)

Clark, T., S. Aiken, B. Jackman and D. Matas, 'International Human Rights Law and Legal Remedies in Expulsion: Progress and Some Remaining Problems with Special Reference to Canada', *NQHR* 15(4) (1997) 429–45

Clark, T. and F. Crépeau, 'Mainstreaming Refugee Rights. The 1951 Refugee Convention and International Human Rights Law', *NQHR* 17(4) (1999) 389–410

Cohen, R., G. Hyden and W. P. Nagan (eds.), *Human Rights and Governance in Africa* (Miami: University Press of Florida, 1993)

Collins, J. S., 'An Analysis of the Voluntariness of Refugee Repatriation in Africa' (Ph.D. thesis, University of Manitoba, 1996)

Conroy, D. K., *The Global and Regional Situation of Women Top Civil Servants* (Vienna: UNDAW, 1989), EGM/EPPDM/1989/WP.3

Crawford, J., 'Democracy and the Body of International Law', in Fox and Roth (eds.), *Democratic Governance* 91–122

Crawford, J., 'Democracy and International Law', *BYIL* 64 (1993) 113–35

Crawford, J. (ed.), *The Right of Peoples* (Oxford: Oxford University Press, 1988)

Crisp, J., 'Africa's Refugees: Patterns, Problems and Policy Challenges', Working Paper No. 28, *New Issues in Refugee Research* (New York: UNHCR, 2000), www.unhcr.ch

Crocker, C. A., 'Military Dependence: The Colonial Legacy in Africa', *Journal of Modern African Studies* 12(2) (1974) 265–86

Davidson, B., *African Nationalism and the Problems of Nation-Building* (Lagos: Nigerian Institute of International Affairs, 1987)

Deng, F. M., 'The Challenge of the African Experience', in F. M. Deng, (ed.), *Protecting the Dispossessed: A Challenge for the International Community* (Washington, DC: Brookings Institute, 1993) 109–20

Dicklitch, S., 'A Basic Human Rights Approach to Democracy in Uganda', *Journal of Contemporary African Studies* 20(2) (2002) 3–15

Dieng, A., 'Addressing the Root Causes of Forced Population Displacements in Africa: A Theoretical Model', *International Journal of Refugee Law* 7(2) (1995) 119–29

Van Dijk, P., 'The Law of Human Rights in Europe – Instruments and Procedures for a Uniform Implementation', *AEL* 6(2) (1997) 22–50

Donnelly, J., 'The "Right to Development": How Not to Link Human Rights and Development', in Welch and Meltzer (eds.), *Human Rights and Development* 261–83

D'Sa, R., 'The African Refugee Problem, Relevant International Conventions and Recent Activities of the Organization of African Unity', *Netherlands International Law Review* 31 (1984) 378–95

Dugard, J., 'Human Rights, Humanitarian Law and the South African Conflict', *Harvard Human Rights Yearbook* 2 (1989) 101–10

Dugard, J., 'The Organisation of African Unity and Colonialism: An Inquiry into the Plea of Self-Defence as a Justification for the Use of Force in the Eradication of Colonialism', *ICLQ* 16 (1967) 157–90

Dumor, E. K., *Ghana, OAU and Southern Africa. An African Response to Apartheid* (Accra: Ghana Universities Press, 1991)

Dunbar, S. R., 'Role of Women in Decision-Making in the Peace Process', in S. Wölte (ed.), *Human Rights Violations against Women during War and Conflict* (Geneva: Women's International League for Peace and Freedom, 1997) 12–18

Dunn, K. C., 'Introduction: Africa and International Relations Theory', in K. C. Dunn and T. M. Shaw, *Africa's Challenge to International Relations Theory* (Basingstoke: Palgrave, 2001) 1–10

Egan, S., 'Human Rights Considerations in Extradition and Expulsion Cases: The European Convention on Human Rights Revisited', *Contemporary Issues in Irish Law and Politics* 1 (1998) 188–215

van Eijk, R., 'The United Nations and the Reconstruction of Collapsed States in Africa', *AJICL* 9(3) (1997) 573–99

Einarsen, T., 'The European Convention on Human Rights and the Notion of an Implied Right to De Facto Asylum', *International Journal of Refugee Law* 3 (1990) 361–75

Elias, T. O., *Africa and the Development of International Law*, 2nd edn., ed. R. Akinjide (The Hague: Martinus Nijhoff, 1988)

Elias, T. O., *Africa before the World Court* (Nairobi: University of Nairobi, 1981)

Elias, T. O., 'The Commission of Mediation, Conciliation and Arbitration of the OAU', *BYIL* 40 (1964) 336

Elias, T. O., 'The Charter of the Organization of African Unity', *AJIL* 59 (1965) 243–67

Elias, T. O., *Government and Politics in Africa* (London: Asia Publishing House, 1961)

Elias, T. O., *New Horizons in International Law*, 2nd edn. (Dordrecht: Martinus Nijhoff, 1992)

Emerson, R., 'The Fate of Human Rights in the Third World', *World Politics* 27(2) (1975) 201–26

Emerson, R., 'Pan-Africanism', *International Organisation* 16 (1962) 275–90

Enemo, I., 'Self-Determination as the Fundamental Basis of the Concept of Legitimate Governance under the African Charter on Human and Peoples' Rights', in Quashigah and Okafor (eds.), *Legitimate Governance in Africa* 403–18

Engo, P. B., 'Peaceful Co-existence and Friendly Relations among States: The African Contribution to the Progressive Development of Principles of International Law', in El-Ayouty and Brooks (eds.), *Africa* 29–47

Eriksson, L.-G., G. Melander and P. Nobel, *An Analysing Account of the Conference on the African Refugee Problem, Arusha, May 1979* (Uppsala: Scandinavian Institute of African Affairs, 1981)

Esiemokhai, E., 'Towards Adequate Defence of Human Rights in Africa', *Quarterly Journal of Administration* 24(4) (1980) 451–61

Evans, M., T. Ige and R. Murray, 'The Reporting Mechanism of the African Charter on Human and Peoples' Rights', in Evans and Murray (eds.), *The African Charter* 36–60

Evans, M. and R. Murray (eds.), *The African Charter on Human and Peoples' Rights. The System in Practice 1986–2000* (Cambridge: Cambridge University Press, 2002)

Eze, O. C., *Human Rights in Africa. Some Selected Problems* (Lagos: Nigerian Institute of International Affairs and Macmillan Nigeria, 1984)

Eze, O. C., 'The Organization of African Unity and Human Rights: Twenty Five Years After', *Nigerian Journal of International Affairs* 14 (1988) 163–4

Ezetah, C. R., 'Legitimate Governance and Statehood in Africa: Beyond the Failed State and Colonial Self-Determination', in Quashigah and Okafor (eds.), *Legitimate Governance in Africa* 419–59

Fitzpatrick, J., 'Temporary Protection of Refugees: Elements of a Formalized Regime', *AJIL* 94(2) (2000) 279–306

Fleck, D. (ed.), *Handbook of Humanitarian law Armed Conflicts* (Oxford; Oxford University Press, 1995)

Flinterman, C. and E. Ankumah, *The African Charter on Human and Peoples' Rights*, in H. Hannum (ed.), *Guide to International Human Rights Practice* (Philadelphia: University of Philadelphia Press, 1992) 159–69

Fonteyne, J. P., 'Burden Sharing: An Analysis of the Nature and Function of International Solidarity in Cases of Mass Influx of Refugees', *Australian Yearbook of International Law* 8 (1983) 162–88

Fox, G., 'The Right to Political Participation in International Law', *Yale Journal of International Law* 17 (1992) 570–87

Fox, G. H., 'The Right to Political Participation in International Law', in Fox and Roth (eds.), *Democratic Governance* 48–90

Fox, H., 'The Settlement of Disputes by Peaceful Means and the Observance of International Law: African Attitudes', *International Relations* 3(6) (1968) 389–400

Fox, D., N. Hasci and P. Magnarella, *The Challenges of Women's Activism and Human Rights in Africa* (New York: Edwin Mellen Press, 1999)

Fox, G. H. and B. R. Roth (eds.), *Democratic Governance and International Law* (Cambridge: Cambridge University Press, 2000)

Franck, T., 'Afference, Efference and Legitimacy in Africa', in El-Ayouty and Brooks (eds.), *Africa* 3–10

Franck, T., 'The Emerging Right to Democratic Governance', *AJIL* 86 (1992) 44–91

Gallagher, A., 'Ending the Marginalization: Strategies for Incorporating Women into the United Nations Human Rights System', *HRQ* 19 (1997) 283–333

Gardham, J., 'The Law of Armed Conflict: A Gendered Regime?', in D. Dallmeyer (ed.), *Reconceiving Reality: Women and International Law* (Washington, DC: American Society of International Law, 1993) 171–93

Gareau, F. H., 'The Impact of the United Nations Upon Africa', *Journal of Modern African Studies* 16(4) (1978) 565–78

Geisler, G., 'Fair? What has Fairness got to do with it? Vagaries of Election Observations and Democratic Standards', *Journal of Modern African Studies* 31(4) (1993) 613–37

Geisler, G., 'Troubled Sisterhood: Women and Politics in Southern Africa: Case Studies from Zambia, Zimbabwe and Botswana', *African Affairs* 95 (1995) 545–78

Geiss, I., *The Pan-African Movement. A History of Pan-Africanism in America, Europe and Asia* (New York: Africana Publishing Company, 1968)

Geissler, N., 'The International Protection of Internally Displaced Persons', *International Journal of Refugee Law* 11(3) (1999) 451–78

Ginther, K., 'Sustainable Development and Good Governance: Development and Evolution of Constitutional Orders', in Ginther et al. (eds.), *Sustainable Development* 150–77

Ginther, K. and W. Benedek, *New Perspectives and Conceptions of International law: An Afro-Asian Dialogue* (Vienna and New York: Springer-Verlag, 1983)

Ginther, K., E. Denters and P. J. I. M. de Waart (eds.), *Sustainable Development and Good Governance* (Dordrecht: Martinus Nijhoff, 1995)

Gittleman, R., 'Peoples' Rights: A Legal Analysis', *Virginia Journal of International Law*, 22 (1982) 667–714

Gonidec, P. F., 'Relationship of International Law and National Law in Africa', *RADIC* 10 (1998) 244–9

Gonidec, P. F., 'Towards a Treatise of African International Law', *AJICL* 9(4) (1997) 807–21

Goodwin-Gill, G., 'International Law and Human Rights: Trends Concerning International Migrants and Refugees', *International Migration Review* 23(3) (1989) 526–46

Goodwin-Gill, G., *The Refugee in International Law*, 2nd edn. (Oxford: Oxford University Press, 1996)

Gorlick, B., 'The Convention and the Committee against Torture: A Complementary Protection Regime for Refugees', *International Journal of Refugee Law* 11(3) (1999) 479–95

Gorlick, B., 'Human Rights and Refugees: Enhancing Protection through International Human Rights Law', Working Paper No. 30, *New Issues in Refugee Research* (New York: UNHCR, October 2000), www.unhcr.ch

Gorman, R. F., 'Beyond ICARA II: Implementing Refugee-Related Development Assistance', *International Migration Review* 20(2) (1986) 283–98

Gose, M., 'The African Charter on the Rights and Welfare of the Child: An Assessment of the Legal Value of its Substantive Provisions by Means of a Direct Comparison to the Convention on the Rights of the Child', Community Law Centre (2002), http://www.communitylawcentre.org.za/children/publications/african_charter.pdf

Gowlland-Debbas, V. (ed.), *The Problem of Refugees in the Light of Contemporary International Law Issues* (The Hague: Martinus Nijhoff, 1996)

Griffiths, I. L. L., *The African Inheritance* (London: Routledge, 1995)

Griffiths, I. L. L., *An Atlas of African Affairs* (London and New York: Methuen, 1984)

Gutto, S., 'Current Concepts, Core Principles, Dimensions, Processes and Institutions of Democracy and the Inter-Relationship between Democracy and Modern Human Rights', Seminar on the Interdependence between Democracy and Human Rights (Geneva, 25–26 November 2002), www.unhchr.ch

Gutto, S., 'The OAU's New Mechanisms for Conflict Prevention, Management and Resolution and the Controversial Concept of Humanitarian Intervention in International Law', *African Society of International and Comparative Law Proceedings* 7 (1995) 348–51

Gutto, S., 'The Rule of Law, Democracy and Human Rights: Whither Africa?', *East African Journal of Peace and Human Rights* 3(1) (1996) 130–9

Haile, M., 'Human Rights, Stability and Development in Africa: Some Observations on the Concept and Reality', *Virginia Journal of International Law* 24(3) (1984) 575–615

Hamalengwa, M., *The International Law of Human Rights in Africa: Basic Documents and Annotated Bibliography* (Dordrecht and Boston: Martinus Nijhoff, 1988)

Hamrell, S., *Refugee Problems in Africa* (Uppsala: Scandinavian Institute of African Studies, 1967)

Hansen, A., 'African Refugees: Defining and Defending their Human Rights', in Cohen, Hyden and Nagan (eds.), *Human Rights and Governance* 139–67

Harbeson, J. W. and D. Rothchild, *Africa in World Politics. The African State System in Flux* (Oxford: Westview Press, 2000)

Harbeson, J. W., D. Rothchild and N. Chazan, *Civil Society and the State in Africa* (Boulder: Lynne Rienner Publishers, 1994)

Harrell-Bond, B. E., 'Repatriation: Under What Conditions is it the Most Desirable Solution for Refugees? An Agenda for Research', *African Studies Review* 32(1) (1989) 41–69

Harrell-Bond, B., *Towards the Economic and Social 'Integration' of Refugee Populations in Host Countries in Africa* (Muscatine, IA: Stanley Foundation, 2002), http://reports.stanleyfoundation.org/hrp/HRP02B.pdf

Harrington, J., 'The African Court on Human and Peoples' Rights', in Evans and Murray (eds.), *The African Charter* 305–34

Harvey, C. J., 'Dissident Voices: Refugees, Human Rights and Asylum in Europe', *Social and Legal Studies* 9(3) (2000) 367–96

Harvey, C. J., 'Strangers at the Gate: Human Rights and Refugee Protection', *Irish Studies in International Affairs* 10 (1999) 7–20

Hatchard, J., 'Reporting under International Human Rights Instruments by African Countries', *JAL* 38 (1994) 61–3

Hathaway, J. C., *Reconceiving International Refugee Law* (The Hague: Martinus Nijhoff, 1997)

Hefny, M., 'Enhancing the Capabilities of the OAU Mechanism for Conflict Prevention, Management and Resolution: An Immediate Agenda for Action', *African Society of International and Comparative Law Proceedings* 7 (1995) 176–80

Held, D., *Models of Democracy* (London: Polity Press, 1996)

Helton, A. C., *The Price of Indifference. Refugees and Humanitarian Action in the New Century* (Oxford: Oxford University Press, 2002)

Helton, A. C., 'Protecting the World's Exiles: Human Rights of Non-Citizens', *HRQ* 22 (2000) 280–301

Henkin, L., 'International Law: Politics, Values and Functions, *Collected Courses of the Hague Academy of International Law* 216 (1989) 3–16

Henry, P. M., 'The UN and the Problem of African Development', *International Organisation* 16(2) (1962) 362–74

Herbert, R., *Implementing NEPAD: A Critical Assessment* (Pretoria: South Africa Institute of International Affairs, June 2002), www.iss.co.za

Hernández-Truyol, B. E., 'Women's Rights as Human Rights, Realities and the Role of Culture: A Formula for Reform', *Brooklyn Journal of International Law*, 21 (1996) 605–77

Higgins, R., *UN Peacekeeping 1946–1967. Africa* (Oxford: Oxford University Press, 1980)

Holleman, J. F., *Issues in African Law* (The Hague: Mouton, 1974)

Holmes, J., 'The Impact of the Commonwealth on Emergence of Africa', *International Organisation* 16(2) (1962) 291–302

Holsti, O. R. and J. N. Rosenau, 'The Foreign Policy Beliefs of Women in Leadership Positions', *Journal of Politics* 43 (1981) 326–40

Houser, G. M., 'Human Rights and the Liberation Struggle: The Importance of Creative Tension', in E. McCarthy-Arnolds, D. R. Penna and D. J. Cruz Sobrepeña (eds.), *Africa, Human Rights and the Global System. The Political Economy of Human Rights in a Changing World* (Westport, CT: Greenwood Press, 1994) 11–22

Hovell tot Westerflier, W., 'Africa and Refugees: The OAU Refugee Convention in Theory and Practice', *NQHR* 7(2) (1989) 11–32

Hovet, T., 'Effect of the African Group of States on the Behaviour of the United Nations', in El-Ayouty and Brooks (eds.), *Africa* 11–17

Howard, R. E., 'Evaluating Human Rights in Africa: Some Problems of Implicit Comparisons', *HRQ* 6 (1984) 160–79

Howard, R. E., *Human Rights in Commonwealth Africa* (Totowa, NJ: Rowman & Littlefield, 1986)

Howard, R. E., 'Is there an African Concept of Human Rights?', in R. J. Vincent (ed.), *Foreign Policy and Human Rights: Issues and Responses* (Cambridge: Cambridge University Press, 1986) 11–32

Howard, R. E., 'Women's Rights and the Right to Development', in Cohen, Hyden and Nagan (eds.), *Human Rights and Governance* 111–38

Human Rights Watch, *Protectors or Pretenders: Human Rights Institutions in Africa* (London: Human Rights Watch, 2001)

Hutchinson, M. R., 'Restoring Hope: UN Security Council Resolutions for Somalia and an Expanded Doctrine of Humanitarian Intervention', *Harvard International Law Journal* 34 (1993) 624–40

Hyden, G. and M. Bratton, *Governance and Politics in Africa* (Boulder: Lynne Rienner Publishers, 1992)

Hyndman, J. and B. V. Nylund, 'UNHCR and the Status of Prima Facie Refugees in Kenya', *International Journal of Refugee Law* 10(1) (1998) 21–48

Ibhawoh, B., 'Between Culture and Constitution: Evaluating the Cultural Legitimacy of Human Rights in the African State', *HRQ* 22(3) (2000) 838–60

ICJ, *Human Rights in One Party State* (London: International Commission of Jurists, 1978)

Ige, T., 'NEPAD and African Women: Mechanism for Engagement Input and Ownership', http://www.unesco.org/women/NEPAD/tokunbo.htm

Ihonvbere, J., *Multiparty Democracy and Political Change: Constraints to Democratisation in Africa* (Aldershot: Ashgate, 1998)

Ihonvbere, J., *The Political Economy of Crisis and Underdevelopment in Africa: Selected Works of Claude Ake* (Lagos: JAD Publishers Ltd, 1989)

Jackson, I., *The Refugee Concept in Group Situations* (The Hague: Martinus Nijhoff, 1999)

Jacobsen, K., 'Factors Influencing the Policy Responses of Host Governments to Mass Refugee Influxes', *International Migration Review* 30(3) (1996) 655–78

Jacobson, R., 'Women's Political Participation: Mozambique's Democratic Transition', *Gender and Development* 3(3) (1995) 29–35

Jesseman, C., 'The Protection and Participation Rights of the Child Soldier: An African and Global Perspective', *African Human Rights Law Journal* 1(1) (2001) 140–54

Jessup, P. C., 'The Estrada Doctrine', *AJIL* 25 (1931) 719

Jjuuko, F. W., 'The State, Democracy and Constitutionalism in Africa', *East African Journal of Peace and Human Rights* 2(1) (1995) 1–40

Jonah, J. O. C., 'The OAU: Peacekeeping and Conflict Resolution', in El-Ayouty (ed.), *OAU after Thirty Years* 3–14

Jonah, J. O. C., 'The UN and the OAU: Roles in the Maintenance of International Peace and Security in Africa', in El-Ayouty and Brooks (eds.), *Africa* 127–51

Juma, M. K., 'Migration, Security and Refugee Protection: A Reflection', prepared for discussion at Stanley Foundation Conference, Refugee Protection in Africa: How to Ensure Stability and Development for Refugees and Hosts (Entebbe, 10–14 November 2002), http://reports.stanleyfoundation.org/HRP02A.pdf

Kaballo, S., 'Human Rights and Democratization in Africa', in D. Beetham (ed.), Politics and Human Rights, *Political Studies* 43 (Special Issue) (1995) 189–203

Kabera, J. B., 'Education of Refugees and their Expectations in Africa: The Case of Returnees with Special Reference to Uganda', *African Studies Review* 32(1) (1989) 31–9

Kamanu, O. S., 'Secession and the Right of Self-Determination: An OAU Dilemma', *Journal of Modern African Studies* 12(3) (1974) 355–76

Kasmann, E. and M. Korner, *Gender-Aware Approaches to Relief and Rehabilitation: Guidelines* (Bonn: InterAktion, 1996)

Khushalani, Y., 'Human Rights in Africa and Asia' *HRLJ* 4 (1983) 403–42

Kibreab, G., *African Refugees* (Trenton, NJ: Africa World Press, 1985)

Kiwanuka, R. N., 'Note, The Meaning of "People" in the African Charter on Human and Peoples' Rights', *AJIL* 82 (1988) 80–101

Klabbers, J. and R. Lefeber, 'Africa: Lost between Self-determination and Uti Possidetis', in C. Brolmann (ed.), *Peoples and Minorities in International Law* (Leiden: Brill, 1993) 37–54

Kloman, E. H., 'African Unification Movements', *International Organisation* 16(2) (1962) 387–404

Knop, K., *Diversity and Self-Determination in International Law* (Cambridge: Cambridge University Press, 2000)

Kois, L., 'Article 18 of the African Charter on Human and Peoples' Rights: A Progressive Approach to Women's Human Rights', *East African Journal of Peace and Human Rights* 2 (1996) 115–29

Kongolo, T., 'WTO Doha Ministerial Declaration and Intellectual Property: African Perspectives', *African Yearbook of International Law* 9 (2001) 185–211

Kouassi, E. K., 'OAU-UN Interaction over the Last Decade', in El-Ayouty (ed.), *OAU after Thirty Years* 139–46

Kumari, R., *Women in Decision-Making* (London: Vikas Publishing House, 1997)

Kunig, P., 'The Protection of Human Rights by International Law in Africa', *German Yearbook of International Law* 25 (1982) 138–68

Kunig, P., W. Benedek and E. R. Mahalu, *Regional Protection of Human Rights by International Law: The Emerging African Systems* (Baden Baden: Nomos Verlagsgesellschaft, 1985)

Kwakwa, E., 'Internal Conflicts in Africa: Is there a Right of Humanitarian Intervention?', *African Yearbook of International Law* 2 (1994) 9–21

Ladouceur, P., 'Seminar on African Refugee Problems', *Journal of Modern African Studies* 8(2) (1970) 298–301

Lang, D., *Sustainable Development and International Law* (London: Kluwer Law International, 1995)

Langley, W., 'The Rights of Women, the African Charter and the Economic Development of Africa', *B. C. Third World Law Journal* 7 (1987) 215–21

Lauterpacht, H., *Recognition in International Law* (Cambridge: Cambridge University Press, 1947)

Lawyers' Committee for Human Rights, *African Exodus. Refugee Crisis, Human Rights and the 1969 OAU Convention* (New York: Lawyers' Committee for Human Rights, 1995)

Lee, L. T., 'The Right to Compensation: Refugees and Countries of Asylum', *AJIL* 80(3) (1986) 532–67

Legesse, A. M., 'Human Rights in African Political Culture', in K. W. Thompson (ed.), *The Moral Imperative of Human Rights: A World Survey* (Washington, DC: Press of America, 1980) 125–8

Legum, C., *Pan-Africanism* (New York: Praeger, 1965)

Leijenaar, M., *How to Create a Gender Balance in Political Decision-Making: A Guide to Implementing Policies for Increasing Participation of Women in Political Decision-Making* (Brussels: European Union, 1997)

Levitt, J., 'Conflict Prevention, Management and Resolution: African Regional Strategies. Cases of OAU, ECOWAS', *Duke Journal of International and Comparative Law* 11 (2001) 39–50

Lillich, I., *Human Rights of Aliens in Contemporary International Law* (Manchester: Manchester University Press, 1984)

Lloyd, A., 'Evolution of the African Charter on the Rights and Welfare of the Child and the African Committee of Experts. Raising the Gauntlet', *International Journal of Children's Rights* 10 (2002) 179–98

Lloyd, A., 'Recent Developments: The First Meeting of the African Committee of Experts on the Rights and Welfare of the Child', *African Human Rights Law Journal* 2(2) (2002) 13–22

Lloyd, A., 'Recent Developments: The Second Ordinary Session in the African Committee of Experts', *African Human Rights Law Journal* 3(2) (2003) 31–48

Lloyd, A., 'Regional Developments on the Rights and Welfare of Children in Africa: A General Report on the African Charter on the Rights and Welfare of the Child and the African Committee of Experts', http://www.uwe.ac.uk/law/research/acr/report.htm

Lloyd, A., 'A Theoretical Analysis of the Reality of Children's Rights in Africa: An Introduction to the African Charter on the Rights and Welfare of the Child', *African Human Rights Law Journal* 2 (2002) 11–32

Loescher, G., *The UNHCR and World Politics. A Perilous Path* (Oxford: Oxford University Press, 2001)

Macrae, J., 'Aiding Peace . . . and War: UNHCR, Returnee Reintegration, and the Relief-Development Debate', Working Paper No. 14, *New Issues in Refugee Research* (New York: UNHCR, 1999), www.unhcr.ch

Mahmud, S. S., 'The State and Human Rights in Africa in the 1990s: Perspectives and Prospects', *HRQ* 15 (1993) 485–98

Makinda, S. M., 'Democracy and Multi-Party Politics in Africa', *Journal of Modern African Studies* 34(4) (1996) 555–73

Makonnen, Y., *International Law and the New States of Africa* (Addis Ababa: UNESCO, 1983)

Malan, M., 'The OAU and Subregional Organisations: A Closer Look at the Peace Pyramid', Occasional Paper No. 36 (Pretoria: Institute for Security Studies, January 1999), http://www.iss.co.za/Pubs/PAPERS/36/Paper36.html

Maluwa, T., 'International Law Making in the Organisation of African Unity: An Overview', *RADIC* 12 (2000) 201–5

Maluwa, T., *International Law in Post-Colonial Africa* (The Hague: Kluwer, 1999)

Maluwa, T., 'The Peaceful Settlement of Disputes among African States, 1963–1983: Some Conceptual Issues and Practical Trends', *ICLQ* 38 (1989) 299–320

Maluwa, T., 'Reimagining African Unity: Some Preliminary Reflections on the Constitutive Act of the African Union', *African Yearbook of International Law* 9 (2001) 3–38

Mann, K. and R. Roberts, *Law in Colonial Africa* (London: Heinmann, 1991)

Mama, A., 'The Need for Gender Analysis: A Component on the Prospects for Peace, Recovery and Development in the Horn of Africa', in M. Doornbos et al. (eds.), *Beyond Conflict in the Horn* (The Hague: Institute of Social Studies, 1992), 72–7

Mamdani, M., 'The Social Basis of Constitutionalism in Africa', *Journal of Modern African Studies* 28(3) (1990) 259–374

Mamdani, M., *Social Movements and Constitutionalism in the African Context* (Kampala: Centre for Basic Research, 1989)

Marantis, D., 'Human Rights, Democracy and Development: The European Community Model', *Harvard Human Rights Journal* 7 (1994) 1– 32

Markakis, J., 'The Organisation of African Unity: A Progress Report', *Journal of Modern African Studies* 4(2) (1966) 135–53

Marks, S., *Riddle of All Constitutions. International Law, Democracy and the Critique of Ideology* (Oxford: Oxford University Press, 2000)

Martin, G., 'International Solidarity and Cooperation Assistance to African Refugees: Burden Sharing or Burden Shifting?', *International Journal of Refugee Law* 7(2) (1995) 250–73

Mathews, K., 'The Organization of African Unity' in D. Mazzeo (ed.), *African Regional Organizations* 49–84

Mazrui, A., *Africa's International Relations. The Diplomacy of Dependency and Change* (London: Heinemann, 1977)

Mazrui, A., 'The Africa State as a Political Refugee in Institutional Collapse and Human Displacement, *International Journal of Refugee Law* 21 (Special Issue) (1995) 3–23

Mazrui, A., 'Comment: Africa: In Search of Self-Pacification', *African Affairs* 93 (1994) 39–42

Mazrui, A., 'Global Africa: From Abolitionists to Reparationists', *African Studies Review* 37(3) (1994) 1–18

Mazrui, A., 'Towards Containing Conflict in Africa: Methods, Mechanisms and Values', *East African Journal of Peace and Human Rights* 2 (1995) 81–90

Mazrui, A., *Towards a Pax Africana: A Study of Ideology and Ambition* (Chicago: University of Chicago Press, 1967)

Mazzeo, D. (ed.), *African Regional Organizations* (Cambridge: Cambridge University Press: 1984)

Mbaku, J. M. and J. O. Ihonvbere, *Multiparty Democracy and Political Change. Constraints to Democratization in Africa* (Aldershot: Ashgate, 1998)

Mbaye, K., 'Human Rights in Africa', in K. Vasak and P. Alston (eds.), *The International Dimensions of Human Rights* (Westport, CT and Paris: Greenwood Press and UNESCO, 1982) 583–90

M'Buyinga, E., *Pan Africanism or Neo-Colonialism: The Bankruptcy of the OAU* (London: Zed Books, 1982)

McCorquodale, R., *Self-Determination in International Law* (Dartmouth: Ashgate, 2000)

McGoldrick, D., 'Sustainable Development and Human Rights: An Integrated Conception', *ICLQ* 45 (1996) 796–835

McKay, S., 'Gendering Peace Psychology', *Peace and Conflict: Journal of Peace Psychology* 2(2) (1996) 93–107

McKay, S., 'Women's Voices in Peace Psychology: A Feminist Agenda', *Peace and Conflict: Journal of Peace Psychology* 1(1) (1995) 67–84

McMorrow, M., 'Global Poverty, Subsistence Rights, and Consequent Obligations for Rich and Poor States', in E. McCarthy-Arnolds, D. R. Penna and D. J. C. Cruz Sobrepeña (eds.), *Africa, Human Rights and the Global System. The Political Economy of Human Rights in a Changing World* (Westport, CT: Greenwood Press, 1994) 37–60

Mekenkamp, M., P. van Tongeren and H. van de Veen, *Searching for Peace in Africa. An Overview of Conflict Prevention and Management Activities* (Utrecht: European Platform for Conflict Prevention and Transformation, 1999)

Melander, G. and P. Nobel, *African Refugees and the Law* (Uppsala: The Scandinavian Institute of African Studies, 1978)

Meltzer, R. I., 'International Human Rights and Development: Evolving Conceptions and their Application to Relations between the European Community and the African–Caribbean–Pacific States', in Welch and Meltzer (eds.), *Human Rights and Development* 208–25

Meron, T., 'On the Inadequate Reach of Humanitarian and Human Rights Law in the Need for a New Instrument', *AJIL* 77 (1983) 589

Mertus, J., 'The State and the Post Cold War Refugee Regime: New Models, New Questions', *International Journal of Refugee Law* 10(3) (1998) 321–48

Meyers, B. D., 'Intraregional Conflict Management by the Organization of African Unity', *International Organisation* 28(3) (1974) 345–73

Mikell, G., 'African Women's Rights in the Context of Systemic Conflict', *ASIL Proceedings* 89 (1995) 490–500

Mohammed, B., *Africa and Non-Alignment. A Study in the Foreign Relations of New Nations* (Kano: Triumph Publishing Company, 1982)

Motala, Z., 'Human Rights in Africa: A Cultural, Ideological, and Legal Examination', *Hastings International and Comparative Law Review* 12 (1989) 373–410

Msekwa, P., 'The Doctrine of the One-Party State in Relation to Human Rights and the Rule of Law', in ICJ, *Human Rights* 33–55

Mubako, S. V., 'Zambia's Single Party Constitution: A Search for Unity and Development', *Zambia Law Journal* 5 (1973) 67–85

Murphy, S. D., 'Democratic Legitimacy and the Recognition of States and Governments', in Fox and Roth (eds.), *Democratic Governance* 123–54

Murray, R., *The African Commission on Human and Peoples' Rights* (Oxford: Hart Publishing, 2000)

Murray, R., 'A Comparison between the African and European Courts of Human Rights', *African Human Rights Law Journal* 2(2) (2002) 192–222

Murray, R., 'Report of the 31st Ordinary Session of the African Commission on Human and Peoples' Rights', South Africa, May 2002', on file with the author

Murray, R. and M. Evans, *Documents of the African Commission on Human and Peoples' Rights* (Oxford: Hart Publishing, 2001)

Musgrave, T. D., *Self-Determination and National Minorities* (Oxford: Oxford University Press, 1997)

Mushkat, M., 'The African Approach to Some Basic Problems of Modern International Law', *Indian Journal of International Law* 7 (1967) 335–68

Mushkat, M., 'Some Remarks on Factors Influencing the Emergence and Evolution of International Law', *Netherlands International Law Review* 7(9) (1961) 341–60

Mutero, J. (ed.), *Looking at Peace through Women's Eyes* (Nairobi: UNIFEM/AFWIC, 1996)

Mutharika, A. P., 'The Role of International Law in the Twenty-First Century: An African Perspective', *Fordham International Law Journal* 18 (1995) 1706s

wa Mutua, M., 'The Banjul Charter and the African Cultural Fingerprint: An Evaluation of the Language of Duties', *Virginia Journal of International Law* 35 (1995) 339–80

wa Mutua, M., 'Human Rights and Politics in Africa: Democratizing the Rights Discourse', *East African Journal of Peace and Human Rights* 1(2) (1993) 250–5

wa Mutua, M., 'The Ideology of Human Rights: Toward Post Liberal Democracy?', in Quashigah and Okafor (eds.), *Legitimate Governance* 109–64

wa Mutua, M., 'Putting Humpty Dumpty Back Together Again: The Dilemmas of the Post-Colonial African State', *Brooklyn Journal of International Law* 21 (1995) 505–36

wa Mutua, M., 'Reformulating the Discourse of the Human Rights Movement', *East African Journal of Peace and Human Rights* 3(2) (1996) 306–12

Nagan, W. P., 'The African Human Rights Process: A Contextual Policy-Oriented Approach', in Cohen et al. (eds.), *Human Rights and Governance in Africa* 87–110

Naldi, G., *Documents of the Organization of African Unity* (Dordrecht: Martinus Nijhoff, 1999)

Naldi, G., *The Organization of African Unity* (Dordrecht: Martinus Nijhoff, 1999)

Naldi, G., *The Organization of African Unity. An Analysis of its Role*, 2nd edn. (London: Mansell, 1999)

Nanda, V. P., 'Civil War in Liberia: A Re-examination of the Doctrine of Non-intervention', in E. McCarthy-Arnolds, D. R. Penna and D. J. Cruz Sobrepeña (eds.), *Africa, Human Rights, and the Global System. The Political Economy of Human Rights in a Changing World* (Westport, CT: Greenwood Press, 1994) 61–80

Nathwani, N., 'The Purpose of Asylum', *International Journal of Refugee Law* 12(3) (2000) 353–79

Ndiaye, B., 'The Place of Human Rights in the Charter of the Organization of African Unity', in K. Vasak and P. Alston (eds.), *The International Dimensions of Human Rights* (Westport, CT and Paris: Greenwood Press and UNESCO, 1982) 601–15

Neff, C. S., 'Human Rights in Africa: Thoughts on the African Charter on Human and Peoples' Rights in the Light of Case Law from Botswana, Lesotho and Swaziland', *ICLQ* 33 (1984) 331–47

Neuwahl, N., and A. Rosas (eds.), *The European Union and Human Rights* (The Hague: Martinus Nijhoff, 1995)

Ngu, A., 'Inauguration of African Women's Committee on Peace and Development', *Resolving Conflicts: OAU Conflict Management Bulletin* 2(6) (1998) 29–30

Nhlapo, R. T., 'International Protection of Human Rights and the Family: African Variations on a Common Theme', *International Journal of the Law and Family* 3(2) (1989) 1–20

Niarchos, C., 'Women, War and Rape: Challenges Facing the International Tribunal for the Former Yugoslavia', *HRQ* 17 (1995) 659–90

Niemann, M., 'Regional Integration and the Right to Development in Africa', in E. McCarthy-Arnolds, D. R. Penna and D. J. Cruz Sobrepeña (eds.), *Africa, Human Rights and the Global System. The Political Economy of Human Rights in a Changing World* (Westport, CT: Greenwood Press, 1994) 107–30

Nizami, A. (ed.), *The Emergence of Africa in International Politics* (New Delhi: Mittal, 1993)

Nkrumah, K., 'United we Stand', address, Proceedings of the Summit Conference of Independent African States, Addis Ababa, vol. 1, Section 2, Summit CIAS/GEN/INF/36, May 1963

Nmehielle, V., *The African Human Rights System: Its Law, Practices and Institutions* (The Hague: Kluwer, 2001)

Nobel, P., *Refugees and Development in Africa* (Uppsala: Scandinavian Institute of African Studies, 1987)

Noll, G. and J. Vedsted-Hansen, 'Non-Communitarians: Refugee and Asylum Policies', in Alston (ed.), *The EU and Human Rights* 359–410

Northrup, T. A., 'Personal Security, Political Security: The Relationship among Conceptions of Gender, War and Peace', *Research in Social Movements, Conflict and Change* 12 (1990) 267–99

Nwankwo, C., 'The OAU and Human Rights', *Journal of Democracy* 4 (1993) 50–4

Nyamu, C. I., 'Rural Women in Kenya and the Legitimacy of Human Rights Discourse and Institutions', in Quashigah and Okafor (eds.), *Legitimate Governance* 263–308

Nyangoni, W. W., *Africa in the United Nations System* (Cranbury, NJ: Associated University Presses, 1985)

Nyerere, J. K., 'Democracy and the Party System', in J. K. Nyerere, *Freedom and Unity: A Selection from Writings and Speeches, 1952–1966* (New York: Oxford University Press, 1966)

Nyongo, P. A. and J. A. Nyang'oya, 'Comprehensive Solutions to Refugee Problems in Africa', *International Journal of Refugee Law* (1995) 164–89

Obiozor, G. A. and A. Ajala (eds.), *Africa and the United Nations System: The First Fifty Years* (Lagos: Nigerian Institute of International Affairs, 1998)

Ocheje, P., 'Exploring the Legal Dimensions of Political Legitimacy: A "Rights" Approach to Governance in Africa', in Quashigah and Okafor (eds.), *Legitimate Governance* 165–205

Okafor, O. C., *Redefining Legitimate Statehood: International Law and State Fragmentation in Africa* (The Hague: Martinus Nijhoff, 2000)

Okoth-Obbo, G., 'The OAU/UNHCR Symposium on Refugees and Forced Displacements in Africa – A Review Article', *International Journal of Refugee Law* (special issue, 1995) 274–99

Okoth-Obbo, G., 'Thirty Years On: A Legal Review of the 1969 OAU Refugee Convention', *African Yearbook of International Law* 8 (2000) 3–70

Okoth-Ogendo, H. W. O., 'Governance and Sustainable Development in Africa', in Ginther et al. (eds.), *Sustainable Development* 105–10

Okoth-Ogendo, H. W. O., 'Human and Peoples' Rights: What Point is Africa Trying to Make?', in Cohen et al. (eds.), *Human Rights and Governance in Africa* 74–86

Okoth-Ogendo, H. W. O., 'The Quest for Constitutional Government', in G. Hyden, D. Olowu and H. W. O. Okoth-Ogendo (eds.), *African Perspectives on Governance* (Trenton, NJ: Africa World Press, 2000) 33–60

Oloka-Onyango, J., 'Beyond the Rhetoric: Reinvigorating the Struggle for Economic and Social Rights in Africa', *California West International Law Journal* 27 (1997) 32–67

Oloka-Onyango, J., 'Human Rights, the OAU Convention and the Refugee Crisis in Africa: Forty Years After Geneva', *International Journal of Refugee Law* 3 (3) (1991) 453–60

Oloka-Onyango, J., 'Human Rights and Sustainable Development in Contemporary Africa', *Buffalo Human Rights Law Review* 6 (2000) 39–50

Oloka-Onyango, J., 'Human Rights and Sustainable Development in Contemporary Africa: A New Dawn or Retreating Horizons', Human Development Report 2000 Background Paper (UNDP, 2000), http://www.undp.org/docs/publications/background_papers/Oloka-Onyango2000.html

Oloka-Onyango, J., 'The Place and Role of the OAU Bureau for Refugees in the African Refugee Crisis', *International Journal of Refugee Law* 6 (1994) 34–52

Oloka-Onyango, J., 'The Plight of the Larger Half: Human Rights, Gender Violence and the Legal Status of the Refugee and Internally Displaced Women in Africa', *Denver Journal of International Law* 24 (1996) 349–94

Oloka-Onyango, J. and S. Tamale, '"The Personal is Political", or Why Women's Rights are Indeed Human Rights: An African Perspective on International Feminism', *HRQ* 17(4) (1995) 691–731

Olsen, G. R., 'Promoting Democracy, Preventing Conflict: The European Union and Africa', *International Politics* 39(3) (2002) 311–28

Olsen, G. R., 'Western Europe's Relations with Africa since the End of the Cold War', *Journal of Modern African Studies* 35(2) (1997) 299–319

O'Neill, W., 'Conflict in West Africa: Dealing with Exclusion and Separation', *International Journal of Refugee Law* 12(1) (2000) 171–94

O'Neill, W., B. Rutinwa and G. Verdirame, 'The Great Lakes: A Survey of the Application of the Exclusion Clauses in the Central African Republic, Kenya and Tanzania', *International Journal of Refugee Law* 12(1) (2000) 135–70

Organization of African Unity/UNHCR, 'The Addis Ababa Symposium 1994', *International Journal of Refugee Law* (1995)

Orwa, D. K., 'The Search for African Unity', in J. C. B. O. Ojo, D. K. Orwa and C. M. B. Utete (eds.), *African International Relations* (London: Longman, 1985), chapter 5

Owusu, M., 'Democracy and Africa – A View from the Village', *Journal of Modern African Studies* 30(3) (1992) 369–96

Perluss, D. and J. Hartman, 'Temporary Refuge: Emergence of a Customary Norm', *Virginia Journal of International Law* 26 (1986) 488–503

Peter, C. M., *Human Rights in Africa. A Comparative Study of the African Human and Peoples' Rights Charter and the New Tanzanian Bill of Rights* (New York: Greenwood Press, 1990)

Peter, C. M., 'The Proposed African Court of Justice – Jurisprudential, Procedural, Enforcement Problems and Beyond', *East African Journal of Peace and Human Rights* 1 (1993) 117–36

Petersmann, E.-U., 'Human Rights and International Economic Law in the 21st Century', *Journal of International Economic Law* 4(1) (2001) 3–25

Pogge, T., 'Creating Supra-National Institutions Democratically: Reflections on the European Union's "Democratic Deficit"', *Journal of Political Philosophy* 5(2) (1997) 3–25

Polemus, J. H., 'The Provisional Secretariat of the OAU, 1963–4', *Journal of Modern African Studies* 12(2) (1974) 287–95

Pomerance, N., *Self-Determination in Law and Practice. The New Doctrine of the United Nations* (Leiden: Brill, 1982)

Quashigah, E. K., 'Legitimate Governance in Africa: The Responsibility of the International Community', in Quashigah and Okafor (eds.), *Legitimate Governance in Africa* 461–85

Quashigah, E. K., 'Protection of Human Rights in the Changing International Scene: Prospects in Sub-Saharan Africa', *RADIC* 6 (1994) 93–114

Quashigah, E. K. and O. C. Okafor, 'Legitimate Governance in Africa – International and Domestic Legal Perspectives: An Introduction', in Quashigah and Okafor (eds.), *Legitimate Governance* 3–19

Quashigah, E. K. and O. C. Ofakor (eds.), *Legitimate Governance in Africa: International and Domestic Legal Perspectives* (The Hague: Kluwer Law, 1999)

Quigley, J., 'Mass Displacement and the Individual Right of Return', *BYIL* 68 (1997) 65–125

Ratner, S. R., 'Drawing a Better Line: Uti Possidetis and the Borders of New States', *AJIL* 90 (1996) 590–621

Rich, R., 'The Right to Development: A Right of Peoples?', in Crawford (ed.), *The Right of Peoples* 17–38

Roberts-Wray, K. O., *Commonwealth and Colonial Law* (London: Stevens & Sons, 1966)

Rogge, J. R. and J. O. Akol, 'Repatriation: Its Role in Resolving Africa's Refugee Dilemma', *International Migration Review* 23(2) (1989) 184–200

Rothchild, D. and M. Chazan, *The Precarious Balance. State and Society in Africa* (Boulder: Westview Press, 1988)

Russell, M. and C. O'Cinneide, 'Positive Action to Promote Women in Politics. Some European Comparisons', *ICLQ* 52 (2003) 587–614

Rutinwa, B., 'The End of Asylum? The Changing Nature of Refugee Policies in Africa', Working Paper No. 5, *New Issues in Refugee Research* (New York: UNHCR, 1999), www.unhcr.ch

Rutinwa, N., 'Refugee Protection through the Rule of Law in Africa: Problems and Prospects', *Commonwealth Judicial Journal* 12(3) (1998) 10–20

Rwelamira, M., '1989 – The Anniversary Year: The 1969 OAU Convention on the Specific Aspects of Refugee Problems in Africa', *International Journal of Refugee Law* 1 (1989) 557–61

Rwezaura, B., 'The Concept of the Child's Best Interests in the Changing Economic and Social Context of Sub-Saharan Africa', *International Journal of the Law and Family* 8 (1994) 82–116

Sagay, I., *International Law and the Struggle for the Freedom of Man in Africa* (Ife: Ife University Press, 1983)

Sandbrook, R., *Democratization and Development in Africa* (London: Zed Books, 2000)

Sands, P., 'International Law in the Field of Sustainable Development', *BYIL* 65 (1994) 303–81

Sands, P. and P. Klein, *Bowett's Law of International Institutions*, 5th edn. (London: Sweet & Maxwell, 2001)

Sano, H.-O., 'Development and Human Rights: The Necessary, but Partial Integration of Human Rights and Development', *HRQ* 22 (2000) 734–52

Schmidt, P. R., 'African Configurations in the Right to a Cultural Heritage', *East African Journal of Peace and Human Rights* 2(1) (1995) 41–52

Schmitter, P. C., *How to Democratize the European Union . . . And Why Bother?* (Lanham: Rowman & Littlefield, 2000)

Schnably, S., 'Constitutionalism and Democratic Government in the Inter-American System', in Fox and Roth (eds.), *Democratic Governance* 155–98

Schultheis, M. J., 'Refugees in Africa: The Geopolitics of Forced Displacement', *African Studies Review* 32(1) (1989) 3–29

Scoble, H., 'Human Rights Non-Governmental Organizations in Black Africa: Their Problems and Prospects in the Wake of the Banjul Charter', in Welch and Meltzer (eds.), *Human Rights* 177–203

Scott-Thompson, W. and R. Bissell, 'Legitimacy and Authority in the OAU', *African Studies Review* 15(1) (1972) 17–42

Sen, A., *Development as Freedom* (Oxford: Oxford University Press, 2000)

Sesay, A., O. Ojo and O. Fasehun, *The OAU After Twenty Years* (Boulder: Westview Press, 1984)

Shaw, M., 'International Law and Intervention in Africa', *International Relations* 8 (1984) 341–67

Shaw, M., *Title to Territory in Africa. International Legal Issues* (Oxford: Clarendon Press, 1986)

Shelton, D., 'Representative Democracy and Human Rights in the Western Hemisphere', *HRLJ* 12 (1991) 353–9

Shepherd Jr., G. W. and M. O. C. Anikpo, *Emerging Human Rights. The African Political Economy Context* (New York: Greenwood Press, 1990)

Sherlock, A., 'Deportation of Aliens and Article 8 ECHR', *European Law Review* 23 (1998) 62–75

Shihata, I. F. L., 'The Attitude of New States towards the International Court of Justice', *International Organization* 19(2) (1965) 203–22

Shivji, I. G., *The Concept of Human Rights in Africa* (London: CODRESIA Book Series, 1989)

Sikkink, K., 'The Power of Principled Ideas: Human Rights Policies in the United States and Europe', in J. Goldstein and R. Keohane (eds.), *Ideas and Foreign Policy: Beliefs, Institutions and Political Change* (Ithaca: Cornell University Press, 1995)

Smock, D. R. and A. Crocker, *African Conflict Resolution* (New York: US Institute of Peace Press, 1995)

Soderbaum, F., *Handbook of Regional Organisations in Africa* (Oslo: Nordic Africa Institute, 1996)

Sohn, L. B., *Basic Documents of African Regional Organisations* (Westport, CT: Oceana Publications, 1988)

Solf, W., 'Human Rights in Armed Conflict: Some Observations on the Relationship between Human Rights Law and the Law of Armed Conflict', in H. Han (ed.), *World in Transition: Challenges to Human Rights, Development and World Order* (Washington, DC: University Press of America, 1979) 41–53

Spencer, J. H., 'Africa at the UN: Some Observations', *International Organization* 16(2) (1962) 375–86

Stein, B. N., 'Durable Solutions for Developing Country Refugees', *International Migration Review* 20(2) (1986) 264–82

Stiehm, J. H., 'Men and Women and Peacekeeping: A Research Note', *International Peacekeeping* 2(4) (1995) 564–9

Stoltenberg, T., 'Refugees and Human Rights', *International Journal of Refugee Law* 2(2) (1998) 274–8

Storey, H. and R. Wallace, 'War and Peace in Refugee Law Jurisprudence', *AJIL* 95(2) (2001) 349–66

Takahashi, S., 'Recourse to Human Rights Treaty Bodies for Monitoring of the Refugee Convention', *NQHR* 20(1) (2002) 53–74

Tandon, Y., 'Peace-Keeping: A Third World Perspective', in Nizami (ed.), *Emergence of Africa* 60–81

Tamale, S., 'Towards Legitimate Governance in Africa: The Case of Affirmative Action and Parliamentary Politics in Uganda', in Quashigah and Okafor (eds.), *Legitimate Governance* 235–62

Theodoropoulos, C. (ed.), *Human Rights in Europe and Africa: A Comparative Analysis* (Athens: Hellenic University Press, 1992)

Thompson, B., 'Africa's Charter on Children's Rights: A Normative Break with Cultural Traditionalism', *ICLQ* 41 (1992) 432–45

Tolentino, A. S., 'Good Governance through Popular Participation in Sustainable Development', in Ginther et al. (eds.), *Sustainable Development and Good Governance* 137–49

Tomasevski, K., *Between Sanctions and Elections: Aid Donors and their Human Rights Performance* (London: Continuum International Publishing Group, 1997)

Tomasevski, K., *Human Rights Violations and Development Aid: From Politics towards Policy* (London: Commonwealth Secretariat, 1990)

Tomuschat, C., *Modern Law of Self-Determination* (Leiden: Brill, 1993)

Tordoff, W., *Government and Politics in Africa*, 3rd edn. (Basingstoke: Macmillan Press, 1997)

Touval, S., 'The Organization of African Unity and African Borders', *International Organization* 11(1) (1967) 102–27

Udechuku, E. C., *African Unity and International Law* (London: African Press, 1974)

Udogu, E. I., *Democracy and Democratization in Africa: Towards the 21st Century* (New York: Brill, 1997)

Udombana, N. J., 'The Third World and the Right to Development: Agenda for the Next Millennium', *HRQ* 22 (2000) 753–87

Umozurike, U. O., 'The African Charter on Human and Peoples' Rights', *AJIL* 77 (1983) 902–112

Umozurike, U. O., *The African Charter on Human and Peoples' Rights* (The Hague: Martinus Nijhoff, 1998)

Umozurike, U. O., *International Law and Colonialism in Africa* (Enugu, Nigeria: Nwamife Publishers, 1979)

Umozurike, U. O., *Self-Determination in International Law* (Hamden: Archon, 1972)

UNDP, 'Deepening Democracy in a Fragmented World', Human Development Report (New York: UNDP, 2002)

United Nations, 'Women in Power and Decision-Making. Regional Preparatory Meeting on 2000 Review of Implementation of the Beijing Platform for Action, 19–21 January 2000', paper prepared for the Economic Commission for Europe, J. Lovenduski and J. Regulska, IPU/FEM/EUR/2000.2

United Nations Office at Vienna Centre for Social Development and Humanitarian Affairs, *Women in Politics and Decision-Making in the Late Twentieth Century* (Dordrecht: Martinus Nijhoff, 1992)

Viljoen, F., 'The Realisation of Human Rights in Africa through Inter-Governmental Institutions' (LLD thesis, University of Pretoria, 1997)

Viljoen, F., 'The Realisation of Human Rights in Africa through Sub-Regional Institutions', *African Yearbook of International Law* 7 (1999) 185–214

Viljoen, F., 'Why South Africa Should Ratify the African Charter on the Rights and Welfare of the Child', *South African Law Journal* 11(6)(1999) 660–4

Wali, S., 'Women in Conditions of War and Peace: Challenges and Dilemmas', in M. Schuler (ed.), *From Basic Needs to Basic Rights: Women's Claim to Human Rights* (Washington, DC: Institute for Women, Law and Development, 1995)

Wallerstein, I., 'The Decline of the Party in Single-Party African States', in J. Palambara and M. Weiner (eds.), *Political Parties and Political Development* (Princeton: Princeton University Press, 1966) 201–14

Wallerstein, I., 'The Role of the Organization of African Unity in Contemporary African Politics', in El-Ayouty and Brooks (eds.), *Africa* 18–28

van Walraven, K., *Dreams of Power. The Role of the Organization of African Unity in the Politics of Africa 1963–1993* (Aldershot: Ashgate, 1999)

Wanda, B. P., 'The One-Party State and the Protection of Human Rights in Africa with Particular Reference to Political Rights', *AJICL* 3(4) (1991) 756–70

Wani, I. J., 'The Rule of Law and Economic Development in Africa', *East African Journal of Peace and Human Rights* 1 (1993) 52–79

Weinstein, W., 'Africa's Approach to Human Rights at the United Nations', *Issue* 6(4) (1976) 14–21

Weiss, P., 'The Convention of the Organization of African Unity Governing Specific Aspects of Refugee Problems in Africa', *Human Rights Journal* 3(3) (1970) 449–61

Welch, C. E., 'The African Commission on Human and Peoples' Rights: A Five-Year Report and Assessment', *HRQ* 14 (1992) 43–61

Welch, C. E., 'Continuity and Discontinuity in African Military Organisation', *Journal of Modern African Studies* 12 (1975) 224–45

Welch, C. E., 'Human Rights and African Women: A Comparison of Protection under Two Major Treaties', *HRQ* 15 (1993) 549–74

Welch, C. E., 'The OAU and Human Rights: Towards a New Definition', *Journal of Modern African Studies* 19(3) (1981) 401–20

Welch, C. E., *Protecting Human Rights in Africa: Strategies and Roles of Non-Governmental Organizations* (Philadelphia: University of Pennsylvania Press, 1995)

Welch, C. E. and R. I. Meltzer (eds.), *Human Rights and Development in Africa* (Albany: State University of New York Press, 1984)

Weller, M., *Regional Peacekeeping and International Enforcement: The Liberian Crisis* (Cambridge: Grotius, 1994)

Wembou, M.-C. D., 'The OAU and International Law', in El-Ayouty (ed.), *OAU after Thirty Years* 15–26

West, H. G. and K.W. Thompson, *Conflict and its Resolution in Contemporary Africa* (Lanham: University Press of America, 1997)

Wheatley, S., 'Democracy and International Law: A European Perspective', *ICLQ* 51 (2002) 225–47

Wilkins, G. L., *African Influence in the United Nations 1967–1975. The Politics and Techniques of Gaining Compliance to UN Principles and Resolutions* (Washington, DC: University Press of America, 1981)

Wilson, H. S., *African Decolonization* (London: Edward Arnold, 1994)

Wolfers, M., *Politics in the Organization of African Unity* (London: Metheun & Co. Ltd., 1976)

Wunsch, J. S. and D. Olowu, *The Failure of the Centralized State. Institutions and Self-Governance in Africa* (San Francisco: Westview Press, 1990)

Young, C., *The African Colonial State in Comparative Perspective* (New Haven and London: Yale University Press, 1994)

Zarsky L. (ed.), *Human Rights and the Environment. Conflicts and Norms in a Globalizing World* (London: Earthscan Publications, 2002)

Zartman, I. W., *International Relations in the New Africa* (Englewood Cliffs, NJ: Prentice-Hall, 1966)

INDEX

Printed in the United States
142218LV00002B/11/A